Advanced Operating Systems and Kernel Applications:
Techniques and Technologies

Yair Wiseman
Bar–Ilan University, Israel

Song Jiang
Wayne State University, USA

INFORMATION SCIENCE REFERENCE

Hershey · New York

Director of Editorial Content:	Kristin Klinger
Senior Managing Editor:	Jamie Snavely
Assistant Managing Editor:	Michael Brehm
Publishing Assistant:	Sean Woznicki
Typesetter:	Sean Woznicki
Cover Design:	Lisa Tosheff
Printed at:	Yurchak Printing Inc.

Published in the United States of America by
Information Science Reference (an imprint of IGI Global)
701 E. Chocolate Avenue
Hershey PA 17033
Tel: 717-533-8845
Fax: 717-533-8661
E-mail: cust@igi-global.com
Web site: http://www.igi-global.com/reference

Library of Congress Cataloging-in-Publication Data

Advanced operating systems and kernel applications : techniques and technologies / Yair Wiseman and Song Jiang, editors.
    p. cm.
  Includes bibliographical references and index.
  Summary: "This book discusses non-distributed operating systems that benefit researchers, academicians, and practitioners"--Provided by publisher.

  ISBN 978-1-60566-850-5 (hardcover) -- ISBN 978-1-60566-851-2 (ebook) 1.
Operating systems (Computers) I. Wiseman, Yair, II. Jiang, Song.
  QA76.76.O63A364 2009
  005.4'32--dc22
                          2009016442

British Cataloguing in Publication Data
A Cataloguing in Publication record for this book is available from the British Library.

Table of Contents

Section 1
Kernel Security and Reliability

Section 2
Efficient Memory Management

Section 3
Systems Profiling

Section 4
I/O Prefetching

Section 5
Page Replacement Algorithms

Detailed Table of Contents

Section 1
Kernel Security and Reliability

Chapter 1

Yair Wiseman, Bar-Ilan University, Israel
Joel Isaacson, Ascender Technologies, Israel
Eliad Lubovsky, Bar-Ilan University, Israel
Pinchas Weisberg, Bar-Ilan University, Israel

The Linux kernel stack has a fixed size. There is no mechanism to prevent the kernel from overflowing the stack. Hackers can exploit this bug to put unwanted information in the memory of the operating system and gain control over the system. In order to prevent this problem, the authors introduce a dynamically sized kernel stack that can be integrated into the standard Linux kernel. The well-known paging mechanism is reused with some changes, in order to enable the kernel stack to grow.

Chapter 2

Michael M. Swift, University of Wisconsin—Madison, USA

Despite decades of research in extensible operating system technology, extensions such as device drivers remain a significant cause of system failures. In Windows XP, for example, drivers account for 85% of recently reported failures. This chapter presents Nooks, a layered architecture for tolerating the failure of drivers within existing operating system kernels. The design consists techniques for isolating drivers from the kernel and for recovering from their failure. Nooks isolates drivers from the kernel in a lightweight kernel protection domain, a new protection mechanism. By executing drivers within a domain, the kernel is protected from their failure and cannot be corrupted. Shadow drivers recover from device driver failures. Based on a replica of the driver's state machine, a shadow driver conceals the driver's failure from applications and restores the driver's internal state to a point where it can process requests as if it had never failed. Thus, the entire failure and recovery is transparent to applications.

Chapter 3

The authors demonstrate a new class of attacks and also present a novel automated technique to detect them. The attacks do not explicitly exhibit hiding behavior but are stealthy by design. They do not rely on user space programs to provide malicious functionality but achieve the same by simply manipulating kernel data. These attacks are symbolic of a larger systemic problem within the kernel, thus requiring comprehensive analysis. The author's novel rootkit detection technique based on automatic inference of data structure invariants, which can automatically detect such advanced stealth attacks on the kernel.

With the rise of the Internet, computer systems appear to be more vulnerable than ever from security attacks. Much attention has been focused on the role of the network in security attacks, but evidence suggests that the computer server and its operating system deserve closer examination since it is ultimately the operating system and its core defense mechanisms of authentication and authorization which are compromised in an attack. This chapter provides an exploratory and evaluative discussion of the authentication and authorization features of two widely used server operating systems: Windows and Linux.

Section 2
Efficient Memory Management

Most computer systems use the global page replacement policy based on the LRU principle to reduce page faults. The LRU principle for the global page replacement dictates that a Least Recently Used (LRU) page, or the least active page in a general sense, should be selected for replacement in the entire user memory space. However, in a multiprogramming environment under high memory load, an indiscriminate use of the principle can lead to system thrashing, in which all processes spend most of their time waiting for the disk service instead of making progress. In this chapter, we will rethink the application of the

LRU principle on global paging to identify one of root causes for thrashing, and describe a mechanism, named as swap token, to solve the issue. The mechanism is simple in its design and implementation but highly effective in alleviating or removing thrashing. A key feature of the swap token mechanism is that it can distinguish the conditions for an LRU page, or a page that has not been used for relatively long period of time, to be generated and accordingly categorized LRU pages into two types: true and false LRU pages. The mechanism identifies false LRU pages to avoid use of the LRU principle on these pages, in order to remove thrashing.

Chapter 6

Song Jiang, Wayne State University, USA

As the hard disk remains as the mainstream on-line storage device, it continues to be the performance bottleneck of data-intensive applications. One of existing most effective solutions to ameliorate the bottle¬neck is to use the buffer cache in the OS kernel to achieve two objectives: reduction of direct access of on-disk data and improvement of disk performance. These two objectives can be achieved by applying both temporal locality and spatial locality in the management of the buffer cache. Traditionally only temporal locality is exploited for the purpose, and spatial locality is largely ignored. As the throughput of access of sequentially-placed disk blocks can be an order of magnitude higher than that of access to randomly-placed blocks, the missing of spatial locality in the buffer management can cause the performance of applications without dominant sequential accesses to be seriously degraded. In the chapter, we introduce a state-of-the-art technique that seamlessly combines these two locality properties embedded in the data access patterns into the management of the kernel buffer cache management to improve I/O performance.

Chapter 7

Moses Reuven, Bar-Ilan University, Israel
Yair Wiseman, Bar-Ilan University, Israel

A technique for minimizing the paging on a system with a very heavy memory usage is proposed. When there are processes with active memory allocations that should be in the physical memory, but their accumulated size exceeds the physical memory capacity. In such cases, the operating system begins swapping pages in and out the memory on every context switch. The authors lessen this thrashing by placing the processes into several bins, using Bin Packing approximation algorithms. They amend the scheduler to maintain two levels of scheduling - medium-term scheduling and short-term scheduling. The medium-term scheduler switches the bins in a Round-Robin manner, whereas the short-term scheduler uses the standard Linux scheduler to schedule the processes in each bin. The authors prove that this feature does not necessitate adjustments in the shared memory maintenance. In addition, they explain how to modify the new scheduler to be compatible with some elements of the original scheduler like priority and real-time privileges. Experimental results show substantial improvement on very loaded memories.

Section 3
Systems Profiling

Chapter 8

Timothy R. Leschke, University of Maryland, Baltimore County, USA

There are two forces that are demanding a change in the traditional design of operating systems. One force requires a more flexible operating system that can accommodate the evolving requirements of new hardware and new user applications. The other force requires an operating system that is fast enough to keep pace with faster hardware and faster communication speeds. If a radical change in operating system design is not implemented soon, the traditional operating system will become the performance bottle-neck for computers in the very near future. The Exokernel Operating System, developed at the Massachusetts Institute of Technology, is an operating system that meets the needs of increased speed and increased flexibility. The Exokernel is extensible, which means that it is easily modified. The Exokernel can be easily modified to meet the requirements of the latest hardware or user applications. Ease in modification also means the Exokernel's performance can be optimized to meet the speed requirements of faster hardware and faster communication. In this chapter, the author explores some details of the Exokernel Operating System. He also explores Active Networking, which is a technology that exploits the extensibility of the Exokernel. His investigation reveals the strengths of the Exokernel as well as some of its design concerns. He concludes his discussion by embracing the Exokernel Operating System and by encouraging more research into this approach to operating system design.

Chapter 9

Daniel G. Waddington, Lockheed Martin, USA
Nilabja Roy, Vanderbilt University, USA
Douglas C. Schmidt, Vanderbilt University, USA

As software-intensive systems become larger, more parallel, and more unpredictable the ability to analyze their behavior is increasingly important. There are two basic approaches to behavioral analysis: static and dynamic. Although static analysis techniques, such as model checking, provide valuable information to software developers and testers, they cannot capture and predict a complete, precise, image of behavior for large-scale systems due to scalability limitations and the inability to model complex external stimuli. This chapter explores four approaches to analyzing the behavior of software systems via dynamic analysis: compiler-based instrumentation, operating system and middleware profiling, virtual machine profiling, and hardware-based profiling. The authors highlight the advantages and disadvantages of each approach with respect to measuring the performance of multithreaded systems and demonstrate how these approaches can be applied in practice.

Section 4
I/O Prefetching

Chapter 10

Feng Chen, The Ohio State University, USA

Xiaoning Ding, The Ohio State University, USA

Song Jiang, Wayne State University, USA

As the major secondary storage device, the hard disk plays a critical role in modern computer system. In order to improve disk performance, most operating systems conduct data prefetch policies by tracking I/O access pattern, mostly at the level of file abstractions. Though such a solution is useful to exploit application-level access patterns, file-level prefetching has many constraints that limit the capability of fully exploiting disk performance. The reasons are twofold. First, certain prefetch opportunities can only be detected by knowing the data layout on the hard disk, such as metadata blocks. Second, due to the non-uniform access cost on the hard disk, the penalty of mis-prefetching a random block is much more costly than mis-prefetching a sequential block. In order to address the intrinsic limitations of file-level prefetching, we propose to prefetch data blocks directly at the disk level in a portable way. The authors' proposed scheme, called DiskSeen, is designed to supplement file-level prefetching. DiskSeen observes the workload access pattern by tracking the locations and access times of disk blocks. Based on analysis of the temporal and spatial relationships of disk data blocks, DiskSeen can significantly increase the sequentiality of disk accesses and improve disk performance in turn. They implemented the DiskSeen scheme in the Linux 2.6 kernel and show that it can significantly improve the effectiveness of file-level prefetching and reduce execution times by 20-53% for various types of applications, including grep, CVS, and TPC-H.

Chapter 11

Fengguang Wu, Intel Corporation, China

Sequential prefetching is a well established technique for improving I/O performance. As Linux runs an increasing variety of workloads, its in-kernel prefetching algorithm has been challenged by many unexpected and subtle problems; As computer hardware evolves, the design goals should also be adapted. To meet the new challenges and demands, a prefetching algorithm that is aggressive yet safe, flexible yet simple, scalable yet efficient is desired. In this chapter, the author explores the principles of I/O prefetching and present a demand readahead algorithm for Linux. He demonstrates how it handles common readahead issues by a host of case studies. Both static, logic and dynamic behaviors of the readahead algorithm are covered, so as to help readers building both theoretical and practical views of sequential prefetching.

Chapter 12

Wei Wu, Singapore-MIT Alliance, and School of Computing, National University of Singapore,
  Singapore
Kian-Lee Tan, Singapore-MIT Alliance, and School of Computing, National University of
  Singapore, Singapore

Caching and prefetching are two effective ways for mobile peers to improve access latency in mobile environments. With short-range communication such as IEEE 802.11 and Bluetooth, a mobile peer can communicate with neighboring peers and share cached or prefetched data objects. This kind of cooperation improves data availability and access latency. In this chapter the authors review several cooperative caching and prefetching schemes in a mobile environment that supports broadcasting. They present two schemes in detail: CPIX (Cooperative PIX) and ACP (Announcement-based Cooperative Prefetching). CPIX is suitable for mobile peers that have limited power and access the broadcast channel in a demand-driven fashion. ACP is designed for mobile peers that have sufficient power and prefetch from the broadcast channel. They both consider the data availability in local cache, neighbors' cache, and on the broadcast channel. Moreover, these schemes are simple enough so that they do not incur much information exchange among peers and each peer can make autonomous caching and prefetching decisions.

Section 5
Page Replacement Algorithms

Chapter 13

Yannis Smaragdakis, University of Massachusetts, Amherst, USA
Scott Kaplan, Amherst College, USA

Replacement algorithms are a major component of operating system design. Every replacement algorithm, however, is pathologically bad for some scenarios, and often these scenarios correspond to common program patterns. This has prompted the design of adaptive replacement algorithms: algorithms that emulate two (or more) basic algorithms and pick the decision of the best one based on recent past behavior. The authors are interested in a special case of adaptive replacement algorithms, which are instances of adaptive replacement templates (ARTs). An ART is a template that can be applied to any two algorithms and yield a combination with some guarantees on the properties of the combination, relative to the properties of the component algorithm. For instance, they show ARTs that for any two algorithms A and B produce a combined algorithm AB that is guaranteed to emulate within a factor of 2 the better of A and B on the current input. They call this guarantee a robustness property. This performance guarantee of ARTs makes them effective but a naïve implementation may not be practically efficient—e.g., because it requires significant space to emulate both component algorithms at the same time. In practice, instantiations of an ART can be specialized to be highly efficient. The authors demonstrate this through a case study. They present the EELRU adaptive replacement algorithm, which pre-dates ARTs but is truly a highly optimized multiple ART instantiation. EELRU is well-known in the research literature and outperforms the well-known LRU algorithm when there is benefit to be gained, while emulating LRU otherwise.

Chapter 14
Enhancing the Efficiency of Memory Management in a Super-Paging Environment

Moshe Itshak, Bar-Ilan University, Israel
Yair Wiseman, Bar-Ilan University, Israel

The concept of Super-Paging has been wandering around for more than a decade. Super-Pages are supported by some operating systems. In addition, there are some interesting research papers that show interesting ideas how to intelligently integrate Super-Pages into modern operating systems; however, the page replacement algorithms used by the contemporary operating system even now use the old Clock algorithm which does not prioritize small or large pages based on their size. In this chapter an algorithm for page replacement in a Super-Page environment is presented. The new technique for page replacement decisions is based on the page size and other parameters; hence is appropriate for a Super-Paging environment.

Preface

Operating Systems research is a vital and dynamic field. Even young computer science students know that Operating Systems are the core of any computer system and a course about Operating Systems is more than common in any Computer Science department all over the world.

This book aims at introducing subjects in the contemporary research of Operating Systems. One-processor machines are still the majority of the computing power far and wide. Therefore, this book will focus at these research topics i.e. Non-Distributed Operating Systems. We believe this book can be especially beneficial for Operating Systems researchers alongside encouraging more graduate students to research this field and to contribute their aptitude.

A probe of recent operating systems conferences and journals focusing on the "pure" Operating Systems subjects (i.e. Kernel's task) has produced several main categories of study in Non-Distributed Operating Systems:

- Kernel Security and Reliability
- Efficient Memory Utilization
- Kernel Security and Reliability
- I/O prefetching
- Page Replacement Algorithms

We introduce subjects in each category and elaborate on them within the chapters. The technical depth of this book is definitely not superficial, because our potential readers are Operating Systems researchers or graduate students who conduct research at Operating System labs. The following paragraphs will introduce the content and the main points of the chapters in each of the categories listed above.

KERNEL SECURITY AND RELIABILITY

Kernel Stack Overflows Elimination

The kernel stack has a fixed size. When too much data is pushed upon the stack, an overflow will be generated. This overflow can be illegitimately utilized by unauthorized users to hack the operating system. The authors of this chapter suggest a technique to prevent the kernel stack from overflowing by using a kernel stack with a flexible size.

Device Driver Reliability

Device Drivers are certainly the Achilles' heel of the operating system kernel. The writers of the device drivers are not always aware of how the kernel was written. In addition, many times, only few users may have a given device, so the device driver is actually not indeed battle-tested. The author of this chapter suggests inserting an additional layer to the kernel that will keep the kernel away from the device driver failures. This isolation will protect the kernel from unwanted malfunctions along with helping the device driver to recover.

Identifying Systemic Threats to Kernel Data: Attacks and Defense Techniques

Installing a malware into the operating system kernel by a hacker can has devastating results for the proper operation of a computer system. The authors of this chapter show examples of dangerous malicious code that can be installed into the kernel. In addition, they suggest techniques how to protect the kernel from such attacks.

EFFICIENT MEMORY MANAGEMENT

Swap Token: Rethink the Application of the LRU Principle on Paging to Remove System Thrashing

The commonly adopted approach to handle paging in the memory system is using the LRU replacement algorithm or its approximations, such the CLOCK policy used in the Linux kernels. However, when a high memory pressure appears, LRU is incapable of satisfactorily managing the memory stress and a thrashing can take place. The author of this chapter proposes a design to alleviate the harmful effect of thrashing by removing a critical loophole in the application of the LRU principle on the memory management.

Application of both Temporal and Spatial Localities in the Management of Kernel Buffer Cache

With the objective of reducing the number of disk accesses, operating systems usually use a memory buffer to cache previously accessed data. The commonly used methods to determine which data should be cached are utilizing only the temporal locality while ignoring the spatial locality. The author of this chapter proposes to exploit both of these localities in order to achieve a substantially improved I/O performance, instead of only minimizing number of disk accesses.

Alleviating the Trashing by Adding Medium-Term Scheduler

When too much memory space is needed, the CPU spends a large portion of its time swapping pages in and out the memory. This effect is called Thrashing. Thrashing's result is a severe overhead time and as a result a significant slowdown of the system. Linux 2.6 has a breakthrough technique that was suggested by one of these book editors - Dr. Jiang and handles this problem. The authors of this chapter took this known technique and significantly improved it. The new technique is suitable for much more cases and also has better results in the already handled cases.

KERNEL FLEXIBILITY

The Exokernel Operating System and Active Networks

The micro-kernel concept is very old dated to the beginning of the seventies. The idea of micro-kernels is minimizing the kernel. I.e. trying to implement outside the kernel whatever possible. This can make the kernel code more flexible and in addition, fault isolation will be achieved. The possible drawback of this technique is the time of the context switches to the new kernel-aid processes. Exokernel is a micro-kernel that achieves both flexibility and fault isolation while trying not to harm the execution time. The author of this chapter describes the principles of this micro-kernel.

I/O PREFETCHING

Exploiting Disk Layout and Block Access History for I/O Prefetch

Prfetching is a known technique that can reduce the fetching overhead time of data from the disk to the internal memory. The known fetching techniques ignore the internal structure of the disk. Most of the disks are maintained by the Operating System in an indexed allocation manner meaning the allocations are not contiguous; hence, the oversight of the internal disk structure might cause an inefficient prefetching. The authors of this chapter suggests an improvement to the prefetching scheme by taking into account the data layout on the hard disk.

Sequential File Prefetching in Linux

The Linux operating system supports autonomous sequential file prefetching, aka readahead. The variety of applications that Linux has to support requires more flexible criteria for identifying prefetchable access patterns in the Linux prefetching algorithm. Interleaved and cooperative streams are example patterns that a prefetching algorithm should be able to recognize and exploit. The author of this chapter proposes a new prefetching algorithm that is able to handle more complicated access patterns. The algorithm will continue to optimize to keep up with the technology trend of escalating disk seek cost and increasingly popular multi-core processors and parallel machines.

PAGE REPLACEMENT ALGORITHMS

Adaptive Replacement Algorithm Templates and EELRU

With the aim of facilitating paging mechanism, the operating system should decide on "page swapping out" policy. Many algorithms have been suggested over the years; however each algorithm has advantages and disadvantages. The authors of this chapter propose to adaptively change the algorithm according to the system behavior. In this way the operating system can avoid choosing inappropriate method and the best algorithm for each scenario will be selected.

Enhancing the Efficiency of Memory Management in a Super-Paging Environment by AMSQM

The traditional page replacement algorithms presuppose that the page size is a constant; however this presumption is not always correct. Many contemporary processors have several page sizes. Larger pages that are pointed to by the TLB are called Super-Pages and there are several super-page sizes. This feature makes the page replacement algorithm much more complicated. The authors of this chapter suggest a novel algorithm that is based on recent constant page replacement algorithms and is able to maintain pages in several sizes.

This book contains surveys and new results in the area of Operating System kernel research. The books aims at providing results that will be suitable to as many operating systems as possible. There are some chapters that deal with a specific Operating System; however the concepts should be valid for other operating systems as well.

We believe this book will be a nice contribution to the community of operating system kernel developers. Most of the existing literature does not focus on operating systems kernel and many operating system books contain chapters on close issues like distributed systems etc. We believe that a more concentrated book will be much more effective; hence we made the effort to collect the chapters and publish the book.

The chapters of this book have been written by different authors; but we have taken some steps like clustering similar subjects to a division, so as to make this book readable as an entity. However, the chapters can also be read individually. We hope you will enjoy the book as it was our intention to select and combine relevant material and make it easy to access.

Acknowledgment

First of all, we would like to thank the authors for their contributions. This book would not have been published without their outstanding efforts. We also would like to thanks IGI Global and especially to Joel Gamon and Rebecca Beistline for their intense guide and help. Our thanks are also given to all the other people who have help us and we did not mention. Finally, we would like to thank our families who let us have the time to devote to write this interesting book.

Yair Wiseman
Bar-Ilan University, Israel

Song Jiang
Wayne State University, USA

Section 1
Kernel Security and Reliability

Chapter 1
Kernel Stack Overflows Elimination

Yair Wiseman
Bar-Ilan University, Israel

Joel Isaacson
Ascender Technologies, Israel

Eliad Lubovsky
Bar-Ilan University, Israel

Pinchas Weisberg
Bar-Ilan University, Israel

ABSTRACT

The Linux kernel stack has a fixed size. There is no mechanism to prevent the kernel from overflowing the stack. Hackers can exploit this bug to put unwanted information in the memory of the operating system and gain control over the system. In order to prevent this problem, the authors introduce a dynamically sized kernel stack that can be integrated into the standard Linux kernel. The well-known paging mechanism is reused with some changes, in order to enable the kernel stack to grow.

INTRODUCTION

The management of virtual memory and the relationship of software and hardware to this management is an old research subject (Denning, 1970). In this chapter we would like to focus on the kernel mode stack. Our discussion will deal with the Linux operating system running on an IA-32 architecture machine. However, the proposed solutions may be relevant for other platforms and operating systems as well.

The memory management architecture of IA-32 machines uses a combination of segmentation (memory areas) and paging to support a protected multitasking environment (Intel, 1993). The x86 enforces the use of segmentation which provides a mechanism of isolating individual code, data and stack modules.

Therefore, Linux splits the memory address space of a user process into multiple segments and assigns a different protection mode for each of them. Each segment contains a logical portion of a process, e.g. the code of the process. Linux uses the

DOI: 10.4018/978-1-60566-850-5.ch001

paging mechanism to implement a conventional demand-paged, virtual-memory system and to isolate the memory spaces of user processes (IA-32, 2005).

Paging is a technique of mapping small fixed size regions of a process address space into chunks of real, physical memory called page frames. The size of the page is constant, e.g. IA-32 machines use 4KB of physical memory.

In point of fact, IA-32 machine support also large pages of 4MB. Linux (and Windows) do not use this ability of large pages (also called super-pages) and actually the 4KB page support fulfills the needs for the implementation of Linux (Winwood et al., 2002).

Linux enables each process to have its own virtual address space. It defines the range of addresses within this space that the process is allowed to use. The addresses are segmented into isolated section of code, data and stack modules.

Linux provides processes a mechanism for requesting, accessing and freeing memory (Bovet and Cesati, 2003), (Love, 2003). Allocations are made to contiguous, virtual addresses by arranging the page table to map physical pages. Processes, through the kernel, can dynamically add and remove memory areas to its address space. Memory areas have attributes such as the start address in the virtual address space, length and access rights. User threads share the process memory areas of the process that has spawned them; therefore, threads are regular processes that share certain resources. The Linux facility known as "kernel threads" are scheduled as user processes but lack any per-process memory space and can only access global kernel memory.

Unlike user mode execution, kernel mode does not have a process address space. If a process executes a system call, kernel mode will be invoked and the memory space of the caller remains valid. Linux gives the kernel a virtual address range of 3GB to 4GB, whereas the processes use the virtual address range of 0 to 3GB. Therefore, there will be no conflict between the virtual addresses of the kernel and the virtual addresses of whichever process.

In addition, a globally defined kernel address space becomes accessible which is not process unique but is global to all processes running in kernel mode. If kernel mode has been entered not via a system call but rather via a hardware interrupt, a process address space is defined but it is irrelevant to the current kernel execution.

VIRTUAL MEMORY

In yesteryears, when a computer program was too big and there was no way to load the entire program into the memory, the overlays technique was used. The programmer had to split the program into several portions that the memory could contain and that can be executed independently. The programmer also was in charge of putting system calls that could replace the portions in the switching time.

With the aim of making the programming work easier and exempting the programmer from managing the portions of the memory, the virtual memory systems have been created. Virtual memory systems automatically load the memory portions that are necessary for the program execution into the memory. Other portions of the memory that are not currently needed are saved in a second memory and will be loaded into the memory only if there is a need to use them.

Virtual memory enables the execution of a program that its size can be up to the virtual address space. This address space is set according to the size of the registers that are used by CPU to access the memory addresses. E. g. by using a processor with 32 bits, we will be able to address 4GB, whereas by using a 64 bits processor, we will be able to address 16 Exabytes. In addition to the address space increase, since, when an operating system uses a virtual memory scheme there is no need to load the entire program, there will be a possibility to load more programs and to execute them concurrently. Another advantage is that the program can start the execution even just after only a small portion of the program memory has been loaded

In a virtual memory system any process is executed in a virtual machine that is allocated only for the process. The process accesses addresses in the virtual address space. And it can ignore other processes that use the physical memory at the same time. The task of the programmer and the compiler becomes much easier because they do not need to delve into the details of memory management difficulties.

Virtual memory systems easily enable to protect the memory of processes from an access of other processes, whereas on the other hand virtual memory systems enable a controlled sharing of memory portions between several processes. This state of affairs makes the implementation of multitasking much easier for the operating system.

Nowadays, computers usually have large memories; hence, the well-known virtual memory mechanism is mostly utilized for secure or shared memory. The virtual machine interface also benefits the virtual memory mechanism, whereas the original need of loading too large processes into the memory is not so essential anymore (Jacob, 2002).

Virtual memory operates in a similar way to the cache memory. When there is a small fast memory and a large slow memory, a hierarchy of memories will be assembled. In virtual memory the hierarchy is between the RAM and the disk. The portion of the program that a chance of accessing to them is higher will be saved in the fast memory; whereas the other portions of the program will be saved in the slow memory and will be moved to the fast memory just if the program accesses them. The effective access time to the memory is the weighted average that based on the access time of the fast memory, the access time of the slow memory and the hit ratio of the fast memory. The effective access time will low if the hit ratio is high.

A high hit ratio will be probably produced because of the locality principle which stipulates that programs tend to access again and again instructions and data that they have accessed them lately. There is a time locality and position locality. Time locality means the program might access again the same memory addresses in a short time. Position locality means the program might access again not only the same memory address in a short time, but also the nearby memory addresses might be accessed in a short time. According to the locality principles, if instructions or data have been loaded into the memory, there is a high chance that these instructions or data will be accessed soon again. If the operating system loads also program portions that contain the "neighborhood" of the original instructions or data, the chances to increase the hit ratio, will be even higher.

With the purpose of implementing virtual memory, the program memory space is split into pieces that are moved between the disk and the memory. Typically, the program memory space is split into equal pieces called pages. The physical memory is also split into pieces in the same size called frames.

There is an option to split the program into unequal pieces called segments. This split is logical; therefore, it is more suitable for protection and sharing; however on the other hand, since the pieces are not equal, there will be a problem of external fragmentation. To facilitate both of the advantages, there are computer architectures that use segments of pages.

When a program tries to access a datum in an address that is not available in the memory, the computer hardware will generate a page fault. The operating system handles the page fault by loading the missing page into the memory while emptying out a frame of the memory if there is a need for that. The decision of which page should be emptied out is typically based on LRU. The time needed by the pure LRU algorithm is too costly because we will need to update too many data after every memory access, so instead most of the operating systems use an approximation of LRU. Each page in the memory has a reference bit that the computer hardware set whenever the page is accessed. According to the CLOCK algorithm (Corbato, 1968), (Nicola et al., 1992), (Jiang et al., 2005), the pages are arranged in a circular list so as to select a page for swapping out from the memory, the operating system moves on the page list and select the first page that its reference bit is unset. While the operating system moves on the list, it will unset the reference bits of the pages that it sees during the move. At the next search for a page for swapping out, the search will continue from the place where the last search was ended. A page that is being used now will not be swapped out because its reference bit will be set before the search will find it again. CLOCK is still dominating the vast majority of operating systems including UNIX, Linux and Windows (Friedman, 1999).

Virtual memory is effective just when not many page faults are generated. According to the locality principle the program usually access memory addresses at the nearby area; therefore, if the pages in the nearby area are loaded in the memory, just few page faults will occur. During the execution of a program there are shifts from one locality to another. These shifts usually cause to an increase in the number of the page faults. In any phase of the execution, the pages that are included in the localities of the process are called the Working Set (Denning, 1968).

As has been written above, virtual memory works very similar to cache memory. In cache memory systems, there is a possibility to implement the cache memory such that each portion of the memory can be put in any place in the cache. Such a cache is called Fully Associative Cache. The major advantage of Fully Associative Cache is its high hit ratio; however Fully Associative Cache is more complex, the search time in it is longer and its power consumption is higher. Usually, cache memories are Set Associative meaning each part of the memory can be put only in predefined

locations, typically just 2 or 4. In Set Associative Cache the hit ratio is smaller, but the search time in it is shorter and the power consumption is lower. In virtual memory, the penalty of missing a hit is very high because it causes an access to a mechanical disk that is very slow; therefore, a page can be located in any place in the memory even though this will make the search algorithm more complex and longer.

In the programmer's point of view, the programs will be written using only virtual addresses. When a program is executed, there is a need to translate the virtual addresses into physical addresses. This translation is done by a special hardware component named MMU (Memory Management Unit). In some cases the operating system also participates in the translation procedure. The basis for the address translation is a page table that the operating system prepares and maintains. The simpler form of the page table is a vector that its indices are the virtual page numbers and every entry in the vector contains the fitting physical page number. With the aim of translating a virtual address into a physical address, there is a need to divide the address into a page number and an offset inside the page. According to the page number, the page will be found in the page table and the translation to a physical page number will be done. Concatenating the offset to the physical page number will yield the desired physical address.

Flat page table that maps the entire virtual memory space might occupy too much space in the physical memory. E. g. if the virtual memory space is 32 bits and the page size is 4KB, there will be needed more than millions entries in the page table. If each entry in the page table is 4 bytes, the page table size of each process will be 4MB. There is a possibility to reduce the page table size by using registers that will point to the beginning and the end of the segment that the program makes use of. E. g. UNIX BSD 4.3 permanently saves the page tables of the processes in the virtual memory of the operating system. The page table consists of two parts - one part maps the text, the data and the heap section that typically occupy a continuous region at the beginning of the memory; whereas the second part maps the stack that occupy a region beginning at the end of the virtual memory. This make a large "hole" in the middle of the page table between the heap region and the stack region and the page table is reduced to just two main areas. Later systems have also needs of dynamic libraries mapping and thread support; therefore the memory segments of the program are scattered over the virtual memory address space. With the aim of mapping a sparse address space and yet reducing the page table size, most of the modern architectures make use of a hierarchy page table. E. g. Linux uses a three level architecture independent page table scheme (Hartig et al., 1997). The tables in the lower levels will be needed just if they map addresses that the process accesses. E. g. Let us assume a hierarchy page table of two levels that the higher level page table contains 1024 pointers to lower level page tables and each page table in the lower level also contains 1024 entries. An address of 32 bits will be split into 10 bits that will contain the index of the higher level page table where a pointer to a page table in a lower level will reside, more 10 bits that will contain an index to a lower level page table where a pointer to the physical frame in the memory will reside and 12 bits that will contain the offset inside the physical page. If the address space is mapped by 64 bits, two levels page table will not be enough and more levels should be added in order to reduce the page table into a reasonable size. This may make the translation time longer, but a huge page table will occupy too much memory space and will be an unnecessary waste of memory resources.

STACK ALLOCATIONS

Fixed Size Allocations

User space allocations are transparent with a large and dynamically growing stack. In the Linux kernel's environment the stack is small-sized and fixed. It is possible to determine the stack size as from 2.6.x kernel series during compile time choosing between 4 to 8KB. The current tendency is to limit the stack to 4KB.

The allocation of one page is done as one non-swappable base-page of 4KB. If a 8KB stack is used, two non-swappable pages will be allocated, even if the hardware support an 8KB super-page (Itshak and Wiseman, 2008); in point of fact, IA-32 machines do not support 8KB super-pages, so 8KB is the only choice.

The rational for this choice is to limit the amount of memory and virtual memory address space that is allocated in order to support a large number of user processes. Allocating an 8KB stack increases the amount of memory by a factor of two. In addition the memory must be allocated as two contiguous pages which are relatively expensive to allocate.

A process that executes in kernel mode, i.e. executing a system call, will use its own kernel stack. The entire call chain of a process executing inside the kernel must be capable of fitting on the stack. In an 8KB stack size configuration, interrupt handlers use the stack of the process they interrupt. This means that the kernel stack size might need to be shared by a deep call chain of multiple functions and an interrupt handler. In a 4KB stack size configuration, interrupts have a separate stack, making the exception mechanism slower and more complicated (Robbins, 2004).

The strict size of the stack may cause an overflow. Any system call must be aware of the stack size. If large stack variables are declared and/or too many function calls are made, an overflow may occur (Baratloo et al., 2000), (Cowan et al., 1998).

Memory corruption caused by a stack overflow may cause the system to be in an undefined state (Wilander and Kamkar, 2003). The kernel makes no effort to manage the stack and no essential mechanism oversees the stack size.

In (Chou et al., 2001) the authors present an empirical study of Linux bugs. The study compares errors in different subsections of Linux kernels, discovers how bugs are distributed and generated, calculates how long, on average, bugs live, clusters bugs according to error types, and compares the Linux kernel bugs to the OpenBSD kernel bugs. The data used in this study was collected from snapshots of the Linux kernel across seven years. The study refers to the versions until the 2.4.1 kernel series, as it was published in 2001. 1025 bugs were reported in this study. The reason for 102 of these bugs is large stack variables on the fixed-size kernel stack. Most of the fixed-size stack overflow bugs are located in device drivers. Device drivers are written by many developers who may understand the device more than the kernel, but are not aware of the kernel stack limitation. Hence, no attempt is made to confront this setback. In addition, only a few users may have a given device; thus, only a minimal check might be made for some device drivers. In addition, Cut-and-Paste bugs are very common in device drivers and elsewhere (Li et al., 2004); therefore, the stack overflow bugs are incessantly and unwarily spread.

The goal of malicious attackers is to drive the system into an unexpected state, which can help the attacker to infiltrate into the protected portion of the operating system. Overflowing the kernel stack can provide the attacker this option which can have very devastating security implications (Coverity, 2004). The attackers look for rare failure cases that almost never happen in normal system operations. It is hard to track down all the rare cases of kernel stack overflow, thus the operating system remains vulnerable. This leads us to the unavoidable conclusion: Since the stack overflows are difficult to detect and fix,

the necessary solution is letting the kernel stack grow dynamically.

A small fixed size stack is a liability when trying to port code from other systems to Linux. The kernel thread capability would seem offer an ideal platform for porting user code and non-Linux OS code. This facility is limited both by the lack of a per-process memory space and by a small fixed sized size stack.

An example of the inadequacy of the fixed size stack is in the very popular use of the Ndiswrapper project (Fuchs and Pemmasani, 2005) to implement Windows kernel API and NDIS (Network Driver Interface Specification) API within the Linux kernel. This can allow the use of a Windows binary driver for a wireless network card running natively within the Linux kernel, without binary emulation. This is frequently the solution used when hardware manufacturers refuse to release detail of their product so a native Linux driver is not available.

The problem with this approach is that the Windows kernel provides a minimum of 12KB kernel stack whereas Linux in the best case uses an 8KB stack. This mismatch of kernel stack sizes can and cause system stack corruptions leading to kernel crashes. This would ironically seem to be the ultimate revenge of an OS (MS Windows) not known for long term reliability on an OS (Linux) which normally is known for its long term stability.

Current Solutions

Currently, Operating Systems developers have suggested several methods how to tackle the kernel stack overflows. They suggest to change the way of writing the code that supposed to be executed in kernel mode instead of changing the way that kernel stack is handled. This is unacceptable - the system must cater for its users!

The common guidance for kernel code developers is not to write recursive functions. Infinite number of calls to a recursive function is a common bug and it will cause very soon a kernel stack overflow. Even too deep recursive call can easily make the stack growing fast and overflowing. This is also correct for deeply nested code. The kernel stack size is very small and even the kernel stack of Windows that can be 12KB or 24KB might overflow very quickly if the kernel code is not written carefully.

Also a common guidance is not to use local variables in kernel code. Global variables are not pushed upon the kernel stack; therefore they will save space on the kernel stack and will not cause a kernel overflow. This guidance is definitely against software engineering rules. A code with only global variables is quite hard to be read and quite hard to be checked and rewritten; however since the kernel stack space is so precise and even a tiny exceeding will be terribly devastating, kernel code developers agree to write an unclear code instead of having a buggy code.

Another frequent guidance is not to declare local variables as a single character or even as a string of characters if the intention is to create a local buffer for a function in the kernel code. Instead, the buffer should be put in a paged or a non-paged pool and then a declaration of a pointer to that buffer can be made. In this way, when a call from this kernel function is made, not all the buffer will be pushed upon the kernel stack and only the pointer will actually be pushed upon the stack.

This is also one of the reasons why the kernel code is not written in C++. C++ needs large memory space for allocations of classes and structures. Sometimes, these allocations can be too large and from time to time they can be a source for kernel stack overflows.

There were some works that suggested to dedicate a special kernel stack for specific tasks e.g. (Draves et al., 1991); however, these additional kernel stacks make the code very complex and the possibilities for bugs in the kernel code become more likely to happen.

Some works tried to implement a hardware solution e.g. (Frantzen and Shuey, 2001); however

such a solution can be difficult to implementation because of the pipelined nature of the nowadays machines. In order to increase the rate of computers, many manufacturers use the pipeline method (Jouppi and Wall, 1989), (Kogge, 1981), (Wiseman, 2001), (Patterson and Hennessy, 1997). This method enables performing several actions in a machine in parallel mode. Every action is in a different phase of its performing. The action is divided into some fundamental sub-actions which can be performed in one clock cycle. In every clock cycle, from every action, the machine will perform a new sub-action. A pipeline machine can perform different sub-actions in parallel. In every clock cycle, the machine performs sub-actions for different actions. The stack handling is complicated because it is depended on the braches to functions which are not easy to be predicted; however, some solutions have been suggested to this difficulty e.g. (McMahan, 1998).

Dynamic Size Allocations

In the 1980s, a new operating system concept was introduced: the microkernels (Liedtke, 1996), (Bershad et al., 1995). The objective of microkernels was to minimize the kernel code and to implement anything possible outside the kernel. This concept is still alive and embraced by some operating systems researchers (Leschke, 2004), although the classic operating systems like Linux still employ the traditional monolithic kernel.

The microkernels concept has two main advantages: First, the system is flexible and extensible, i.e. the operating system can easily adapt a new hardware. Second, many malfunctions are isolated like in a regular application; because many parts of the operating system are standard processes and thus are independent. A permanent failure of a standard process does not induce a reboot; therefore, the microkernel based operating systems tend to be more robust (Lu and Smith, 2006).

A microkernel feature that is worthy of note is the address space memory management (Liedtke,

1995). A dedicated process is in charge of the memory space allocation, reallocations and free. The process is executed in user mode; thus, the page faults are forwarded and handled in user mode and cannot cause a kernel bug. Moreover, most of the kernel services are implemented outside the kernel and specifically the device drivers; hence these services are executed in user mode and are not able to use the kernel stack.

Although the microkernel has many theoretical advantages (Hand et al., 2005), its performance and efficiency are somewhat disappointing. Nowadays, most of the modern operating systems use a monolithic kernel. In addition, even when an operating system uses a microkernel scheme, there still will be minimal use of the kernel stack.

We propose an approach that suggests a dynamically growing stack. However, unlike the microkernel approach, we will implement the dynamically growing stack within the kernel.

Real Time Considerations

Linux is designed as a non-preemptive kernel. Therefore, by its nature, is not well suited for real time applications that require deterministic response time.

The 2.4.x Linux kernel versions introduced several new amendments. One of them was the preemptive patch which supports soft real-time applications (Anzinger and Gamble, 2000). This patch is now a standard in the new Linux kernel versions (Kuhn, 2004). The objective of this patch is executing the scheduler more often by finding places in the kernel code that preemptions can be executed safely. On such cases more data is pushed onto the kernel stack. This additional data can worsen the kernel overflow problem. In addition, these cases are hard to be predicted (Williams, 2002).

For hard real-time applications, RTLinux (Dankwardt, 2001) or RTAI (Mantegazz et al., 2000) can be used. These systems use a nano-kernel that runs Linux as its lowest priority

execution thread. This thread is fully preemptive hence real-time tasks are never delayed by non-real-time operations.

Another interesting solution for a high-speed kernel-programming environment is the KML (Kernel Mode Linux) project (Maeda, 2002a), (Maeda, 2002b), (Maeda, 2003). KML allows executing user programs in kernel mode and a direct access to the kernel address space. The kernel mode execution eliminates the system call overhead, because every system call is merely a function call. The main disadvantage of KML is that any user can write to the kernel memory. In order to trim down the aforementioned problem, the author of KML suggests using TAL (Typed Assembly Language) which checks the program before loading. However, this check does not always find the memory leak. As a result, the security is very poor. It is difficult to prevent illegal memory access and illegal code execution. On occasion, memory illegal accesses are done deliberately, but they also can be performed accidentally.

Our approach to increase the soft real-time applications responsiveness is to run them as kernel threads while using fundamental normal process facilities such as a large and dynamically growing stack. While running in kernel context, it is possible to achieve a better predictive response time as the kernel is the highest priority component in the system. The solution provides the most important benefits you find in the KML project, although this solution is a more intuitive and straightforward implementation.

IMPLEMENTATION

The objective of this implementation is to support the demand paging mechanism for the kernel mode stack. The proposed solution is a patch for the kernel that can be enabled or disabled using the kernel configuration tools. In the following sections the design, implementation and testing utilities are described.

Figure 1. Kernel Memory Stack and the Process Descriptor

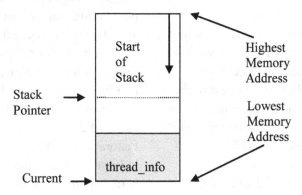

Process Descriptor

In order to manage its processes, Linux has for each process a process descriptor containing the information related to this process (Gorman, 2004). Linux stores the process descriptors in a circular doubly linked list called the task list. The process descriptor's pointer is a part of a structure named "thread_info" that is stored under the bottom of the kernel mode stack of each process as shown in Figure 1.

This feature allows referencing the process descriptor using the stack pointer without any memory referencing. The reason for this method of implementation is improved performance. The stack pointer address is frequently used; hence, it is stored in a special purpose register. In order to get a reference for the current process descriptor faster, the stack pointer is used. This is done by a macro called "current".

In order to benefit the performance and leave the "current" mechanism untouched, a new allocation interface is introduced which allocates one physical page and a contiguous virtual address space that is aligned to the new stack size.

The new virtual area of the stack size can be of any size. The thread_info structure is set to the top of the highest virtual address minus the thread_info structure size. The stack pointer starts from beneath the thread_info. Additional physical pages will be allocated and populated in the virtual address space if the CPU triggers a page fault exception.

Exceptions

The IA-32 architecture provides 4 protection levels of code execution. Usually they are called "rings" and numbered as 0,1,2,3 whereas 0 is the most privileged ring and 3 is the least privileged. Linux uses just ring 0 and 3. Ring 0 is used when the kernel is executed, whereas 3 is used for non-privileged user space applications.

When a process is executed and an exception occurs, the ring is switched from 3 to 0. One of the consequences of this switch is changing of the stack. The process' user space stack is replaced by the process' kernel mode stack while the CPU pushes several registers to the new stack. When the execution is completed, the CPU restores the interrupted process user space stack using the registers it pushed to the kernel stack.

If an exception occurs during a kernel execution in the kernel mode stack, the stack is not replaced because the task is already running in ring 0. The CPU cannot push the registers to the kernel mode stack, thus it generates a double fault exception. This is called the stack starvation problem.

Interrupt Task

Interrupts divert the processor to code outside the normal flow of control. The CPU stops what it is currently doing and switches to a new activity. This activity is usually held in the context of the process that is currently running, i.e the interrupted process. As mentioned, current scheme may lead to a stack starvation problem if a page fault exception happens in the kernel mode stack.

The IA-32 provides a special task management facility to support process management in the kernel. Using this facility while running in the kernel mode causes the CPU to switch an execution context to a special context, therefore preventing the stack starvation problem.

The current Linux kernel release uses this kind of mechanism to handle double fault exceptions that are non-recoverable exceptions in the kernel. This mechanism uses a system segment called a Task State Segment that is referenced via the IDT (Interrupt Descriptor Table) and the GDT (Global Descriptor Table) tables. This mechanism provides a protected way to manage processes although it is not widely used because of a relatively larger context switch time.

We suggest adding the special task management facility to handle page fault exceptions in the kernel mode stack. Using this mechanism it is possible to handle the exceptions by allocating a new physical page, mapping it to the kernel page tables and resuming the interrupted process. Current user space page faults handling will remains as is.

EVALUATION

First, we used the BYTE UNIX benchmark (BYTE, 2005) in order to check that we did not introduce unnecessary performance degradation in the system's normal flow of execution. The benchmark that was used checks system performance by the following criteria (as can be seen in the following figures 2, 3): system call overhead, pipe throughput, context switching, process creation (spawn) and execl.

Results measurements are presented in lps (loops per second). We executed the benchmark on two different platforms. The first test was executed on a Pentium 1.7GHz with 512MB RAM and a cache of 2MB running Linux kernel 2.6.9 with Fedora core 2 distribution. The detailed results are in Figure 2. Blue columns represent the original kernel whereas the green columns represent the patched kernel.

We also executed the BYTE benchmark on a Celeron Pentium 2.4GHz with 256MB RAM and a cache of 512KB running Linux kernel 2.6.9 with Fedora core 2 distribution. The results of this test can be seen in Figure 3. Examination of the results found no performance degradation in the new mechanism integrated into the Linux kernel and the results of all tests were essentially unchanged.

Second, we performed a functionality test to check that when the CPU triggers a page fault in the kernel mode stack, a new page is actually allocated and mapped to the kernel page tables.

This feature was accomplished by writing a kernel module and intentionally overloading the stack by a large vector variable. We then added printing to the page fault handler and were able to assess that the new mechanism worked as expected.

It has to be noted that only page faults that are in the kernel mode stack are handled using the task management facility, whereas page faults triggered from user space processes are handled as in the original kernel.

Triggering of page faults from the user processes stack and even more so from the kernel mode stack rarely happens. In both scenarios performance decrement in the system is negligible.

In spite of the aforementioned, we obtained several measurements to ensure that the new mechanism does not demonstrate anomalous results.

Figure 2. BYTE Unix benchmark for Pentium 1.7GHz.

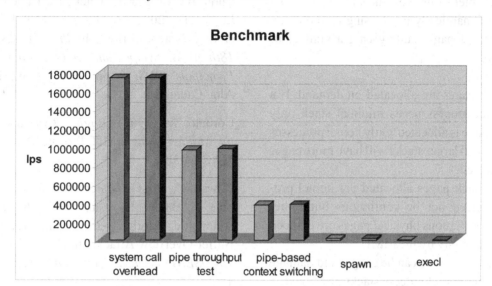

Page fault latency measurements showed that the original page fault time is averagely 3.55 microseconds on the Pentium 1.7GHz we used in the previous test, whereas the page fault time of the kernel stack is averagely 7.15 microseconds i.e. the kernel stack page fault time is apparently roughly double.

CONCLUSION

An overflow in kernel stack is a common bug in the Linux operating system. These bugs are difficult to detect because they are created as a side effect of the code and not as an inherent mistake in the algorithm implementation.

Figure 3. BYTE Unix benchmark for Pentium 2.4GHz.

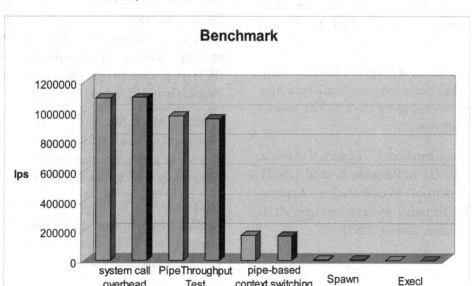

This chapter shows how the size of the kernel stack can dynamically grow using the common mechanism of page faults giving a number of advantages:

1. Stack pages are allocated on demand. If a kernel process needs minimal stack only one page is allocated. Only kernel processes that need larger stacks will have more pages allocated.
2. The stack pages allocated per kernel process need not be contiguous but rather non-contiguous physical pages are mapped contiguously by the MMU.
3. Stack overflows can be caught and damage to other kernel process stacks prevented.
4. Larger kernel stacks can be efficiently provided. This facilitates porting of code that has not been designed for minimal stack usage into the Linux kernel.

REFERENCES

Analysis of the Linux kernel (2004). San Francisco, CA: Coverity Corporation.

Anzinger, G., & Gamble, N. (2000). *Design of a Fully Preemptable Linux Kernel*. MontaVista Software.

Baratloo, A., Tsai, T., & Singh, N. (2000). Transparent Run-Time Defense Against Stack Smashing Attacks. In *Proceedings of the USENIX annual Technical Conference*.

Bershad, B. N., Chambers, C., Eggers, S., Maeda, C., McNamee, D., & Pardyak, P. et al (1995). SPIN - An Extensible Microkernel for Application-specific Operating System Services. *ACM Operating Systems Review, 29*(1).

Chou, A., Yang, J. F., Chelf, B., Hallem, S., & Engler, D. (2001). An Empirical Study of Operating Systems Errors. In *Proceedings of the 18th ACM, Symposium on Operating System Principals (SOSP)*, (pp. 73-88), Lake Louise, Alta. Canada.

Corbato, A. (1968). *Paging Experiment with the Multics System*. MIT Project MAC Report, MAC-M-384.

Cowan, C., Pu, C., Maier, D., Hinton, H., Walpole, J., Bakke, P., et al. (1998). StackGuard: Automatic Adaptive Detection and Prevention of Buffer-Overflow Attacks. In *Proceedings of the 7th USENIX Security Conference,* San Antonio, TX.

Dankwardt, K. (2001). *Real Time and Linux, Part 3: Sub-Kernels and Benchmarks*. Retrieved from

Denning, P. (1970). Virtual Memory. [CSUR]. *ACM Computing Surveys, 2*(3), 153–189. doi:10.1145/356571.356573

Denning, P. J. (1968). The Working Set Model for Program Behavior. *Communications of the ACM, 11*(5), 323–333. doi:10.1145/363095.363141

Draves, R. P., Bershad, B. N., Rashid, R. F., & Dean, R. W. (1991). Using continuations to implement thread management and communication in operating systems. In *Proceedings of the thirteenth ACM symposium on Operating systems principles,* Pacific Grove, CA, (pp. 122-136).

Frantzen, M., & Shuey, M. (2001). StackGhost: Hardware facilitated stack protection. In *Proceedings of the 10th conference on USENIX Security Symposium* – Washington, D.C. (Vol. 10, p. 5).

Friedman, M. B. (1999). Windows NT Page Replacement Policies. In *Proceedings of 25th International Computer Measurement Group Conference*, (pp. 234-244).

Fuchs, P., & Pemmasani, G. (2005). *NdisWrapper*. Retrieved from http://ndiswrapper.sourceforge. net/

Gorman, M. (2004). Understanding The Linux Virtual Memory Manager. Upper Saddle River, NJ: Prentice Hall, Bruce Perens' Open Source Series.

Hand, S. Warfield, A. Fraser, K. Kotsovinos E. & Magenheimer, D. (2005). Are Virtual Machine Monitors Microkernels Done Right? In *Proceedings of the Tenth Workshop on Hot Topics in Operating Systems (HotOS-X)*, June 12-15, Santa-Fe, NM.

Hartig, H. Hohmuth, M. Liedtke, J. Schonberg, & S. Wolter, J. (1997). The Performance of μ-Kernel-Based Systems. In *Proceedings of the sixteenth ACM symposium on Operating systems principles*, Saint Malo, France, (p.66-77).

Intel Pentium Processor User's Manual. (1993). Mt. Prospect, IL: Intel Corporation. *IA-32 Intel Architecture Software Developer's Manual*, (2005). Volume 3: System Programming Guide. Mt. Prospect, IL: Intel Corporation.

Itshak, M., & Wiseman, Y. (2008). AMSQM: Adaptive Multiple SuperPage Queue Management. In *Proc. IEEE Conference on Information Reuse and Integration (IEEE IRI-2008)*, Las Vegas, Nevada, (pp. 52-57).

Jacob, B. (2002). Virtual Memory Systems and TLB Structures. In *Computer Engineering Handbook*. Boca Raton, FL: CRC Press.

Jiang, S., Chen, F., & Zhang, X. (2005). CLOCK-Pro: an Effective Improvement of the CLOCK Replacement. In *Proceedings of 2005 USENIX Annual Technical Conference*, Anaheim, CA (pp. 323-336).

Jouppi, N. P., & Wall, D. W. (1989). Available Instruction Level Parallelism for Superscalar and Superpipelined Machines. In *Proc. Third Conf. On Architectural Support for Programming Languages and Operation System IEEE/ACM*, Boston, (pp. 82-272).

Kogge, P. M. (1981). The Architecture of Pipelined Computers. New-York: McGraw-Hill.

Kuhn, B. (2004). *The Linux real time interrupt patch*. Retrieved from http://linuxdevices.com/ articles/AT6105045931.html.

Leschke, T. (2004). Achieving speed and flexibility by separating management from protection: embracing the Exokernel operating system. *Operating Systems Review*, *38*(4), 5–19. doi:10.1145/1031154.1031155

Li, Z., Lu, S., Myagmar, S., & Zhou, Y. (2004). CP-Miner: A Tool for Finding Copy-paste and Related Bugs in Operating System Code. In *The 6th Symposium on Operating Systems Design and Implementation (OSDI '04)*, San Francisco, CA.

Liedtke, J. (1995). On Micro-Kernel Construction. In *Proceedings of the 15th ACM Symposium on Operating System Principles*. New York: ACM.

Liedtke, J. (1996). Toward Real Microkernels. *Communications of the ACM*, *39*(9). doi:10.1145/234215.234473

LINUX Pentiums using BYTE UNIX Benchmarks (2005). Winston-Salem, NC: SilkRoad, Inc.

Love, R. (2003). *Linux Kernel Development* (1st Ed.). Sams.

Lu, X., & Smith, S. F. (2006). A Microkernel Virtual Machine: Building Security with Clear Interfaces. *ACM SIGPLAN Workshop on Programming Languages and Analysis for Security*, Ottawa, Canada, June 10, (pp. 47-56).

Maeda, T. (2002). *Safe Execution of User programs in Kernel Mode Using Typed Assembly Language.* Master Thesis, The University of Tokyo, Tokyo, Japan.

Maeda, T. (2002). *Kernel Mode Linux: Execute user process in kernel mode.* Retrieved from http://www.yl.is.s.u-tokyo.ac.jp/~tosh/kml/

Maeda, T. (2003). Kernel Mode Linux. *Linux Journal, 109,* 62–67.

Mantegazz, P., Bianchi, E., Dozio, L., Papacharalambous, S., & Hughes, S. (2000). *RTAI: Real-Time Application Interface.* Retrieved from http://www.linuxdevices.com/articles/ AT6605918741.html.

McMahan, S. (1998). Cyrix Corp. *Branch Processing unit with a return stack including repair using pointers from different pipe stage.* U.S. Patent No. 5,706,491.

Nicola, V. F., Dan, A., & Diaz, D. M. (1992). Analysis of the generalized clock buffer replacement scheme for database transaction processing. *ACM SIGMETRICS Performance Evaluation Review, 20*(1), 35–46. doi:10.1145/149439.133084

Patterson, D. A., & Hennessy, J. L. (1997). *Computer Organization and Design* (pp. 434-536). San Francisco, CA: Morgan Kaufmann Publishers, INC.

Robbins, A. (2004). *Linux Programming by Example.* Upper Saddle River, NJ: Pearson Education Inc.

Wilander, J., & Kamkar, M. (2003). A Comparison of Publicly Available Tools for Dynamic Buffer Overflow Prevention. In *Proceedings of the 10th Network and Distributed System Security Symposium (NDSS'03)*, San Diego, CA, (pp. 149-162).

Williams, C. (2002). *Linux Scheduler Latency.* Raleigh, NC: Red Hat Inc.

Winwood, S. J., Shuf, Y., & Franke, H. (2002). Multiple page size support in the Linux kernel. *Proceedings of Ottawa Linux Symposium,* Ottawa, Canada. Bovet, D. P. & Cesati, M. (2003). Understanding the Linux Kernel (2nd Ed). Sebastol, CA: O'reilly.

Chapter 2
Device Driver Reliability

Michael M. Swift
University of Wisconsin—Madison, USA

ABSTRACT

Despite decades of research in extensible operating system technology, extensions such as device drivers remain a significant cause of system failures. In Windows XP, for example, drivers account for 85% of recently reported failures. This chapter presents Nooks, a layered architecture for tolerating the failure of drivers within existing operating system kernels. The design consists techniques for isolating drivers from the kernel and for recovering from their failure. Nooks isolates drivers from the kernel in a light-weight kernel protection domain, a new protection mechanism. By executing drivers within a domain, the kernel is protected from their failure and cannot be corrupted. Shadow drivers recover from device driver failures. Based on a replica of the driver's state machine, a shadow driver conceals the driver's failure from applications and restores the driver's internal state to a point where it can process requests as if it had never failed. Thus, the entire failure and recovery is transparent to applications.

INTRODUCTION

Improving reliability is one of the greatest challenges for commodity operating systems, such as Windows and Linux. System failures are commonplace and costly across all domains: in the home, in the server room, and in embedded systems, where the existence of the OS itself is invisible. At the low end, failures lead to user frustration and lost sales. At the high end, an hour of downtime from a system failure can lead to losses in the millions.

Computer system reliability remains a crucial but unsolved problem. This problem has been exacerbated by the adoption of commodity operating systems, designed for best-effort operation, in environments that require high availability. While the cost of high-performance computing continues to drop because of commoditization, the cost of failures (e.g., downtime on a stock exchange or e-commerce server, or the manpower required to service a help-

DOI: 10.4018/978-1-60566-850-5.ch002

desk request in an office environment) continues to rise as our dependence on computers grows. In addition, the growing sector of "unmanaged" systems, such as digital appliances and consumer devices based on commodity hardware and software, amplifies the need for reliability.

Device drivers are a leading cause of operating system failure. Device drivers and other extensions have become increasingly prevalent in commodity systems such as Linux (where they are called *modules*) and Windows (where they are called *drivers*). Extensions are optional components that reside in the kernel address space and typically communicate with the kernel through published interfaces. Drivers now account for over 70% of Linux kernel code, and over 35,000 different drivers with over 112,000 versions exist on Windows XP desktops. Unfortunately, most of the programmers writing drivers work for independent hardware vendors and have significantly less experience in kernel organization and programming than the programmers that build the operating system itself.

In Windows XP, for example, drivers cause 85% of reported failures. In Linux, the frequency of coding errors is up to seven times higher for device drivers than for the rest of the kernel. While the core operating system kernel can reach high levels of reliability because of longevity and repeated testing, the *extended* operating system cannot be tested completely. With tens of thousands of drivers, operating system vendors cannot even identify them all, let alone test all possible combinations used in the marketplace. In contemporary systems, any fault in a driver can corrupt vital kernel data, causing the system to crash.

This chapter presents Nooks, a driver reliability subsystem that allows existing device drivers to execute safely in commodity kernels (Swift, Bershad & Levy, 2005). Nooks acts as a layer between drivers and the kernel and provides two key services: isolation and recovery. Nooks allows the operating system to tolerate driver failures by isolating the OS from device drivers. With

Nooks, a bug in a driver cannot corrupt or otherwise harm the operating system. Nooks contains driver failures with a new isolation mechanism, called a *lightweight kernel protection domain*, that is a privileged kernel-mode environment with restricted write access to kernel memory.

When a driver failure occurs, Nooks detects the failure with a combination of hardware and software checks and triggers automatic recovery. A new kernel agent, called a *shadow driver*, conceals a driver's failure from its clients while recovering from the failure (Swift et al, 2006). During normal operation, the shadow tracks the state of the real driver by monitoring all communication between the kernel and the driver. When a failure occurs, the shadow inserts itself *temporarily* in place of the failed driver, servicing requests on its behalf. While shielding the kernel and applications from the failure, the shadow driver restarts the failed driver and restores it to a state where it can resume processing requests as if it had never failed.

DEVICE DRIVER OVERVIEW

A device driver is a kernel-mode software component that provides an interface between the OS and a hardware device. In most commodity operating systems, device drivers execute in the kernel for two reasons. First, they require privileged access to hardware, such as the ability to handle interrupts, which is only available in the kernel. Second, they require high performance, which is achieved via direct procedure calls into and out of the kernel.

Driver Software Structure

A driver converts requests from the kernel into requests to the hardware. Drivers rely on two interfaces: the interface that drivers *export* to the kernel, which provides access to the device, and the kernel interface that drivers *import* from the operating system. The kernel invokes the functions exported by a driver to requests its services. Similarly, a driver invokes functions imported from the kernel to request its services. For example, Figure 1(a) shows the kernel calling into a sound-card driver to play a tone; in response, the sound driver converts the request into a sequence of I/O instructions that direct the sound card to emit a sound.

In addition to processing I/O requests, drivers also handle configuration requests. Configuration requests can change both driver and device behavior for future I/O requests. As examples, applications may configure the bandwidth of a network card or the volume of a sound card.

In practice, most device drivers are members of a *class*, which is defined by its interface. Code that can invoke one driver in the class can invoke any driver in the class. For example, all network drivers obey the same kernel-driver interface, and

all sound-card drivers obey the same kernel-driver interface, so no new kernel or application code is needed to invoke new drivers in these classes. This class orientation allows the OS and applications to be device-independent, as the details of a specific device are hidden from view in the driver.

In Linux, there are approximately 20 common classes of drivers. However, not all drivers fit into classes; a driver may extend the interface for a class with proprietary functions, in effect creating a new sub-class of drivers. Drivers may also define their own semantics for standard interface functions, known only to applications written specifically for the driver. In this case, the driver is in a class by itself. In practice, most common drivers, such as network, sound, and storage drivers, implement only the standard interfaces.

Device drivers are either *request-oriented* or *connection-oriented*. Request-oriented drivers, such as network drivers and block storage driv-

Figure 1. (a) a sound device driver, showing the common interface to the kernel and to all sound drivers, (b) states of a network driver and sound driver

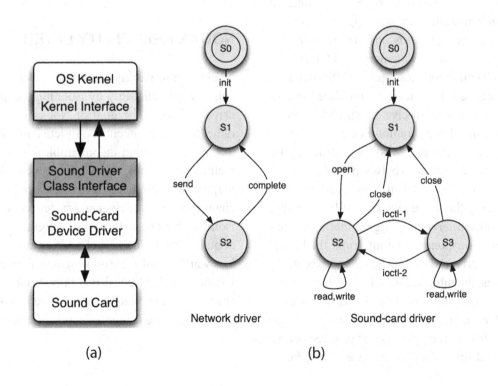

(a)

(b)

ers, maintain a single hardware configuration and process each request independently. In contrast, connection-oriented drivers maintain separate hardware and software configurations for each client of the device. Furthermore, requests on a single connection may depend on past requests that changed the connection configuration.

Devices attach to a computer through a *bus*, such as PCI (Peripheral Component Interconnect) or USB (Universal Serial Bus), which is responsible for detecting attached devices and making them available to software. When detected, the operating system locates and loads the appropriate device driver. Communication between the driver and its device depends on the connection bus. For PCI devices, the driver communicates directly with the device through regions of the computer's physical address space that are mapped onto the PCI bus or through I/O ports. Thus, loads and stores to these addresses and ports cause communication with a device. For USB devices, drivers create request packets that are sent to the device by the driver for the USB bus.

Most drivers rely on three types of communication with devices. First, drivers communicate control information, such as configuration or I/O commands, through reads and writes to *device registers* in ports or I/O memory for PCI devices or through command messages for USB devices. Device registers are a device's interface to share information and to receive commands from a driver. Second, drivers communicate data through DMA (Direct Memory Access) by instructing the device or bus to copy data between the device and memory; the processor is not involved in copying, reducing the processing cost of I/O. Finally, devices raise *interrupts* to signal that they need attention. In response to an interrupt, the kernel schedules a driver's interrupt handler to execute. In most cases, the interrupt signal is *level triggered*, in that an interrupt raised by the device is only lowered when the driver instructs the device to do so. Thus, interrupt handling must proceed before any normal processing, because enabling inter-

rupts in the processor will cause another interrupt until the driver dismisses the interrupt.

Device drivers can be modeled as abstract state machines; each input to the driver from the kernel or output from the driver reflects a potential state change in the driver. For example, the left side of Figure 1(b) shows a state machine for a network driver as it sends packets. The driver begins in state S0, before the driver has been loaded. Once the driver is loaded and initialized, the driver enters state S1. When the driver receives a request to send packets, it enters state S2, where there is a packet outstanding. When the driver notifies the kernel that the send is complete, it returns to state S1. The right side of Figure 1(b) shows a similar state machine for a sound-card driver. This driver may be opened, configured between multiple states, and closed. The state-machine model aids in designing and understanding a recovery process that seeks to restore the driver state by clarifying the state to which the driver is recovering. For example, a mechanism that unloads a driver after a failure returns the driver to state S0, while one that also reloads the driver returns it to state S1.

NOOKS RELIABILITY LAYER

Nooks is a reliability layer that seeks to greatly enhance OS reliability by isolating the OS from driver failures. The goal of Nooks is practical: rather than guaranteeing complete fault tolerance through a new (and incompatible) OS or driver architecture, Nooks seeks to prevent the vast majority of driver-caused crashes with little or no change to existing driver and system code. Nooks isolates drivers within lightweight protection domains inside the kernel address space, where hardware and software prevent them from corrupting the kernel. After a driver fails, Nooks invokes shadow drivers, a recovery subsystem, to recover by restoring the driver to its pre-failure state.

Figure 2. The Nooks Isolation Manager as a layer between device drivers and the kernel. The black lines indicate the minor changes needed to each.

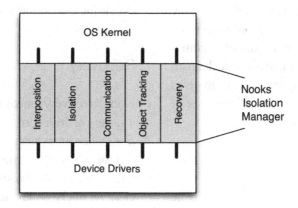

Design

Nooks operates as a layer that is inserted between drivers and the OS kernel. This layer intercepts all interactions between drivers and the kernel to facilitate isolation and recovery. Figure 2 shows this new layer, called the *Nooks Isolation Manager* (NIM). Above the NIM is the operating system kernel. The NIM function lines jutting up into the kernel represent kernel-dependent modifications, if any, the OS kernel programmer makes to insert Nooks into a particular OS. These modifications need only be made once. Underneath the NIM is the set of isolated drivers. The function lines jutting down below the NIM represent the changes, if any, the driver writer makes to interface a specific driver or driver class to Nooks. In general, no modifications should be required at this level.

The NIM provides five major architectural functions, as shown in Figure 2: interposition, isolation, communication, object tracking, and recovery.

Interposition

The Nooks interposition mechanisms transparently integrate existing extensions into the Nooks environment. Interposition code ensures that: (1)

all driver-to-kernel and kernel-to-driver control flow occurs through the communication mechanism, and (2) all data transfer between the kernel and driver is viewed and managed by Nooks' object-tracking code (described below).

The interface between the extension, the NIM, and the kernel is provided by a set of *wrapper stubs* that are part of the interposition mechanism. Wrappers resemble the stubs in an RPC system that provide transparent control and data transfer across address space (and machine) boundaries. Nooks' stubs provide safe and transparent control and data transfer between the kernel and driver. Thus, from the driver's viewpoint, the stubs appear to be the kernel's extension API. From the kernel's point of view, the stubs appear to be the driver's function entry points.

In addition, wrapper stubs provide support for recovery. When the driver functions correctly, wrappers pass information about the state of the driver to shadow drivers. During recovery, wrappers disable communication between the driver and the kernel to ensure that the kernel is isolated from the recovery process.

Isolation

The Nooks isolation mechanisms prevent driver faults from damaging the kernel (or other isolated drivers). Every driver in Nooks executes within its own *lightweight kernel protection domain*. This domain is an execution context with the same processor privilege as the kernel but with write access to a limited portion of the kernel's address space. The major task of the isolation mechanism is protection-domain management. This involves the creation, manipulation, and maintenance of lightweight protection domains.

Communication

The Nooks communication mechanisms enable procedure calls between lightweight protection domains. Unlike system calls, which are always initiated by an application, the kernel frequently calls into drivers. These calls may generate callbacks into the kernel, which may then generate a call into the driver, and so on. This complex communication style is handled by a new kernel service, called the *Extension Procedure Call* (XPC) - a control transfer mechanism specifically tailored to isolating driver within the kernel. An XPC combines both a protection domain change and a procedure call. This mechanism resembles a system call, in that parameters must be verified on entry to the kernel. However, XPC also occurs from the kernel into the driver as well.

Object Tracking

Nooks object-tracking functions oversee all kernel resources used by drivers. In particular, object-tracking code: (1) maintains a list of kernel data structures that are manipulated by a driver, (2) controls all modifications to those structures, and (3) provides object information for cleanup when a driver fails. Protection domains prevent drivers from directly modifying kernel data structures. Therefore, object-tracking code must copy kernel objects into a driver domain so they can be modified and copy them back after changes have been applied. When possible, object-tracking code verifies the type and accessibility of each parameter

that passes between the driver and kernel. Kernel routines can then avoid scrutinizing parameters, executing checks only when called from unreliable drivers.

Recovery

Nooks' recovery functions detect and recover from a variety of driver errors. Nooks detects a *software fault* when an extension invokes a kernel service improperly (e.g., with invalid arguments) or when an extension consumes too many resources. In this case, recovery policy determines whether Nooks triggers recovery or returns an error code to the driver, which can already handle the failure of a kernel function. Triggering recovery prevents further corruption, but may degrade performance by recovering more frequently. Nooks detects a *hardware fault* when the processor raises an exception during driver execution, e.g., when a driver attempts to read unmapped memory or to write memory outside of its protection domain. Unmodified drivers are unable to handle their own hardware faults, so in such cases Nooks always triggers a higher-level recovery.

Nooks relies on *shadow drivers* to recover from the failure of a driver. Shadow drivers are a recovery service that leverage the shared properties of a class of drivers for recovery. The architecture consists of three components: shadow drivers, taps, and a shadow recovery manager.

A *shadow driver* is a kernel agent that facilitates recovery for an entire class of device drivers. A shadow driver instance is a running shadow driver that recovers for a single, specific driver. The shadow instance compensates for and recovers from a driver that has failed. When a driver fails, its shadow restores the driver to its pre-failure state. This allows, for example, the recovered driver to complete requests made before the failure.

Figure 3. Control flow of driver and kernel wrappers

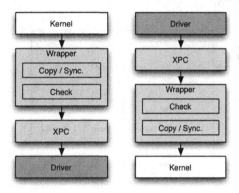

Implementation

Nooks was implemented within the Linux 2.4.18 kernel on the Intel x86 architecture. The kernel provides over 700 functions callable by drivers and other extensions and more than 650 extension-entry functions callable by the kernel. Moreover, few data types are abstracted, and drivers directly access fields in many kernel data structures.

The Linux kernel supports standard interfaces for many extension classes. For example, there is a generic interface for block, character, and network device drivers. The interfaces are implemented as C language structures containing a set of function pointers.

Most interactions between the kernel and drivers take place through function calls, either from the kernel into drivers or from drivers into exported kernel routines. Drivers directly access only a few global data structures, such as the current task structure As a result, Nooks can interpose on most kernel-driver interactions by intercepting the function calls between the driver and kernel.

Interposition

Interposition allows Nooks to intercept and control communication between drivers and the kernel. Nooks interposes on kernel-driver control transfers with *wrapper stubs*. Wrappers provide transparency by preserving existing kernel-driver procedure-call interfaces while enabling the protection of all control and data transfers in both directions.

When loading a module, Nooks links the driver against wrappers rather than to normal kernel functions. This ensures that Nooks intercepts all function calls from the driver into the kernel. Similarly, the kernel's module initialization code explicitly invokes a Nooks wrapper on the initialization call into a driver, enabling the driver to execute within its lightweight protection domain. Following initialization, wrappers replace all function pointers passed from the driver to the kernel with pointers to other wrappers. This causes the kernel to call wrapper functions instead of driver functions directly.

In addition to interposing on control transfers, Nooks must interpose on some data references. Drivers are linked directly to global kernel variables that they read but do not write (e.g., the current time). For global variables that drivers modify, Nooks creates a shadow copy of the kernel data structure within the driver's domain that is synchronized to the kernel's version. For example, Nooks uses this technique for the queue of packets sent and received by a network driver. The object tracker synchronizes the contents of the kernel and driver version of this structure before and after XPCs into a network driver.

As noted above, Nooks inserts wrapper stubs between kernel and driver functions. There are

Figure 4. Protection of the kernel address space. Drivers can read and write their private heap and stacks, but only read from the kernel.

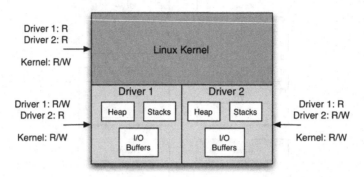

two types of wrappers: *kernel wrappers*, which are called by drivers to execute kernel-supplied functions; *driver wrappers*, which are called by the kernel to execute driver-supplied functions. In both cases, a wrapper functions as an XPC stub that appears to the caller as if it were the target procedure in the called domain.

Both wrapper types perform the body of their work within the kernel protection domain. Therefore, the domain change occurs at a different point depending on the direction of transfer, as shown in Figure 3. When a driver calls a kernel wrapper, the wrapper performs an XPC on entry so that the body of the wrapper (i.e., object checking, copying, etc.) can execute in the kernel's domain. Once the wrapper's work is done, it calls the target kernel function directly with a regular procedure call. In the opposite direction, when the kernel calls a driver wrapper, the wrapper executes within the kernel's domain. When it is done, the wrapper performs an XPC to transfer to the target function within the driver.

Wrappers perform four basic tasks. First, wrappers implement the shadow driver tap mechanism (described later in this chapter). Second, wrappers check parameters for validity by verifying with the object tracker and memory manager that pointers are valid. Third, they implement *call-by-value-result* semantics for XPC, by creating a copy of kernel objects on the local heap or stack within

the driver's protection domain. These semantics ensure that updates to kernel objects are transactional, because they are only applied after the driver completes, when the wrappers copy the results back to the kernel. Fourth, wrappers perform an XPC into the kernel or driver to execute the desired function, as shown in Figure 3.

While wrappers must copy data between protection domains, no marshaling or unmarshaling is necessary, because the driver and kernel share the same address space. Instead, wrappers may directly allocate and reference memory in either the kernel or the driver protection domains. The code for synchronizing simple objects is placed directly in the wrappers, while the object tracker provides synchronization routines for complex objects with many pointers. As an optimization, wrappers may pass parameters that are only read but not written by drivers without modification, as any attempt to modify the parameter will cause a memory access fault.

To improve performance, the wrappers rely on several techniques for moving complex objects between protection domains. In some cases, Nooks copies objects into the driver's protection domain, following embedded pointers as appropriate. It is generally unnecessary to copy the complete transitive closure of an object; while drivers read pointers more than one level removed from a parameter, they generally do not write to them.

In other cases, Nooks avoids copying entirely by changing the protection on the page containing an object. A "page tracker" mechanism within the object tracker remembers the state of these mapped pages and grants and revokes driver access to the pages. Nooks uses this mechanism to avoid copying network packets and disk blocks.

Writing a wrapper requires knowing how drivers use a parameter: whether it is live across multiple calls to the drivers, whether it can be passed to other threads or back to the kernel, and which fields of the parameter can be modified. This analysis can be manual or performed by static analysis tools that determine these properties by analyzing an existing set of drivers.

Isolation

The isolation component of Nooks provides memory management to implement lightweight kernel protection domains with virtual memory protection.

Figure 4 shows the Linux kernel with two lightweight kernel protection domains, each containing a single driver. All components exist in the kernel's address space. However, memory access rights differ for each component: e.g., the kernel has read-write access to the entire address space, while each driver is restricted to read-only kernel access and read-write access to its local domain.

To provide drivers with read access to the kernel, Nooks' memory management code maintains a synchronized copy of the kernel page table for each domain. Each lightweight protection domain has private structures, including a domain-local heap, a pool of stacks for use by the driver, memory-mapped physical I/O regions, and kernel memory buffers, such as socket buffers or I/O blocks, that are currently in use by the driver.

Nooks protects against bugs but not against malicious code. Lightweight protection domains reflect this design. For example, Nooks prevents a driver from writing kernel memory, but it does not prevent a malicious driver from replacing the

domain-local page table explicitly by reloading the hardware page table base register.

Furthermore, Nooks currently does not protect the kernel from Direct Memory Access (DMA) by a device into the kernel address space. Isolation is provided through virtual memory page tables, but devices use DMA to directly access physical memory. Preventing a rogue DMA requires an IO memory management unit (IOMMU), which is not common on PC-class x86 computers. However, Nooks tracks the set of pages writable by a driver and could use this information to restrict DMA on a machine with the suitable hardware support.

Communication

Nooks uses the extension procedure call (XPC) mechanism to transfer control between driver and kernel domains. The wrapper mechanism makes the XPC mechanism invisible to both the kernel and drivers, which continue to interact through their original procedural interfaces.

Two functions internal to Nooks manage XPC control transfer: one to transfer from the kernel into a driver, and one to transfer from drivers into the kernel. These functions take a function pointer, an argument list, and a protection domain. They execute the function with its arguments in the specified domain. The transfer routines save the caller's context on the stack, find a stack for the calling domain (which may be newly allocated or reused when calls are nested), change page tables to the target domain, and then call the function. XPC performs the reverse operations when the call returns.

Changing protection domains requires a change of page tables. The Intel x86 architecture flushes the TLB on such a change, and hence there is a substantial cost to entering a lightweight protection domain, both from the flush and from subsequent TLB misses. This cost could be mitigated in a processor architecture with a tagged TLB, such as the MIPS or Alpha, or with single-address-space protection support, such as the IA-64 or PA-RISC.

However, because Nooks' lightweight protection domains execute on kernel threads that share the kernel address space, they reduce the costs of scheduling and data copying on a domain change when compared to normal cross-address space or kernel-user RPCs.

To reduce the performance cost of XPC, Nooks supports *deferred calls*, which batch many calls into a single domain crossing. Nooks can defer function calls that have no visible side effects to the call. Wrappers queue deferred function calls for later execution, either at the entry or exit of a future XPC. Each domain maintains two queues: a driver-domain queue holds delayed kernel calls, and a kernel-domain queue holds delayed driver calls. As an example, Nooks changes the packet-delivery routine used by the network driver to batch the transfer of message packets from the driver to the kernel. When a packet arrives, the driver calls a wrapper to pass the packet to the kernel. The wrapper queues a deferred XPC to deliver the packet after the driver completes interrupt processing.

Object Tracking

The object tracker facilitates the recovery of kernel objects following a driver failure. The Nooks object tracker performs two independent tasks. First, it records the *addresses* of all objects in use by a driver in a database. As an optimization, objects used only for the duration of a single XPC call are recorded on the kernel stack. Objects with long lifetimes are recorded in a per-protection-domain hash table. Second, for objects that drivers may modify, the object tracker creates and manages a driver version of the object and records an association between the kernel and driver versions. Wrappers rely on this association to map parameters between the driver's protection domain and the kernel's protection domain.

The Nooks implementation supports many kernel object types, such as tasklets, PCI devices, inodes, and memory pages. For each of the 52 object types used by drivers, there is a unique type identifier and code to release instances of that type during recovery. Complex types also have a routine to copy changes between a kernel and driver instance of the type.

When an object "dies" and is no longer usable by a driver, the object tracker must remove the object from its database. Determining when an object will no longer be used requires a careful examination of the kernel-driver interface. This task is possible because the kernel requires the same information to safely reclaim shared objects. For example, some objects are accessible to the driver only during the lifetime of a single XPC call from the kernel. In this case, Nooks adds the object to the tracker's database when the call begins and removes it on return. Other objects are explicitly allocated and deallocated by the driver, in which case Nooks knows their lifetimes exactly. In still other cases, Nooks relies in the semantics of the object and its use. For example, drivers allocate a timer data structure to register for a future callback. Nooks adds this object to the object tracker when a driver calls the kernel to add the timer and removes it when the timer fires, at which point it is no longer used. The object-tracking code is conservative, in that it may under-estimate the lifetime of an object and unnecessarily add and remove the same object from the database multiple times. It will not, however, allow a driver to access an object that the kernel has released.

In addition to tracking objects in use by drivers, the tracker must record the status of locks that are shared with the kernel. When a driver fails, Nooks releases all locks acquired by the driver to prevent the system from hanging. As a result, calls to lock kernel data structures require an XPC into the kernel to acquire the lock, synchronize the kernel and driver versions of the data structure, and record that the lock was acquired.

Recovery

The recovery code in Nooks consists of three components. First, the isolation components detect driver failures and notify the controller. Second, the object tracker and protection domains support cleanup operations that release the resources in use by a driver. This functionality is available to the third component, a *recovery manager*, whose job is to recover after a failure. The recovery manager may be customized to a specific driver or class of drivers.

Failure Detection

Nooks triggers recovery when it detects a failure through software checks (e.g., parameter validation or livelock detection), processor exceptions, or notification from an external source. Specifically, the wrappers, protection domains, and object tracker notify the Nooks isolation manager of a failure when:

- The driver passes a bad parameter to the kernel, such as accessing a resource it had freed or unlocking a lock not held.
- The driver allocates too much memory, such as an amount exceeding the physical memory in the computer.
- The driver executes too frequently without an intervening clock interrupt (implying livelock).
- The driver generates an invalid processor exception, such as an illegal memory access or an invalid instruction.

In addition, it is possible to implement an external failure detector, such as a user- or kernel-mode agent, that notifies the controller of a failure. In all cases, the controller invokes the driver's recovery manager.

Recovery Managers

The recovery manager is tasked with returning the system to a functioning state. Nooks supports three recovery managers. The *default recovery manager* is a kernel service that simply unloads the failed driver, leaving the system running but without the services of the driver. The *restart recovery manager* is a user-mode agent that similarly unloads the failed driver but then executes a script to reload and restart the driver. The *shadow recovery manager* performs complete recovery in the kernel, oblivious to applications and the kernel itself. Shadow driver recovery is described in more detail in the next section.

The XPC, object tracking, and protection domain code all provide interfaces to the recovery managers. The XPC service allows a manager to signal all the threads that are currently executing in the driver or have called through the driver and back into the kernel. The signal causes the threads to unwind out of the driver by returning to the point where they invoked the driver without executing any additional driver code.

The object tracker provides an interface to recovery managers to enumerate the objects in use by a driver at the time of failure and to garbage collect the objects by releasing them to the kernel. The manager may choose both the set of objects it releases and the order in which to release them. Thus, it may preserve objects for use by the driver after recovery, such as memory-mapped I/O buffers that a hardware device continues to access.

Lightweight kernel protection domains provide similar support for recovery. The domains record the memory regions accessible to a driver and provide interfaces for enumerating the regions and for releasing the regions to the kernel.

Summary of Nooks

Device drivers are a major source of failure in modern operating systems. Nooks is a new reliability layer intended to significantly reduce driver-related failures. Nooks isolates drivers in lightweight kernel protection domains and relies on hardware and software checks to detect failures. After a failure, Nooks recovers by unloading and then reloading the failed driver. Nooks focuses on achieving *backward compatibility*, that is, it sacrifices complete isolation and fault tolerance for compatibility and transparency with existing kernels and drivers. As a result, Nooks has the potential to greatly improve the reliability of today's operating systems by removing their dependence on driver correctness.

Shadow Driver Recovery

Isolation techniques can reduce the frequency of system crashes, but *applications* using the failed driver may continue to crash. Applications receive erroneous results following a failure, and the driver loses application state when it restarts. Most applications are unprepared to cope with either situation. Rather, applications reflect the conventional failure model: drivers and the operating system either fail together or not at all. The restart recovery manager recovers from driver failure by unloading and then reloading the failed driver. However, reloading failed drivers is effective at preventing system crashes. However, users of a computer are not solely interested in whether the operating system continues to function. Often, users care more about *the applications* with which they interact. If applications using drivers fail, then I have only partially achieved my goal of improving reliability.

With the restart recovery manager, calls into a driver that fails and subsequently recovers may return error codes because the recovery manager unloads the driver and invalidates open connections to the driver during recovery. As a result, clients of a recovered driver would themselves fail if they depend on the driver during or after recovery. For example, audio players stopped producing sound when a sound-card driver failed and recovered. For the same reason, the restart recovery manager cannot restart drivers needed by the kernel, such as disk drivers. Requests to the disk driver fail while the driver is recovering. When the Linux kernel receives multiple errors

from a disk driver used for swapping, it assumes that the device is faulty and crashes the system.

In addition, any settings an application or the OS had downloaded into a driver are lost when the driver restarts. Thus, even if the application reconnects to the driver, the driver may not be able to process requests correctly.

These weaknesses highlight a fundamental problem with a recovery strategy that reveals driver failures to their clients: the clients may not be prepared to handle these failures. Rather, they are designed for the more common case that either drivers never fail, or, if they fail, the whole system fails.

To address these problems, *shadow drivers* are a transparent recovery mechanism for driver failures. Their design for shadows reflects three principles:

- *Device driver failures should be concealed from the driver's clients.* If the operating system and applications using a driver cannot detect that it has failed, they are unlikely to fail themselves.
- *Driver recovery logic should be generic.* Given the huge number and variety of device drivers, it is not practical to implement per-driver recovery code. Therefore, the architecture must enable a single shadow driver to handle recovery for a large number of device drivers.
- *Recovery services should have low overhead when not needed.* The recovery system should impose relatively little overhead for the common case (that is, when drivers are operating normally).

Overall, these design principles aim to protect applications and the OS from driver failure, while minimizing the cost required to make and use shadow drivers.

Shadow drivers only apply to device drivers that belong to a class and share a common calling interface. They recover after a failure by restarting the driver and replaying past requests and hence, can only recover from failures that are both transient and fail-stop. Deterministic failures may recur when the driver recovers, again causing a failure. Recoverable failures must be fail-stop, because shadow drivers must detect a failure in order to conceal it from the OS and applications. Hence, shadow drivers require an isolation subsystem to detect and stop failures before they are visible to applications or the operating system.

Shadow Driver Operation

Shadow drivers execute in one of two modes: *passive* or *active*. Passive mode is used during normal (non-faulting) operation, when the shadow driver monitors all communication between the kernel and the device driver it shadows. This monitoring is achieved via replicated procedure calls, called *taps*: a kernel call to a device driver function causes an automatic, identical call to the corresponding shadow driver function. Similarly, a driver call to a kernel function causes an automatic, identical call to a corresponding shadow driver function. These passive-mode calls are transparent to the device driver and the kernel and occur only to track the state of the driver as necessary for recovery. Based on the calls, the shadow tracks the state transitions of the shadowed device driver.

Active mode is used during recovery from a failure. Here, the shadow performs two functions. First, it *impersonates* the failed driver, intercepting and responding to calls for service. Therefore, the kernel and higher-level applications continue operating as though the driver had not failed. Second, the shadow driver restarts the failed driver and brings it back to its pre-failure state. While the driver restarts, the shadow impersonates the kernel to the driver, responding to its requests for service. Together, these two functions hide recovery from the driver, which is unaware that a shadow driver is restarting it after a failure, and from the kernel and applications, which continue to receive service from the shadow.

Once the driver has restarted, the active-mode shadow returns the driver to its pre-failure state. For example, the shadow re-establishes any configuration state and then replays pending requests. Shadow drivers rely on the state machine model of drivers. Whereas the default and restart recovery managers seek to restore the driver to its unloaded state or initialized state, shadow drivers seek to restore drivers to their state at the time of failure.

A shadow driver is a *class driver*, aware of the interface to the drivers it shadows but *not* of their implementations. The class orientation has two key implications. First, a single shadow driver implementation can recover from a failure of any driver in its class, meaning that a handful of different shadow drivers can serve a large number of device drivers. As previously mentioned, Linux, for example, has only 20 driver classes. Second, implementing a shadow driver does not require a detailed understanding of the internals of the drivers it shadows. Rather, it requires only an understanding of those drivers' interactions with the kernel. Thus, they can be implemented by kernel developers with no knowledge of device specifics and have no dependencies on individual drivers. For example, if a new network interface card and driver are inserted into a PC, the existing network shadow driver can shadow the new driver without change. Similarly, drivers can be patched or updated without requiring changes to their shadows.

Taps

As previously described, a shadow driver monitors communication between a functioning driver and the kernel and impersonates one to the other during failure and recovery. This is made possible by a new mechanism, called a *tap*. Conceptually, a tap is a T-junction placed between the kernel and its drivers. It is implemented as a callout from wrapper stubs. During a shadow's passive-mode operation, the tap: (1) invokes the original

Figure 5. (a) A sample shadow driver operating in passive mode. (b) A sample shadow driver operating in active mode.

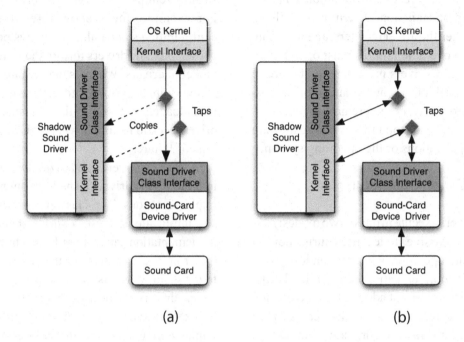

(a)   (b)

driver, and then (2) invokes the corresponding shadow with the parameters and results of the call, as shown in Figure 5(a). In active mode, a tap always invokes the shadow driver, as shown in Figure 5(b).

The Shadow Recovery Manager

The *shadow recovery manager* is responsible for coordinating recovery with shadow drivers. The Nooks Isolation Manager notifies the shadow recovery manager that it has detected a failure in a driver. The shadow recovery manager then transitions the shadow driver to active mode and closes the taps. In this way, requests for the driver's services are redirected to the corresponding shadow driver. The shadow recovery manager then initiates the shadow driver's recovery sequence to restore the driver. When recovery completes, the shadow recovery manager returns the shadow driver to passive-mode operation and re-opens its taps so that the driver can resume service.

Shadow Drivers

Each shadow driver is a single module written with knowledge of the behavior (interface) of a class of device drivers, allowing it to conceal a driver failure and restart the driver after a failure. A shadow driver, when passive, monitors communication between the kernel and the driver. It becomes active when a driver fails and then both proxies requests for the driver and restores the driver's state.

Passive-Mode Monitoring

In passive mode, a shadow driver monitors the current state of a device driver by observing its communication with the kernel. In order to return the driver to its state at the time of failure, the shadow records the inputs to the driver in a log. These inputs are then replayed during recovery. With no knowledge of how drivers operate, the shadow would have to log all inputs to the driver. However, because the shadow is implemented with knowledge of the driver's interface, and

Figure 6. The State machine transitions for a sound-card shadow driver. Those recorded for recovery are shown in **boldface**.

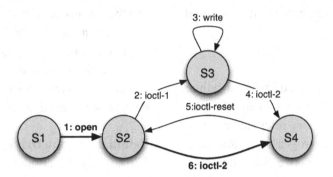

hence its abstract state machine, not all inputs must be logged. Instead, the shadow only records inputs needed to return a driver to its state at the time of failure. The shadow drops requests that do not advance the driver's state or whose impact has been superseded by later inputs, for example transitions on a loop in the abstract state machine.

Figure 6 shows an example of the state machine transitions for a sound-card driver. The transitions, made when the kernel issues requests to the driver, are numbered. The final state of the sequence is S4, but there is a loop through state S3. As a result, the shadow may drop requests 2 through 5 from its log, because they do not affect the final state of the driver.

To implement this state machine, the shadow driver maintains a log in which it records several types of information. First, it tracks I/O requests made to the driver, enabling pending requests to be re-submitted after recovery. An entry remains in the log until the corresponding request has been handled. In addition, for connection-oriented drivers, the shadow driver records the state of each active connection, such as offset or positioning information.

The shadow driver also records configuration and driver parameters that the kernel passes into the driver. The shadow relies on this information to reconfigure the driver to its pre-failure state during recovery. For example, the shadow sound-card driver logs ioctl calls (command numbers and arguments) that configure the driver.

For stateful devices, such as a hard disk, the shadow does not create a copy of the device state. Instead, a shadow driver depends on the fail-stop assumption to preserve persistent state (e.g., on disk) from corruption. In other cases, the shadow may be able to force the device's clients to recreate the state after a failure. For example, a windowing system can recreate the contents of a frame buffer by redrawing the desktop.

In many cases, passive-mode calls do no work and the shadow returns immediately to the caller. For example, the kernel maintains a queue of outstanding requests to a disk driver, and hence the shadow driver for an IDE disk does little in passive mode. For the network shadow driver, too, the Nooks object-tracking system performs much of the work to capture driver state by recording outstanding packets.

Opaque parameters can pose problems for recovery as they did for isolation. However, the class-based approach allows shadow drivers to interpret most opaque pointers. The standardized interface to drivers ensures that a client of the interface that has no knowledge of a driver's implementation can still invoke it. Hence, clients must know the real type of opaque parameters. The shadow implementer can use the same knowledge to interpret them. For example, the Linux Open Sound System interface defines opaque pointer parameters to the ioctl call for sound-card drivers. The shadow sound-card driver relies on this standard to interpret and log ioctl requests.

Active-Mode Recovery

The shadow enters active mode when a failure is detected in a driver. A driver typically fails by generating an illegal memory reference or passing an invalid parameter across a kernel interface. Nooks' failure detectors notice the failure and notify the Nooks Isolation Manager, which in turn invokes the shadow recovery manager. This manager immediately locates the corresponding shadow driver and directs it to recover the failed driver. The shadow driver's task is to restore the driver to the state it was in at the time of failure, so it can continue processing requests as if it had never failed. The three steps of recovery are: (1) stopping the failed driver, (2) reinitializing the driver from a clean state, and (3) transferring relevant shadow driver state into the new driver. Unlike Nooks' restart recovery manager, a shadow driver does not completely unload the failed driver.

Stopping the Failed Driver

The shadow recovery manager begins recovery by informing the responsible shadow driver that a failure has occurred. It also closes the taps, isolating the kernel and driver from one another's subsequent activity during recovery. After this point, the tap redirects all kernel requests to the shadow until recovery is complete.

Informed of the failure, the shadow driver first invokes the isolation service to preempt threads executing in the failed driver. It also disables the hardware device to prevent it from interfering with the OS while not under driver control. For example, the shadow disables the driver's interrupt request line. Otherwise, the device may continuously interrupt the kernel and prevent recovery. On hardware platforms with I/O memory mapping, the shadow also removes the device's I/O mappings to prevent DMAs into kernel memory.

In preparation for recovery, the shadow garbage collects resources held by the driver. To ensure that the kernel does not see the driver "disappear" as it is restarted, the shadow retains objects that the kernel uses to request driver services. For example, the shadow does not release the device object for network device drivers. The remaining resources, not needed for recovery, are released.

Reinitializing the Driver

The shadow driver next "boots" the driver from a clean state. Normally, booting a driver requires loading the driver from disk. However, the disk driver may not be functional during recovery. Hence, the driver code and data must already be in memory before a failure occurs. For this reason, the shadow caches a copy of the device driver's initial, clean data section when the driver is first loaded. These data sections tend to be small. The driver's code is already loaded read-only in the kernel, so it can be reused from memory.

The shadow boots the driver by repeating the sequence of calls that the kernel makes to initialize a driver. For some driver classes, such as sound-card drivers, this consists of a single call into the driver's initialization routine. Other drivers, such as network interface drivers, require additional calls to connect the driver into the network stack.

As the driver restarts, the shadow reattaches the driver to the kernel resources it was using before the failure. For example, when the driver calls the kernel to register itself as a driver, the taps redirect these calls to the shadow driver, which reconnects the driver to existing kernel data structures. The shadow reuses the existing driver registration, passing it back to the driver. For requests that generate callbacks, such as a request to register the driver with the PCI subsystem, the shadow emulates the kernel and calls the driver back in the kernel's place. The shadow also provides the driver with its hardware resources, such as interrupt request lines and memory-mapped I/O regions. If the shadow had disabled these resources in the first step of recovery, the shadow re-enables them, e.g., enabling interrupt handling for the device's interrupt line. In essence, the shadow driver initializes the recovering driver by calling and responding as the kernel would when the driver starts normally.

Transferring State to the New Driver

The final recovery step restores the driver to the state it was in at the time of the failure, permitting it to respond to requests as if it had never failed. Thus, any configuration that either the kernel or an application had downloaded to the driver must be restored. The shadow driver walks its log and issues requests to the driver that to restore its state.

The details of this final state transfer depend on the device driver class. Some drivers are connection oriented. For these, the state consists of the state of the connections before the failure. The shadow re-opens the connections and restores the state of each active connection with configuration calls. Other drivers are request oriented. For these, the shadow restores the state of the driver by replaying logged configuration operations and then resubmits to the driver any requests that were outstanding when the driver crashed.

As an example, to restart a sound-card driver, the shadow driver resets the driver and all its open connections back to their pre-failure state. Specifically, the shadow scans its list of open connections and calls the open function in the driver to reopen each connection. The shadow then walks its log of configuration commands for each connection and replays commands that set driver properties.

For some driver classes, the shadow cannot completely transfer its state into the driver. However, it may be possible to compensate in other, perhaps less elegant, ways. For example, a sound-card driver that is recording sound stores the number of bytes it has recorded since the last reset. After recovery, the sound-card driver initializes this counter to zero. Because the interface

has no call that sets the counter value, the shadow driver must insert its "true" value into the return argument list whenever the application reads the counter to maintain the illusion that the driver has not crashed. The shadow can do this because it receives control (on its replicated call) before the kernel returns to user space.

After resetting driver and connection state, the shadow must handle requests that were either outstanding when the driver crashed or arrived while the driver was recovering. If a driver crashes after submitting a request to a device but before notifying the kernel that the request has completed, the shadow cannot know whether the device completed the request. As a result, shadow drivers cannot guarantee exactly once behavior and must rely on devices and higher levels of software to absorb duplicate requests. So, the shadow driver has two choices during recovery: restart in-progress requests and risk duplication, or cancel the request and risk lost data. For some device classes, such as disks or networks, duplication is acceptable. However, other classes, such as printers, may not tolerate duplicates. In these cases, the shadow driver cancels outstanding requests and returns an error to the kernel or application in a manner consistent with the driver interface.

After this final step, the driver has been re-initialized, linked into the kernel, reloaded with its pre-failure state, and is ready to process commands. At this point, the shadow driver notifies the shadow recovery manager, which sets the taps to restore kernel-driver communication and reestablish passive-mode monitoring.

Active-Mode Proxying of Kernel Requests

While a shadow driver is restoring a failed driver, it is also acting as a proxy for the driver to conceal the failure and recovery from applications and the kernel. Thus, the shadow must respond to any request for the driver's service in a way that satisfies and does not corrupt the driver's caller. The shadow's response depends on the driver's

Table 1. The proxying actions of the shadow sound-card driver.

Request	Action
read / write	suspend caller
interrupt	drop request
query capability ioctl	answer from log
query buffer ioctl	act busy
reset ioctl	queue for later / drop duplicate

interface and the request semantics. In general, the shadow will take one of five actions:

1. Respond with information that it has recorded in its log.
2. Report that the driver is busy and that the kernel or application should try again later.
3. Suspend the requesting thread until the driver recovers.
4. Queue the request for processing after recovery and return success.
5. Silently drop the request.

The choice of strategy depends on the caller's expectations of the driver.

Writing the proxying code requires knowledge of the kernel-driver interface, its interactions, and its requirements. For example, the kernel may require that some driver functions never block, while others always block. Some kernel requests are idempotent (e.g., many ioctl commands), permitting duplicate requests to be dropped, while others return different results on every call (e.g., many read requests). The writer of a shadow for a driver class uses these requirements to select the response strategy.

Device drivers often support the concept of being "busy." This concept allows a driver to manage the speed difference between software running on the computer and the device. For example, network drivers in Linux may reject requests and turn themselves off if packets are arriving from the kernel to quickly and their queues are full. The kernel then refrains from sending packets until the

driver turns itself back on. The notion of being "busy" in a driver interface simplifies active proxying. By reporting that the device is currently busy, shadow drivers instruct the kernel or application to block calls to a driver. The shadow network driver exploits this behavior during recovery by returning a "busy" error on calls to send packets. IDE storage drivers support a similar notion when request queues are full. Sound drivers can report that their buffers are temporarily full.

The shadow sound-card driver uses a mix of all five strategies for proxying functions in its service interface. Table 1 shows the shadow's actions for common requests. The shadow suspends kernel read and write requests, which play and record sound samples, until the failed driver recovers. It processes ioctl calls itself, either by responding with information it captured or by logging the request to be processed later. For ioctl commands that are idempotent, the shadow driver silently drops duplicate requests. Finally, when applications query for buffer space, the shadow responds that buffers are full. As a result, many applications block themselves rather than blocking in the shadow driver.

Shadow Driver Summary

Shadow drivers provide an elegant mechanism that leverages the properties of device drivers for recovery. Based on an abstract state machine modeling an entire class of drivers, shadow drivers monitor the communication between the kernel and driver to obtain the driver state dur-

Table 2. The number of non-comment lines of source code in Nooks and Shadow Drivers.

Nooks Components	# Lines
Domain Management	2,391
Object Tracking	1,498
Extension Procedure Call	928
Wrappers	14,484
Recovery	1,849
Build tools	1,762
Linux Kernel Changes	924
Miscellaneous	1,629
Shadow driver components	**# Lines**
Shadow recover manager	600
Tap-generation tools	750
Shared shadow driver code	750
Sound shadow driver	666
Network shadow driver	198
Storage shadow driver	321
Total number of lines of code	**28,800**

ing normal operation. When a driver fails, the shadow relies on this state to conceal the failure by proxying for the driver. At the same time, the shadow recovers by restarting the driver, and then replaying requests to bring the driver back to its pre-failure state.

EVALUATION OF NOOKS AND SHADOW DRIVERS

Any new operating system mechanism must be evaluated according to the increase in complexity it adds to the system relative the benefit it provides and its performance.

Code Size and Complexity

Table 2 shows the size of the Nooks and shadow driver implementation. This code can tolerate the failure of fourteen device drivers. The Nooks reliability layer comprises less than 26,000 lines of code.

Shadow drivers have been implemented for three classes of device drivers: sound-card drivers, network interface drivers, and IDE storage drivers. Table 2 shows, for each class, the size in lines of code unique to the shadow driver for the class. Of the 177 taps, only 31 required actual code in a shadow; the remainder were no-ops because the calls did not significantly impact kernel or driver state.

In contrast, the kernel itself has 2.4 million lines, and the Linux 2.4 distribution has about 30 million. For comparison, the Linux 2.4.18 kernel includes 118,981 lines of sound driver code, 264,500 lines of network driver code, and 29,000 lines of IDE storage code. Relative to a base kernel and its drivers, the Nooks reliability layer introduces only a modest amount of additional system complexity. This demonstrates the leverage that Nooks and shadow drivers provide by implementing fault tolerance for a much larger body of driver code.

Figure 7. The reduction in system crashes observed using Nooks.

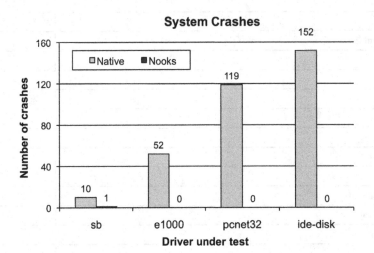

Reliability

The primary goal of Nooks and shadow drivers is to improve the reliability of an operating system and applications. This section evaluates the ability of Nooks and shadow drivers to tolerate driver failures. In the experiments reported below, Nooks is used to isolate three classes of device drivers: network, sound card, and IDE storage drivers. Reliability and performance results for five representatives of the three driver classes are presented: *sb* (SoundBlaster 16 sound card), *audigy* (SoundBlaster Audigy sound card), *pcnet32* (AMD PCnet32 10/100 Ethernet card), e1000 (Intel Pro/1000 Gigabit Ethernet card), and *ide-disk* (IDE disk driver).

Three platforms are used to evaluate Nooks and shadow drivers, all based on the Linux 2.4.18 kernel:

1. *Linux-Native* is the unmodified Linux kernel.
2. *Linux-Nooks* is a version of *Linux-Native* that includes the Nooks fault isolation subsystem and the restart recovery manager. When a driver fails, this system restarts the driver but does not attempt to conceal its failure.

3. *Linux-SD* includes Nooks, the shadow driver recovery manager, and the three shadow drivers.

Nooks was tested with synthetic *fault injection* to insert artificial faults into drivers. The fault injector automatically changes single instructions in driver code to emulate a variety of common programming errors, such as uninitialized local variables, bad parameters, and inverted test conditions. The output of the fault injection tests is a metric of *coverage*, not reliability. The tests measure the fraction of faults (failure causes) that can be detected and isolated, not the fraction of existing failures that can be tolerated.

System Survival

This section evaluates Nooks' ability to isolate the kernel from driver failure. The goal of these tests is to measure the survival rate of the operating system. The application-level workload consists of programs that stress the sound-card driver, the network driver, and the storage driver. The first program plays a short MP3 file. The second performs a series of ICMP-ping and TCP stream-

Table 3. The applications used for evaluating shadow drivers.

Device Driver	Application Activity
Sound	mp3 player (*zinf*) playing 128kb/s audio
(audigy driver)	audio recorder (*audacity*) recording from microphone
	speech synthesizer (*festival*) reading a text file
	strategy game (*Battle of Wesnoth*)
Network	network file transfer (*scp*) of a 1GB file
	remote window manager (*vnc*)
	network analyzer (*ethereal*) sniffing packets
Storage	compiler (*make/gcc*) compiling 788 C files
(ide-disk driver)	encoder (*LAME*) converting 90 MB file .wav to .mp3
	database (*mySQL*) processing the *Wisconsin Benchmark*

ing tests, while the third untars and compiles a number of files.

To measure isolation, test trials inject faults into extensions running under two different Linux configurations, both running the *Linux-Nooks* kernel. In the first, called "native," the Nooks isolation services were present but unused. In the second, called "Nooks," the isolation services were enabled for the extension under test. For each driver, 400 trials inject five random faults into the driver and exercised the system. Not all fault-injection trials cause faulty behavior, e.g., bugs inserted on a rarely (or never) executed path will rarely (or never) produce an error.

A system crash is the most extreme and easiest problem to detect, as the operating system panics, becomes unresponsive, or simply reboots. In an ideal world, every system crash caused by a fault-injection trial under native Linux would result in a recovery under Nooks. As previously discussed, in practice Nooks may not detect or recover from certain failures caused by very bad programmers or very bad luck.

Figure 7 shows the number of system crashes caused by the fault-injection experiments for each of the extensions running on native Linux and Nooks. Of the 333 crashes observed with native Linux, Nooks eliminated 332, or 99%. In the remaining crashes, the system deadlocked when the driver went into a tight loop with interrupts disabled. Nooks does not detect this type of failure.

In addition, 206 trials caused applications to fail without crashing the system under native Linux. Nooks was able to reduce this to 102 application failures. These failure manifest as the driver misbehaving, but not performing illegal operations. Nooks generally does not detect such problems (nor is it intended to). However, when Nooks' simple failure detectors do detect such problems, its recovery services can safely restart the faulty extensions.

Figure 7 also illustrates a substantial difference in the number of system crashes that occur for *sb* driver under Linux, compared to *e1000*, *pcnet32*, and *ide-disk*. This difference reflects the way in which Linux responds to kernel failures. The *e1000*, *pcnet32* and *ide-disk* extensions are *interrupt oriented*, i.e., kernel-mode extension code is run as the result of an interrupt. The *sb* driver is *process oriented*, i.e., kernel-mode extension code is run as the result of a system call from a user process. Linux treats exceptions in interrupt-oriented code as fatal and crashes the system, hence the large number of crashes in *e1000*, *pcnet32*, and *ide-disk)*. Linux treats exceptions in process-oriented code as non-fatal, continuing to run the kernel but terminating the offending

Table 4. The observed behavior of several applications following the failure of the device drivers on which they depend.

Device Driver	Application Activity	Application Behavior		
		Linux-Native	Linux-Nooks	Linux-SD
Sound	mp3 player	CRASH	MALFUNCTION	√
(audigy driver)	audio recorder	CRASH	MALFUNCTION	√
	speech synthesizer	CRASH	√	√
	strategy game	CRASH	MALFUNCTION	√
Network	network file transfer	CRASH	√	√
(e1000 driver)	remote window manager	CRASH	√	√
	network analyzer	CRASH	MALFUNCTION	√
IDE	compiler	CRASH	CRASH	√
(ide-disk driver)	encoder	CRASH	CRASH	√
	database	CRASH	CRASH	√

process even though the exception occurred in the kernel. This behavior is unique to Linux. Other operating systems, such as Microsoft Windows XP, deal with kernel processor exceptions more aggressively by always halting the operating system. In such systems, exceptions in *sb* would cause system crashes.

Application Survival

The previous section evaluated the ability of the operating system to survive extension failures. This section answers the question of whether applications that use a device driver continue to run even after the driver fails and recovers. Shadow driver recovery is tested in the presence of simple failures to show the benefits of shadow drivers compared to the simple restart recovery manager.

The crucial question for shadow drivers is whether an application can continue functioning following the failure of a device driver on which it relies. To answer this question, the 10 applications in Table 3 were tested on each of the three configurations, *Linux-Native*, *Linux-Nooks*, and *Linux-SD*.

In each test, common driver bugs were simulated by injecting a null pointer dereference bug

into a device driver while an application using that driver was running. Because both *Linux-Nooks* and *Linux-SD* depend on the same isolation and failure-detection services, their recovery capabilities are differentiated by simulating failures that are easily isolated and detected.

Application Survival Results

Table 4 shows the three application behaviors observed. When a driver failed, each application continued to run normally (√), failed completely ("CRASH"), or continued to run but behaved abnormally ("MALFUNCTION"). In the latter case, manual intervention was typically required to reset or terminate the program.

This table demonstrates that shadow drivers (*Linux-SD*) enable applications to continue running normally even when device drivers fail. In contrast, all applications on *Linux-Native* failed when drivers failed. Most programs running on *Linux-Nooks* failed or behaved abnormally, illustrating that restart recovery protects the kernel, which is constructed to tolerate driver failures, but does not protect applications. The restart recovery manager lacks two key features of shadow drivers: (1) it does not advance the driver to its pre-fail state, and (2) it has no component to "pinch hit" for the failed driver during recovery. As a result, *Linux-Nooks* handles driver failures by returning an error to the application, leaving it to recover by itself. Unfortunately, few applications can do this.

Some applications on *Linux-Nooks* survived the driver failure but in a degraded form. For example, *mp3 player*, *audio recorder* and *strategy game* continued running, but they lost their ability to input or output sound until the user intervened. Similarly, *network analyzer*, which interfaces directly with the network device driver, lost its ability to receive packets once the driver was reloaded.

A few applications continued to function properly after driver failure on *Linux-Nooks*. One application, *speech synthesizer*, includes the code to reestablish its context within an unreliable sound-card driver. Two of the network applications survived on *Linux-Nooks* because they access the network device driver through kernel services (TCP/IP and sockets) that are themselves resilient to driver failures.

Unlike *Linux-Nooks*, *Linux-SD* can recover from disk driver failures. Recovery is possible because the IDE storage shadow driver instance maintains the failing driver's initial state. During recovery the shadow copies back the driver's initial data and reuses the driver code, which is already stored read-only in the kernel. In contrast, *Linux-Nooks* illustrates the risk of circular dependencies from rebooting drivers. Following these failures, the restart recovery manager, which had unloaded the *ide-disk* driver, was then required to reload the driver off the IDE disk. The circularity could only be resolved by a system reboot. While a second (non-IDE) disk would mitigate this problem, few machines are configured this way.

In general, programs that directly depend on driver state but are unprepared to deal with its loss benefit the most from shadow drivers. In contrast, those that do not directly depend on driver state or are able to reconstruct it when necessary benefit the least. Experience suggests that few applica-

tions are as fault-tolerant as *speech synthesizer*. Were future applications to be pushed in this direction, software manufacturers would either need to develop custom recovery solutions on a per-application basis or find a general solution that could protect any application from the failure of a device driver.

Application Behavior During Driver Recovery

Although shadow drivers can prevent application failure, they are not "real" device drivers and do not provide complete device services. As a result, applications often observe a slight timing disruption while the driver recovered. At best, output was queued in the shadow driver or the kernel. At worst, input was lost by the device. The length of the delay depends on the recovering device driver itself, which, on initialization, must first discover and then configure the hardware.

Few device drivers implement fast reconfiguration, which can lead to brief recovery delays. For example, the temporary loss of the *e1000* network device driver prevented applications from receiving packets for about five seconds while the driver reinitializes. Programs using files stored on the disk managed by the *ide-disk* driver stalled for about four seconds during recovery. In contrast, the normally smooth sounds produced by the *audigy* sound-card driver were interrupted by a pause of about one-tenth of one second, which sounded like a slight click in the audio stream.

The significance of these delays depends on the application. Streaming applications may become unacceptably "jittery" during recovery. Those processing input data in real-time might become lossy. Others may simply run a few seconds longer in response to a disk that appears to be operating more sluggishly than usual.

Performance

This section presents benchmark results that evaluate the performance cost of the Nooks and shadow

Figure 8. Comparative application performance of Linux-SD relative to Linux-Native. The X-axis crosses at 80%.

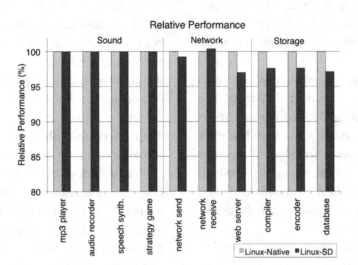

drivers. The experiments use existing benchmarks and tools to compare the performance of a system using Nooks to one that does not. Tests ran on a Dell 3 GHz Pentium 4 PC running Linux 2.4.18. The machine includes 1 GB of RAM, a Sound-Blaster Audigy sound card, an Intel Pro/1000 Gigabit Ethernet adapter, and a single 7200 RPM, 80 GB IDE hard disk drive

The same application reliability benchmarks are used to evaluate system performance with the

exception of the network applications. For the network driver, throughput is a more useful metric; therefore, the throughput-oriented *network send* and *network receive* benchmarks are substituted. In addition, the *web server* benchmark measures network application performance.

For each benchmark, Nooks isolates a *single* driver. The benchmark executes both on native Linux without Nooks (*Linux-Native*) and then again on a version of Linux with Nooks and shadow

Figure 9. Absolute CPU utilization by application.

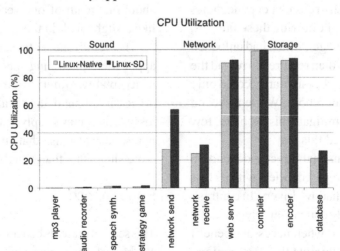

drivers enabled (*Linux-SD*). Figure 8 shows the performance of Linux-SD relative to Linux-Native either in wall clock time or throughput, depending on the benchmark. Figure 9 shows CPU utilization measured during benchmark execution (which is only accurate to a few percent). These figures show that Nooks achieves 97% and 100% of the performance of native Linux for these tests.

The primary performance difference is in the CPU utilization of the benchmarks. As the isolation services are primarily imposed at the point of the XPC, the rate of XPCs offers a telling performance indicator. Thus, the benchmarks fall into two broad categories characterized by the rate of XPCs: low frequency (a hundred to thousands XPCs per second), and high frequency (tens of thousands of XPCs per second).

The sound and storage driver benchmarks exhibit low XPC rates; between 300 and 1000 per second. At this low rate, the additional CPU utilization is negligible. For the many low-bandwidth devices in a system, such as keyboards, mice, Bluetooth devices, modems, and sound cards, Nooks offers improved reliability with almost no performance cost.

The network send and receive benchmarks are examples of high XPC-frequency applications. Network receive performance was measured with the *netperf* performance tool, where the receiving node used an isolated Ethernet driver to receive a stream of 32KB TCP messages using a 256KB buffer. The machine is bandwidth, not CPU limited, and hence there is no reduction in throughput. However, overall CPU utilization increase of 7 percentage points for receiving packets and 29 percentage points for sending packets.

The added cost comes from two factors: executing more code, to implement Nooks isolation, and executing existing code more slowly. A single XPC may take thousands of cycles, because it must copy data between the kernel and the driver as well as change the page table. This causes both kernel and driver code to execute more slowly, because the x86 architecture must flush the TLB after the page

table changes, leading to subsequent TLB misses. In addition, the additional code and data copying puts pressure on the processor caches, leading to more misses and lower performance.

Performance Summary

This section used a small set of benchmarks to quantify the performance cost of Nooks. Nooks imposed a performance penalty of less than 3%, although CPU utilization doubled for some workloads. The rate of XPCs is a key factor in the performance impact, as XPCs impose a high burden, due to cost of flushing the x86 TLB in the current implementation. The performance costs of Nooks' isolation services depend as well on the CPU utilization imposed by the workload. If the CPU is saturated, the additional cost can be significant, because there is no spare capacity to absorb Nooks overhead.

Summary of Nooks and Shadow Drivers

Overall, Nooks provides a substantial reliability improvement at low cost for common drivers. The results demonstrate that: (1) the performance overhead of Nooks during normal operation is small for many drivers and moderate for other extensions, (2) applications and the OS survived driver failures that otherwise would have caused the OS, application, or both to fail. Overall, Nooks and shadow drivers prevented 99% of system crashes, with an average performance cost of 1% for drivers.

DRIVER FAULT TOLERANCE IN COMMERCIAL SYSTEMS

While Nooks remains a research project, several commercial operating systems provide run-time mechanisms to isolate the kernel from driver failures. These mechanisms can be categorized into two major categories: user-mode drivers to

Figure 10. (a) Microsoft Windows User-Mode Driver Framework. Applications call standard Win32 I/O APIs, and the kernel I/O manager invokes a UMDF device object that forwards the request to user mode. (b) Linux Userspace I/O (UIO) architecture. Applications link to driver libraries, which use the Posix I/O APIs to communicate to the UIO manager in the kernel.

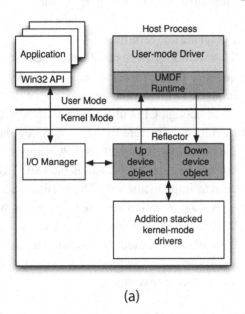

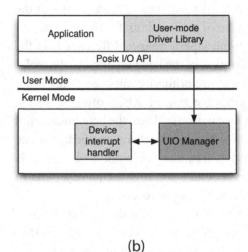

(a)   (b)

remove driver code from the kernel, and virtual machine isolation of drivers.

User-Mode Drivers

While drivers for most commodity operating systems are written in kernel-mode, Windows, Linux and MacOS X all have limited support for user-mode drivers. This section describes the support in Windows and Linux.

Microsoft Windows UMDF

In response to driver reliability problems, Microsoft implemented the User-mode Driver Framework (UMDF) for Windows XP and Vista (Microsoft, 2007). As shown in Figure 10a, UMDF adds a *reflector* to the device driver stack that forwards requests to a user-mode driver *host process*. I/O requests from applications are sent first to the I/O manager in the Windows kernel, which dispatches requests to specific drivers. For

devices with UMDF drivers, the I/O manager sends requests to the reflector, which forwards the request to a user-level runtime, which in turn invokes the UMDF driver.

UMDF drivers are specified as a set of COM (Component Object Model) interfaces. As a result, UMDF simplifies driver development by supporting the C++ language and by providing runtime support for common driver operations. However, it therefore cannot provide fault tolerance for existing kernel-mode drivers, which must be written in C.

User-move driver support in Windows is complicated by the existence of *stacked drivers*. In this model, a device is served by a layered set of drivers, each providing additional functionality. For example, a driver for a USB device layer over a generic USB interface driver, which layers over a driver for the specific host interface attached to the device. In UMDF, only the top-most driver in a stack may execute at user-level; the rest must execute in the kernel.

In addition, UMDF does not support drivers requiring interrupt handling, because Windows cannot field interrupts at user level. Drivers also cannot use DMA, because a driver could bypass kernel memory protection. These three limitations restrict UMDF drivers to devices accessed over serial ports, USB buses, or a network. In addition, drivers accessed internally within the kernel, such as storage and network devices, cannot be supported. Thus, UMDF supports portable storage devices, such as PDAs and cell phones, portable media players, USB bulk transfer devices, and auxiliary display/video devices, but not network devices or hard disks.

Linux UIO

Starting with the 2.6.23 kernel, Linux includes the Userspace I/O (UIO) driver model that can execute some driver code in user mode (Koch, 2008). With UIO, drivers consist of a kernel module containing an interrupt handler and a user-level library for the remainder of the driver. At startup, a kernel module registers an interrupt handler and a list of I/O memory addresses with the UIO manager. The UIO manager exports this information through an entry named in the /dev/uioX, where X is the index of the device. Reading from the device file returns the number of interrupts since it was last read, or blocks if there have been none. Memory mapping the device file provides access to the device's memory regions.

In the UIO driver model, all driver functionality *except* dismissing interrupts executes at user level. The kernel portion of a UIO driver is solely responsible for telling the device to stop interrupting, at which point it signals that the user-level driver should execute. The driver model provides no specific API to access device functionality; the driver code may be linked directly in with applications. As a result, UIO drivers cannot be accessed through standard file system interface, and therefore require changes to application code

to be used. Figure 10(b) illustrates the UMDF architecture.

Like Nooks, executing driver code at user level with UIO isolates the kernel from driver bugs. However, UIO has substantial limitations not present with Nooks. First, UIO is only available for devices with a character interface, but not block or network interfaces. Second, UIO provides no fault-detection or recover mechanisms. Finally, UIO requires writing new driver, so does not preserve the existing investment in drivers. Nonetheless, the UIO framework is compact, consisting of 800 lines of code, and can isolate the kernel from the failure of drivers.

Xen Hypervisor Drivers

Virtual machines raise unique issues for I/O. Most virtual machine monitors and hypervisors virtualize devices to share them between multiple guest virtual machines (Barham et al, 2003, and Fraser et al, 2004). As a result, guest operating systems talk to a *virtual device* rather than communicating directly with a physical device. In some virtual machine monitor architectures, device drivers execute within the virtual machine monitor itself. This poses the same reliability problems as executing drivers unprotected within an OS kernel, as a driver failure may cause the VMM and all guest VMs to crash. Hosted VMMs rely on a host operating system for device access. In this architecture, too, the failure of a driver can lead the host OS, the VMM, and all guest virtual machines to crash.

The Xen hypervisor addresses this problem by executing device drivers in virtual machines, rather than within the hypervisor. As shown in Figure 11, the guest OS kernel runs a *virtual driver* that exports an interface identical to a real device driver. Like shadow drivers, a virtual driver represents a *class* of devices, such as a network interface card. Thus, only one virtual driver is required per class. Instead of using processor

Figure 11. Xen architecture for device driver isolation. Drivers execute in a special driver virtual machine, called an Isolated Driver Domain (IDD)..

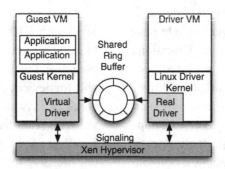

I/O operations, the virtual driver communicates with a real driver executing in an *isolated driver domain*, a virtual machine specific to that driver or to a set of drivers. Data communication takes place through a ring buffer, and control is communicated through the Xen Hypervisor.

In the driver VM, the *real driver* runs inside a standard operating system, and the Xen hypervisor provides it with access to physical devices. Xen also provides code to receive incoming I/O requests from guest VMs and invoke the real driver. A failure of the driver may cause the operating system and other drivers in the driver VM to fail, but the guest OS and its applications are unaffected.

This architecture provides several distinct benefits:

1. The driver VM can execute unmodified device drivers, providing compatibility with existing code.
2. The operating system in the guest VM and the driver VM may be different, enabling drivers for one operating system (e.g., Linux in the driver VM) to be used for device access a different guest OS (e.g., Solaris).
3. The code in the guest OS is relatively simple. In contrast to the thousands of lines of wrapper code in Nooks, Xen requires only a small virtual driver. In addition, this virtual driver is easier to port between operating

systems or versions of a single operating system.
4. Performance is comparable to Nooks, as passing data to a driver requires changing memory protection or copying, and invoking a driver requires changing page tables when changing virtual machines.

However, this architecture also imposes additional performance costs by running an entire operating system in the driver's protection domain. This requires additional memory and may require additional administration, to apply patches to this OS.

RESEARCH DIRECTIONS

Within the operating research community, two further approaches for driver fault tolerance have been investigated: pushing user-mode drivers further, to remove all drivers from the kernel; and applying language-level protections, such as type safety, to driver code.

User-Mode Drivers in Microkernels

All preceding approachs to driver reliability were constrained by the need to execute within an existing monolithic operating system. The Minix 3 operating system is a research system investigating the reliability benefits of a small-kernel design (Herder et al 2006). Only code needed for securely multiplexing hardware, such as interrupt handling, process creation and scheduling, and inter-process communication, is included in the kernel. All other services, including networking, file systems, and device access, execute in separate user-level processes.

Minix executes driver code similarly to Windows UMDF; an I/O request goes through the Minix kernel to a user-level driver process (Herder et al, 2007). However, Minix removes the restrictions of UMDF and allows all drivers to execute at user level. First, it traps device interrupts in the kernel and instead sends a message to a waiting driver process. These messages do not interrupt a driver process, but instead are retrieved the next time the driver waits for an event. This removes the need to write re-entrant driver code. Second user-level code is granted access to I/O hardware through the kernel. Rather than reading or writing a device register directly, drivers make a system call to access the device. In contrast, UMDF provides no access to devices from user-level. In addition, Minix 3 depends on hardware support to prevent a user-level driver from using DMA to corrupt memory, while UMDF prohibits DMA completely.

In addition to isolation, Minix 3 provides recovery mechanisms similar to Nooks. The OS includes a *reincarnation server* that (1) is notified by the kernel when a driver process crashes, and (2) polls all drivers periodically to determine if they still function. If a driver fails, the reincarnation server kills and restarts the driver process. Unlike shadow drivers, the failure is not concealed from applications.

Minix 3 demonstrates that, with a full-system redesign and hardware support, drivers can execute safely and with high performance in user mode.

Type-Safe Drivers

The preceding driver reliability systems all depend on hardware memory protection, in the form of virtual memory protection and processor privilege levels, to prevent drivers from corrupting the kernel. In contrast, SafeDrive and Singularity provides reliable execution of device drivers by verifying type safety at statically, at compile time, and dynamically, at runtime.

SafeDrive targets existing drivers for the Linux operating system, and relies on programmer annotations to enable compiler type checking (Zhou et al, 2006). Rather than relying on hardware memory protection like Nooks, SafeDrive uses a compiler to (1) verify the type safety of a driver statically, when possible, and (2) generate code to enforce type safety at runtime. Like Nooks, SafeDrive is compatible with existing drivers and requires only minor modifications to annotate driver data structures. In addition, it provides a recovery mechanism similar to Nooks' default recovery manager that safely unloads a failed driver. Compared to Nooks, SafeDrive imposes lower performance overhead for drivers with frequent kernel interactions, such as network drivers. However, it only detects memory errors and not invalid parameters or livelock problems.

Singularity, like Minix 3, is a new microkernel operating system (Hunt & Larus, 2007). It requires that all code, including the OS kernel, device drivers, and applications be written in Sing#, a variant of the C# programming language, which is type safe. As a result, memory protection can be enforced statically through the compiler, rather than with hardware at runtime. Similar to Minix 3, drivers execute in separate processes (Spear et al, 2006), which are isolate through type safety rather than virtual memory protection. The communication channel between drivers and other processes is specified as a contract, allowing compilers to statically ensure that the driver obeys the interface contract. This reduces the frequency of coding errors by catching them at compile time,

43

and reduces the likelihood that a faulty driver will corrupt other processes.

CHAPTER SUMMARY

Reliability has become a critical challenge for commodity operating systems. The competitive pressure on these systems and their huge installed base, though, prevents the adoption of traditional fault-tolerance techniques.

This chapter presents a new approach to improving the reliability of operating systems that is at once efficient and backwards compatible. Rather than tolerate all possible failures, Nooks targets the most common failures and thereby improve reliability at very low cost. In today's commodity operating systems, device driver failures are the dominant cause of system failure.

Nooks prevents drivers from forcing either the OS or applications to restart. It uses hardware and software techniques to isolate device drivers, trapping many common faults and permitting extension recovery. Shadow drivers ensure that the OS and applications continue to function during and after recovery. Dynamic driver update ensures that applications and the OS continue to run when applying driver updates.

The Nooks system focuses on *backward compatibility*. That is, Nooks sacrifices complete isolation and fault tolerance for compatibility and transparency with existing kernels and drivers. Nevertheless, Nooks demonstrates that it is possible to realize an extremely high level of operating system reliability with low performance lost for common device drivers.

REFERENCES

Barham, P., Dragovic, B., Fraser, K., Hand, S., Harris, T., Ho, A., et al. (2003). Xen and the art of virtualization. In *Proceedings of the 19th ACM Symposium on Operating Systems Principles*.

Fraser, K., Hand, S., Neugebauer, R., Pratt, I., Warfield, A., & Williamson, M. (2004). Safe hardware access with the Xen virtual machine monitor. In *Workshop on Operating System and Architectural Support for the On-Demand IT Infrastructure*.

Herder, J. N., Bos, H., Gras, B., Homburg, P., & Tanenbaum, A. S. (2006). Minix 3: a highly reliable, self-repairing operating system. *ACM Operating Systems Review*, *40*(3), 80–89. doi:10.1145/1151374.1151391

Herder, J. N., Bos, H., Gras, B., Homburg, P., & Tanenbaum, A. S. (2007). Failure resilience for device drivers. In *The 37th Annual IEEE/IFIP International Conference on Dependable Systems and Networks*, (pp. 41-50).

Hunt, G., & Larus, J. (2007). Singularity: Rethinking the software stack. *Operating Systems Review*, *41*(2), 37–49. doi:10.1145/1243418.1243424

Koch, H.-J. (2008). The Userspace I/O HOWTO. Revision 0.5. In *Linux kernel DocBook documentation*.

Microsoft (2006). *Architecture of the user-mode driver framework*. Version 0.7. Redmond, WA: Author.

Spear, M., Roeder, T., Hodson, O., Hunt, G., & Levi, S. (2006). Solving the starting problem: Device drivers as self-describing artifacts. In *Proceedings of the 2006 EuroSys Conference*, pages 45-58.

Swift, M., Annamalau, M., Bershad, B. N., & Levy, H. M. (2006). Recovering device drivers. *ACM Transactions on Computer Systems*, *24*(4). doi:10.1145/1189256.1189257

Swift, M. M., Bershad, B. N., & Levy, H. M. (2005). Improving the reliability of commodity operating systems. *ACM Transactions on Computer Systems*, *23*(1). doi:10.1145/1047915.1047919

Zhou, F., Condit, J., Anderson, Z., Bagrak, I., Ennals, R., Harren, M., et al. (2006). SafeDrive: Safe and recoverable extensions using language-based techniques. In *Proceedings of the 7th USENIX Symposium on Operating Systems Design and Implementation.*

Chapter 3
Identifying Systemic Threats to Kernel Data:
Attacks and Defense Techniques

Arati Baliga
Rutgers University, USA

Pandurang Kamat
Rutgers University, USA

Vinod Ganapathy
Rutgers University, USA

Liviu Iftode
Rutgers University, USA

ABSTRACT

The authors demonstrate a new class of attacks and also present a novel automated technique to detect them. The attacks do not explicitly exhibit hiding behavior but are stealthy by design. They do not rely on user space programs to provide malicious functionality but achieve the same by simply manipulating kernel data. These attacks are symbolic of a larger systemic problem within the kernel, thus requiring comprehensive analysis. The author's novel rootkit detection technique based on automatic inference of data structure invariants, which can automatically detect such advanced stealth attacks on the kernel.

INTRODUCTION

Integrity of the operating system kernel is critical to the security of all applications and data on the computer system. Tampering with the kernel is traditionally performed by malware, commonly known as rootkits. The term "rootkit" was originally used to refer to a toolkit developed by the attacker, which

DOI: 10.4018/978-1-60566-850-5.ch003

would help conceal his presence on the compromised system. The rootkit was typically installed after the attacker obtained "root" level control and attempted to hide the malicious objects belonging to him, such as files, processes and network connections.

A rootkit infested system can be exploited by remote attackers stealthily, such as exfiltration of sensitive information or system involvement in fraudulent or malicious activities without the user's knowledge or permission. The lack of appropriate

Figure 1. Evolution of rootkit attack techniques

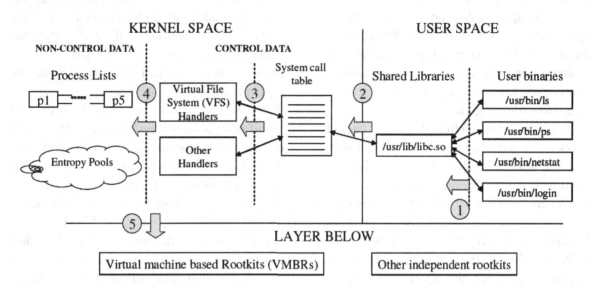

detection tools allows such systems to stealthily lie within the attackers realm for indefinite periods of time. Recent studies have shown a phenomenal increase in the number of malware that use stealth techniques commonly employed by rootkits. For example, a report by MacAfee Avert Labs (MacAfee, 2006) observes a 600% increase in the number of rootkits in the three year period from 2004-2006. Indeed, this trend continues even today; according to the forum antirootkit. com (Antirootkit, n.d.), over 200 rootkits were discovered in the first quarter of 2008 alone.

Rootkit Evolution

Rootkits attack techniques have matured over the past few years, posing a realistic threat to commodity operating systems. Comprehensive detection of such advanced rootkits is still an open research problem. The new attack techniques used by rootkits have in turn triggered the development of novel techniques to detect their presence. The evolution of rootkits and techniques to detect them continues to be an arms race between attackers and defenders. Figure 1 shows the evolution in rootkit attack techniques. Rootkits have evolved

from manipulating user space binaries and shared libraries to modifying control and non-control data in the kernel. The latest rootkits install themselves below the operating system.

Early rootkits operate by modifying system binaries and shared libraries replacing them with trojaned versions. The goal of these trojaned binaries is to hide malicious objects or grant privileged access to malicious processes. For example, a trojaned *ps* binary will not list the malicious processes running on the system. A trojaned *login* process can give root privileges to a malicious user. To detect trojaned system binaries and shared libraries, tools such as Tripwire (Kim, 1994) and AIDE (Aide, n.d.) were developed. These tools generate checksums of authentic binaries when run on a clean system and store them in a database. A user can examine the system at later points in time, using these tools, and compare the checksums of system binaries with those previously stored in the database. A mismatch in checksum indicates the presence of the trojaned binary. Other detection tools used an anti-virus like approach, where the presence of a rootkit is detected using a database of known signatures, such as a specific sequence of bytes in memory, or by the presence of certain files on disk. This approach does not protect the system against newer unknown rootkits. Rootkits could thwart such detectors by using polymorphic and metamorphic techniques for code obfuscation, traditionally used by viruses to escape detection from anti-virus programs.

To escape detection from disk based integrity checkers, rootkits have evolved to make modifications to kernel code and certain well known immutable data structures in the kernel, such as the system call table, to achieve the same goals. These rootkits are known as kernel-level rootkits because they modify the kernel. Modifications to the kernel make the rootkit powerful enough to control all application level views. For example, intercepting the file related system calls, allows the rootkit to control all files accesses by all applications on the system. The rootkit can intercept these accesses and perform the necessary filtering to hide its malicious objects. Since the rootkit manipulates the kernel, which is the trusted computing base of the system, it can also manipulate any user level applications on the system. Such applications include the rootkit detection tools that run in user space. Therefore, researchers proposed isolating the rootkit detectors from the operating system by either moving them onto a secure co-processor that does not rely on the operating system (Petroni, 2004), (Zhang, 2002) or isolating them using the virtualization architecture where the detector is run in a separate virtual machine (Garfinkel, 2003), (Payne, 2008). The rootkit detectors, built to detect the kernel level rootkits, use a checksum/secure hash based method to detect corruption of the kernel code or other well known immutable data structures in the kernel, such as the system call table. The hashes are pre-computed over the memory locations of a clean system, where the code and data structures are stored. They are periodically recomputed and compared with the stored hashes to detect code or data structure corruption (Petroni, 2004),(Garfinkel, 2003).

To further thwart detection tools, rootkit authors have adopted stealthier techniques. Since detection tools solely checked the integrity of the kernel code and some well known data structures, such as the system call table, rootkits delved deeper into the kernel and altered data structures that were less known. For example, instead of modifying file related system calls in the system call table, rootkits modified hooks in the virtual file system layer instead. For a while, the arms race continued where the rootkit explored a new data structure that it could exploit, while the detector had to incorporate the newly discovered data structure in its verification list. Most of the data that the rootkits modified was immutable control data i.e. function pointers used by various layers in the kernel. An automated approach was later developed to uniformly check for manipulation of all control data in the kernel, by validating every function pointer against a valid kernel function address (Petroni, 2007).

Since the integrity of mostly immutable control data can be verified, rootkit authors have advanced another step and have built innovative attacks that work by solely manipulating data structures that are mutable (Butler, 2005). This defeats the existing integrity checking mechanism of storing checksums and performing periodic comparisons because these data structures are also modified by authentic kernel code. We demonstrated some attacks that work by modifying relatively immutable non-control data (Baliga, 2007), (Baliga, 2009). These attacks modify variable values to alter the behavior of kernel algorithms. They escape detection because they manipulate non-control data within data structures not typically monitored by rootkit detectors. Detection approach was built to detect these advanced attacks using manual specifications, as long as the attack obeys some constraint (Petroni, 2006). This approach is effective as long as a manual security expert is capable of analyzing, anticipating and specifying the constraints on data structures that might become the target of future attacks.

More recent trends have shown rookits that operate below the operating system layer. Researchers have demonstrated rootkits that use the virtual machine technology to subvert the system (King, 2006), (Rutkowska, 2006) and rootkits that work independently of the operating system without requesting its services or affecting its state (David, 2008). While these indicate a new trend in the development of rootkits, they are likely to be unpopular because they are highly platform specific and depend on specific hardware features for their deployment. The operating system is still an attractive target because kernel level rootkits work independent of the hardware and can therefore be easily ported across different platforms. The kernel also provides a large code base and numerous amounts of complex data structures, providing the rootkit authors with several avenues for building stealthy innovative attacks.

Our Contribution

The focus of this chapter is on attacks that alter code and data structure in the operating system kernel. Conventionally, rootkits provide all malicious functionality as user space programs. To conceal their presence, rootkits tamper with the kernel. This involves modifying kernel code or data structures in the system call paths that are capable of affecting the user's view of the system. Typically, rootkits intercept control by installing hooks within the system call control path, which provide them with the capability of filtering requests and responses. The most common data structure manipulated by rootkits for this purpose is the system call table. As detection techniques matured to monitor the well known data structures targeted by rootkits, rootkits evolved to modify other less known data structures for control interception. Others evolved to modify non-control data to achieve similar goals.

While the data structures that are tampered have changed over the years, the intent of tampering is still the same, namely to hide the malicious files,

process and network connections. These rootkits can be easily detected by tools that use the hiding behavior as a symptom for detection. In fact, tools such as Strider Ghostbuster (Wang, 2005) detect the presence of rootkits, merely from their attempt to hide.

In this chapter, we demonstrate a new class of attacks and also present a novel automated technique to detect them. The attacks do not explicitly exhibit hiding behavior but are stealthy by design. They do not rely on user space programs to provide malicious functionality but achieve the same by simply manipulating kernel data. These attacks are symbolic of a larger systemic problem within the kernel, thus requiring comprehensive analysis. Our novel rootkit detection technique based on automatic inference of data structure invariants, which can automatically detect such advanced stealth attacks on the kernel. We have built a prototype Gibraltar, which evaluates our approach. Gibraltar has automatically detected all publicly known rootkits as well as other stealth attacks discussed by us and proposed in other research literature.

ATTACKS

In this section, we present four stealth attacks that we designed and one designed by another research group (Shellcode, 2006), all of which achieve their malicious objectives by solely changing kernel data. None of them explicitly exhibit hiding behavior and therefore cannot be detected by tools that use hiding behavior as a symptom for detection. These attacks span different subsystems in the kernel and are indicative of a more systemic threat posed by future rootkits.

Disable Firewall

This attack hooks into the *netfilter* framework of the Linux kernel and stealthily disables the firewall installed on the system. The user cannot

Figure 2. Hooks provided for the Linux netfilter framework

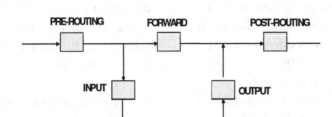

determine this fact by inspecting the system using *iptables*. The rules still appear to be valid and the firewall appears to be in effect. In designing this attack, the goal of the attacker is to disable the network defense mechanisms employed by the target systems, thereby making them vulnerable to other attacks over the network.

Background: *Netfilter* is a packet filtering framework in the Linux kernel. It provides hooks at different points in the networking stack. This was designed for kernel modules to hook into and provide different functionality such as packet filtering, packet mangling and network address translation. These hooks are provided for each protocol supported by the system. The *netfilter* hooks for the IP protocol are shown in Figure 2. Each of the hooks, *Pre-routing, Input, Forward, Output and Post-routing*, are hooks at different points in the packets traversal. *Iptables* is a firewall management command line tool available on Linux. *Iptables* can be used to set the firewall rules for incoming and outgoing packets. *Iptables* uses the netfilter framework to enforce the firewall rules. Packets are filtered according to the rules provided by the firewall.

Attack Description: The pointers to the *netfilter* hooks are stored in a global table called *nf_hooks*. This is an array of pointers that point to the handlers registered by kernel modules to handle different protocol hooks. This data structure is exported even by the latest 2.6 Linux kernel. We modified the hook corresponding to the IP protocol and redirected it to our dummy code, effectively disabling the firewall.

The firewall rules that we used during this experiment are shown in Figure 3. The INPUT rules deny admission for incoming traffic to the web server running on the system. Before the attack, we were unable to access this web server externally. After we inserted the attack module, we could access the web content hosted by the web server running on http port (port 80). Running *iptables* command to list the firewall rules still shows that the same rules are in effect (as shown in Figure 3). The user has no way of knowing that the firewall is disabled as the rules appear to be in effect.

Impact: A stealthy attack such as the one described cannot be detected by the existing set of tools. Since our attack module is able to filter all packets without passing it to the firewall, it can run other commands upon receipt of a specially crafted packet sent by the remote attacker.

Resource Wastage

This attack causes resource wastage and performance degradation on applications by generating artificial memory pressure, which can lead to a thrashing (Wiseman, 2009), (Jiang, 2009). The goal of this attack is to show that it is possible to stealthily influence the kernel algorithms by simply manipulating data values. This attack targets the zone balancing logic, which ensures that there are always enough free pages available in the system memory.

Background: Linux divides the total physical memory installed on a machine into nodes. Each

Figure 3. Firewall rules deny admission to web server port

```
Chain INPUT (policy ACCEPT)
target prot opt source     destination
ACCEPT tcp  --  anywhere   anywhere tcp dpt:ssh
ACCEPT tcp  --  anywhere   anywhere tcp dpt:telnet
ACCEPT tcp  --  anywhere   anywhere tcp dpt:24
REJECT tcp  --  anywhere   anywhere tcp dpt:http reject-with
                                        icmp-port-unreachable

Chain FORWARD (policy ACCEPT)
target      prot opt source     destination

Chain OUTPUT (policy ACCEPT)
target      prot opt source     destination
```

node corresponds to one memory bank. A node is further divided into three zones: zone dma, zone normal and zone highmem. Zone dma is the first 16MB reserved for direct memory access (DMA) transfers. Zone normal spans from 16MB to 896MB. This is the zone that is used by user applications and dynamic data requests within the kernel. This zone and zone dma are linearly mapped in the kernel virtual address space. Zone highmem is memory beyond 896MB. This zone is not linearly mapped and is used for allocations that require a large amount of contiguous memory in the virtual address space.

Each zone is always kept balanced by the kernel memory allocator called the *buddy allocator* and the page swapper *kswapd*. The balance is achieved using zone watermarks, which are basically indicators for gauging memory pressure in the particular zone. The zone watermarks have different values for all the three zones. These are initialized on startup depending on the number of pages present in the zones. These three watermarks are called *pages_min*, *page low* and *pages_high* respectively as shown in Figure 4. When the number of free pages in the zones, drops below *pages_low* pages, *kswapd* is woken up. *kswapd* tries to free pages by swapping unused pages to the swap store. It continues this process until the number of pages reaches *pages_high* and then goes back to sleep.

When the number of pages reaches *pages_min*, the buddy allocator tries to synchronously free pages. Note that sometimes the number of free pages can go below the *pages_min*, due to atomic allocations requested by the kernel.

Attack Description: The zone watermarks for each zone are stored in a global data structure called *zone_table*. *Zone_table* is an array of *zone_t* data structures that correspond to each zone. Zone watermarks are stored inside this data structure. This symbol is exported even by the 2.6 kernel. The location of this table can be found by referring to the System.map file. We wrote a simple kernel module to corrupt the zone watermarks for the zone normal memory zone. The original and new values for these watermarks are shown in Table 1. We push the *pages_min* and the *pages_low* watermarks very close to the *pages_high* watermark. We also make the *pages_high* watermark very close to the total number of pages in that zone.

This forces the zone balancing logic to maintain the number of free pages close to the total number of pages in that zone, essentially wasting a big chunk of the physical memory. Table 1 shows that 210065 (820.56 MB) pages are maintained in the free pool. This attack can be similarly carried out for other zones as well, wasting almost all memory installed on the system. The table indicates that only about 60MB is used and the rest is main-

Figure 4. Kernel Memory Allocation: Zone balancing logic and usage of zone watermarks

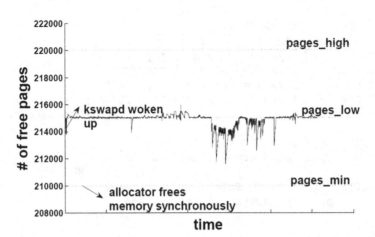

Table 1. Watermark values and free page count before and after the resource wastage attack for the normal zone

Watermark	Original Value	Modified Value
pages_min	255	210000
pages_low	510	21500
pages_high	765	220000
total free pages	144681	210065
total number of pages in zone: 225280		

tained in the free pool, causing applications to constantly swap to disk. This attack also imposes a performance overhead on applications as shown in Table 2. The three tasks that we used to measure the performance overhead are file copy of a large number of files, compilation of the Linux kernel and file compression of a directory. The table shows the time taken when these tasks were carried out on a clean kernel and after the kernel was tampered. The performance degradation imposed by this attack is considerable.

Impact: This attack resembles a stealthier version of the resource exhaustion attack, which traditionally has been carried out over the network (Schuba, 1997), (Wang, 2002), (Moore, 2006). We try to achieve a similar goal i.e to overwhelm the compromised system subtly by creating artificial memory pressure. This leads to a considerable performance overhead on the system. This also causes a large amount of memory to be unused all the time to maintain the high number of pages in the free pool, leading to resource wastage. The attacker could keep the degradation subtle enough to escape detection over extended periods.

Entropy Pool Contamination

This attack contaminates the entropy pool and the polynomials used by the Pseudo-Random Number Generator (PRNG) to stir the pools. The goal of

Table 2. Performance degradation exhibited by applications after the resource wastage attack

Application	Before Attack	After Attack	Degradation (%)
file copy	49s	1m 3s	28.57
compilation	2m 33s	2m 56s	15.03
file compression	8s	23s	187.5

Figure 5. The Linux Random Number Generator

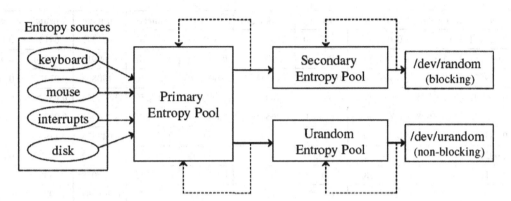

this attack is to degrade the quality of the pseudo random numbers that are generated by the PRNG. The kernel depends on the PRNG to supply good quality pseudo random numbers, which are used by all security functions in the kernel as well as by applications for key generation, generating secure session id's, etc. All applications and kernel functions that depend on the PRNG are in turn open to attack.

Background: The PRNG provides two interfaces to user applications namely */dev/random* and */dev/urandom* as shown in Figure 5. The PRNG depends on three pools for its entropy requirements: the primary pool, the secondary pool and the urandom pool. The */dev/random* is a blocking interface and is used for very secure applications. The device maintains an entropy count and blocks if there is insufficient entropy available. Entropy is added to the primary pool from external events such as keystrokes, mouse movements, disk activity and network activity. When a request is made for random bytes, bytes are moved from the primary pool to the secondary and the urandom pools. The */dev/urandom* interface on the other hand is non-blocking. The contents of the pool are stirred when the bytes are extracted from the pools. A detailed analysis of the Linux random number generator is available in (Gutterman, 2006).

Attack Description: This attack constantly contaminates the entropy pool by writing zeroes into all the pools. This is done by loading an attack module that consists of a kernel thread. The thread constantly wakes up and writes zeroes into the entropy pools. It also attacks the polynomials that are used to stir the pool. Zeroing out these polynomials nullifies a part of the extraction algorithm used by the PRNG. The location of the entropy pool is not exported by the Linux kernel. We can find the location by simply scanning kernel memory. Entropy pool has the cryptographic property of being completely random (Shamir, 1999). Since we know the size of the entropy pools, this can be found by running a sliding window of the same sizes through memory and calculating the entropy of the data within the window. Kernel code and data regions are more ordered than the entropy pools and have a lower entropy value. The pool locations can therefore be successfully located.

We measured the quality of the random numbers generated by using the diehard battery of tests (Marsaglia, 1996). The results are summarized in Table 3. Diehard is the suite of tests used to measure the quality of random numbers generated. Any test that generates a value extremely close to 0 or 1 represents a failing sequence. More about the details of these tests can be found in (Marsaglia, 1996). We run the tests over ten different 10MB files that were generated by reading from the */dev/random* device. The table shows that the sequence that is generated after attack, fails

Table 3. Results from running the Diehard battery of tests after contamination of the entropy pool

File#	bday	operm	binrnk6x8	cnt1s	parkinglot	mindist	sphere	squeeze	osum	craps
1	0.765454	0.497607	0.197306	0.000000	0.159241	0.000000	0.893287	0.423572	0.641313	0.147407
2	0.044118	0.180747	0.143452	0.000000	0.012559	0.000000	0.055361	0.769919	0.002603	0.066102
3	0.079672	0.999996	0.467953	0.000000	0.132155	0.000000	0.001550	0.190808	0.032007	0.468605
4	0.009391	0.000334	0.010857	0.000000	0.400118	0.000000	0.000258	0.573443	0.051299	0.057709
5	0.059726	0.996908	0.754544	0.000000	0.065416	0.000000	0.212797	0.276961	0.009343	0.389614
6	0.384023	0.975071	0.003450	0.000000	0.004431	0.000000	0.021339	0.047575	0.139662	0.082087
7	0.002450	0.458676	0.014060	0.000000	0.002061	0.000000	0.000010	0.044232	0.068223	0.836221
8	0.001195	0.840548	0.115478	0.000000	0.192544	0.000000	0.001535	0.024058	0.000078	0.214631
9	0.427721	0.553566	0.138635	0.000000	0.311526	0.000000	0.071177	0.296367	0.003107	0.679244
10	0.654884	0.106287	0.212463	0.000000	0.072483	0.000000	0.212785	0.338967	0.122016	0.710536

miserably in two of the tests: *cnt1s* and *mindist* and partially in the others. A failure in any one of the tests means that the PRNG is no longer cryptographically secure.

Impact: After the attack, the generated pseudo random numbers are of poor quality, leaving the system and applications vulnerable to cryptanalysis attacks.

Disable Pseudo-Random Number Generator

This attack overwrites the addresses of the device functions registered by the Pseudo-Random Number Generator (PRNG) with the function addresses of the attack code. The original functions are never invoked. These functions always return a zero when random bytes are requested from the */dev/random* or */dev/urandom* devices. Note that though this appears similar to the attack by traditional rootkits that hook into function pointers, there is a subtle difference. Since this particular device does not affect user-level view of objects, this is not a target for achieving hiding behavior and hence, not monitored by kernel integrity monitors.

Background: Linux provides a flexible architecture where different file systems and devices can use a common interface. This interface is provided by a layer called the virtual file system (VFS) layer. A new file system or a device provides a set of hooks when registering with the VFS layer. Figure 6 depicts two file systems *ext3* and *MS-DOS* and one device */dev/random* that are registered with the VFS layer. This enables user applications to access files residing on both file systems and the access to the device file with a common set of system calls. The system call is first handled by the VFS code. Depending on where the file resides, the VFS layer invokes the appropriate function registered by the file system or device during registration. Some system calls such as the *close* system call are directly handled by the VFS layer, which simply requires release of resources.

Attack Description: The kernel provides functions for reading and writing to the */dev/random* and */dev/urandom* devices. The data structures used to register the device functions are called *random_state_ops* and *urandom_state_ops* for the devices */dev/random* and */dev/urandom* respectively. These symbols are exported by the 2.4 kernel but are not exported by the 2.6 kernel. We could find this data structure by first scanning for function opcodes of functions present within *random_state_ops* and *urandom_state_ops*. We then used the function addresses in the correct order to find the data structure in memory. Once

Figure 6. File and device hooks in the Linux virtual file system (vfs) layer

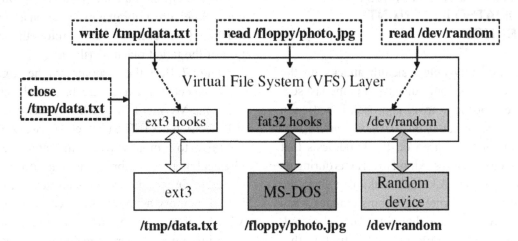

these data structures are located in memory, the attack module replaces the genuine function provided by the character devices with the attack function. The attack function for reading from the device simply returns a zero when bytes are requested. After the attack, every read from the device returns a zero.

Impact: All security functions within the kernel and other security applications rely on the PRNG to supply pseudo random numbers. This attack stealthily compromises the security of the system, without raising any suspicions from the user.

Adding a New Binary Format

The goal of this attack is to invoke malicious code each time a new process is created on the system (Shellcode, 2006). While rootkits typically achieve this form of hooking by modifying kernel control data, such as the system call table, this attack works by inserting a new binary format into the system.

Attack. This attack operates by introducing a new binary format into the list of formats supported by the system. The handler provided to support this format is malicious in nature. The binary formats supported by a system are maintained by the kernel

in a global linked list called formats. The binary handler, specific to a given binary format, is also supplied when a new format is registered.

A new process is created on the system, the kernel creates the process address space, sets up credentials and in calls the function *search_binary_handler*, which is responsible for loading the binary image of the process from the executable file. This function iterates through the formats list to look for an appropriate handler for the binary that it is attempting to load. As it traverses this list, it invokes each handler in it. If a handler returns an error code ENOEXEC, the kernel considers the next handler on the list; it continues to do so until it finds a handler that returns the code SUCCESS.

This attack works by inserting a new binary format in the formats list and supplying the kernel with a malicious handler that returns the error code ENOEXEC each time it is invoked. Because the new handler is inserted at the head of the *formats* list, the malicious handler is executed each time a new process is executed.

Impact: The attacker is able to successfully invoke malicious code each time a new process is created on the system.

ROOTKIT DETECTION VIA AUTOMATED INVARIANT INFERENCE

To automatically detect stealth attacks on the kernel such as the ones discussed in the last section, we propose a novel approach based upon *automatic inference of data structure invariants*. This approach is based on the hypothesis that kernel data structures exhibit invariants during its normal operation. A kernel rootkit that alters the behavior of the kernel algorithms violates some of these invariants and therefore can be detected. This approach can uniformly detect rootkits that modify both control and non-control data. To evaluate this hypothesis, we built a prototype Gibraltar, whose design and implementation, we discuss below.

The key idea is to monitor the values of kernel data structures during a training phase, and hypothesize invariants that are satisfied by these data structures. These invariants serve as specifications of data structure integrity. For example, an invariant could state that the values of elements of the system call table are a constant (an example of a control data invariant). Similarly, an invariant could state that all the elements of the running-tasks linked list (used by the kernel for process scheduling) are also elements of the all-tasks linked list that is used by the kernel for process accounting (an example of a non-control data invariant) (Butler, 2005),

(Petroni, 2006). These invariants are then checked during an enforcement phase; violation of an invariant indicates the presence of a rootkit. Because invariants are inferred *automatically* and *uniformly across both control and non-control data structures*, the approach presented in this section, overcomes the shortcomings of prior rootkit detection techniques.

Because Gibraltar aims to detect rootkits, it must execute on an entity that is outside the control of the monitored kernel, such as a coprocessor (Petroni, 2004), (Zhang, 2002) or inside

a separate virtual machine (Garfinkel, 2003). In our architecture, Gibraltar executes on a separate machine (the *observer*) and monitors the execution of the target machine (the *target*) as shown in Figure 7. Both the observer and the target are interconnected via a secure back-end network using the Myrinet PCI intelligent network cards (Myricom, n.d.) 1. The back end network allows Gibraltar to remotely access the target kernel's physical memory. Gibraltar is built to infer data structure invariants when supplied with raw kernel memory as input. Since coprocessor and VMM based external monitors use a similar asynchronous monitoring technique to read the target memory, Gibraltar can be easily adapted to work with these infrastructures.

Figure 8 presents the architecture of Gibraltar. It operates in two modes, namely, a *training* mode and an *enforcement* mode. In the training mode, Gibraltar infers invariants on data structures of the target's kernel. Training happens in a controlled environment on an uncompromised target (e.g. a fresh installation of the kernel on the target machine). In the enforcement mode, Gibraltar ensures that the data structures on the target's kernel satisfy the invariants inferred during the training mode.

As shown in Figure 8, Gibraltar consists of four key components (shown in the boxes with solid lines). The *page fetcher* responds to requests by the *data structure extractor* to fetch kernel

memory pages from the target. The data structure extractor, in turn, extracts values of data structures on the target's kernel by analyzing raw physical memory pages. The data structure extractor also accepts as input the data type definitions of the kernel running on the target machine and a set of root symbols that it uses to traverse the target's kernel memory pages. Both these inputs are obtained via an off line analysis of the source code of the kernel version executing on the target machine. The output of the data structure extractor is the set of kernel data structures on the target. The *invariant generator* processes these data structures

Figure 7. Gibraltar running on the Observer remotely fetches kernel snapshots from the target via the Myrinet back end network

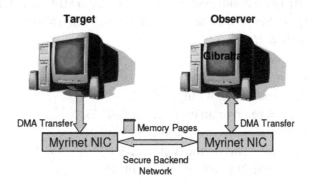

and infers invariants. These invariants represent properties of both individual data structures, also called *objects*, (e.g. scalars, such as integer variables and arrays and aggregate data structures, such as structs) as well as collections of data structures (e.g. linked lists). During enforcement, the *monitor* uses the invariants as specifications of kernel data structure integrity, which raises an alert when an invariant is violated by a kernel data structure. The following sections elaborate on the design of each of these components.

The Page Fetcher

Gibraltar executes on the observer, which is isolated from the target system. Gibraltar's page fetcher is a component that takes a physical memory address as input, and obtains the corresponding memory page from the target. The target runs a Myrinet PCI card to which the page fetcher issues a request for a physical memory page. Upon receiving a request, the firmware on the target initiates a DMA request for the requested page. It sends the contents of the physical page to the observer upon completion of the DMA. The Myrinet card on the target system runs an enhanced version of

Figure 8. Boxes with solid lines show components of Gibraltar. Boxes with dashed lines show data used as input or output by the different components

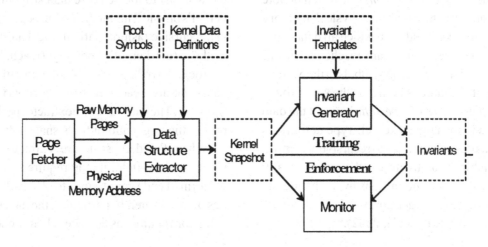

Figure 9. Algorithm used by the data structure extractor

> **Input:** (a) R: addresses of roots; (b) Data structure definitions.
> **Output:** Set of all data structures reachable from R.
> 1.   *worklist = R*;
> 2.   *visited = ϕ*;
> 3.   *snapshot = ϕ*;
> 4.   **while** *worklist* is not empty **do**
> 5.   *addr* = remove an entry from *worklist*;
> 6.   *visited = visited $\cup$ {addr}*;
> 7. M = physical memory page containing *addr*;
> 8.   *obj* = object at address *addr* in M;
> 9.   *snapshot = snapshot $\cup$ value of obj*;
> 10.   **foreach** pointer p in *obj* **do**
> 11.   **if** $p \notin$ *visited*
> 12.   *worklist = worklist $\cup$ {p}*;
> 13.   **return** *snapshot*;

the original firmware. Our enhancement ensures that when the card receives a request from the page fetcher, the request is directly interpreted by the firmware and serviced.

The Data Structure Extractor

This component reconstructs snapshots of the target kernel's data structures from raw physical memory pages. The data structure extractor processes raw physical memory pages using two inputs to locate data structures within these pages. First, it uses a set of *root symbols*, which denote kernel data structures whose physical memory locations are fixed, and from which all data structures on the target's heap are reachable. In our implementation, we use the symbols in the *System. map* file of the target's kernel as the set of roots. Second, it uses a set of *type definitions* of the data structures in the target's kernel. Type definitions are used as described below to recursively identify all reachable data structures. We automatically extracted 1292 type definitions by analyzing the source code of the target Linux-2.4.20 kernel using a CIL module (Necula, 2002).

The data structure extractor uses the roots and type definitions to recursively identify data structures in physical memory using a standard worklist algorithm as shown in Figure 9. The extractor first adds the addresses of the roots to a worklist; it then issues a request to the page fetcher for memory pages containing the roots. It extracts the values of the roots from these pages, and uses their type definitions to identify pointers to more (previously-unseen) data structures. For example, if a root is a C *struct*, the data structure extractor adds all pointer-valued fields of this *struct* to the worklist to locate more data structures in the kernel's physical memory. This process continues in a recursive fashion until all the data structures in the target kernel's memory (reachable from the roots) have been identified. A complete set of data structures reachable from the roots is called a *snapshot*. The data structure extractor periodically probes the target and outputs snapshots.

When the data structure extractor finds a pointer-valued field, it may require assistance in the form of code annotations to clarify the semantics of the pointer. In particular, the data structure extractor requires assistance when it encounters linked lists, implemented in the Linux kernel using the *list_head* structure. In Linux, other kernel data structures (called *containers*) that must be organized as a linked list simply include the list head data structure. The kernel provides functions to add, delete, and traverse list head data structures. Such linked lists are problematic for the data structure extractor. In particular, when it encounters a list head structure, it will be unable to identify the container data structure. To handle such linked lists, we use the *Container* annotation. The annotation explicitly specifies the type of the container data structure and the field within this type, to which the list head pointers refer. The extractor uses this annotation and locates the container data structure. In our experiments, we annotated all 163 annotations of the *list_head* data structure in the Linux-2.4.20 kernel.

In addition to linked lists, Gibraltar may also require assistance to disambiguate opaque pointers (void *), dynamically allocated arrays and untagged unions. For example, the extractor would require the length of dynamically-allocated arrays in order to traverse and locate objects in the array. We plan to add support for dynamic arrays, opaque pointers and untagged unions in future work.

Because the page fetcher obtains pages from the target asynchronously (without halting the target), it is likely that the data structure extractor will encounter inconsistencies, such as pointers to non-existent objects. Such invalid pointers are problematic because the data structure extractor will incorrectly fetch and parse the memory region referenced by the pointer (which will result in more invalid pointers being added to the work list of the traversal algorithm). To remedy this problem, we currently place an upper bound on the number of objects traversed by the extractor. In our experiments, we found that on an idle system, the number of data structures in the kernel varies between 40,000 and 65,000 objects. We therefore place an upper bound of 150,000; the data structure extractor aborts the collection of new objects when

this threshold is reached. In our experiments, this threshold was rarely reached, and even so, only when the system was under heavy load.

The Invariant Generator

In the training mode, the output of the data structure extractor is used by the invariant generator, which infers likely data structure invariants. These invariants are used as specifications of data structure integrity.

To extract data structure invariants, we adapted Daikon (Ernst, 2006), a state of the art invariant inference tool. Daikon was developed to dynamically infer invariants for application programs. An invariant is a property that holds at a certain point or points in a program; these are often used in assert statements and for formal specifications. For application programs, invariants can be useful mainly in program understanding. It can also be used for generating test cases, predicting incompatibilities in component integration, automating theorem proving and repairing inconsistent data structures.

Daikon attempts to infer likely program invariants by observing the values of variables during multiple executions of a program. Daikon first instruments the program to emit a trace that contains the values of variables at selected *program points*, such as the entry points and exits of functions. It then executes the program on a test suite, and collects the traces generated by the program. Finally, Daikon analyzes these traces and hypothesizes invariants—properties of variables that hold across all the executions of the program. The invariants produced by Daikon conform to one of several *invariant templates*. For example, the template $x == const$ checks whether the value of a variable x equals a constant value const (where const represents a symbolic constant; if x has the constant value 5, Daikon will infer $x == 5$ as the invariant). Daikon also infers invariants over *collections* of objects. For example, if it observes that the field bar of all objects of type struct foo at a program point have the value 5, it will infer the invariant "The fields bar of all objects of type struct foo have value 5."

We had to make three key changes to adapt Daikon to infer invariants over kernel data structures.

- **Inference over snapshots.** Daikon is designed to analyze multiple execution traces obtained from instrumented programs and extract invariants that hold across these traces. We cannot use Daikon directly in this mode because the target's kernel is not instrumented to collect execution traces. Rather, we obtain values of data structures by asynchronously observing the memory of the target kernel. To adapt Daikon to infer invariants over these data structures, we represent all the data structures in one snapshot of the target's memory as a single Daikon trace. As described in 3.2, the data structure extractor periodically reconstructs snapshots of the target's memory. Multiple snapshots therefore yield multiple traces. Daikon processes all these traces and hypothesizes properties that hold across all traces, thereby yielding invariants over kernel data structures

- **Naming data structures.** Because Daikon analyzes instrumented programs, it represents invariants using global variables and the local variables and formal parameters of functions in the program. However, because Gibraltar aims to infer invariants on data structures reconstructed from snapshots, the invariants output by Gibraltar must be represented using the root symbols. Gibraltar represents each data structure in a snapshot using its name relative to one of the root symbols. For example, Gibraltar represents the head of the all-tasks linked list, using the name

init tasks->next task (here, init tasks is a root symbol). The extractor names each data structure as it is visited for the first time.

In addition, Gibraltar also associates each name with the virtual memory address of the data structure that it represents in the snapshot. These addresses are used during invariant inference, where they help identify cases where the same name may represent different data structures in multiple snapshots. This may happen because of deallocation and reallocation. For example, suppose that the kernel deallocates (and reallocates, at a different address) the head of the all-tasks linked list. Because the name init tasks->next task will be associated with different virtual memory addresses before and after allocation, it represents different data structures; Gibraltar ignores such objects during invariant inference.

- **Linked data structures.** Linked lists are ubiquitous in the kernel and, as demonstrated later in 4.2, can be exploited subtly by rootkits. It is therefore important to preserve the integrity of kernel linked lists. Daikon, however, does not infer invariants over linked lists. To overcome this shortcoming, we represented kernel linked lists as arrays in Daikon trace files, and leveraged Daikon's ability to infer invariants over arrays. We then converted the invariants that Daikon inferred over these arrays to invariants over linked lists.

Daikon infers invariants that conform to 75 different templates (Ernst, 2006), and infers several thousand invariants over kernel data structures using these templates. In the discussion below, and in the experimental results reported in section 4, we focus on five templates; in the templates below, *var* denotes either a scalar variable or a field of a structure.

- **Membership template (var $\in$ {a, b, c}).** This template corresponds to invariants that state that var only acquires a fixed set of values (in this case, a, b or c). If this set is a singleton {a}, denoting that var is a constant, then Daikon expresses the invariant as var == a.
- **Non-zero template (var != 0).** The non-zero template corresponds to invariants that determine that a var is a non-NULL value (or not 0, if var is not a pointer).
- **Bounds template (var <= const), (var >= const).** This template corresponds to invariants that determine lower and upper bounds of the values that var acquires.

The three example templates discussed above correspond to invariants over variables and fields of C struct data structures. These invariants can be inferred over individual objects, as well as over collections of data structures (e.g. the fields bar of all objects of type struct foo have value 5). Invariants over collections describe a property that hold for *all members* of that collection across *all snapshots*.

- **Length template (length(var) == const).** This template describes invariants over lengths of linked lists.
- **Subset template (coll1 TODO-SUBSET coll2).** This template represents invariants that describe that the collection $coll_1$ is a subset of collection $coll_2$. This is used, for instance, to represent invariants that describe that every element of one linked list is also an element of another linked list.

The last two example templates are used to describe properties of kernel linked lists. As reported in section 4, in our experiments, invariants that conformed to the Daikon templates sufficed to detect all the conventional and the modern stealth attacks on the kernel that we tested. However, to accommodate for rootkits that only violate invariants that conform to other kinds of templates, we may need to extend Gibraltar with more templates in the future. Fortunately, Daikon supports an extensible architecture. Newer invariant templates can be supplied to Daikon, thereby allowing Gibraltar to detect more attacks.

The Monitor

During enforcement, the monitor ensures that the data structures in the target's memory satisfy the invariants obtained during training. As with the invariant generator, the monitor obtains snapshots from the data structure extractor, and checks the data structures in each snapshot against the invariants. This ensures that any malicious modifications to kernel memory that cause the violation of an invariant are automatically detected.

Persistent vs. Transient Invariants

The invariants inferred by Gibraltar can be categorized as either *persistent* or *transient*. persistent invariants represent properties that are valid across reboots of the target machine, provided that the target's kernel is not reconfigured or recompiled between reboots. All the examples in Figures 11-15 are persistent invariants.

An invariant is persistent if and only if the names of the variables in the invariant persist across reboots *and* the property represented by the invariant holds across reboots. Thus, a transient invariant either expresses a property of a variable whose name does not persist across reboots or represents a property that does not hold across reboots. For example, consider the invariant in Figure 10, which expresses a property of a *struct* file operations object. This invariant is transient because it does not persist across reboots. The name of this object changes across reboots as it appears at different locations in kernel linked lists; consequently, the number of *next* and *prevs* that appear in the name of the variable differ across reboots.

Figure 10. Example of a transient invariant. The name of the variable changes across reboots.

Init_fs->root->d_sb->s_dirty.next->i_dentry.next ->
d_child.prev->d_inode->i_fop.read == 0xeff9bf60

The distinction between persistent and transient invariants is important because it determines the number of invariants that must be inferred each time the target machine is rebooted. In our experiments, we found that out of a total of approximately 718,000 invariants extracted by Gibraltar, approximately 40,600 invariants persist across reboots of the target system.

Although it is evident that the number of persistent invariants is much smaller than the total number of invariants inferred by Gibraltar (thus necessitating a training each time the target is rebooted), we note that this does not reflect poorly on our approach. In particular, the persistent invariants can be enforced as Gibraltar infers transient invariants after a reboot of the target machine, thus providing protection during the training phase as well. The cost of retraining to obtain transient invariants can potentially be ameliorated with techniques such as live-patching (Chen, 2006), (Arnold, 2008), which can be used to apply patches to a running system.

EXPERIMENTAL RESULTS

This section presents the results of experiments to test the effectiveness and performance of Gibraltar at detecting rootkits that modify both control and non-control data structures. We focus on three concerns:

Detection accuracy. We tested the effectiveness of Gibraltar by using it to detect both publicly available rootkits as well as those proposed in the research literature (Shellcode, 2006), (Baliga, 2007), (Petroni, 2007). Gibraltar detected all these rootkits (Section 4.2).

False positives. During enforcement Gibraltar raises an alert when it detects an invariant violation; if the violation was not because of a malicious modification, the alert is a false positive. Our experiments showed that Gibraltar has a false positive rate of 0:65% (Section 4.3).

Performance. We measured three aspects of Gibraltar's performance and found that it imposes a negligible monitoring overhead (Section 4.4).

All our experiments are performed on a target system with a Intel Xeon 2.80GHz processor with 1GB RAM, running a Linux-2.4.20 kernel (infrastructure limitations prevented us from upgrading to the latest version of the Linux kernel). The observer also has an identical configuration.

Experimental Methodology

Our experiments with Gibraltar proceeded as follows. We first ran Gibraltar in training mode and executed a workload that emulated user behavior (described below) on the target system. We configured Gibraltar to collect fifteen snapshots during training. Gibraltar analyzes these snapshots and infers invariants. We then configured Gibraltar to run in enforcement mode using the invariants obtained from training. During enforcement, we installed rootkits on the target system, and observed the alerts generated by Gibraltar. Finally, we studied the false positive rate of Gibraltar by executing a workload consisting of benign applications.

Workload. We chose the Lmbench (McVoy, 1996) benchmark as the workload that runs on the target system. This workload consists of a micro benchmark suite that is used to measure operating system performance. These micro

Table 4. Conventional rootkits for Linux, publicly available and found in research literature (Petroni, 2006). This table shows the data structures modified by the rootkit. Gibraltar successfully detects all the rootkits.

Attack Name	Data Structures Affected
Rootkits from Packet Storm [5].	
Adore-0.42, All-root, Kbd, Kis 0.9, Linspy2, Modhide, Phide, Rial, Rkit 1.01, Shtroj2, Synapsys-0.4, THC Backdoor	System call table
Adore-ng	Vfs hooks, udp recvmsg
Knark 2.4.3	System call table, proc hooks
Rootkits from research literature [19].	
Hiding Process Attack	all-tasks list

benchmarks measure bandwidth and latency for common operations performed by applications, such as copying to memory, reading cached files, context switching, networking, file system operations, process creation, signal handling and IPC operations. This benchmark therefore exercises several kernel subsystems and modifies several kernel data structures as it executes.

Detection Accuracy

We report the results obtained in the use of the inferred invariants to detect conventional rootkits and modern stealth attacks proposed by us and other research literature (Shellcode, 2006), (Baliga, 2007), (Petroni, 2007).

Detecting conventional rootkits. We used fourteen publicly-available rootkits (Packetstorm, n.d.) that modify kernel data structures to test the effectiveness of Gibraltar. Most of these rootkits hide user level objects by modifying function pointers in the kernel. We also included one rootkit proposed in the research literature (Petroni, 2006); this rootkit hides malicious processes by altering non-control data. This rootkit relies on the fact that process accounting utilities, such as *ps*, and the kernel's task scheduler consult different process lists. The process descriptors of all tasks running on a system belong to a linked list called the *all-tasks* list (represented in the kernel

by the data structure *init_tasks->next task*). This list contains process descriptors headed by the first process created on the system. The all-tasks list is used by process accounting utilities. In contrast, the scheduler uses a second linked list, called the *run-list* (represented in the kernel by *run_queue_head->next*), to schedule processes for execution. This rootkit removes the process descriptor of a malicious user-space process from the *all-tasks* list (but not from the *run-list*). This ensures that the process is not visible to process accounting utilities, but that it will still be scheduled for execution. This technique is also used by the Windows rootkit named *fu* (Butler, 2005).

Table 4 summarizes the list of the conventional rootkits that we used in our experiments. Gibraltar successfully detects all the above rootkits. Each of these rootkits violated a persistent invariant. All rootkits, except for the process hiding attack, violated a object invariant conforming to the template *var == constant*, where var is a function pointer within the data structures modified by the rootkit and constant is the value of the function pointer. The process hiding attack violates the subset invariant, *run-list TODO-SUBSET all-tasks*, which states that each element in the *run-list* is also an element of the *all-tasks* list. The process hiding attack violates this invariant by removing an entry from the all-tasks list and is therefore detected by Gibraltar.

Table 5. Modern stealth attacks on kernel data (Shellcode, 2006), (Baliga, 2007). This table shows the data structure modified by the attack, the type of invariant violated and the template that the invariant conforms to.

Attack Name	Data Structures Affected	Invariant Type	Template
Disable Firewall	struct nf_hooks[]	Object	Membership (constant)
Resource Wastage	struct zone_struct	Object	Membership (constant)
Entropy Pool Contamination	struct poolinfo	Collection	Membership
Disable PRNG	struct random_state_ops	Object	Membership (constant)
Adding Binary Format	formats list	Collection	Length

Detecting modern stealth attacks. We used five stealth attacks developed by us and those discussed in prior work (Shellcode, 2006), (Baliga, 2007) to test Gibraltar. Table 5 summarizes these attacks, and shows the data structures modified by the attack, the invariant type (collection/object) violated, and the template that classifies the invariant. Each of the invariants that was violated was a persistent invariant, which survives a reboot of the target machine. We discuss the invariants violated by each attack in detail below. The details of the first four attacks mentioned below are described earlier in this chapter (Section 2).

Disable Firewall Attack

Gibraltar inferred the invariant shown in Figure 11 on the *netfilter* framework for the disable firewall attack. This attack overwrites the hook with the attack function, thereby violating the invariant, which states that the function pointer *nf_hooks[2][1].next. hook* is a constant. Because this attack modifies kernel function pointers, it can also be detected by SBCFI (Petroni, 2007), which automatically extracts and enforces kernel control flow integ-

rity. In fact, function pointer invariants inferred by Gibraltar implicitly determine a control flow integrity policy that is equivalent to SBCFI.

Resource Wastage Attack

Gibraltar identifies the invariants shown in Figure 12 for the three watermarks, manipulated by the resource wastage attack. These values are initialized upon system startup, and typically do not change in an uncompromised kernel. The attack sets the pages min, pages low and pages high watermarks to 210,000, 215,000 and 220,000 respectively. The values of these watermarks are close to 225,280, which is the total number of pages available on our system. Gibraltar detects this attack because the invariants shown in Figure 12 are violated.

Entropy Pool Contamination Attack

Figure 13 shows the invariants that Gibraltar identifies for the coefficients of the polynomial that is used to stir entropy pools in an uncompromised kernel (the *poolinfo* data structure shown

Figure 11. An invariant inferred on the netfilter hook. Firewalls are disabled by modifying the function pointer, thereby violating the invariant.

nf hooks[2][1].next.hook == 0xc03295b0

Figure 12. Invariants inferred by Gibraltar for zone_table[1], a data structure of type zone_struct (Gibraltar infers similar invariants for the other elements of the zone_table array).

```
zone table[1].pages min  == 255
zone table[1].pages low  == 510
zone table[1].pages high == 765
```

Figure 13. The invariants satisfied by the coefficients of the polynomial used by the stirring function in the PRNG. The coefficients are the fields of the struct poolinfo data structure, shown above as poolinfo.

```
poolinfo.tap1 ∈ {26, 103}
poolinfo.tap2 ∈ {20, 76}
poolinfo.tap3 ∈ {14, 51}
poolinfo.tap4 ∈ {7, 25}
poolinfo.tap5 == 1
```

in this Figure is represented in the kernel by one of *random_state->poolinfo* or *sec_random_state->poolinfo*). The coefficients are initialized upon system startup, and must never be changed during the execution of the kernel. The attack violates these invariants when it zeroes the coefficients of the polynomial. Gibraltar detects this attack when the invariants are violated.

Disable PRNG Attack

The invariants inferred by Gibraltar on our system for the random fops and urandom fops are shown in Figure 14. The attack code changes the values of the above two function pointers, violating the invariants. As with Attack 1, this attack can also be detected using SBCFI.

Adding Binary Format Attack

Gibraltar infers the invariant shown in Figure 15 on the formats list on our system, which has two registered binary formats. The size of the list is constant after the system starts, and changes only when a new binary format is installed. Because this attack inserts a new binary format, it changes the length of the formats list violating the invariant in Figure 10; consequently, Gibraltar detects this attack.

Invariants and False Positives

Invariants. As discussed in Section 3, Gibraltar uses Daikon to infer invariants; these invariants express properties of both individual objects, as well as collections of objects (e.g., all objects of the same type; invariants inferred over linked

Figure 14. Invariants inferred for the PRNG function pointers. These are replaced to point to attacker specified code, thereby disabling the PRNG.

```
random_fops.read  == 0xc028bd48
urandom_fops.read == 0xc028bda8
```

Figure 15. Invariants inferred on the formats list; the attack modifies the length of the list

$$length(formats) == 2$$

lists are also classified as invariants over collections). Table 6 reports the number of invariants inferred by Gibraltar on individual objects as well as on collections of objects. Table 6 also presents a classification of invariants by templates; the length and subset invariants apply only to linked lists. As this table shows, Gibraltar *automatically* infers several thousand invariants on kernel data structures.

False Positives. To evaluate the false positive rate of Gibraltar, we designed a test suite consisting of several benign applications, that performed the following tasks: (a) copying the Linux kernel source code from one directory to another; (b) editing a text document (an interactive task); (c) compiling the Linux kernel; (d) downloading eight video files from the Internet; and (e) perform file system read/write and meta data operations using the IOZone benchmark (Norcott, 2001). This test suite ran for 42 minutes on the target. We enforced the invariants inferred using the

Table 6. Invariants and false positives classified by the type of invariant and the template used to mine the invariant. Gibraltar infers a total of 718,940 invariants. Average false positive rate: 0.65%.

| Templates | Invariants | | False Positives | |
	Object	Collection	Object	Collection
Membership	*643,622*	*422*	*0.71%*	*1.18%*
Non-zero	*49,058*	*266*	*0.17%*	*2.25%*
Bounds	*16,696*	*600*	*0%*	*0%*
Length	*NA*	*4,696*	*NA*	*0.66%*
Subset	*NA*	*3,580*	*NA*	*0%*

workload described in 4.1.

The false positive rate is measured as the ratio of the number of invariants for which violations are reported and the total number of invariants inferred by Gibraltar. Table 6 presents the false positive rate, further classified by the type of invariant (object/collection) that was erroneously violated by the benign workload, and the template that classifies the invariant. As this table shows, the overall false positive rate of Gibraltar was 0.65%.

Performance

We measured three aspects of Gibraltar's performance: (a) training time, i.e. the time taken by Gibraltar to observe the target and infer invariants; (b) detection time, i.e. the time taken for an alert to be raised after the rootkit has been installed; and (c) performance overhead, i.e. the overhead on the target system as a result of periodic page fetches via DMA.

Training time. The training time is calculated as the cumulative time taken by Gibraltar to gather kernel data structure snapshots and infer invariants when executing in training mode. Overall, the process of gathering 15 snapshots of the target kernel's memory requires approximately 25 minutes, followed by 31 minutes to infer invariants, resulting in a total of 56 minutes for training.

Training is currently a time-consuming process because our current prototype invokes Daikon to infer invariants after collecting all the kernel snapshots. Training time can potentially be reduced by adapting Daikon to use an incremental approach to infer invariants. In this approach, Daikon would hypothesize invariants using the first snapshot, in parallel with the execution of the workload to produce more snapshots. As more snapshots are produced, Daikon can incrementally refine the set of invariants. We leave this enhancement for future work.

Detection time. We measure the detection time as the interval between the installation of the rootkit and Gibraltar detecting that an invariant has been violated. Because Gibraltar traverses the data structures in a snapshot and checks invariants over each data structure, detection time is proportional to the number of objects in each snapshot and the order in which they are encountered by the traversal algorithm. Gibraltar's detection time varied from a minimum of fifteen seconds (when there were 41,254 objects in the snapshot) to a maximum of 132 seconds (when there were 150,000 objects in the snapshot). On average, we observed a detection time of approximately 20 seconds.

Monitoring overhead. The Myrinet PCI card fetches raw physical memory pages from the target using DMA; because DMA increases contention on the memory bus, the target's performance will potentially be affected. We measured this overhead using the Stream benchmark (McCalpin, 1995), a synthetic benchmark that measures sustainable memory bandwidth. Measurement is performed over four vector operations, namely, copy, scale, add and triad and averaged over 100 executions. The vectors are chosen so that they clear the last-level cache in the system, forcing data to be fetched from main memory. Gibraltar imposes a negligible overhead of 0.49% on the operation of the target system.

CONCLUSION

Conventionally, rootkits tamper with the kernel to achieve stealth, while most of the malicious functionality is provided by accompanying user space programs. Therefore, stealth is achieved by trying to hide the objects, such as files, processes and network connections present in user space be-

longing to the attacker. Since user space programs can access or modify user space objects using system calls, the rootkit is limited to manipulating code or data structures that are reachable from the system call paths alone.

We demonstrated a new class of stealth attacks that do not employ the traditional hiding behavior used by rootkits but are stealthy by design. They manipulate data within several different subsystems in the kernel to achieve their malicious objectives. They are based upon the observation that kernel rootkits need not necessarily be limited to manipulation of data structures that lie within the system call paths. Other subsystems within the kernel are also vulnerable to such attacks. To demonstrate this threat, we built several new attacks. We have designed attack prototypes to demonstrate that such attacks are realistic and indicative of a more systemic problem in the kernel.

Previously proposed rootkit detection techniques largely detect attacks that modify kernel control data; techniques that detect non-control data attacks, especially on dynamically-allocated data structures, require specifications of data structure integrity to be supplied manually. In this chapter, we presented a novel rootkit detection technique that detects rootkits uniformly across control and non-control data. The approach is based on the hypothesis that several invariants are exhibited by kernel data structures at runtime during its correct operation. A rootkit that modifies the behavior of the kernel algorithms violates some of these invariants. We presented a prototype Gibraltar, a tool that automatically infers and enforces specifications of kernel data structure integrity. Gibraltar infers invariants uniformly across control and non-control kernel data, and enforces these invariants as specifications of data structure integrity. Our experiments showed that Gibraltar successfully detects rootkits that modify both control and non-control data structures, and does so with a low false positive rate and negligible performance overhead.

FUTURE WORK

Research over the past few years has made significant strides in the development of stealth attacks and tools and techniques for monitoring the integrity of the kernel. Numerous novel research challenges have also emerged that show promise towards building more robust and comprehensive kernel integrity monitors. Below, we discuss some interesting directions for future work in this area.

Data Structure Repair

Detection of rootkits that tamper with the kernel data structures has received a lot of attention over the past five years. Detection techniques are able to identify the data structures that are modified by the attack. While some work has been done in containment of ongoing attacks (Baliga, 2008), the commonly employed approach in the face of such attacks is to format the disk and install a new operating system image. The current response procedure besides being tedious and time consuming does not scale with the current attack growth rate.

Kernel integrity monitors such as Gibraltar discussed in this chapter monitor invariants exhibited by kernel data. These are used as integrity specifications and are checked during runtime. The monitor can therefore, identify the data structure and the invariant that is violated when an alert is raised by the system. In such cases, repair of the data structure comprises of restoring the invariant that is violated. For example, if a data structure exhibits the constancy invariant, then a violation occurs when the rootkit replaces this value with a different one. The repair action comprises of restoring the old value. While restoring other more complex invariants might require sophisticated methods, we believe that data structure repair is a promising research direction.

To secure the monitor, current approaches isolate it from the system that it monitors. As a result, the monitor is limited to external asynchronous memory based scans. It is unable to acquire locks from the operating system that is concurrently executing and modifying the data structures that are monitored. Repairing data structures requires the monitor to be able to make modifications to kernel data structures without affecting the correctness of kernel code. This also requires the invention of better mechanisms for realizing inline data structure repairs.

Mining Complex Invariants

Complex invariants that express conjunction or disjunction between simple invariants might express interesting properties. It is also possible to mine more complex invariants that express relationships between different data structure fields or between different data structures altogether. Invariants might also be mined using more complex invariant templates. Verifying a large number of invariants has performance implications for the monitor. Therefore a careful study of the kind of invariants that are more likely to be violated by attacks will provide some insight into the type of invariants that are more interesting than others.

REFERENCES

Anti rootkit software, news, articles and forums. *(n.d.) Retrieved from* http://antirootkit.com/.

Arnold, J. B. (2008). *Ksplice: An automatic system for rebootless linux kernel security updates.* Retrieved from http://web.mit.edu/ksplice/doc/ksplice.pdf.

Baliga, A. (2009). *Automated Detection and Containment of Stealth Attacks on the Operating System Kernel.* Ph. D Thesis, Department of Computer Science, Rutgers University.

Baliga, A., Ganapathy, V., & Iftode, L. (2008). Automatic Inference and Enforcement of Kernel Data Structure Invariants. In *Proceedings of the 2008 Annual Computer Security and Applications Conference*, Anaheim, CA.

Baliga, A., Iftode, L., & Chen, X. (2008). Automated Containment of Rootkit Attacks. *Elsevier Journal on Computers and Security*, 27(Nov), 323–334.

Baliga, A., Kamat, P., & Iftode, L. (2007). Lurking in the shadows: Identifying systemic threats to kernel data. In *Proceedings of the 2007 IEEE Symposium on Security and Privacy*, Oakland, CA.

Butler, J. (2005). Fu rootkit. http://www.rootkit.com/project.php?id=12.

Chen, H., Chen, R., Zhang, F., Zang, B., & Yew, P.-C. (2006). Live updating operating systems using virtualization. *Proceedings of the 2nd international conference on Virtual execution environments*, Ottawa, Canada.

Ernst, M. D., Perkins, J. H., Guo, P. J., McCamant, S., Pacheco, C., Tschantz, M. S., & Xiao, C. (2007). The Daikon system for dynamic detection of likely invariants. *Science of Computer Programming*, 69.

Garfinkel, T., & Rosenblum, M. (2003). A virtual machine introspection based architecture for intrusion detection. In *Proceedings of the Network and Distributed Systems Security Symposium*, San Diego, CA.

Gutterman, Z., Pinkas, B., & Reinman, T. (2006). Analysis of the linux random number generator. In *Proceedings of the 2006 IEEE Symposium on Security and Privacy*, Oakland, CA.

MacAfee AVERT Labs. (2006). *Rootkits, part 1 of 3: A growing threat*. MacAfee AVERT Labs Whitepaper.

Marsaglia, G. (1996). *The marsaglia random number cdrom including the diehard battery of tests of randomness*. Retrieved from http://stat.fsu.edu/pub/diehard

McCalpin, J. D. (1995). Memory bandwidth and machine balance in current high performance computers. *IEEE Technical Committee on Computer Architecture newsletter*.

McVoy, L., & Staelin, C. (1996). Lmbench: portable tools for performance analysis. In *Proceedings of the USENIX Annual Technical Conference*, May 1996.

Moore, D., Shannon, C., Brown, D. J., Voelker, G. M., & Savage, S. (2006). Inferring internet denial-of-service activity. *ACM Transactions on Computer Systems*.

Myricom: Pioneering high performance computing. (n.d.). Retrieved from http://www.myri.com

Necula, G. C., McPeak, S., Rahul, S. P., & Weimer, W. (2002). Cil: Intermediate language and tools for analysis and transformation of c programs. In *Proceedings of the 11th International Conference on Compiler Construction*, Grenoble, France.

Nick, J., Petroni, L., Fraser, T., Walters, A., & Arbaugh, W. A. (2006). An architecture for specification-based detection of semantic integrity violations in kernel dynamic data. In *Proceedings of the USENIX Security Symposium*, Vancouver, Canada.

Nick, J., Petroni, L., & Hicks, M. (2007). Automated detection of persistent kernel control-flow attacks. In *Proceedings of the 14th ACM conference on Computer and Communications Security*, Alexandria, VA.

Norcott, W. (2001). *Iozone benchmark*. Retrieved from http://www.iozone.org

Packetstorm. (n.d.). Retrieved from http://packetstormsecurity.org/UNIX/penetration/rootkits/.

Petroni, N., Jr., Fraser, T., Molina, J., & Arbaugh, W. A. (2004). Copilot - a coprocessor-based kernel runtime integrity monitor. In *Proceedings of the USENIX Security Symposium*, San Diego, CA.

Rutkowska, J. (2007). Defeating hardware based ram acquisition. *Blackhat Conference*, Arlington, VA.

Schuba, C. L., Krsul, I. V., & Kuhn, M. G. spafford, E. H., Sundaram, A. & Zamboni, D. (1997). Analysis of a denial of service attack on tcp. In *Proceedings of the 1997 Symposium on Security and Privacy*, Oakland, CA.

Shamir, A., & van Someren, N. (1999). Playing "hide and seek" with stored keys. In *Proceedings of the Third International Conference on Financial Cryptography*, London, UK.

Shellcode Security Research Team. (2006). *Registration weakness in linux kernel's binary formats*. Retrieved from http://goodfellas.shellcode.com.ar/own/binfmt-en.pdf.

Wang, H., Zhang, D., & Shin, K. (2002). Detecting syn flooding attacks. In *Proceedings of the INFOCOM Conference*, Manhattan, NY.

Wang, Y., Beck, D., Vo, B., Roussev, R., & Verbowski, C. (2005). Detecting stealth software with strider ghostbuster. *Proceedings of the 2005 International Conference on Dependable Systems and Networks*, Yokohama, Japan.

Zhang, X., van Doorn, L., Jaeger, T., Perez, R., & Sailer, R. (2002). Secure coprocessor-based intrusion detection. In *Proceedings of the 10th workshop on ACM SIGOPS European workshop*, St-Emilion, France.

Chapter 4
The Last Line of Defense:
A Comparison of Windows and Linux Authentication and Authorization Features

Art Taylor
Rider University, USA

ABSTRACT

With the rise of the Internet, computer systems appear to be more vulnerable than ever from security attacks. Much attention has been focused on the role of the network in security attacks, but evidence suggests that the computer server and its operating system deserve closer examination since it is ultimately the operating system and its core defense mechanisms of authentication and authorization which are compromised in an attack. This chapter provides an exploratory and evaluative discussion of the authentication and authorization features of two widely used server operating systems: Windows and Linux.

THE LAST LINE OF DEFENSE: THE OPERATING SYSTEM

The number of computer security incidents reported from various forms of attacks has increased significantly since the introduction of the Internet (CERT1; Yegneswaran, Barford, & Ullrich, 2003). Though it is clear that the introduction of the Internet coupled with the decreased cost of networking has helped to pave the way for attackers, the end result of most malicious attacks is the alteration of the host operating system. This alteration is often with the intent of propagating the malicious program and continuing the attack (virus, Trojan horse) or potentially damaging, stealing or altering some content on the host machine. While this type of attack may be aided by the network and security weaknesses therein, the attack could not be successful without ultimately compromising the host operating system. While much attention has focused on securing the network, since it is ultimately the operating system which is compromised, a closer examination of the defense mechanisms of the operating system may be warranted (Losocco, Smalley, Mucklebauer, Taylor, Turner, & Farrell, 1998). Security weaknesses in host operating systems are therefore a major concern for the IT practitioner. If unwanted modification of the host system can be prevented, then the attack may be thwarted despite any weaknesses in the network which allows the attacker to contact the host machine.

There has been a distinction drawn in research between application security and operating system security. It has become increasingly clear, however, that such a distinction is academic and that in practice malicious programs and the individuals who create them make no such distinction. Malware such as Code Red exploited weaknesses in both application and operating system security (Staniford, Paxson, & Weaver, 2002). What is required is an end-to-end solution, one that considers not only the distributed nature of the current computing environment and the network, but the close relationship between the application program and the operating system (Howell & Kotz, 2000; Saltzer, Reed, & Clark, 1981; Thompson, 1984). Recent focus on the concept of endpoint security represents an additional effort to understand and mediate these risks (Kadrich, 2007).

This chapter will examine specific security features of the host operating system in a descriptive and exploratory manner. By understanding the security controls available at the operating system level and the security weaknesses in those systems it is possible understand how to better prevent attacks on these systems.

Operating systems and their underlying security mechanisms are clearly a varied landscape which over time can be quite fluid. This chapter will focus on two common server operating systems: Microsoft Windows Server 2003 and Red Hat Enterprise Linux Server 5. Rather than refer to specific versions of these operating systems, this chapter will use the terms Windows and Linux to refer to Windows Server 2003 and Red Hat Enterprise Linux Server 5 respectively.

(As this chapter goes to press, the next version of Windows server operating system, Windows Server 2008, is in Beta 3; the updates to security features in this release considered relevant to this discussion will be identified and evaluated in this chapter.)

Security and Operating System Security Architecture

Early computers operated in closed environments with experienced and generally trusted personnel. The introduction of time-sharing with multiple concurrent processes required the consideration of how to manage the resources of the computer relative to the processes using the computer. Initial computer security concerns had focused on protecting executing tasks or processes from each other. Lampson (1974) expanded on that with a broad definition of protection that involved all resources under control of the operating system: memory, CPU registers, files (disk resources) and password security. Lampson proposed *protection domains* to define access rights and objects and associated object access lists. Under this paradigm, access to objects is enforced in relation to the protection domain of the user. The evaluation of operating system security requires a firm definition of the somewhat nebulous concept of the functionality and purpose of a computer operating system. An expansive definition could complicate qualitative comparisons with other operating systems which have not been developed with such a broad definition. For this reason, this discussion will consider the operating system the set of software which controls access to the hardware resources (CPU, disk, peripherals) of the server and will focus on specific operating system functionality which is of central importance to security, in particular, *authentication* and *authorization* (Lampson, 2004). The definitions used here identify *authenticating* principals as those which involve the process of determining which security principal made a request, and *authorizing* access as the process of determining who is trusted (authorized) to perform specific operations on an object.

In order to evaluate operating system security a set of standard principles is useful to provide a basis for discussion and comparison. Such a standard set of principles was established by Saltzer and Schroeder (1975) and remain relevant today (see Table 1). The evaluation presented here will examine these security principles in relation to the operating security functions of authentication and authorization. This evaluation will add *accountability* to this list since this has evolved as a central tenet of security on multi-user operating systems. This is defined as our ability to trust that the action performed on the system has by a known security principal.

Apples to Oranges: Comparing Windows and Linux

Any assessment of Windows and Linux must take into account the institutional and developmental background of these two operating systems. The Windows operating system is a product of a business entity with specific organizational goals. This business entity seeks to maintain the revenue stream generated by the sale of its software product through continual upgrades to the product. Since users are not compelled to upgrade software, the business entity needs to convince them of the need to upgrade by addressing previous product shortcomings and adding functionality to the product. The design and structure of the Windows operating system reflects this strategy in the continued addition of features to the core operating system. The Internet Information Server Web server, the built-in DNS and DHCP services and Active Directory directory services all represent additions to the core Windows operating system. The functionality and design of many Windows security features also reflect this approach where specific features and functionality have been added as part of the core operating system. This composition of the operating system is a key component of a specific business model chosen by Microsoft. Rather than leave it to customers to piece together a complete computing solution, they make the selection for them and produce a product which is complete, more robust than the previous version and easy to use since components do not need to be added to provide the computing solution the customer is seeking.

The composition of the Linux operating system reflects a different approach. Linux is a Unix

Table 1. Computer security principles

Principle	Description
least privilege	A user's security permissions should only be adequate for the task being performed.
economy of mechanism	The system must be sufficiently small and simple to allow verification and implementation.
complete mediation	Access to each object in the system must be checked by the operating system.
open design	The design of the system must be open to scrutiny by the community.
separation of privilege	A process which requires multiple security conditions to be satisfied is more reliable than a process which only requires one condition to be satisfied.
least common mechanism	The amount of security mechanism in use by more than one task should be minimized.
psychological acceptability	The human interface should be designed for ease-of-use so that excessive complexity does not hinder user acceptance of the security mechanism.
fail-safe defaults.	System defaults should be restrictive such that the default is lack of access.

variant, a version of original Unix developed at Bell Labs in New Jersey in 1971 for academic and research work (Ritchie, 1978). Linux was developed about 20 years after the original Unix and is not a product owned by a single company. Its design is purposely sparse and modular. The core operating system component is the Linux *kernel* and it is this kernel that is packaged with numerous open source operating system utilities and programs to create the various Linux *distributions* available today. There is no overarching business strategy and accompanying update cycle which impacts the development of Linux distributions. This combined with the fact that the business model under which Linux distribution vendors operates is new and volatile have led to a varied landscape of Linux distributions. Though some Linux distributions are marketed as complete solutions, most Linux users will add a variety of additional components to the system to provide the complete solution. Linux distribution vendors consider this a benefit of using a modular, flexible operating system and refer to this approach as a "best-of-breed approach" where the user can choose the components best suited to their environment.

To identify the best approach to developing an operating system or to define which components are truly part of an operating system is beyond the scope of this chapter. But in order to make a valid "apples-to-apples" comparison of Windows and Linux security, it is important to acknowledge the fact that Windows installations commonly use just the components provided with the operating system but Linux installations commonly add components to complete the computing environment. Any assessment of authentication, authorization must take this into consideration and discuss the security components commonly added to complete the Linux computing environment in order to make reasonable comparison. For purposes of this comparison we assume a standard Windows distribution which effectively is bundled with significant security and administration features

such as Active Directory, IIS and DNS, and Red Hat Linux ES with SELinux extensions.

The following sections will provide an evaluation of Windows and Linux security in relation to authentication and authorization. The next section will evaluate authentication, evaluating Windows and then Linux. The section following will evaluate authorization, evaluating Windows and then Linux.

AUTHENTICATION

Windows Authentication

Authentication on Windows allows a user to login to either a local workstation or a network domain of Windows hosts. A login process requests the user name and password interacts with the *local security authority* to request a *security access token* which contains the security identifier (SID) for the user. The Security Account Manager (SAM) database contains user and group names, security identifiers and passwords stored in encrypted form. The SAM database is stored in the Windows registry but is not accessible by system users. In Windows, the login process and local security authority are processes which run in user-space. A security reference monitor is executed in kernel-space and is used to determine whether or not a user has permission to access a system object (WindowsSecurity.com).

In larger installations of Windows clients, Active Directory (AD) is commonly for user authentication and is considered a central component of the Windows server product line. Active Directory is a customization of the LDAP (Lightweight Directory Access Protocol) for storage of user information (user name, password) and Kerberos to provide trusted logins over the network. A detailed description of AD is beyond the scope of this chapter, but key authentication features are relevant to this discussion. AD provides both authentication and authorization features over one or more network segments with the collection of network hosts considered the *domain*. Security rules are related to domains. Users using client computers which use AD for authentication request authentication from an AD server in a network login process which is generally similar to the standard Windows login (without AD). Later revisions of Windows have simplified administration of AD through security trust models which provide a hierarchy of trust relationships with the ability to inherit trust models.

Within Windows, domain security models from multiple domains can be combined to manage security across multiple servers and organizational departments connected over a network. In many cases, users who have authenticated in one domain need to use resources in another domain. This requires one domain to trust another domain's users with what is known as *inter-domain trust*. These trust relationships are transitive by default and are reflected through the hierarchy of the domain tree, thus simplifying administration. Trust relationships can be one-way or reciprocal and hierarchies of trust can be established (NT Security, 2005).

Use of AD enhances Windows security by providing simplified administration of the complex security models of medium to large sized organizations. This improves Windows implementation of the psychological acceptability security principle by making it easier, and thus more likely, to implement a consistent enterprise-wide security model. The secure login process also enhances accountability since we are more certain the user is who they say they are.

Windows authentication is started using a *trusted path* (Loscocco et al, 1998; Yee, 2002), a trusted communication channel between the user and the secure system which can only be initiated by the user. A user name and password prompt are displayed using the GINA (Graphical Identification and Authentication) facility. This is a replaceable DLL which can be substituted with another DLL to provide a different form of authen-

tication (for example, Smartcards or fingerprint readers) (MSDN Tech Report: GINA). The user then enters a user name and password and the local security authority is asked to authenticate the user using the password provided. The local security authority then invokes the authentication package provided with Windows, or may invoke a custom package to provide authentication.

The password provided by the user is converted to a cryptographic hash. The plain text version of password entered by the user is discarded and this cryptographic hash is compared to the cryptographic hash stored in a user database for the user being authenticated. If the entries match, then the *security access token* for that user is returned containing the *security identifier* (SID) for the user. The Windows security identifier uniquely identifies every user and group on the local host or in the domain and is used to determine authorization privileges throughout the system (NT Security, 2005).

Logging in to a Windows domain uses a slightly different approach to the authentication process. Since a domain login will most likely be performed over a network, a *nonce* (a unique number generated only once) is used to reduce the possibility of a replay attack to gain passwords for a system. This nonce is used to encrypt the password before sending it from the client to the domain server. As with the local login, if the encrypted password matches, the user is considered authenticated and the security access token for the user is returned.

An alternative network login facility known as LAN Manager (LM) is supported in Windows for backwards compatibility. This login facility has a number of well-known and significant security weaknesses as revealed by applications which can crack these passwords within 5-15 minutes (Lemos, 2003). Despite these weaknesses, the storage of these weak passwords has persisted for some time as a default option on the many desktop versions of Windows though it is possible to turn the feature off in some versions.

Windows provides a `runas` utility which allows a user to run a program as another user, effectively allowing the user to change their identity to execute a specific program. The user must provide the user name and password of the user identity under which the program will run. This feature raises issues with the several security principles. The user of this feature implies that an unprivileged user has been given access to a privileged account and thereby violating the "least privilege" principle since with the execution of the privileged program the user is now considered a privileged user. This also raises the potential violation of "accountability" since a single user has assumed two identities within a single session.

Linux Authentication

User authentication in the Unix world has traditionally varied from implementation to implementation with a core set of authentication services usually available. This assessment will examine the basic authentication services provided with Linux and then examine the features and functionality provided through common Linux extensions which provide additional security.

Linux basic authentication is performed using a login process which authenticates a user and provides a "shell" in which the user can then operate. The login process checks to see that logins are allowed and prompts for the user name. If the user is attempting to login as `root` (an administrator account), the login process restricts the login to specific terminals or locations. If the user is allowed to continue the process, the plain text password entered and the salt value (a 12 bit random number) retrieved from the password file is added and the result is encrypted with DES or MD5 encryption (depending on how the system is configured). This encrypted value is then checked against a password file. If a match is found, the user id and group id of the user are returned (Bacic, n.d.; Morris & Thompson, 1979).

Earlier Linux versions used a one-way DES encryption algorithm and stored the result along with a user name, user ID and group ID in a file readable by all users (/etc/passwd). It is still possible to do this in Linux but an option to use a more secure MD5 encryption algorithm and store the results in a file readable only by the administrator (/etc/shadow) is available during installation and is recommended by Red Hat (Red Hat Linux Technical Guide). Once the user has logged in, a user id and group id are associated with the user and are later used to determine accessibility rights for objects on the system.

While early versions of Linux used the basic authentication services described in previous paragraphs, most installations now use the Pluggable Authentication Module (PAM). PAM is a product of efforts by the former Open Software Foundation (currently the Open Group) to address shortcomings and variations in authentication, account management, and session management across Unix variants. When PAM is installed, Linux uses an abstraction layer to communicate an authentication request to the PAM subsystem. The PAM subsystem then chooses one or more modules to perform the authentication.

The use of a PAM login module which supports LDAP (Lightweight Directory Access Protocol) is used in many Linux installations to allow network authentication to be performed using an LDAP server. The Kerberos utility is also used for authentication, an approach similar to that of Window's domain authentication and allows authentication realms to be established and inter-realm trust relationships to be configured (Kerberos1). Both PAM and Kerberos provide simplified administration of larger Linux installations, thus enhancing the Linux implementation of the "psychological acceptability" security principle. Kerberos also improves upon accountability since it provides a stronger login mechanism which improves trust.

Linux provides a switch-user (`su`) utility which allows a user in a particular session to authenticate as a new user. This utility requires all users other than the root user to enter the password for the user identity they are trying to assume. Alternatively, a program can run with a set of privileges different than the set of privileges associated with the user without performing authentication as the user. This can be done by setting a specific file system identifier for the program being executed with the `setuid` bit. This feature has the effect of allowing a user executing a program to assume the identity of another user (the owner of the executable file that is the program) without authentication. Though commonly used in early versions of Unix, current security best practices discourages the use of the `setuid` bit. As with the Windows `runas` utility, the use of these features are contrary to the tenets of the "least privilege" principle and reduces the "accountability" of the users on the system.

By default, non-root users, users who do not have super-user privileges, may shutdown the system. Configuration parameters in Linux can be changed to restrict this capability to a specific set of users.

AUTHORIZATION

Windows Authorization

Windows authorization involves a set of user and group identifiers for each user and group on the system. Objects on the system (files, directories, peripherals) have associated access control lists (ACL) which identify which users and groups can access an object. Actions permitted are *reading*, *executing*, *writing*, and *deleting*. Users can belong to one or more group.

Authorization in Windows is enforced by the security reference monitor running in kernel-space. An access control list identifies the users or groups that can access an object. The security reference monitor manages the request for the object by the program (on behalf of the user). First the access denied entries in the list are checked and if any match the security identifier (SID) of the user requesting the resource, no other access control list entries are checked and access is denied. Next the access allowed entries are checked until enough entries are found to grant access to the object. If there are not enough entries found to grant access to the object, or there are no entries found then object access is denied.

An administrator account exists in Windows which provides a supreme (super-user) set of privileges. An administrator can set and change access control lists and can grant or deny user privileges and can access any object on the Windows system regardless of the access control list entries for the object. Windows supports a number of different administrator accounts each with different levels of authorization.

Windows also provides access control facilities to perform certain system actions such as system shutdown or backup. These are referred to as user rights and can be assigned to specific users (Windows Privileges). Windows Integrity Controls (WIC) available in Vista provides capabilities similar to MAC but does not provide the same level of security granularity. WIC is a mandatory access control which overrides discretionary access controls such as file permissions and manages the interaction of objects only allowing the object initiating the action to interact with objects of the same or lower privilege. An object which attempts to interact with an object of higher privilege will be denied regardless of the permissions of the user. WIC authorizations are associated with an object, not the user.

WIC provides stronger authentication and a finer granularity of control than discretionary access controls, but it appears to have been implemented primarily to address the damage caused by malware such as virus and worms and does not go as far as MAC in providing robust control over the interaction of objects. Objects which are considered associated with the Internet are given low WIC priority and thus have difficulty making changes to the operating system. This feature improves Windows implementation of fail-safe defaults in providing mandatory rather than just discretionary controls and also improves the implementation of complete mediation by the operating system by improving the granularity of that mediation. (Note that as this chapter goes to press, it is not clear that WIC will be in Windows Server 2008.)

Linux Authorization

By default, Linux uses a *discretionary access control* approach to authorization. Authorization privileges are either *read*, *write*, or *execute*. The objects under the control of the operating system are files and directories and special files which provide access to device drivers (Bacic, n.d.; Ritchie, 1978). When a program attempts to access an object in Linux, a system call is made which requests that the kernel return a handle (reference) to the object. The request specifies an operation as *read*, *write*, or *execute* for the object. The ability to delete an object is implied by the write permission.

When an object request has been made, the kernel first checks to determine whether or not the user has permission to use the object. If user permissions on the file match the user permissions of the program requesting the object, then the kernel will move to the next step. In this step, the privilege type for the user is evaluated. If the privilege type on the object is suitable for the operation being requested, the object handle is returned to the object. If no user permissions on the file are found to match the user requesting the object, then group permissions are checked. If the group identifier for the user matches that of the file, then the next step is to determine which access privilege will be used. If no suitable access privileges are found which satisfy the access being requested then the program is not permitted to use the object.

Linux Security Modules and Mandatory Access Controls

In response to heightened security concerns and a Linux user-base which is expanding to larger mission critical operations there has been an effort to provide extensible and flexible security features in Linux without having the operating system kernel source code fracture into numerous variants. The Linux Security Module was designed to provide a lightweight, general purpose, access control framework which supports kernel-space mediation of object access (Wright, Cowan, Morris, Smalley, & Kroah-Hartman, 2002).

Linux Security Modules (LSM) provide a pluggable architecture for the enforcement of security authorization by the kernel. A strict, finely-grained authorization model can be substituted using an LSM module, or a less-restrictive, discretionary access model could be used instead by using a different LSM module.

Security-Enhanced Linux (SELinux) provides mandatory access controls (MAC) and role-based access control using LSM. MAC allows a set of permissions to be defined for subjects (users, programs and processes) and objects (files, devices). It is based on the principal of least privilege and allows an administrator to grant an application just the permissions needed to perform its task. Permissions (authorization) can be assigned not to the user but to the application (Karsten, n.d.).

ASSESSMENT

Table 2 summarizes the assessment of the security features of authentication and authorization in Windows and Linux. It is clear from this table that both Windows and Linux have provided adequate solutions for a number of the principles cited by Saltzer and Schroeder.

Recent releases of Windows and Linux have both attempted to improve implementations of least privilege and fail-safe defaults, more no-

Table 2. Summary of assessment

Principle	Windows	Linux
least privilege	Partial	Yes
economy of mechanism	Partial	Partial
complete mediation	Yes	Yes
open design	No	Yes
separation of privilege	Partial	Partial
least common mechanism	n/a	n/a
psychological acceptability	Yes	Partial
fail-safe defaults	No	Yes
accountability	Yes	Yes

tably in Windows where it can be argued that many security exploits took advantages of these weaknesses. Fail-safe defaults have been an issue in previous versions of Windows with the default storage of weak LM passwords. Likewise least privilege was often violated through a dependency of operating system utilities and a number of applications of running at administrator privilege level. Least privilege issues are addressed in the Vista release of Windows through WIC but at this time (prior to the release of Windows Server 2008) it is still unclear that this feature will be in Windows Server 2008 and whether the Vista implementation of mandatory access controls will completely address the problem of persistent least privilege failures in Windows applications. Fail-safe defaults have been addressed partly through various patches to the Windows OS and partly through WIC which will force more careful consideration of access privileges on the part of Windows developers.

Windows developers have put a great deal of effort into easing administration of security policies at the enterprise level. This effort improves the psychological acceptability of Windows and is superior to the Linux environment where in the past it often required installation of one or more packages to implement enterprise-wide security policies (for example Kerberos and LDAP).

Recent efforts by vendors such as Red Hat have addressed this through bundling of packages for security hardened distributions, but Windows AD still has the advantage in ease of administration (psychological acceptability).

While it has no specific bearing on authentication or authorization, the principle of open design is not met by Windows. Though this is not a surprise given the nature of the Windows' development and the view that the underlying source code is the intellectual property of Microsoft, the idea that this diminishes the quality of the security code as proposed by Saltzer and Schroeder has some bearing on this discussion. The following sections will extend this discussion in more detail, assessing these security principles in terms of authentication and authorization.

Evaluation of OS Implementation of Security Principles

The principle of least privilege raises concern with both operating systems. According to Saltzer and Schroeder "every program and every user of the system should operate using the least set of privileges to complete the job" (1975, p. 7). Compliance with this principle is troublesome in a large part because of the history of each operating system.

Windows legacy environment (DOS, Windows 95) is that of a single user computer not necessarily connected to the network where any security that existed was implemented largely through physical security mechanisms (a lock on the computer; the computer in a locked office). These early PC operating systems were single user systems and did not limit accessibility to any part of the system. If a user had access to the computer, the user had access to all components of the computer. Thus programs operating in this environment had access to operating system resources. By nature of this design, any programs running in this legacy Windows environment violated the principle of least privilege.

For business policy reasons, Microsoft has long been committed to providing backwards compatibility with legacy applications. Consequently, in order to run many of these legacy applications in a Windows environment which supports access privileges, these programs must operate with administration privileges, privileges in excess of "what is needed to complete the job" (Saltzer & Schroeder, 1975, p. 6).

Linux provides the ability for a program to assume rights in excess of what the user running the program has available. Whether or not this is required would need to be evaluated on a case to case basis, but it is possible that many of these applications violate the principle of least privilege and their execution under different user accounts provides questionable accountability.

Linux provides a super-user account known as the `root` account, which has access rights and control over all objects on the operating system. The existence of this account violates the principle of least privilege since the actions performed using this account rarely require complete and unfettered access to operating system resources. For example, administration of the printer queue does not require the ability to delete all files on the system as the root account allows.

Linux with MAC provides robust control of privileges by allowing a set of permissions to be defined for security principals (objects) such as users, programs or processes and security objects such files or devices. It is based on the principal of least privilege and allows an administrator to grant an application only the permissions needed to perform its task. This feature also improves the implementation of the principle of complete mediation and fail-safe defaults in providing mandatory rather than just discretionary control over the interaction of operating system objects (security principals). This provides a much better implementation of the least privilege principle than current versions of Windows.

Windows provides a similar set of capabilities with the `administrator` account but provides the ability to create other accounts which have some but not all of the administrator account privileges. Using this capability, administrative accounts could be established with various gradations of security required for administrative tasks (for example, a backup account to perform backups, a network account to perform network maintenance). The proper use of these limited administrative accounts provides better compliance with the principle of least privilege.

Both the Linux `root` account and the Windows `administrator` account exist largely for convenience reasons. The Linux operating system is derived from the Unix operating system which began in an academic research environment where access security was not a major concern. As Unix matured, however, it quickly became a best practices standard to severely limit the use of the root account when running Unix. For this reason, few legacy applications running on Linux use root account privileges and it continues to be widely discouraged.

The ubiquitous buffer overflow attack has been used extensively on Windows platforms over the past five years (CERT2, 2003; CERT3, 2005; Microsoft-1; Yegneswarean et al, 2003). This attack involves exploiting memory bounds within a program (usually a network program) and loading the overrun memory with a different program (Bates, 2004). Once the new program is loaded, the program which has been exploited executes the new program code which has been loaded into the overrun buffer. These exploits are in part due to an inadequate least privilege implementation on the host operating system. Any Windows exploit which involves installation of software on the host operating system is potentially the result of account privileges assigned to an application in excess of what was needed by the application (CERT Incident Note IN-2001-09). Such exploits are rare on Linux and even when they do occur, the exploit does not always achieve root access permissions and are thus limited in the amount of malicious activity which can be performed on the system (CERT Vulnerability Note VU#596387).

The principle of *economy of mechanism* suggests that the system under examination must be small and open to inspection. It is most likely that Saltzer and Schroeder were proposing that the operating system being examined would be sufficiently small as to allow a quick security audit. Both Linux and Windows have grown to be large, complex operating systems with numerous modules used for authentication and authorization. It is not clear that either operating system would fully conform to this principle.

The principle of *complete mediation* applies to the manner in which the core operating system manages security. This operating system operation was a concern when Saltzer and Schroeder wrote their principles in 1975, but modern operating systems provide adequate implementations of this principle. Both Windows and Linux check the permissions of objects in kernel-space. Mediation is thorough and complete in both operating systems.

The principle of *open design* also applies to the ability to audit the security operations of operating system. Linux is an open source operating system which allows examination of its source code and therefore complies with this principle. Windows is proprietary source code and Microsoft does not

generally allow examination of its source code so therefore Windows does not comply with this principle.

The principle of *separation of privilege* recommends that more than one security mechanism should be used to implement security features. In relation to authentication and authorization, Windows and Linux have had limited implementation of this feature. With the addition of WIC and MAC which add mandatory access controls to the legacy discretionary access controls of the operating system, separation of privilege has improved in both operating systems though additional mechanisms could be added, for example defaulting to both biometric and password authentication, or providing multiple levels of authentication for a security principle. (Though WIC is definitely a part of the Windows desktop operating system, it is not clear if it will be part of the Windows Server 2008 release.)

The principle of *least common mechanism* applies to implementation of internal operating system security and control of system tasks. It is not practical to evaluate this principle in relation to authentication and authorization.

With regard to *fail-safe* defaults, both Windows and Linux provide installation default accounts, but unlike previous versions of both operating systems they no longer use default passwords. Passwords are chosen during installation and if password best practices are followed, an acceptable level of authentication security should be maintained. An additional level of security is provided with mandatory access controls. The implementation of these controls in SELinux provides robust control over the default behavior of applications. A Windows (Vista) implementation of this control provides some controls but lacks the complete implementation of MAC and it is uncertain whether this will become part of Windows Server 2008. Currently Linux provides the most complete implementation of this principle.

In evaluating their default password authentication methods, the use of password encryption does differ. Linux uses a password salt, a random value generated and added to the users password before encryption. This increases the difficulty of guessing the password with a brute force attack. Windows does not use a password encryption salt which combined with other weaknesses has led to some well publicized concerns about the ease of cracking Windows passwords (Lemos, 2003). A fair analysis of Windows authentication must however consider the user of AD to provide authentication. AD has become the common method for user authentication for Windows systems. The AD password does not have the password weaknesses of LM passwords and essentially provides a secure authentication process and enhances the authorization process.

Considering the principle of *psychological acceptability*, using Active Directory the Windows network authentication scheme is more robust and flexible, making administration of authentication and authorization easier. Similar domain security administration is possible with Linux (LDAP + Kerberos), but is currently more difficult to administer than its Windows counterpart. Though there are incompatibility issues with using Linux and Windows network authentication together (a common requirement in today's information technology centers), these incompatibilities are not insurmountable and are not severe enough to change this assessment.

Though it does not fall under the categories established by Saltzer and Schroeder (1975), *accountability* issues should be considered under authentication and authorization. General shared user accounts should be limited and discouraged since a user account shared amongst multiple users does not provide accountability for the actions performed by that user account on the system (since it could be one of many users). For this reason, authentication for shared accounts should either be eliminated or severely limited by the system. In Windows, the "guest" account is commonly used as a shared account and is now disabled by default. In Linux, the "nobody" account is commonly used by a number of programs but login is disabled by default.

SUMMARY AND CONCLUSION

In evaluating the authentication and authorization of Windows and Linux on the basis of Saltzer and Schroeder's security principles and accountability, Linux distributions of SELinux using MAC have an advantage in authentication and authorization. The lack of open design in Windows limits the auditability of its authentication and authorization features and is considered a detriment. Malicious software running in user-space is the most common cause of security exploits. Mandatory access controls (MAC) provide a higher level of security which can mitigate weaknesses in application security. These controls add another layer of security to the management of authorization requests by the operating system and thus improve the Linux implementation of separation of privilege and the default behavior of applications (fail-safe defaults). Windows does not currently provide an implementation of MAC in their server product and consideration of this reduces the authentication and authorization security of that operating system.

Windows implementation of network security with AD demonstrates the benefits of psychological acceptability in security features. As Saltzer and Schroeder understood, providing ease of use greatly improves the likelihood that the security feature will be used (psychological acceptability). The ability to create consistent security policies and the ability to implement them throughout an enterprise is a significant benefit. Windows has an advantage in this area as Linux implementations of such features have had limited development and must contend with the predominance of Windows client operating system on the desktop and the persistent interoperability issues that exist in integrating Windows authorization and authentication features with Linux.

Auditing the security of operating systems in complex enterprise environments involves evaluation of a number of factors which is beyond the scope of this chapter. The evaluation presented represents a start. A next step would be the expansion of evaluative criteria in addition to the security principles identified here followed by the assignment of statistical weights for those criteria. The statistical weights used would represent the perceived value of those security criteria to the enterprise. Aggregation of those weights would provide a representative score for each operating system which could then be combined with other qualitative criteria to arrive at a final assessment.

REFERENCES

Bacic, E. M. (n.d.). UNIX & Security. Canadian System Security Centre, Communications Security Establishment. Retrieved January 7, 2005 from http://andercheran.aiind.upv.es/toni/unix/Unix_and_Security.ps.gz

Bates, R. (2004). Buffer overrun madness. *ACM Queue, 2*(3).

CERT1 (2004). CERT, [Data File]. Accessed on December 20, 2004 from http://www.cert.org/cert_stats.html

CERT2 (2003). Incident note IN-2001-09, Code Red II: Another worm exploiting buffer overflow In IIS indexing service DLL. Retrieved on December 20, 2004 from http://www.cert.org/incident_notes/IN-2001-09.html

CERT3 (2005). CERT Vulnerability Note VU#596387, Icecast vulnerable to buffer overflow via long GET request. US-CERT Vulnerability Notes Database. Retrieved on January 4, 2005 from http://www.kb.cert.org/vuls/id/596387

Kadrich, M. (2007). *Endpoint security.* New York: Addison-Wesley Professional.

Howell, J. & Kotz, D. (2000). End-to-end authorization. *Proceedings of the 4th Symposium on Operating Systems Design and Implementation* (151 164). San Diego, CA.

Karsten, W. (n.d.). Fedora Core 2, SELinux FAQ. Retrieved on January 5, 2005 from http://fedora.redhat.com/docs/selinux-faq-fc2/index.html#id3176332

Kerberos1 (n.d.). Kerberos: the Network Authentication Protocol. Retrieved January 5, 2005 from http://web.mit.edu/kerberos/www/

Lampson, B. (1974). Protection. *SIGOPS Operating System Review, 8*, 18-24.

Lampson, B. (2004). Computer security in the real world. *IEEE Computer, 37*, 37-46.

Lemos, R. (2003). Cracking Windows passwords in seconds. CNET News.com. Retrieved July 22, 2003 from http://news.zdnet.com/2100-1009_22-5053063.html

Loscocco, P. A., Smalley, S. D., Mucklebauer, P. A., Taylor, R. C., Turner, S. J., & Farrell, J. F. (1998). The inevitability of failure: The flawed assumption of security in modern computing national security agency.

Microsoft-1, Microsoft Security Bulletin MS03-026, Buffer Overrun In RPC Interface Could Allow Code Execution (823980) revised September 10, 2003, Retrieved on January 7, 2005 from http://www.microsoft.com/technet/security/bulletin/MS03-026.mspx

Microsoft-2, Microsoft, Inc. (2005). *Loading and Running a GINA DLL*. (n.d.). Retrieved January 7, 2005 from http://whidbey.msdn.microsoft.com/library/default.asp?url=/library/en-us/security/security/loading_and_running_a_gina_dll.asp

Morris, R., & Thompson, K. (1979). Password security: A case history. *Communications of the ACM, 22*, 594-597.

MSDN Technical Library, Interactive Authentication (GINA). Retrieved on December 21, 2004 from http://msdn.microsoft.com/library/default. asp?url=/library/en-us/secauthn/security/interactive_authentication.asp

NT Security (2005). Network strategy report: Windows NT security. Retrieved on January 5, 2005 from http://www.secinf.net/windows_security/ Network_Strategy_Report_Windows_NT_Security.html

Red Hat-1, Red Hat Linux Reference Guide, Shadow Passwords. Retrieved January 6, 2005 from http://www.redhat.com/docs/manuals/ linux/RHL-9-Manual/ref-guide/s1-users-groups-shadow-utilities.html

Ritchie, D. M. & Thompson, K. (1978). The UNIX time-sharing system. *The Bell System Technical Journal, 57*, 1905-1920.

Ritchie, D. M. (1979). *On the Security of UNIX*, in UNIX SUPPLEMENTARY DOCUMENTS, AT & T.

Saltzer, J. H., Reed, D. P., & Clark, D. D. (1984). End-to-end arguments in system design. *ACM Transactions on Computer Systems, 2* , 277-288.

Saltzer, J. H., & Schroeder, M. D. (1975). The protection of information in computer systems. *Proceedings of the IEEE, 63*, 1278-1308.

Samar, V. & Schemers, R. (1995). *Unified Login with Pluggable Authentication Modules (PAM)*. Request For Comments: 86.0, Open Software Foundation (October 1995).

Staniford, S., Paxson, V., & Weaver, N. (2002). How to own the Internet in your spare time. *Proceedings of the 11th Usenix Security Symposium*, 149-167.

Thompson, K. (1984). Reflections on trusting trust. *Communication of the ACM, 27*, 761-763.

Wright C., Cowan C., Morris J., Smalley S. & Kroah-Hartman G. (2002). Linux security modules: General security support for the Linux kernel. *Proceedings of Usenix 2002*.

Yee, K. User Interaction Design for Secure Systems 2002

Yegneswaran, V., Barford, P. & Ullrich, J. (2003). *Internet intrusions: Global characteristics and prevalence*, 138-147. New York: ACM Press.

This work was previously published in the Handbook of Research on Information Security and Assurance, edited by J. Gupta and S. Sharma, pp. 518-528, copyright 2009 by Information Science Reference (an imprint of IGI Global).

Section 2
Efficient Memory Management

Chapter 5
Swap Token:
Rethink the Application of the LRU Principle on Paging to Remove System Thrashing

Song Jiang
Wayne State University, USA

ABSTRACT

Most computer systems use the global page replacement policy based on the LRU principle to reduce page faults. The LRU principle for the global page replacement dictates that a Least Recently Used (LRU) page, or the least active page in a general sense, should be selected for replacement in the entire user memory space. However, in a multiprogramming environment under high memory load, an indiscriminate use of the principle can lead to system thrashing, in which all processes spend most of their time waiting for the disk service instead of making progress. In this chapter, we will rethink the application of the LRU principle on global paging to identify one of root causes for thrashing, and describe a mechanism, named as swap token, to solve the issue. The mechnism is simple in its design and implementation but highly effective in alleviating or removing thrashing. A key feature of the swap token mechanism is that it can distinguish the conditions for an LRU page, or a page that has not been used for relatively long period of time, to be generated and accordingly categorize LRU pages into two types: true and false LRU pages. The mechanism identifies false LRU pages to avoid use of the LRU principle on these pages, in order to remove thrashing. A prototype implementation of the swap token mechanism in the Linux kernel as well as some experiment measurements are presented. The experiment results show that the mechanism can consistently reduce the program execution slowdown in a multiprogramming environment including SPEC2000 programs and other memory-intensive applications by up to 67%. The slowdown reductions mainly come from reductions of up to 95% of total page faults during program interactions. This chapter also shows that the mechanism introduces little overhead to program executions, and its implementations on Linux (and Unix) systems are straightforward.

DOI: 10.4018/978-1-60566-850-5.ch005

INTRODUCTION

The virtual memory system allocates physical memory to multiple concurrently running programs in a computer system through a global page replacement algorithm, especially when the aggregate memory demand is larger than the available physical memory space. A commonly used replacement algorithm in a virtual memory management is the global Least Recent Used (LRU) replacement, which selects an LRU memory page, or the least actively used page, for replacement throughout the entire user memory space of the system. According to the observed common memory reference behavior, the LRU replacement policy takes the assumption that a page will not be used again in the near future if it has not been accessed for a certain period of time. In a single programming environment where only one process is running at a time, this assumption as well as the corresponding LRU principle, which always selects LRU pages for replacement -- hold well for many application programs, leading to an efficient memory use for their execution. However, as the assumption and the principle are directly adopted in memory management designs and implementations for multiprogramming systems, many of computing practitioners can experience following difficulty in their program executions. When the aggregate memory demand of multiple concurrently running programs exceeds the available user memory space to a certain degree, the system starts thrashing --- none of the processes are able to establish their working sets, causing a large number of page faults in the system, low CPU utilization, and a long delay for each process. Although a large amount of CPU cycles are wasted due to the excessive page faults in the shared use of the memory, people seem to have accepted this reality, and to believe that these additional cycles are unavoidable due to the memory shortage and due to the fairness requirement for the concurrently running programs.

As the LRU principle is based on access patterns exhibited in one program's execution, a direct application of the principle on the concurrently running programs is problematic and may cause system thrashing. Let us take a close look into the way an LRU replacement policy is implemented in a multiprogramming system. An allocated memory page of a process will become a replacement candidate according to the LRU principle if the page has not been accessed for a certain period of time under two conditions: (1) the process does not need to access the page; and (2) the process is conducting page faults (a sleeping process) so that it is *not able* to access the page although it might have done so without the page faults. We call the LRU pages generated on the first condition *true LRU pages*, and those on the second condition *false LRU pages*. These false LRU pages are produced by the time delay of page faults, not by the access delay of the process. Therefore, this delay does not necessarily hint that the page is not going to be accessed again by the process soon, or the LRU assumption is not applicable for the false LRU pages. However, LRU page replacement implementations do not distinguish these two types of LRU pages, and treats them equally by attempting to replace any LRU pages!

Whenever page faults occur due to memory shortage in a multiprogramming environment, false LRU pages of a process can be generated, which will weaken the ability of the process to achieve its working set. For example, if a process does not access its already obtained memory pages on the false LRU condition, these pages may become replacement candidates (the LRU pages) when the memory space is being demanded by other processes. When the process is ready to use these pages in its execution turn, these LRU pages may have been replaced to satisfy memory demands from other processes. The process then has to ask the virtual memory system to retrieve these pages back probably by generating and replacing false LRU pages from other processes. The false LRU pages may be cascaded among the concurrently running programs, eventually causing system into thrashing, in which processes chaotically compete for pages by swapping in and out pages frequently, but are unable to establish their working sets and make little progress, wasting CPU cycles.

Such a problem can be very serious for the following two reasons. First, these LRU pages are produced by the time delay of page faults, not by the access delay of the process. The LRU assumption is not held. Thus, the probability of accessing these pages soon is much greater than that of accessing true LRU pages, which produces high page fault ratios. Second, the delay from page fault penalty increases with the increase of the number of page faults due to increasingly congested disk. The increased page fault penalty could produce even more false LRU pages. Processes receiving many page faults are the ones that demand memory space dynamically and the ones that incrementally establish their working sets. On the other hand, a process that requests a stable working set in a short period of time and then frequently accesses it in its entire execution, could soon get the working set established and probably keep it, or keep a major part of it in its lifetime. Therefore, it suffers the least from the system thrashing.

BACKGROUNDS OF THRASHING PROTECTIONS

Researchers in the operating system field have proposed several schemes to protect system from thrashing during program interactions, and even implemented some in practical systems. The framework of *local page replacements* [Alderson et al. 1972] and *working set models* [Denning 1968-1] have been designed for the purpose. Once a thrashing is detected, *load controls* [Denning 1968-2] can be used to eliminate it. In this section, we will briefly overview these schemes and techniques, and discuss their limitations, which motivates the design of the swap token mechanism.

Local Page Replacement

Although most paging systems use the global page replacement, the local page replacement has been proposed to protect systems from thrashing in a multiprogramming environment. A local replacement requires that the paging system select pages for a process only from its allocated memory space when no free pages can be found in their memory allotments. Unlike the global replacement policy, the local policy needs a memory allocation scheme to respond to the need of each process. Two commonly used policies are equal and proportional allocations, which cannot capture dynamically changing memory demand of each process [Alderson et al. 1972]. As a result, the memory space may not be well utilized. On the other hand, an allocation dynamically adapting to the memory demands of individual programs will actually turn the scheme into the global replacement. The VMS [Kenah et al. 1984] is a representative operating system using a local replacement policy, in which the memory is partitioned into multiple independent areas, each of which is localized to a collection of processes that compete with one another for memory space. With this scheme, system administrators can guarantee that a process, or a collection of processes, will always at least keep a certain percentage of memory. Unfortunately, this scheme can be difficult to administer [Lazowska et al. 1978]. Allocating too small a number of pages to a partition can result in excessive swapping, whereas setting the number too high can cause underutilization of memory [Lazowska et al. 1978]. Researchers and system practitioners seem to have agreed on that a local policy is not an effective solution for virtual memory management.

The Working Set Model

Denning [Denning 1968-1] proposes the working set model to measure the current memory demand of a running program in the system. A working set of a program is a set of its recently accessed pages. Specifically, at virtual time t, the program's working set W_t, is the subset of all pages of the program which has been accessed in the previous θ virtual time units (the working set window). The task's virtual time is a measure of the duration the program has control of the processor and is executing instructions. A working set replacement algorithm is used to ensure no pages in the working set of a running program will be replaced [Denning 1970]. Since the I/O time caused by page faults is excluded in the working set model, the working set replacement algorithm can theoretically eliminate the thrashing caused by chaotic memory competition. However, the implementation of this model is very expensive because a working set monitoring is required for each individual process based on its virtual time [Morris 1972].

The affordable LRU approximations of working set algorithm, such as two-handed clock, FIFO with second chance, have to replace virtual time with real time in determining the working sets. This approximation leaves a loophole for the false LRU pages.

Load Controls

A commonly used method to protect systems from thrashing is load control, which adjusts the memory demands from multiple processes by changing the multiprogramming level (MPL), or the number of active processes in the system. It suspends/reactivates, even swaps out/in processes to control memory demands after the thrashing is

detected. The 4.4 BSD operating system [McKusick et al. 1996], AIX system in the IBM RS/6000 [IBM 1996], HP-UX 10.0 in HP 9000 [HP 1995] are the examples to adopt this method. In addition, HP-UX system provides a ``serialize()'' command to run the processes once at a time after thrashing is detected.

Advantages of a Lightweight Thrashing Prevention Mechanism

The most destructive aspect of thrashing is that, although thrashing may have been triggered by a brief, random peak in workloads (e.g. all of the users of a system happen to press the Enter keys at the same second), the system might keep thrashing for an indefinitely long time. This could likely happen in a networked system, where multiple users coincidentally run memory-intensive programs simultaneously without coordination on the usage of the memory. Because thrashing is often a result of a sudden spike of memory demand in the workload, a lightweight, dynamic protection mechanism that brings only momentary change to the system behaviors for eliminating thrashing is more desirable than a brute-force action, such as process suspension or even a process removal. This is because suspension-based load control strategy has several limitations. First, a suspension/ reactivation scheme is based on the detection of thrashing. Before certain conditions are detected and the suspension/reactivation actions are taken, the system has been thrashing and its memory has been under-utilized for a period of time. Second, in a multiprogramming environment, a short moment of lack or availability of free memory, or increase or decrease of page fault rates, may not necessarily indicate that thrashing is immediately coming or leaving. Thus, it is hard to determine the timing of suspension/reactivation of processes in the load control strategy, especially for programs of very dynamically changing memory demands. A wrong decision can significantly degrade the system performance because of high costs associated with these operations. Finally, when a process is suspended, a large portion of its entire working set can be replaced for other processes. Re-establishing the working set after its reactivation, particularly for a large suspended program, could involve significant overhead. For these reasons, in the most of today's operating systems, such as Solaris and Linux, only the approximation of global LRU replacement is implemented without a built-in suspension/reactivation-based load control mechanism.

It is noted that the ultimate solution to constant and serious thrashing in a system due to memory shortage is to increase physical memory size, and a thrashing due to a significant memory shortage can only be removed through swapping out processes to reduce memory demands. The swap token mechanism is intended to remove the thrashing which can be considered as a temporary and short-term pathological system condition caused by limited memory shortage. Using the swap token mechanism at the first place, it is possible to eliminate system thrashing at its early stage, minimizing the usage of load control. As a proactive and lightweight mechanism, swap token aims to achieve the same goal as load control for thrashing protection, but without the limitations of load control. Therefore, with the swap token mechanism and load control guarding at two different levels and two different stages, the system performance will become more stable and cost-effective.

In the remaining of the chapter, we will first experimentally show the access behaviors of some typical programs in Section 3. We then show how system thrashing can be developed when multiple of the programs run together in Section 4. Section 5 describes the design of the swap token mechanism, whose effectiveness is experimentally evaluated in Section 6.

EXPERIMENTAL OBSERVATION OF PROGRAM'S ACCESS PATTERNS

The Benchmark Programs

We have selected five memory-intensive application programs, three of which are from SPEC 2000 (*gcc, gzip,* and *vortex*), and the other two are programs for data reordering and matrix computation. All of these programs are both CPU-intensive and memory-intensive, and are briefly described as follows

* *gcc:* an optimized C programming language compiler from SPEC 2000.
* *gzip:* a data compression utility from SPEC 2000.
* *vorte:* a data-oriented database program from SPEC 2000.
* bit-reversals (*bit-r*): This program carries out data reordering operations which are required in many Fast Fourier Transform (FFT) algorithms.
* LU decomposition (*LU*): This is a standard matrix LU decomposition program for solving linear systems.

Experimental System Setup

The machine used in the experiments is a Pentium II at 400 MHz with a physical memory space of 384 MBytes. The operating system is Redhat Linux release 6.1 with the kernel 2.2.14. Program memory space is allocated in units of 4KByte pages. The disk is an IBM Hercules with capacity of 8,450 MB.

When memory related activities in a program execution occur, such as memory accesses and page faults, the system kernel is heavily involved. To gain insights into the memory system behaviors of application programs, program executions are monitored at the kernel level by using some lightweight instrumentation in the kernel. A user monitor program is designed with two functionalities: adjusting user memory space allocation and collecting system data. To flexibly adjust the available memory space for user programs in the experiments, the monitor program requests a memory space of certain pre-defined size, and excludes it from the page replacement with the help from the kernel. The remaining memory is available for executions of application programs in our experiments. The monitor program will not affect the experiment measurements, because (1) it consumes few CPU cycles; (2) Its resident memory is excluded from the global page replacement scope, so its memory usage has no interactions with application programs. The monitor program dynamically collects following memory system statistics once in every one second for each interesting process:

- Memory Allocation Demand (*MAD*): is the total amount of requested memory space, in pages, reflected in the page table of the process. This memory allocation demand is maintained and recorded in the kernel data structure of *task_struct*.
- Resident Set Size (*RSS*): is the total amount of physical memory used by the process, in pages, and can be read from *task_struct*.
- Number of Page Faults (*NPF*): is the number of page faults of the process, and can be read from *task_struct*. There are two types of page faults for each process: minor page faults and major page faults. A minor page fault will cause an operation to relink the requested page in memory into the page table. The cost of a minor page fault is negligible. A major page fault happens when the requested page is not in the memory and has to be retrieved from the disk. We only collect major page fault events for each process.
- Number of Accessed Pages (*NAP*): is the number of accessed pages by the process within the last time interval of one second. During a program execution, a system

routine is periodically called to examine all the reference bits in the process's page table to get the number.

In the experiments each program is first run in a dedicated environment to observe its memory access behavior without occurrence of major page faults and page replacements because the memory demand from a single program is smaller than the available user space.

Memory Access Behavior in The Dedicated Environment

We use memory-time graphs to show the memory usage of the selected programs in the dedicated execution environment. In the graphs, the *x* axis represents the execution time, and the *y* axis represents the number of memory pages for three memory usage curves: memory allocation demand (MAD), resident set size (RSS), and number of accessed pages (NAP). The memory usage curves of the five benchmark programs measured by MAD, RSS, and NAP are presented in Figures 1 and 2. With regard to the development of memory demands, the memory usage patterns for the programs can be classified in three types according to the graphs:

- **Quickly acquiring memory allotments**: This type of programs demands stable memory allocations from the beginning of program executions. When the available space is sufficient, they can quickly acquire their allotments in the early stage of their executions. Programs *bit-r* and *gzip* belong to this type.
- **Gradually acquiring memory allotments**: This type of programs gradually increases their memory allotments as their executions proceed, and accesses their data sets regularly in each stage until their executions complete. When the available space is sufficient, their RSS sizes in each

Figure 1. Memory-time graphs depicting the memory behaviors of programs, gcc, gzip, and vortex, for their dedicated executions.

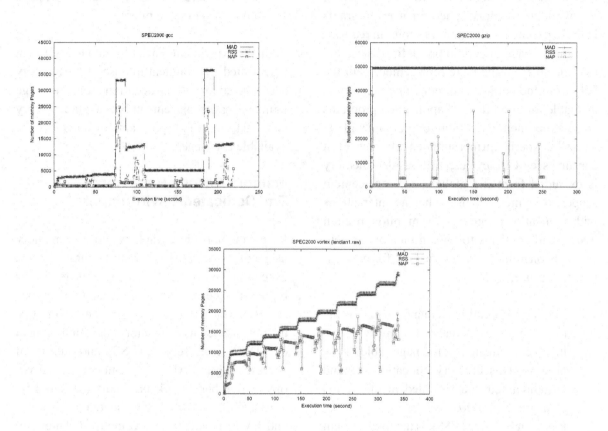

Figure 2. Memory-time graphs depicting the memory behaviors of programs, bit-r and LU, for their dedicated executions.

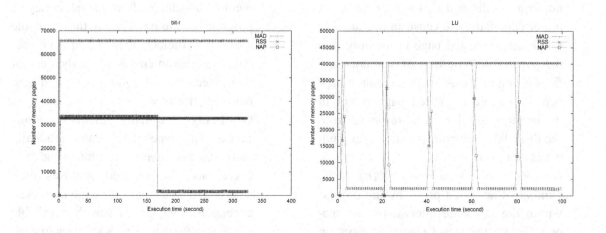

time interval form stair climbing curves as their executions proceed. Program *vortex* belongs to this type.

- **Non-regularly changing memory allotments**: This type of programs has non-regular memory demands in their life times of executions. Their demands on memory sizes are changed dynamically with high variations. When the available space is sufficient, there are multiple ups and downs in the RSS curves in their executions. Programs *gcc* and *LU* belong to this type.

MEMORY PERFORMANCE DUE TO INTERACTIONS OF DIFFERENT TYPES OF PROGRAMS

Performance Metrics

We use *slowdown* to measure the degradation of a program performance due to its concurrent execution, which is defined as the ratio between the execution time of the program in a shared environment and its execution time in a dedicated environment without major page faults. Major sources of the slowdown are the penalty of page faults, shared CPU cycles, processor context switch, and monitoring activity overheads. Among them, we found that context switch and monitoring activity overheads are trivial in our measurements.

Memory Performance of Program Interactions

Recall that we have classified three types of memory usage patterns in programs, namely, type 1: quickly acquiring memory allotments; type 2: gradually acquiring memory allotments; and type 3: non-regularly changing memory allotments. There are seven typical groups of execution interactions between these three types of programs: type 1 and type 2 (group 1), type 1 and type 3 (group 2), type 2 and type 3 (group 3), three types together (group 4), multiple type 1's (group 5), multiple type 2's (group 6), and multiple type 3's (group 7). To provide insights into the LRU page replacement behaviors during program interactions, five representative program interaction groups are described in this chapter. The performance results of many other program interactions are consistent with the reported ones. In order to clearly and concisely present effects of the false LRU pages on the program executions, two programs in each group are selected.

The five selected program interaction groups includes *gzip* with *vortex* (belonging to group 1), *bit-r* with *gcc* (belonging to group 2), *vortex* with *gcc* (belonging to group 3), two *vortex* programs, each with a different input (belonging to group 6), and two *LU* programs (belonging to group 7).

In the experiments, the available user memory space was adjusted by the monitor program accordingly so that each program has considerable performance degradation due to 20% to 50% memory shortage. The shortage ratios are calculated based on the peak memory demands during programs' executions. In practice, the real memory shortage ratios are smaller due to their dynamically changing memory demands, as shown in Figures 1 and 2. As the program execution reaches the shortage range, these memory-constrained programs start thrashing, but are not completely page-fault I/O bound. It is the range where improvements on page replacement algorithms can help the most. The swap token mechanism aims at eliminating thrashing in this situation and intends to leave the true page-fault I/O bound situation to load control.

Figure 3 presents the memory behaviors measured by MAD and RSS of programs *gzip* and *vortex*. In the figures, both RSS curves fluctuate during the concurrent execution, which demonstrates the impact of the gap between memory demands and the limited memory allocations for each process. The gap persists for a long period of time, even though the memory is enough to satisfy the demand for one process at a time.

Figure 3. The memory performance of gzip and vortex in their concurrent execution.

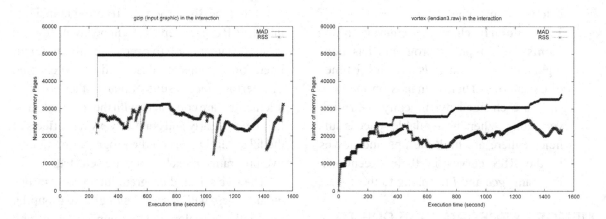

A process gains more memory pages and increases its RSS through page faults. On the other hand, it loses pages when these pages become old. In this way the global page replacement policy attempts to make the memory allocated among multiple processes to conform their respective memory demands.

Unfortunately, what a process loses includes false LRU pages, which are generated during its period of faulting. The losing of these false LRU pages does not reflect the memory demands. This study shows that the proportion of false LRU pages in all the page faults keeps increasing with the increase of memory shortage. Consequently, the dynamic memory allocations are hard to reflect the memory demands of processes. For example, *gzip* established its working set during the period of time between 600th second and 760th second, because we observed that its page fault rate is significantly reduced. Then some of its memory allocation was transferred to *vortex*, illustrated by the lowered *gzip* RSS curve and increased

Figure 4. The memory performance of bit-r and gcc in their concurrent execution.

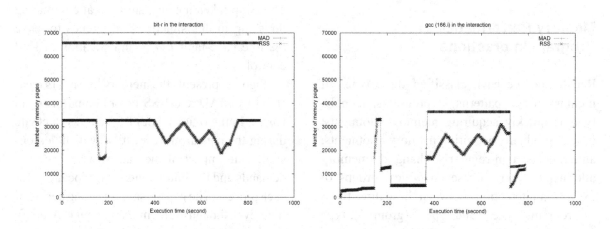

vortex RSS curve after 760th second in Figure 3. We believe the pages *gzip* lost are part of its working set, because it had increased number of page faults and tried to gain some allocation back after then. Though *vortex* can take certain memory spaces from *gzip*, it is unable to build up its working set. This is because it also lost a large number of false LRU pages when it tried to build up its working set, which should not have been lost considering the needs of *vortex*. Unfortunately, we observed that the system ended up with high page fault rates for both processes and a low CPU utilization. We found that a process is powerful to get additional memory allocation in the global replacement policy when it has large memory shortage between its RSS and its working set. However, when it gets more memory, it becomes less powerful, and tends to lose memory. For this reason we see the fluctuating RSS curves for the concurrently running programs in the system thrashing. Our experiments show that the execution times of both programs are significantly increased due to the page faults in the concurrent execution. The slowdown of *gzip* is 5.23, and is 3.85 for *vortex*.

Figure 4 presents the memory usage behavior measured by MAD and RSS of concurrently run-

ning programs *bit-r* and *gcc*. *Gcc* belongs to type 3 which has two spikes in MAD and RSS due to its dynamic memory demands. For *bit-r*, its RSS curve dropped sharply from 32,800 pages to about 16,500 pages at the 165th second caused by the first RSS spike of *gcc* at the same time. After the spike, the RSS of *gcc* was decreased, which allowed *bit-r* to regain its RSS. When the second RSS spike of *gcc* arrived at the 365th second, the RSS of *bit-r* dropped again. However, this time the RSS of *gcc* began to lose its pages at about 450th second before it could establish its working set. After that, both programs exhibited fluctuating RSS curves. The second spike requires only 7% more memory demand than the first spike, which causes a much longer execution delay. Consequently, program *gcc*'s second spike of the MAD and RSS curves were stretched to a delay of 357 seconds due to page faults. During this period, there was a big gap between the RSS and MAD, up to more than 20,000 pages. The experiments consistently show that the execution times of both programs were significantly increased due to the page faults in the interaction. The slowdown of *bit-r* is 2.69, and is 3.63 for *gcc*.

Figure 5 presents the memory behavior measured by MAD and RSS of concurrently running

Figure 5. The memory performance of gcc and vortex in their concurrent execution.

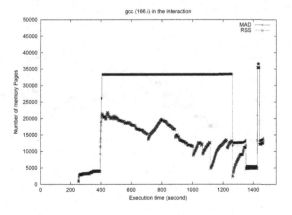

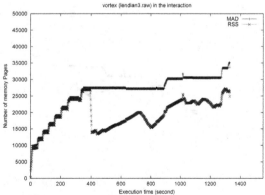

programs *gcc* and *vortex*. Regarding program *vortex*, its RSS curve suddenly dropped to about 14,000 pages after it reached to 26,800 pages due to its memory competition from *gcc*. After that, its RSS curve entered the fluctuating stage. The fluctuating RSS curves of *vortex* and the first spike of *gcc* caused a large number of page faults to both processes, which extended the first spike of *gcc* by 865 seconds, and extended a RSS stair in *vortex* by 563 seconds. The second spike of *gcc* arrived after *vortex* finished its execution. Then it ran smoothly. The experiments consistently show that the execution times of both processes are significantly increased due to their page faults. The slowdown of *gcc* is 5.61, and is 3.37 for vortex.

Figure 6 presents the memory behavior measured by MAD and RSS of *votex1* and *vortex2*, two concurrently running *vortex* programs, each with a different input. Although the input files are different, their memory access patterns are similar. But neither could establish its working set. The experiments again show that the execution times of both programs are significantly increased due to the page faults in the interaction. The slowdown for *vortex1* is 3.58, and is 3.33 for *vortex2*.

Figure 7 presents the memory behavior mea-sured by MAD and RSS of two concurrently running programs *LU*. The experiments show that frequently climbing and dropping slopes of RSS can incur memory reallocations and trigger fluctuating RSS curves, leading to inefficient memory use and low CPU utilization. The dynamic memory demands from the program caused the system to stay in the thrashing state for most of their execution time. The execution times of both processes are significantly increased due to the page faults. The slowdowns for the two *LU* processes are 3.57 and 3.40, respectively.

Development of Thrashing

The experiments have shown that thrashings can be triggered with a moderate amount of memory shortage and can cause significant performance degradations. False LRU pages play their role in the process -- they make global replacement policies blind to a program's true memory needs, and a portion of the working set identified as the false LRU pages mistakenly replaced. Here are certain conditions that probably cause thrashings based on the experimental studies.

Figure 6. The memory performance of two vortex programs (vortex1 and vortex2), each with a different input, in their concurrent execution.

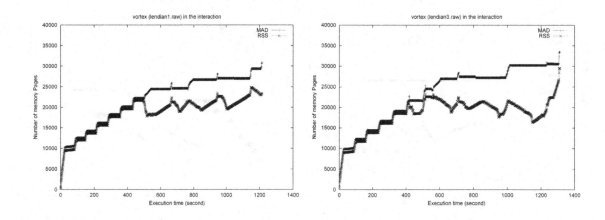

Figure 7. The memory performance of two LU programs in their concurrent execution.

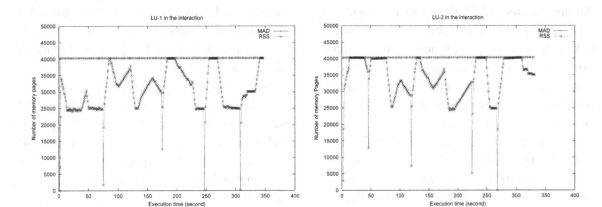

• When the memory demand of a process has a sudden jump for additional memory allocation, its RSS can be easily increased accordingly at the beginning because addition of new pages do not need I/O operations to access data on the disk (zero-filled pages instead of disk-read pages). If the process cannot establish its working set before many false LRU pages are produced, the number of lost pages on the false LRU condition can exceed the number of obtained pages through page faulting, causing its RSS to drop. In addition, the increased memory demand of this process causes other processes in the system to generate more false LRU pages. In this way thrashing is triggered. The examples of this condition include: the starting execution stage of *gzip* in the left figure of Figure 3, the second spike of *gcc* in the *bit-r / gcc* interaction in Figure 4, the first spike of *gcc* in the *gcc / vortex* interaction in Figure 5, and all the RSS jumps of both *LU* processes in Figure 7.

• If memory access patterns of concurrently running programs, in terms of working set size, memory usage behavior, and access frequency, are similar, false LRU pages can be easily generated for both processes, which can trigger the system thrashing. The interactions between two *vortex* processes in Figure 6 and between two *LU* processes in Figure 7 are examples of this condition.

• When the available memory space is significantly less than the aggregate memory demand of the processes, all the processes compete for the limited memory allocations. A small number of page faults may trigger a large number of false LRU pages. This condition will be shown in Figure 8 before the token is taken by a process.

DESIGN AND IMPLEMENTATIONS OF SWAP TOKEN

We choose the Linux OS as a base to evaluate the design and implementation of swap token. The swap token has been implemented in Linux Kernel 2.2 by Song Jiang and in Linux kernel 2.6 by Rik van Riel. As a more thorough evaluation has been conducted for the implementation in Kernel 2.2, the discussions on the topic in the chapter are based on this implementation.

The LRU Page Replacement in Linux

An approximate LRU algorithm is adopted in the Linux kernels as its global page replacement policy. When a page fault occurs, kernel function *do_page_fault()* will be called to handle it. If the page fault is caused by a legal access to a page missed in memory but stored in the swap file on disk, the kernel will try to get a free page in memory and load the requested page from the swap file by kernel function *do_swap_page()*. If there are no free memory pages available, the kernel will make a room for the page by selecting a victim page from the memory for replacement. If the replaced page is dirty, it has to be written back first to the swap file, which also contributes to the number of major page faults (NPF).

To select victim pages, kernel function __*get_free_pages()* is invoked by the swap daemon *kswapd*, which is waken up when the free physical memory space is below a threshold or when a page faulted program cannot find a page from the free page pool. The function will look into the process space of each eligible process in the system to see if it is a candidate from which memory pages can be found for swapping. It always starts from the process with the largest resident pages. The kernel will then check through all of the virtual memory pages in the page table of the selected process. Generally, once the kernel finds that the reference bit of a page table entry is turned off (indicating that the page has not been accessed since it was reset last time by the function), the kernel will select the page for replacement. If the bit is on, the kernel will turn it off, and keep checking the next page in the table. If no pages can be replaced from this process, the next candidate process will be tried. This implementation effectively emulates the behavior of the LRU replacement algorithm with a small overhead. However it also generates false LRU pages during concurrent execution of programs as we have discussed.

Most operating systems have protection mechanisms to resolve serious thrashing problems.

For example, a process will be killed in Linux to release its memory space when the process keeps being denied its requested pages. A process will be swapped out for the same purpose in the 4.4 BSD operating system. If the free page pool cannot be filled in a timely manner, the system will start to swap out or remove processes.

Unfortunately, the existence of false LRU pages makes kernel function __*get_free_pages()* in Linux (and the *pageout* daemon in 4.4 BSD) easily and quickly find "qualified" pages, including many false LRU pages, to fill the free page pool. As the result, the system can be involved in a "pre-thrashing" state for a significantly long period of time before the kernel is awakened to swap out or remove processes. The CPU utilization in the pre-thrashing state can be extremely low due to the large number of page faults. The system developers of the 4.4 BSD operating system points out that the system performance can be much better when the memory scheduling is done by page replacement operations than when the process swapping is used [McKusick et al. 1996]. The swap token mechanism is a page-replacement-oriented memory scheduling scheme to address the thrashing issue before the system has to swap out or remove processes.

The Implementation of the Swap Token in Linux

The basic idea of the swap token mechanism is to keep false LRU pages from spreading over all the concurrently running processes, and to make the working set of at least one process be identified and established. A token is a newly introduced global and mutually exclusive variable in the kernel, which has two states, indicating either the token is available or the token has been taken by a page faulted process. The token is initialized when the system is booted. In the implementation, a process requests the token right before it invokes function *do_swap_page()*, which is called right after a page fault occurs and before the page is loaded from the swap file. This arrangement makes sure that the token only goes to the process in need of memory. The token is only taken by a process when page faults occur due to memory shortage. In other words, a process will not compete for the token until the memory space is insufficient for it. The system functions exactly as the original Linux system when memory space is sufficient for processes. In the implementation, a new status, called *swapping_status*, is introduced for each process to indicate whether the process is in the stage of swapping in/out pages.

As we have explained, false LRU pages are generated for a process in its page swapping period. The process does not access its allocated memory because it does not have a chance to do so due to swapping.

Therefore, these pages should be prevented from swapping out. With the swap token mechanism, a process holding the token can prevent its false LRU pages from being replaced. In the process of searching for and marking LRU pages (by turning off their reference bits) for page replacement, kernel function __get_free_pages() skips the process that holds the token *and* is in the swapping status. In this way the memory pages of the process with the token are protected when and only when it has unsolved page faults, and false LRU pages are eliminated from it.

The LRU pages of a process identified during a normal computing phase are the true LRU pages, which are the replacement candidates targeted by the swap token mechanism. To this end, the privilege for the process holding the token is removed as soon as the process resolves its page faults by turning off its swapping status, which allows __get_free_pages() to include the process in its search for LRU pages for replacement. In our implementation, there is an exception handler. When the privileged process cannot find LRU pages from other processes for replacement, the system will have to select LRU pages for the process from its own resident space.

The swap token mechanism is highly light-weight. Its only additional operations are to set the token/swapping status, and to decide whether the process holding the token should be skipped or not when the system is searching for LRU pages for replacement. Thus, the implementation incurs very little overhead.

Fairness Issue in Memory Usage

If a process has fully established its working set, and it is able to regularly access it, there is a good chance for the process to keep its allocated memory space even with the competition from other processes through their page faults, because it would generate few false LRU pages when the process establishes its working set and has a small number of page faults. Therefore, this process can be expected to efficiently finish its execution and then release its space to other processes, which allows multiple processes to finish their executions one by one with a high CPU utilization even with a considerable memory shortage. Most operating systems make efforts to keep the system away from thrashing and stay in this situation until load controls have to be applied. As a lightweight, proactive thrashing protection mechanism, swap token allows a process to keep the token for the rest of its lifetime once it receives it. When a program exits its execution, the token will be returned for public use.

The fairness issue of memory usage among processes in thrashing is usually addressed in the load control policies, rather than explicitly considered in the global page replacement policies. For example, the 4.4 BSD operating system initially suspends a process after thrashing. If the thrashing continues, additional processes are suspended until enough memory space becomes available. In order to address the issue of fairness, even if there is not enough memory, the suspended processes are allowed to reactivate its execution after about 20 seconds. If the thrashing condition returns, other processes will be selected for suspension to free memory space. As a mechanism to overcome the limitations of the global LRU replacement implementation, the fairness issue remains to be addressed in the load control policies.

A Close Look at the Effect of Swap Token

To show how a swap token functions and its effectiveness, let us take a close look at its running behavior during program interactions. The following program segment is used in the experiment:

```
#define LOOP 1000
#define SIZE (53*1024*1024/
sizeof(double));

double * mem_page;
int size= SIZE;

  mem_page = (double *)calloc(SIZE,
  sizeof(double));
  for (i = 0; i < LOOP; i++){
    for (j = 0; j < SIZE; j += step){
      mem_page[j] = mem_page[j] + 1;
      Other computing work only on mem_
      page[j];
    }
    if ((i+1)%10 == 0)
      SIZE = (long)(0.9*SIZE);
  }
```

This program uses 1000 loop iterations to access a large array. At first the program sequentially accesses its entire data array for ten times. Then for each of its next ten iterations, the program reduces its accessing range over the array by removing 10% of all its accesses at the end of the array. The available user memory space was adjusted to 60 MB. The access pattern produces a large number of page faults when there is a memory shortage. In this experiment, we will demonstrate how the token works to address the serious performance degradation by reducing false LRU pages in program interaction environment.

We let two instances of the program run simultaneously, allocating a 53 MB array for one process (referred as small process hereafter) and a 58 MB array for another process (referred as large process hereafter) by adjusting variable *size* in the program. Closely tracing the page access behaviors of each process before and after the token was set in the system, we present the impact of the token to each of the interacting programs. Figure 8 presents space-time graphs for the small process (left graph) and the large process (right graph) during their interaction, where *y*-axis represents three types of memory pages at different virtual addresses: recently visited pages (or the pages that have been accessed in the last one-second time window}, swapped-out pages, and resident but not recently visited pages, and the *x*-axis represents the execution time sequence. The RSS size of each process can be approximated by the sum of the number of "visited pages" and the number of "resident but not visited pages" at any execution point.

We have observed that each of the processes expanded its RSS through page faulting and meanwhile lost some of its pages under the false LRU condition. The combination of these two activities causes three effects: (1) neither process could establish its working set; (2) the RSS size of each process fluctuated; and (3) little useful work could be done.

The token was set in the system and taken by the small process (left graph in Figure 8) at the execution time of 125th second. After this time, this process successfully kept its useful memory pages and avoided false LRU pages, whose effect is reflected in the increased lightly gray area for "resident but not visited pages". During the same period of time, the large process reduced its number of "resident but not visited pages". Once the small process established its working set, all its obtained pages were frequently visited. The token only avoids swapping out the false LRU pages, but still treats the true LRU pages as replacement candidates. This can be confirmed by observing

Figure 8. The memory behaviors of the process which accesses an array of 53 MB and takes the token in the middle of its execution (left figure) and the other process which accesses an array of 58 MB and does not own the token (right figure) during their execution interaction.

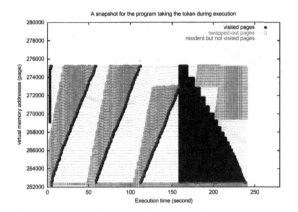
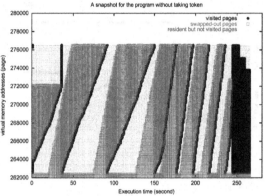

the phase when the small process started reducing its working set. Although the process still held the token, its true LRU pages were migrated to the large process so that the large one can use these released pages. The right graph in Figure7 shows that the large process did increase its RSS size from this time. Then the large process quickly finished its execution after the small process holding the token left the system.

It is interesting to see that the token was also beneficial to the process that did not own the token. The right graph in Figure 8 shows that the large process without the token took about 50 seconds to finish one pass of access to the array before the token was set in the system. After the token was taken by the small process, the one pass access time of the large process was reduced to less than 25 seconds, although its RSS was reduced. The reason for this is as follows. Since the I/O bandwidth of the disk became a bottleneck when a system conducted a large number of page faults for both processes, the page fault penalty increased accordingly. When one process got the token, its number of page faults was significantly reduced, and it consumed much less I/O bandwidth. Thus,

the page fault penalty of the process without the token was also greatly reduced, and more useful work can be done even though its number of page faults may be increased.

PERFORMANCE OF THE SWAP TOKEN MECHANISM

The performance of swap token is experimentally evaluated using the five selected groups of the interacting programs. Each of the experiments has the exactly same condition as its counterpart conducted in Section 4.2, except that swap token is introduced in the experiments.

Figure 9 presents the memory performance measured by MAD and RSS of concurrently running programs *gzip* and *vortex* when the swap token is introduced. At the execution time of 250th second, both programs started page faults due to a memory shortage. The token was taken by *vortex* after then. Figure 8 shows that the once seriously fluctuating RSS curves of *vortex* observed in the original system in Figure 3 disappeared. Although the RSS curve of *vortex* does not exhibit the be-

Figure 9. The memory performance of gzip and vortex in their concurrent execution managed with swap token.

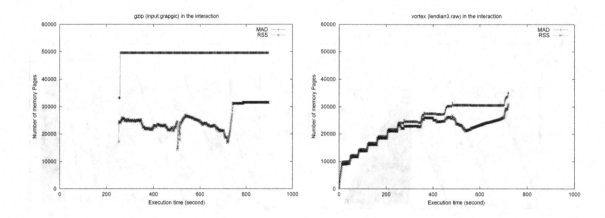

havior as it is shown in the dedicated environment, where its RSS curve was almost overlapped with its MAD curve (see Figures 1 and 2), we believe this RSS curve represents its real memory demands for its effective execution (or its working set size). There are two reasons for this: (1) The page fault rate is significantly lower than that in its counterpart experiment for the original system. Even when RSS curve of *vortex* is considerably lower than its MAD curve after the 470th second, its page fault rates are lowered by at least 70% compared with those measured at the same execution stage in the original system. (2) The RSS curve of *vortex* is consistent with its NAP curve in the dedicated environment. The NAP curve was increased much slowly than MAD curve, which reflects that the recently accessed memory size did not increase as MAD did. Therefore, the gap between its RSS and MAD curves in Figure 9 was enlarged in its late execution stage, where its fluctuation was caused by the content change of its working set. While eliminating the thrashing quickly, the swap token distinguished true and false LRU pages, and only kept the working set of the protected process in the memory, rather than simply pinned all of its pages in memory.

The experiments also show that the execution times of both programs are significantly reduced by the swap token compared with the times in the original Linux. The slowdown of *gzip* is 2.63 (a reduction of 50%), and is 1.83 for *vortex* (a reduction of 52%). The page fault reductions for *gzip* and *vortex* are 45% and 80%, respectively.

Figure 10 presents the memory performance measured by MAD and RSS of concurrently running programs *bit-r* and *gcc* when the swap token is introduced. At the execution time of 146th second, the first RSS spike of *gcc* caused many page faults for both processes due to memory shortage. The token was taken by *gcc* after this moment. Figure 10 shows that *gcc* quickly built up its working set, reflected by keeping its first RSS spike with a short delay after taking the token, while *bit-r* sharply decreased its RSS during this short period of time. Process *gcc* established its working set in its second spike more quickly than it did in its first spike, due to the difference between their reference behaviors: *gcc* accessed its working set more frequently in the second spike than it did in the first spike. The swap token mechanism attempted to reduce false LRU pages without affecting the ability of

Figure 10. The memory performance of bit-r and gcc in their concurrent execution managed with swap token.

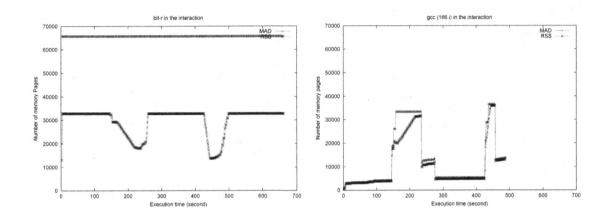

global LRU to reflect memory access patterns of processes. The measurements show that the execution times of both programs are significantly reduced by the swap token compared with the times in the original Linux LRU. The slowdown of *bit-r* is 2.08 (a reduction of 23%), and is 2.25 for *gcc* (a reduction of 38%). The page fault reductions for *bit-r* and *gcc* are 20% and 82%, respectively.

Figure 11 presents the memory performance measured by MAD and RSS of concurrently running programs *gcc* and *vortex* when the swap token is introduced. At the execution time of 397th second, both processes started page faults due to memory shortage. The token was taken by *gcc* after this time.

Figure 11 shows that *gcc* quickly built up its working set, reflected by keeping the first RSS

Figure 11. The memory performance of gcc and vortex in their concurrent execution managed with swap token.

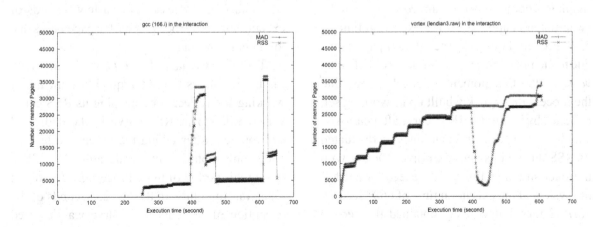

Figure 12. The memory performance of two vortex programs (vortex1 and vortex2), each with a different input, in their concurrent execution managed with swap token.

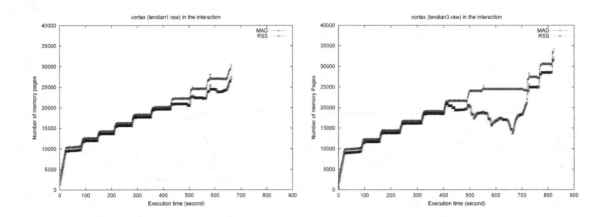

spike narrow after taking the token, while *gzip* sharply reduced its RSS during this short period of time. *Vortex* finished its execution before the second RSS spike of *gcc* arrived. Process *gcc* finished its execution without major page faults after another 42 seconds. The execution times of both processes are significantly reduced by the swap token compared with the ones with the original Linux LRU. The slowdown of *gcc* is 1.85 (a reduction of 67%), and is 1.54 for *vortex* (a reduction of 54%). The page fault reductions for *gcc* and *vortex* are 95% and 79%, respectively.

Figure 12 presents the memory performance measured by MAD and RSS of two concurrent running programs *vortex1* and *vortex2* when the swap token is applied. At the execution time of 433rd second, both processes started page faults due to memory shortage. The token was taken by *vortex1* after this moment. Figure 11 shows that the process then quickly built up its working set, reflected by its climbing RSS curve after the token was taken, while *vortex2* continuously fluctuated its RSS during this period of time. *Vortex1* with the token smoothly finished the execution and left the system at the execution time of 668th second. *Vortex2* then immediately obtained the needed

memory space, reflected by the sharp increase of its RSS, and finished its execution without major page faults after another 161 seconds. The execution times of both programs are significantly reduced by the swap token compared with the ones in the original Linux LRU. The slowdown of *vortex1* is 1.95 (a reduction of 46%), and is 2.08 for *vortex2* (a reduction of 38%). The page fault reductions for *vortex1* and *vortex2* are 93% and 63%, respectively.

Figure 13 presents the memory performance measured by MAD and RSS of two concurrently running programs *LU1* and *LU2* when the swap token is introduced. In the first spikes of both *LU1* and *LU2* processes after a few seconds of executions, both processes started page faults due to memory shortage.

The token was taken by *LU1* after this moment. Figure 12 shows that *LU1* quickly built up its working set, reflected by keeping its RSS curve very similar to its RSS curve in the dedicated environment after taking the token, while *LU2* could only obtain a moderate amount of RSS during this period of time. Process *LU1* with the token ran smoothly. In the last 25 seconds of the execution of *LU1*, its RSS curve was lowered

Figure 13. The memory performance of two LU programs (LU1 and LU2), each with a different input, in their concurrent execution managed with swap token.

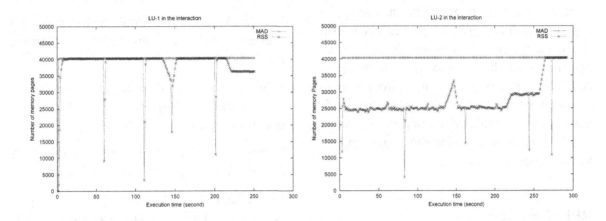

while the RSS curve of *LU2* accordingly rose by obtaining true LRU pages from *LU1*. The measurements show that the execution times of both processes are significantly reduced by the swap token compared with the ones in the original Linux LRU. The slowdown of *LU1* is 2.57 (a reduction of 28%), and is 2.99 for *LU2* (a reduction of 12%). The page fault reductions for *LU1* and *LU2* are 87% and -116%, respectively. It is noted that the execution time of *LU2* was still reduced, though its number of page faults was significantly increased. This is because the page fault penalty was reduced with more available I/O bandwidth after the token was taken by *LU1*.

CONCLUDING REMARKS

Management of memory hierarchies has been an intensive study for several decades. Regarding the large gap in access time between memory and disk, a lot of work has been done to reduce the number of page faults for each program. Research on page replacement algorithms have been a classical topic since 1960s and many improvements over the LRU page replacement policy have been recently proposed, including 2Q, LIRS, and ARC. However, in a multiprogramming environment, the interactions between concurrently running programs can have a large impact on memory usage pattern. Specifically, an uncoordinated use of memory among the processes can lead to the system thrashing when their aggregate memory demand considerably exceeds physical memory.

In the chapter, we have investigated sources of memory performance degradation in program interactions by carefully examining the LRU memory page replacement and its representative implementations in Linux systems. We have experimentally demonstrated that the false LRU pages can be a serious loophole in the LRU replacement implementations because these implementations do not correctly reflect and predict memory access patterns of interacting programs.

In order to overcome the limitations in the LRU replacement in program interactions, the swap token mechanism is designed and implemented in the memory management system of the Linux kernel. Rather than pinning all pages of a token-holding process in memory, the swap token only protects its true LRU pages from swapping to establish an orderly page replacement, and allows its false LRU pages to be selected for replacement no matter whether a process possesses the token. In this way we can avoid the drawbacks of existing brute-force thrashing mechanisms. The experiments show that the swap token mechanism can consistently and significantly reduce the page faults and the execution times of memory-demanding programs in a multiprogramming environment. As the swap token mechanism is not designed specifically for specific operating systems, its implementation can be also applied to other operating systems.

REFERENCES

Alderson, A., Lynch, W. C., & Randell, B. (1972). *Thrashing in a Multiprogrammed System. Operating Systems Techniques*. London: Academic Press.

Coffman, E. G. Jr, & Ryan, T. A. (1972). A Study of Storage Partitioning Using a Mathematical Model of Locality. *Communications of the ACM, 15*(3), 185–190. doi:10.1145/361268.361280

Corporation, H. P. (1995). *HP-UX 10.0*. Memory Management White Paper.

IBM Corporation (1996). *AIX Versions 3.2 and 4 Performance Tuning Guide*.

Denning, P. J. (1968a). The Working Set Model for Program Behavior. *Communications of the ACM, 11*(5), 323–333. doi:10.1145/363095.363141

Denning, P. J. (1968b). Thrashing: Its Causes and Prevention. In *Proceedings of AFIPS Conference,* (pp. 915-922).

Denning, P. J. (1970). Virtual Memory. *Computer Survey, 2*(3), 153–189. doi:10.1145/356571.356573

Kenah, L. J., & Bate, S. F. (1984). *VAX/VMS Internals and Data Structures*. Digital Press.

Lazowska, E. D., & Kelsey, J. M. (1978). *Notes on Tuning VAX/VMS*. Technical Report 78-12-01. Dept. of Computer Science, Univ. of Washington.

McKusick, M. K., Bostic, K., Karels, M. J., & Quarterman, J. S. (1996). *The Design and Implementation of the 4.4 BSD Operating System*. Reading, MA: Addison Wesley.

Morris, J. B. (1972). Demand Paging through Utilization of Working Sets on the MANIAC II. *Communications of the ACM, 15*(10), 867–872. doi:10.1145/355604.361592

Chapter 6
Application of both Temporal and Spatial Localities in the Management of Kernel Buffer Cache

Song Jiang
Wayne State University, USA

ABSTRACT

As the hard disk remains as the mainstream on-line storage device, it continues to be the performance bottleneck of data-intensive applications. One of existing most effective solutions to ameliorate the bottleneck is to use the buffer cache in the OS kernel to achieve two objectives: reduction of direct access of on-disk data and improvement of disk performance. These two objectives can be achieved by applying both temporal locality and spatial locality in the management of the buffer cache. Traditionally only temporal locality is exploited for the purpose, and spatial locality, which refers to the on-disk sequentiality of requested blocks, is largely ignored. As the throughput of access of sequentially-placed disk blocks can be an order of magnitude higher than that of access to randomly-placed blocks, the missing of spatial locality in the buffer management can cause the performance of applications without dominant sequential accesses to be seriously degraded. In the chapter, we introduce a state-of-the-art technique that seamlessly combines these two locality properties embedded in the data access patterns into the management of the kernel buffer cache management. After elaboration on why the spatial locality is needed in addition to the temporal locality, we detail a framework, DULO (DUal LOcality), in which these two properties are taken account of simultaneously. A prototype implementation of DULO in the Linux kernel as well as some experiment results are presented, showing that DULO can significantly increases disk I/O throughput for real-world applications such as Web server, TPC benchmark, file system benchmark, and scientific programs. It reduces their execution times by as much as 53%. We conclude the chapter by identifying and encouraging a new direction for research and practice on the improvement of disk I/O performance, which is to expose more disk-specific data layout and access patterns to the upper-level system software for disk-oriented policies.

DOI: 10.4018/978-1-60566-850-5.ch006

INTRODUCTION

The hard drive is the most commonly used secondary storage device supporting file accesses and virtual memory paging. While its capacity growth pleasantly matches the rapidly increasing data storage demand, its electromechanical nature causes its performance improvements to lag painfully far behind processor speed progress. It is apparent that the disk bottleneck effect is worsening in modern computer systems, while the role of the hard disk as dominant storage device will not change in the foreseeable future, and the amount of disk data requested by applications continues to increase.

The performance of a disk is constrained by its mechanical operations, including disk platter rotation (*spinning*) and disk arm movement (*seeking*). A disk head has to be on the right track through seeking and on the right sector through spinning for reading/writing its desired data. Between the two moving parts of a disk drive affecting its performance, the disk arm is its Achilles' Heel. This is because an actuator has to move the arm accurately to the desired track through a series of actions including acceleration, coast, deceleration, and settle. As an example, for a typical high performance drive of 10,000 RPM, average seek time is 6.5 milliseconds, while its average rotation time is 3 milliseconds. Thus, accessing of a stream of sequential blocks on the same track achieves a much higher disk throughput than that accessing of several random blocks does.

In the current practice, there are several major efforts in parallel to break the disk bottleneck. One effort is to reduce disk accesses through memory caching. By using replacement algorithms to exploit the temporal locality of data accesses, where data are likely to be re-accessed in the near future after they are accessed, requests for on-disk data can be satisfied without actually being passed to disk. To minimize disk activities in the number of requested blocks, all current replacement algorithms are designed by choosing block miss

reduction as the sole objective. However, this can be a misleading metric that may not accurately reflect real system performance. For example, requesting ten sequential disk blocks can be completed much faster than requesting three random disk blocks, where disk seeking is involved. To improve real system performance, spatial locality, a factor that can make a difference as large as an order of magnitude in disk performance, must be considered. However, spatial locality is unfortunately ignored in current buffer cache managements. In the discussion of this chapter, spatial locality specifically refers to the sequentiality of the disk placements of the continuously requested blocks.

Another effort to break the disk bottleneck is reducing disk arm seeks through I/O request scheduling. I/O scheduler reorders pending requests in a block device's request queue into a dispatching order that results in minimal seeks and thereafter maximal global disk throughput. Example schedulers include Shortest-Seek-Time-First (SSTF), C-SCAN, as well as the Deadline and Anticipatory I/O schedulers (Iyer et al. 2001) adopted in the current Linux kernels.

The third effort is prefetching. A prefetching manager predicts future request patterns associated with a file opened by a process. If a sequential access pattern is detected, then the prefetching manager issues requests for the blocks following the current on-demand block on behalf of the process. Because a file is usually contiguously allocated on disk, these prefetching requests can be fulfilled quickly with few disk seeks.

While I/O scheduling and prefetching can effectively exploit spatial locality and dramatically improve disk throughput for workloads with dominant sequential accesses, their ability to deal with workloads mixed with sequential and random data accesses, such as those in Web services, databases, and scientific computing applications, is very limited. This is because these two strategies are positioned at a level lower than the buffer cache. While the buffer cache receives

I/O requests directly from applications and has the power to shape the requests into a desirable I/O request stream, I/O scheduling and prefetching only work on the request stream passed on from the buffer cache and have very limited ability to re-catch the opportunities lost in the buffer cache management. Hence, in the worst case, a stream filled with random accesses makes I/O scheduling and prefetching largely ineffective, because no spatial locality is left for them to exploit.

Concerned with the lack of ability to exploit spatial locality in buffer cache management, the solution to the deteriorating disk bottleneck is a new buffer cache management scheme that exploits both temporal and spatial localities, which is named as *Du*al *LO*cality scheme (*DULO*). DULO introduces dual locality into the caching component in an operating systems by tracking and utilizing disk placements of in-memory pages in its buffer cache management. The objective is to maximize the sequentiality of I/O requests that are serviced by disks. For this purpose, DULO gives preference to random blocks for staying in the cache, while sequential blocks that have their temporal locality comparable to those random blocks are replaced first. With the filtering effect of the cache on I/O requests, DULO influences the I/O requests made by applications so that more sequential block requests and less random block requests are passed to the disk thereafter. The disk is then able to process the requests with stronger spatial locality more efficiently.

CHALLENGES WITH DUAL LOCALITY

Application of dual locality in the cache management raises challenges that do not exist in a traditional system. In the current cache managements, replacement algorithms only consider temporal locality (a position in a queue in the case of LRU) to make a replacement decision. While introduction of spatial locality necessarily has to compromise the weight of temporal locality in a replacement decision, the role of temporal locality must be appropriately retained in the decision. For example, we may give randomly accessed blocks more privilege of staying in cache due to their weak spatial locality (weak sequentiality), even though they have weak temporal locality (large recency). However, we certainly cannot keep them in cache forever if they do not have sufficient re-accesses that indicate temporal locality. Otherwise, they would pollute the cache with inactive data and reduce the effective cache size. The same consideration also applies to the block sequences of different sizes. We prefer to keep a short sequence because it only has a small number of blocks to amortize the cost of an I/O operation. However, how do we make a replacement decision when we encounter a not-recently-accessed short sequence and a recently-accessed long sequence? The challenge is essentially how to make the tradeoff between temporal locality (recency) and spatial locality (sequence size) with the goal of maximizing disk performance.

THE DULO SCHEME

We now present the DULO scheme to exploit both temporal locality and spatial locality simultaneously and seamlessly. Because Least Recently Used (LRU) or its variants are the most widely used replacement algorithms, the DULO scheme is designed by using the LRU algorithm and its data structure --- the LRU stack, as a reference point.

In LRU, newly fetched blocks enter into its stack top and replaced blocks leave from its stack bottom. There are two key operations in the DULO scheme: (1) Forming sequences. A *sequence* is defined as a number of blocks whose disk locations are close to each other and have been accessed sequentially in a series without interruption during a limited time period. Additionally, a sequence is required to be stable so that blocks in

Figure 1. The LRU stack is structured for the DULO replacement algorithm

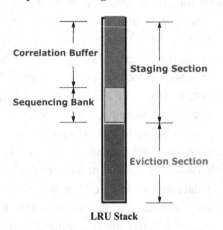

LRU Stack

it would be fetched together next time when they are read from disk. Specifically, a random block is a sequence of size 1. (2) Sorting the sequences in the LRU stack according to their recency (temporal locality) and size (spatial locality), with the objective that sequences of large recency and size are placed close to the LRU stack bottom. Because the recency of a sequence changes while new sequences are being added, the order of the sorted sequence should be adjusted dynamically to reflect the change.

Structuring LRU Stack

To facilitate the operations presented above, DULO partitions the LRU stack into two sections (shown in Figure 1 as a vertically placed queue). The top part is called *staging section* used for admitting newly fetched blocks, and the bottom part is called *eviction section* used for storing sorted sequences to be evicted in their orders. The staging section is again partitioned into two segments. The first segment is called *correlation buffer*, and the second segment is called *sequencing bank*. Its role is to filter high frequency references and to keep them from entering the sequencing bank, so as to reduce the consequential operational cost. The sequencing

bank is used to prepare a collection of blocks to be sequenced, and its size ranges from 0 to a maximum value, *BANK_MAX*.

Suppose in the beginning the staging section of an LRU stack consists of only the correlation buffer (the size of the sequencing bank is 0), and the eviction section holds the rest of the stack. When a block leaves the eviction section and a block enters the correlation buffer at its top, the bottom block of the correlation buffer enters the sequencing bank. When there are BANK_MAX blocks leaving the eviction section, the size of sequencing bank is BANK_MAX. We refill the eviction section by taking the blocks in the bank, forming sequences out of them, and inserting them into the eviction section in a desired order. There are three reasons for us to maintain two interacting sections and use the bank to conduct sequence forming: (1) The newly admitted blocks have a buffering area to be accumulated for forming potential sequences. (2) The sequences formed at the same time must share a common recency, because their constituent blocks are from the same block pool --- the sequencing bank in the staging section. By restricting the bank size, we make sure that the block recency will not be excessively compromised for the sake of spatial locality. (3) The blocks that are leaving the stack are sorted in the eviction section for a replacement order reflecting both their sequentiality and their recency.

Block Table: A Data Structure For Dual Locality

To complement the missing spatial locality in traditional caching systems, we introduce a data structure in the OS kernel called *block table*. The block table is analogous in structure to the multi-level page table used for process address translation. However there are clear differences between them because they serve different purposes: (1) The page table covers virtual address space of a process in the unit of page and page address is an index into the table, while the block table covers disk space in the unit of block, and block disk location is an index into the table. (2) The page table is used to translate a virtual address into its physical address, while the block table is used to provide the times of recent accesses for a given disk block. (3) The requirement on the page table lookup efficiency is much more demanding and performance-critical than that on the block table lookup efficiency because the former supports instruction execution while the latter facilitates I/O operations. That is the reason why a hardware TLB has to be used to expedite page table lookup, but there is no such a need for block table. (4) Each process owns a page table, while each disk drive owns a block table in memory.

In the system we set a global variable called *disk access clock*, which ticks each time a block is fetched into memory. The block being fetched takes the current clock time. We then record the timestamp in an entry at the leaf level of the block table corresponding to the block disk location, which we called BTE (*Block Table Entry*). When the block is being released, we reset the information recorded for that block to prevent new blocks allocated to the same location inheriting stale information. Each BTE allows at most two most recent access times recorded in it. Whenever a new time is added, the oldest time is replaced if the BTE is full. In addition, to manage efficiently the memory space held by block table(s), a timestamp is set in each table entry at directory levels. Each time the block table is looked up in a hierarchical way to record a new access time, the time is also recorded as a timestamp in each directory entry that has been passed. In this way, each directory entry keeps the most recent timestamp among those of all its direct/indirect children entries when the table is viewed as a tree. The entries of the table are allocated in an on-demand fashion.

The memory consumption of the block table can be flexibly controlled. When system memory pressure is too high and the system needs to reclaim memory held by the table, it traverses the table with a specified clock time threshold for reclamation. Because the most recent access times are recorded in the directories, the system will remove a directory once it finds its timestamp is smaller than the threshold, and all the subdirectories and BTEs under it will be removed.

Forming Sequences

When the bank is full, it is the time to traverse all the blocks in the bank to collect all the sequences. To ensure the sequentiality and the stability requirement of a sequence, the algorithm determines that the last block (*A*) of a developing sequence should not be coalesced with the closest block (*B*) in the bank if the two blocks belong to one of the following cases:

- Block B is not close enough to block A. This includes the case that the LBN (*Logical Block Number*) of block B is less than that of block A, where a long rotation time is involved to move the disk head from block A to block B. Currently, DULO uses 4 as the distance threshold. The reason is that, if the distance between block B and block A is within the threshold, the read-ahead mechanism in most hard drives, which is enabled by default, can fetch block B into disk caches automatically after it fetches block A. So the cost of reading of block B is very cheap.
- Block B and block A are not sequentially fetched from disk this time. If the most recent time stamp of block B is not greater than the most recent time stamp of block A by 1, the accesses of block A and block B are intersected by the access of the third block, and high cost disk head seeks are involved.
- Block B and block A were not sequentially fetched from disk last time. This includes the case where one and only one of the two blocks was not accessed before the current

clock time (i.e., it has only one timestamp), and the case that their non-recent time stamps have a difference larger than 1.

- The current sequence size reaches 128, which is the maximal allowed sequence size and we deem to be sufficient to amortize a disk operation cost.

If any one of the conditions is met, a complete sequence has been formed and a new sequence starts to be formed. Otherwise, block B becomes part of the sequence, the following blocks will be tested continuously.

The DULO Replacement Algorithm

There are two challenging issues to be addressed in the design of the DULO replacement algorithm.

The first issue is the potentially prohibitive overhead associated with the DULO scheme. In the strict LRU algorithm, both missed blocks and hit blocks are required to move to the stack top. This means that a hit on a block in the eviction section is associated with a bank sequencing cost and a cost for sequence ordering in the eviction section. These additional costs that can incur in a system with few memory misses are unacceptable. In fact, the strict LRU algorithm is seldom used in real systems because of its overhead associated with every memory reference (Jiang et al. 2005). Instead, its variant, the CLOCK replacement algorithm, has been widely used in practice. In CLOCK, when a block is hit, it is only flagged as *young* block without being moved to the stack top. When a block has to be replaced, the block at the stack bottom is examined. If it is a young block, it is moved to the stack top and its ``young block'' status is revoked. Otherwise, the block is replaced. It is known that CLOCK simulates LRU behaviors very closely and its hit ratios are very close to those of LRU. For this reason, we build the DULO replacement algorithm based on the CLOCK algorithm. That is, it delays the movement of a hit block until it reaches the stack

bottom. In this way, only block misses could trigger sequencing and the eviction section refilling operations. While being compared with the miss penalty, these costs are very small.

The second issue is how the sequences in the eviction section are ordered for replacement according to their temporal and spatial locality. We adopt an algorithm similar to *GreedyDual-Size* used in Web file caching (Cao et al. 2007). It makes its replacement decision by considering the recency, size, and fetching cost of cached files. In our case, file size is equivalent to sequence size, and file fetching cost is equivalent to the I/O operation cost for a sequence access. For sequences whose sizes are distributed in a reasonable range, which is limited by bank size, we currently assume their fetching cost is the same. Our algorithm can be modified to accommodate cost variance if necessary in the future.

The DULO algorithm associates each sequence with a value H, where a relatively small value indicates the sequence should be evicted first. The algorithm has a global inflation value L, which records the H value of the most recent evicted sequence. When a new sequence s is admitted into the eviction section, its H value is set as $H(s) = L + 1/size(s)$, where $size(s)$ is the number of the blocks contained in s. The sequences in the eviction section are sorted by their H values with sequences of small H values at the LRU stack bottom. In the algorithm a sequence of large size tends to stay at the stack bottom and to be evicted first. However, if a sequence of small size is not accessed for a relatively long time, it will be replaced. This is because a newly admitted long sequence could have a larger H value due to the L value, which is continuously being inflated by the evicted blocks. When all sequences are random blocks (i.e., their sizes are 1), the algorithm degenerates into the LRU replacement algorithm.

As we have mentioned before, once a bank size of blocks are replaced from the eviction section, we take the blocks in the sequencing bank to form sequences and order the sequences by their

H values. Note that all these sequences share the same current *L* value in their *H* value calculations. With a merge sorting of the newly ordered sequence list and the ordered sequence list in the eviction section, we complete the refilling of the eviction section, and the staging section ends up with only the correlation buffer.

PERFORMANCE RESULTS

To demonstrate the performance improvements of DULO on a modern operating system, we implement it in the recent Linux kernel 2.6.11. To exhibit the impact of introducing spatial locality into replacement decisions under different circumstances, we run two types of applications, whose I/O operations are mostly file accesses and VM paging respectively. As file system fragmentation may have substantial impact on system performance, we also test DULO on an aged file system.

The DULO Implementation

As many other Unix variants, Linux uses an LRU variant as its replacement policy, which brings up some implementation issues. So let's start with a brief description of the implementation of the Linux replacement policy.

Linux Caching

Linux adopts an LRU variant similar to the 2Q replacement (Johnson el al. 1994). The Linux 2.6 kernel groups all the process pages and file pages into two LRU lists called the *active list* and the *inactive list*. As their names indicate, the active list is used to store recently actively accessed pages, and the inactive list is used to store those pages that have not been accessed for some time. A faulted-in page is placed at the head of the inactive list. The replacement page is always selected at the tail of the inactive list. An inactive page is promoted into the active list when it is accessed as a file page, or it is accessed as a process page and its reference is detected at the inactive list tail. An active page is demoted to the inactive list if it is determined to have not been recently accessed. Linux uses an adaptive method to refill inactive list with pages picked from active list. When the page reclaiming at the tail of the inactive list becomes difficult, more pages are picked from active list to inactive list.

Implementation Issues

In our prototype implementation of DULO, we do not replace the original Linux page frame reclaiming code with a faithful DULO scheme implementation. Instead, we opt to keep the existing data structure and policies mostly unchanged, and seamlessly adapt DULO into them. We make this choice, which has to tolerate some compromises of the original DULO design, to serve the purpose of demonstrating what improvements a dual locality consideration could bring to an existing spatial-locality-unaware system without changing its basic underlying replacement policy.

In Linux, we partition the inactive list into a staging section and an eviction section because the list is the place where new blocks are added and old blocks are replaced. To keep DULO effective and make it cooperate well with existing policies in Linux, both staging section and eviction section need to have reasonable lengths, which are now limited by inactive list. The length of eviction section presents DULO's ability to control the eviction order of the pages. The longer the eviction is, the more power DULO has to protect the high-cost random blocks from being evicted. Different with other LRU variants, where newly fetched pages enter the head of the only list, inactive list provides a shorter evaluation period for newly fetched pages, during which frequently referenced ones are re-visited and promoted to active list and unfrequently referenced ones are evicted.

The anonymous pages that do not yet have mappings on disk are treated as random blocks until they are swapped out and are associated with some disk locations. To map the LBN (Logical Block Number) of a block into a one-dimensional physical disk address, we use a technique described in (Schindler et al. 2002) to extract track boundaries. To characterize accurately block location sequentiality, all the defective and spare blocks on disk are counted. We also artificially place a dummy block between the blocks on a track boundary in the mapping to show the two blocks are non-sequential.

The experiment is conducted on a Dell desktop with a single 3.0GHz Intel Pentium 4 processor, 512MB memory, and a Western Digital 7200 RPM IDE disk with a capacity of 160GB. The read-ahead mechanism built in the hard drive is enabled. The operating system is Redhat WS4 with its kernel updated to Linux 2.6.11. The file system is Ext2. In the experiments, we change the memory sizes available for benchmarks to observe their performance with different memory sizes.

Experiment Results on File Accesses

In the evaluation of impact of DULO on the performance of file access, we select benchmarks that represent different access patterns, including almost-all sequential accesses (*TPC-H*), almost all random accesses (*diff*), and mixed I/O access patterns (*BLAST, PostMark, LXR*). DULO shows the most performance advantages with benchmarks that have considerable amount of both short sequences and long sequences by increasing the number of disk accesses to long sequences and keeping data of short sequence in memory.

Here are insights on the experiment results. First, the increases of sequence sizes are directly correlated to the improvement of the execution times or I/O throughputs. Let us take BLAST as an example. With a memory size of 512MB, Linux has 8.2% accesses whose sequence sizes equal to 1, while DULO reduces this percentage

to 3.5%. At the same time, in DULO there are 57.7% sequences whose sizes are larger than 32, compared with 33.8% in Linux. Accordingly, there is a 20.1% execution time reduction by DULO. In contrast, with the memory size of 192MB DULO reduces random accesses from 15.2% to 4.2% and increases sequences longer than 32 from 19.8% to 51.3%. Accordingly, there is a 53.0% execution time reduction. The correlation clearly indicates that the size of requested sequence is a critical factor affecting disk performance and DULO makes its contributions through increasing sequence sizes. Second, DULO increases the sequence size without excessively compromising temporal locality. This is demonstrated by the small difference of hit ratios between Linux and DULO. For example, DULO reduces the hit ratios of PostMark by 0.53%~1.6%, while it slightly increases the hit ratio of BLAST by 1.1% ~ 2.2%. In addition, this observation also indicates that reduced execution times and increased server throughputs are results of the improved disk I/O efficiency, rather than the reduced I/O operations in terms of the number of accessed blocks, which is actually the objective of traditional caching algorithms. Third, sequential accesses are important in leveraging the buffer cache filtering effect by DULO. We observe that DULO achieves more performance improvement for BLAST than it does for PostMark and LXR. BLAST has over 40% sequences whose sizes are larger than 16 blocks, while PostMark and LXR have only 30% and 15% such sequences. The small portion of sequential accesses in PostMark and LXR make DULO less capable of keeping random blocks from being replaced because there are not sufficient number of sequentially accessed blocks to be replaced first.

Meanwhile, DULO has only limited or little influence on the performance of workloads with almost-all-sequential and a random accesses. Take TPC-H and diff as examples. Workload TPC-H has more than 85% of the sequences that are longer than 16 blocks. For this almost-all-sequential workload, DULO can only slightly increase the sizes of short sequences, and accordingly reduce execution time by 2.1% with a memory size of 384MB. However, for the almost-all-random workload diff, more than 80% of the sequences are shorter than 4 blocks. Unsurprisingly, DULO cannot create sequential disk requests from workload requests consisting of purely random blocks. As expected, DULO cannot reduce the execution time.

Experiment Results with an Aged File System

The free space of an aged file system is usually fragmented, and sometimes it is difficult to find a large chunk of contiguous space for creating or extending files. This usually causes large files to consist of a number of fragments of various sizes, and files in the same directory to be dispersed on the disk. This non-contiguous allocation of logically related blocks of data worsens the performance of I/O-intensive applications. However, it could provide DULO more opportunities to show its effectiveness by trying to keep small fragments in memory.

The experiments with an aged file system shows that, for workloads dominated with long sequential accesses such as TPC-H, an aged file system degrades its performance. For example, with a memory size of 448MB, the execution time of TPC-H on an aged file system is 107% more than on a fresh file system. This is because on an aged file system large data files scanned by TPC-H are broken into pieces of various sizes. Accessing of small pieces of data on disk significantly increases I/O times. Dealing with sequences of various sizes caused by aged file system, DULO can reduce execution time by a larger percentage than it does on a fresh file system. For TPC-H, with a fresh file system DULO can hardly reduce the execution time. However, with an aged file system DULO manages to identify sequences of small sizes and give them a high caching priority, so that their high I/O costs can be avoided. This results in a

16.3% reduction of its execution time with the memory size of 448MB.

For workloads with patterns mixed of sequential accesses and random accesses, such as BLAST and PostMark, an aged file system has different effects on DULO's performance, depending on sequentiality of the workloads and memory sizes. For BLAST, which abounds in long sequences, DULO reduces its execution time by a larger percentage on an aged file system than it does on a fresh file system when memory size is large. For workloads with a relatively small percentage of long sequences, the reduction of long sequences makes its access pattern close to that in almost-all-random applications, where the lack of sufficient long sequences causes short sequences to be replaced quickly. Thus we expect that DULO may reduce less execution time with an aged file system than it does with a fresh file system. This is confirmed by our experimental results.

While programs and file systems are designed to preserve sequential accesses for efficient disk accesses, DULO is important in keeping system performance from degradation due to an aged file system and to help retaining the expected performance advantage associated with sequential accesses.

Experiments on Virtual Memory Paging

In order to study the influence of the DULO scheme on VM paging performance, we use a representative scientific computing benchmark --- sparse matrix multiplication (SMM) from an NIST benchmark suite SciMark2. The total working set, including the result vector and the index arrays, is around 348MB.

To cause the system paging and stress the swap space accesses, we have to adopt small memory sizes, from 336MB to 440MB, including the memory used by the kernel and applications.

To increase spatial locality of swapped-out pages in the disk swap space, Linux tries to allocate contiguous swap slots on disk to sequentially reclaimed anonymous pages in the hope that they would be efficiently swapped-in in the same order. However, the data access pattern in SMM foils the system effort. The swap-in accesses of the vector arrays recording the positions of elements in a matrix turn into random accesses, while the elements of matrix elements are still sequentially accessed. This explains why DULO can significantly reduce the execution times of the program (by up to 38.6%). This is because DULO detects the random pages in the vector array and caches them with a higher priority. Because the matrix is a sparse one, the vector array cannot obtain sufficiently frequent reuses to allow the original kernel to keep them from being paged out. In addition, the similar execution times between the two kernels when there is enough memory (exceeding 424MB) to hold the working set shown in the figure suggest that DULO's overhead is small.

RESEARCH ON IMPROVING AND EXPOSING ON-DISK LAYOUT FOR UPPER-LEVEL SOFTWARES

We know that the disk head seek time far dominates I/O data transfer time, and the efficiency of accessing sequential data on the disk can be one order of magnitude higher than that of accessing of random data. As the hard disk has been and is expected to continue to be the mainstream on-line storage device in the foreseeable future, efforts on making sure on-disk data are sequentially accessed are critical to maintain a high I/O performance. Exposing information from the lower layers up for better utilization of hard disk is an active research topic.

Most of the existing work focuses on using disk-specific knowledge for improving data placements on disk that facilitate the efficient servicing of future requests. For example, Fast File System (FFS) and its variants allocate related data and metadata into the same cylinder group to minimize seeks (Mckusick et al. 1994; Ganger et al. 1997).

There have been many other techniques to control the data placement on disk (Arpaci-Dusseau et al. 2003; Black et al. 1991) or reorganize selected disk blocks (Hsu el al. 2003), so that related objects are clustered and the accesses to them become more sequential. Traxtent-aware file system excludes track boundary block from being allocated for better disk sequential access performance (Schindler et al. 2002). The effort on improving access sequentiality through statically arranging data layout on the disk is effective only when the actually accesses take place in the assumed order. If not or the access order changes from time to time, many random accesses can still occur.

As the techniques focusing only on the disk alone cannot fully solve the issue, another complimentary effort, represented by DULO, is to expose the data layout information to the upper-lever software such as the buffer cache management module in the OS kernel, so that they can leverage the information in their policies for a higher I/O throughput. Besides DULO, DiskSeen is another example of such effort (Ding et al. 2007). DiskSeen improves the effectiveness of prefetching by using the disk layout knowledge to find the on-disk data access sequences. In addition to the conventional file-level prefetching, the disk-level prefetching provides substantially higher I/O performance for many patterns of accesses, especially for access of a large number of small files. It is noted that the two efforts are complementary and synergistic.

While statically improvement data layout on the disk provides the opportunity of long sequence of data access, leveraging the layout information in the upper-level software can maximize the performance potential of sequential access and minimize the performance penalty incurred by access random data.

We believe that exposing more detailed information on the storage system, such as the configuration of disk array, the data layout on a disk, and buffer cache size on the storage controller, to the various software layers of the I/O stack, including kernel of OS, would be of great potential for improving I/O performance and removing the painful I/O bottleneck. A challenge in the approach is how to make it reconcile with the virtualization technologies and effectively deal with portability issues, which all require isolation from the low-level details to some extent.

CONCLUSION

In this chapter, we identify a serious weakness of lacking spatial locality exploitation in I/O caching, and propose a new and effective memory management scheme, DULO, which can significantly improve I/O performance by exploiting both temporal and spatial locality. Our experiment results show that DULO can effectively reorganize application I/O request streams mixed with random and sequential accesses in order to provide a more disk-friendly request stream with high sequentiality of block accesses. We present an effective DULO replacement algorithm to carefully tradeoff random accesses with sequential accesses and evaluate it using traces representing representative access patterns. The results of experiments on a prototype implementation of DULO in a recent Linux kernel show that DULO can significantly improve the I/O performance for many applications from different areas. As DULO represents a promising effort in removing the I/O barrier for many I/O-intensive applications, more research in this direction is called to reveal its full potential and address its issues.

REFERENCES

Arpaci-Dusseau, R. H., Arpaci-Dusseau, N. C., Burnett, T. E., Denehy, T. J., Engle, H. S., Gunawi, J., & Nugent, F. I. Popovici. (2003). *Transforming Policies into Mechanisms with Infokernel.* 19th ACM Symposium on Operating Systems Principles.

Black, D., Carter, J., Feinberg, G., MacDonald, R., Mangalat, S., Sheinbrood, E., et al. (1991). *OSF/1 Virtual Memory Improvements.* USENIX Mac Symposium.

Cao, P., & Irani, S. (1997). *Cost-Aware WWW Proxy Caching Algorithms.* USENIX Annual Technical Conference.

Ding, X., Jiang, S., Chen, F., Davis, K., & Zhang, X. (2007). *DiskSeen: Exploiting Disk Layout and Access History to Enhance I/O Prefetch.* USENIX Annual Technical Conference.

Ganger, G., & Kaashoek, F. (1997). *Embedded Inodes and Explicit Groups: Exploiting Disk Bandwidth for Small Files.* USENIX Annual Technical Conference.

Hsu, W. W., Young, H. C., & Smith, A. J. (2003). *The Automatic Improvement of Locality in Storage Systems.* Technical Report CSD-03-1264, UC Berkeley.

Iyer, S., & Druschel, P. (2001). Anticipatory Scheduling: A Disk Scheduling Framework to Overcome Deceptive Idleness in Synchronous I/O. *18th ACM Symposium on Operating Systems Principles.*

Jiang, S., Chen, F., & Zhang, X. (2005). *CLOCK-Pro: An Effective Improvement of the CLOCK Replacement.* USENIX Annual Technical Conference.

Johnson, T., & Shasha, D. (1994). 2Q: A Low Overhead High Performance Buffer Management Replacement Algorithm. In *International Conference on Very Large Data Bases,* (pp. 439-450).

Mckusick, M. K., Joy, W. N., Leffler, S. J., & Fabry, R. S. (1884). A Fast File System for UNIX. *Transactions on Computer Systems, 2*(3).

Schindler, J., Griffin, J. L., Lumb, C. R., & Ganger, G. R. (2002). *Track-Aligned Extents: Matching Access Patterns to Disk Drive Characteristics.* USENIX Conference on File and Storage Technologies.

Chapter 7
Alleviating the Thrashing by Adding Medium-Term Scheduler

Moses Reuven
Bar-Ilan University, Israel

Yair Wiseman
Bar-Ilan University, Israel

ABSTRACT

A technique for minimizing the paging on a system with a very heavy memory usage is proposed. When there are processes with active memory allocations that should be in the physical memory, but their accumulated size exceeds the physical memory capacity. In such cases, the operating system begins swapping pages in and out the memory on every context switch. The authors lessen this thrashing by placing the processes into several bins, using Bin Packing approximation algorithms. They amend the scheduler to maintain two levels of scheduling - medium-term scheduling and short-term scheduling. The medium-term scheduler switches the bins in a Round-Robin manner, whereas the short-term scheduler uses the standard Linux scheduler to schedule the processes in each bin. The authors prove that this feature does not necessitate adjustments in the shared memory maintenance. In addition, they explain how to modify the new scheduler to be compatible with some elements of the original scheduler like priority and real-time privileges. Experimental results show substantial improvement on very loaded memories.

INTRODUCTION

One of the most substantial computer resources is the RAM. Multitasking operating system executes several processes simultaneously. Each one of the processes uses several sections of the memory. The connection of the memory and the scheduling strategy is an old subject for research (Zahorjan et al., 1991), (Wiseman and Feitelson, 2003).

Usually, most of the processes do not make use of the entire memory that has been allocated for them. This shows the way to the principle of virtual memory (Denning, 1970): Many processes have allocations in the virtual memory, but only the pages which are currently required will be physically stored in the memory; therefore, many more processes can be executed in parallel, while occupying less physical memory space.

DOI: 10.4018/978-1-60566-850-5.ch007

Various operating systems implement the virtual memory concept using the paging model i.e. the operating system will load a memory page into the physical memory only if a process asks for it. If no free memory frame is available, the operating system will swap out a page from the physical memory to the secondary memory (hard disk). Different techniques for choosing which pages the operating system will swap out to the disk have been suggested over the years (Belady, 1966).

When large memory space is needed, swapping pages in and out the memory will consume a large portion of the CPU cycles. This situation is called Thrashing (Abrossimov et al., 1989). Thrashing causes a severe overhead time and as a result a substantial slowdown of the system. Some studies for alleviating the unwanted consequences of the thrashing have been carried out over the years (Galvin and Silberschatz, 1998).

In (Jiang and Zhang, 2001), (Jiang and Zhang, 2002), (Jiang, 2009), the authors propose giving one of the interactive processes a privilege. The process's pages will not be swapped out. As a result, the privileged process will be executed faster and therefore will free its memory allocation earlier. This feature may assist the operating system freeing enough memory fast and to get back to a normal behavior. However, this technique will be advantageous only if the memory allocations slightly exceed the physical memory. This technique will work like a First-In-First-Out scheduler if many processes produce a large memory excess. In such cases this FIFO continues and the system will keep on thrashing. Linux 2.6 version has a similar mechanism and its scheduler is described in section 2.

In (Batat and Feitelson, 2000) the authors suggest not admitting jobs that do not fit into the current available memory. The system waits for several processes to finish their execution and only when enough memory is freed, a new job can be admitted. The authors also discuss the dilemma how a memory size needed by a new job can be assessed. This technique is essentially very similar to the VMS technique that uses the "Balance Sets" method. However, the authors of this paper have implemented the "Balance Sets" concept for distributed systems.

In (Nikolopoulos, 2003) the author handles the thrashing problem by adjusting the memory needs of a process to the current available memory. This solution is quite different from the other solutions, because it modifies the processes instead of modifying the operating system.

Some hardware solutions for trashing are also have been suggested which are implemented in the cache (Gonzalez et al., 1997), (Chu and Ito, 2000). Typically LRU is the basic scheme that both hardware and software victim selection algorithms employ. However, the LRU algorithm is manipulated differently by hardware and software implementations. Naturally, hardware solutions must be much simpler for implementation; but on the other hand, hardware solutions can use data that the operating system does not know e.g. the cache can distinguish between an instructions block and a data block; while the operating system does not distinguish. Clearly, this parameter can be very useful for victim selection algorithms.

This chapter suggests a technique that modifies the traditional process scheduling method by adding a new a layer of scheduling (Reuven and Wiseman, 2005), (Reuven and Wiseman, 2006). By using this modification, the operating system can swap in and out fewer pages; therefore alleviating the slowdown stemming from thrashing. The technique suggested in this chapter is not restricted to a specific operating system; therefore, any multitasking paging system can employ it. The figures and the results given in this chapter have been produced by running benchmarks on the Linux operating system (Card et al., 1998). However, as has been noted, Linux is just an example to show the feasibility of our concept.

The rest of the chapter is organized as follow. Section 1 describes the Linux scheduling algorithms. Section 2 explains the Bin Packing problem. Section 3 presents the reduced paging algorithm. Finally, section 4 gives the results and evaluates them.

THRASHING IN THE LINUX OPERATING SYSTEM

Traditionally, UNIX scheduler is priority based (Vahalia, 1996). The process scheduling algorithm of Linux is based on the traditional UNIX scheduler. The Linux scheduler is well-known and a description of it can be found in many places e.g. (Beck at el. 1998), (Komarinski and Collett 1998).

Linux virtual memory mechanism along with the paging techniques gives Linux the ability to manage many processes, even when the real memory requirements are larger than the available physical memory. However, the virtual memory mechanism cannot handle some circumstances. If the memory space required is too much over a short time, the swapping mechanism cannot satisfy the memory requirements quickly; therefore pages are swapped in and out time and again and a little progress is made.

Linux will kill processes if thrashing occurs and the system is out of swap space. In some sense there is nothing else that the kernel is able to do in such situation, because memory is needed but no more physical or swap memory is available (Gorman, 2004), (Marti, 2002). If a thrashing occurs, Linux kernel will kill the most memory consuming processes. This feature is very harsh; therefore its implications might be drastic. For example, if a server runs several applications with mutual dependencies, killing one of these applications may yield unexpected results.

Linux 2.6 version has implemented the token-ordered LRU policy (Jiang and Zhang, 2005). The key idea of this policy is eliminating page swapping at some cases called by the developers "false LRU pages". Sometimes, a page of a sleeping process is swapped out, even though it would have not

been swapped out if the process was not sleeping. The concept of the token-ordered LRU policy is setting one or multiple tokens in the system. The token is taken by one process when a page fault occurs. The system prevents the false LRU pages for the process holding the token from occurring. This feature allows the process holding the token a quick establishing of its working set. By giving this privilege to a process, the total number of false LRU pages is reduced and the pool of the competing pages is getting ordered. However, this policy can be beneficial only when the memory needs slightly exceed the physical memory space. A large memory excess of many processes will be treated by this method as First-In-First-Out, while other processes still vie for memory allocations and thrash; therefore, in (Jiang and Zhang, 2005) the traditional killing approach is of Linux is kept for severe situations. In this chapter another technique is suggested that can also handle the cases that were handled by the killing methods.

Another problem is that the process selection algorithm of Linux can mistakenly select a process executing an endless loop. Such a selection will even worsen the thrashing. Also selecting a very long process that is executed for some hours will be damaging. The selection algorithm can just estimate which the shortest process is, but its estimation might be wrong.

BIN PACKING

The suggested technique needs a set of all the processes that are currently in the virtual memory. This set is split into several groups, such that the total memory size of each group is as close as possible to the size of the available real memory.

These groups of processes can be built as followed: There is a set of processes P_i, each with a memory allocation. Let M_i denote the maximal working set size that might be needed by process P_i. We need an algorithm which splits these M_i's into as few groups as possible, with the sum of the M_is in each group not exceeding the size of the real memory. Practically, the kernel and some other daemons occupy part of the memory, so the sum should not exceed a smaller memory size. This splitting problem is well known and called the Bin Packing problem (Scholl et al., 1997).

The Bin Packing problem is defined as a set of numbers X_1, X_2, ..., X_n, with $X_i \in [0, 1]$ for each i. The problem is finding the smallest natural number m for which:

- X_1, X_2, ..., X_n can be partitioned into m sets.
- The sum of the members of each set is not higher than one.

The Bin Packing problem is NP-hard (Karp, 1972). However, some polynomial time approximations have been introduced over the years, such as (Fekete and Schepers, 2001), (Gent, 1998) and (Martello and Toth, 1990). The approximation algorithms use no more than $(1+E)*OPT(I)$ number of bins, where $OPT(I)$ is the number of bins in the optimal solution for case I. If E is smaller, the result will be closer to the optimal solution, but unfortunately good approximations are usually time consuming (Coffman et al., 1997). We would like to choose one of the approximation algorithms which is not time consuming, but yet tries minimizing $(1+E)*OPT(I)$.

A simple idea of an approximation algorithm for the Bin Packing problem is the greedy approach (Albers and Mitzenmacher, 2000), also known as the First-Fit approach. This algorithm is defined as follow:

- Sort the vector X_1, X_2, ..., X_n by the allocated memory size.
- Open a new bin and put the highest number in it.
- While there are more numbers
- If adding the current number to one of the existing bins exceeds the size of the bin
  - ○ Open a new bin and put the current number in it.
- Else
  - ○ Put the current number in the current bin.

In our tests, we used a version of this approximation algorithm with a slight modification. We usually achieved the minimal number of bins and the cost of execution time was usually low. Below we describe the version that has been use in this chapter..

BIN PACKING BASED PAGING

It is well known that increasing the level of multitasking in any operating system may sometimes cause thrashing. In order to avoid thrashing, we would like to suggest a new approach: All the processes will be split into several groups such that the sum of physical memory demands within each group will not be higher than the amount of physical memory available on the machine. In (Alverson et al., 1995) the authors give some ideas to use a Bin Packing approximation (First Fit) to improve the Backfilling scheduling of a specific Operating System (Tera). We would like to use the Bin Packing Algorithms to improve the Linux scheduling using more approximations.

Medium-Term Scheduler

A new scheduler procedure will be added to the Linux operating system. The new scheduler will operate in the manner of the medium-term scheduler, which was part of some operating systems (Stallings, 1998). The medium-term scheduler will load the groups into the Ready queue of the Linux scheduler in a Round-Robin manner. The traditional Linux scheduler will do the scheduling within the current group in the same way the scheduling is originally done on Linux machines. The time slice of each group in the medium-term scheduler will be significantly higher than the average time allocated to the processes by the original Linux scheduler. The processes in the real memory will not be able to cause thrashing during the execution of the group, because their total size is not higher than the size of the available physical memory i.e. the size of each bin. Only at the beginning of each group execution there will be an intensive swapping, because the new group's pages are swapped into the memory. This approach can improve the system ability to support memory-consuming processes in a more tolerant way than killing them.

There are some methods to calculate the working set size needed by each process. One of these methods can be found in (Zhou et al., 2004). In this paper, the authors suggest a way that adds 7-10% overhead. Obviously, such an overhead is time consuming and not suitable for the concept of the bin packing approach. The scheduler needs to know the working set size on every context switch and calculating this working set often is costly. We use another simple approach. The resident size of each process was taken from /proc/PROCESS_NO/status file. This size is the process' last pages total size. This size is not accurate and if the system is not busy, the resident size may include large portions of stale pages that are not currently essential. However, when the system is not busy, there will be no thrashing and this overestimation will make no harm.

In our implementation, the group time slice was half a second or one second, whereas the Linux scheduler gives time slices of some dozen milliseconds. When Linux thrashes, any context switch causes many page faults, whereas with the medium-term scheduler, intensive swapping will occur only when switching between groups. This lets the operating system in our implementation swapping a significant amount of pages only in a few percents of the cases, in contrast to conventional Linux during thrashing conditions.

The processes which are not in the current group should be kept on a different queue, so that Linux scheduler will not be able to see them. In order to implement this feature, we added a new record to Linux kernel code. This record has the same structure as the "active" and "expired" records described in (Beck et al., 1998) and it holds the hidden processes.

When the last group finishes its execution, the medium-term scheduler is invoked, and rebuilds the process groups, taking into account any changes to the old processes (e.g. exited or stopped) and adding any new processes to the groups.

Sometimes the current group finishes executing all the processes within the time slice awarded to it by the medium-term scheduler. Even if there are still some processes in the group, these processes might be sleeping. If not all the processes in the group are ready to be executed, the Linux scheduler has been modified to invoke the medium-term scheduler, which promptly switches to the next waiting group.

The medium-term scheduler takes the sum of the memory sizes that are currently needed by the processes and divides this sum by the available physical memory size. The quotient is taken to be the number of bins. After that, the medium-term scheduler scatters the processes between these bins. The medium-term scheduler uses the greedy algorithm until the medium-term scheduler is unable to fit another process into the bins. Next, the medium-term scheduler tries to find room for all the remaining processes in the existing bins. If it fails to find room in one of the existing bins, it exceeds the size of the smallest bin by adding the unfitting process to it. The original Bin Packing problem does not allow such an excess, but in this case it might be preferable to have a few page faults within a group than adding an additional bin.

One of our assumptions for a working solution is that there exist a considerable number of processes for a good bin packing, and some small memory demands processes are even better. However, if one process demand is larger than the available memory size, the solution will not be effective and the process will thrash within itself. In fact, most of the thrashing cases are not caused by one process. However, if such a case does occur, none of the solutions that have been presented in section 1 can be useful. In such a case, only the original Linux solution that kills such a process will be beneficial, but it can be harmful if the process is essential.

Swapping Management

When the time slice of a group ends, a context switch of groups will be performed. This context switch will probably cause many page faults: The kernel uses its swap management to make room for the processes of the new group and this procedure might be long and fatiguing. The previous group of processes has most probably used up most of the available physical memory, and when the swap thread executes the LRU function to find the best pages to swap out to the disk, it will probably find pages of the old group. This procedure is wasteful because the paging function is performed separately for every new required page. Linux kernel does not know at the context switch time that the recently used pages of the previous group will not be needed for a long time, and can be swapped out.

In order to overcome this Linux kernel management, we modified Linux kernel as follow: when the medium-term scheduler is invoked, it calls the Linux swap management functions to swap out all of the pages that belong to the processes of the previous group. This gives Linux a significant amount of empty frames for the new group. This swapping management approach is much quicker than incrementally loading the pages of the new process group, and for each page fault searching for the oldest page in the physical memory to swap out. When a round of the medium-term scheduler is completed, the medium-term scheduler will rebuild the process groups and some processes may migrate from one group to another; hence the

medium-term scheduler does not call the Linux swap management at this point, because it might swap out pages that may be needed again for the next group.

Shared Memory

Often, two or more processes share some memory. Shared memory widely exists in most of the operating systems and Linux has some tools to handle it too.

When using the medium-term scheduler, it will be inefficient to put two processes that share a large piece of memory into two different groups of processes. For example, consider the following scenario:

Suppose processes A and B share a piece of memory, process A is of group #1 and process B is of group #3. After group #1 completes its execution, the pages of group #1 are swapped out and the pages of group #2 are loaded and placed in the physical memory instead, as we explained in the previous section. The same swapping happens when the operating system replaces group #2 by groups #3. The pages of process B are loaded by demand, so the same pages, albeit not all of them, are loaded and swapped twice, once for process A and once again for process B.

This situation is illogical and inefficient; hence, the medium-term scheduler must put processes with a large shared memory in the same group.

In order to tackle this situation we must know which processes share pages, and which pages they share. Each process that uses a page increments the "count" field of the page (Bovet and Cesati, 2003), so reading this field can easily let the Linux know which pages are shared. However, the medium-term scheduler must still know which processes use the page. A naive approach would be searching the page table of all the processes, in order to extract the addresses of the given pages. Obviously, this will be very time consuming and will probably impair the medium-term scheduler efficiency.

Figure 1. shared memory size of common processes

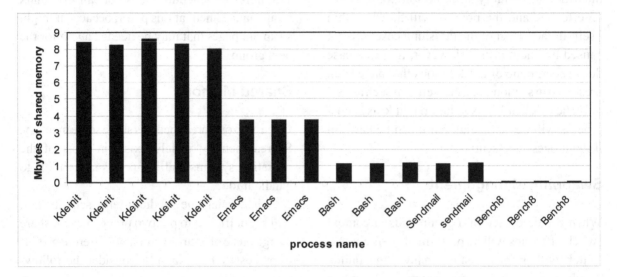

It frequently happens that applications which share a piece of memory will have an almost equal size of shared memory. If the shared memory stems from a 'fork' system call, the child process will be created from its parent; hence the size of the shared memory in the parent process and the child process will be almost equal, unless the child or the parents allocate a large piece of new shared memory. The same will be correct, if processes share an IPC or a common text segment. If there is no other shared memory obtained by just one the processes, the shared memory size will be almost equal.

Figure 1 shows the shared memory size in some common cases. The data was obtained from a running Linux machine that serves the Computer Science department in Bar-Ilan University. Many processes do not have shared memory and they have been omitted from the figure. However, when processes do share memory, it can be seen that they usually have the same size of shared memory.

Linux calculates the shared memory size of each process. Based on the shared size characteristic, we would like to suggest a simple solution for the issue of large shared memory. When the medium-term scheduler recalculates the bins of the processes, it will first sort the vector of the processes by the shared memory size. Then, using the greedy approximation, the processes with almost equal shared memory size will usually be in the same bin or in adjacent bins; hence no swapping will be needed when replacing the pages of two processes with shared memory.

We have chosen to use insertion sort for this. Since we use the old sorted list of processes, insertion sort is executed in the shortest time (Manber, 1989).

Group Time Slice

Sometimes we can be lucky and the sizes of the total memory needs in all the different groups are almost equal. This is the best situation, because a fixed time slice that will be given to the groups is usually quite fair. However, when the sizes of the total memory allocations are significantly different, some processes might get an implicit high priority. When the medium-term scheduler uses the greedy approximation, such a situation usually occurs when the last processes are assigned to a bin. The last bin is sometimes almost empty; hence the processes in this bin gain precedence, because in the time slice of this bin, there are less processes vying for CPU cycles. It should be noted that when the size of the last bin is not small, this solution will function efficiently.

One possible solution is breaking up small groups and scattering processes belong to the small groups in other groups. This solution can be good if the size of the small group is not big and when there is just one small group. If the size of the small group is big, scattering it might cause thrashing in the other groups.

A better solution can be a dynamic group time slices, instead of a constant time slice. E.g. if the size vector is [1,1,0.5] and the default group time slice is one second, the medium-term scheduler should assign each of the first two groups one second, whereas the last group will get only 0.5 second. (The vector represents the group's memory size as the total memory allocations divided by the total memory available for user application). This solution gave us the best results; therefore it has been implemented.

Interactive Processes

The interactive processes should be dealt with differently. If we treat them the same way as the non-interactive processes, they will not be able to be executed as long as their group is not current. Interactive processes need fast response time and a few seconds delay can be a major drawback.

To remedy this drawback, the scheduler allows an interactive process which can be identified by directly quantifying the I/O between an application and the user (keyboard, mouse and screen activity) (Etsion et al., 2004), to run in each of the process groups. So, actually the process will belong to all the groups, but with a smaller time slice in each group:

p->time_slice = time_slice(p)/num_of_groups;

This feature can assure us a short response time for interactive processes while keeping fairness towards other processes. The resident

pages of interactive processes will be marked as low priority swappable, so the kernel will not swap out interactive processes when a group context switch is done. However, the scheduler has to calculate the memory needs of interactive processes in every group.

When a new process is admitted, it will be handled as an interactive process. The operating system cannot know whether the new process is interactive and if the execution of this process is delayed, it will be irritating for interactive processes. After one round of the bins, the scheduler can assess the nature of the process and treat it accordingly.

Real Time Processes

The handling of real time processes is somewhat similar to interactive processes. Real time processes must get the CPU as fast as possible. The management of these processes will be the same as interactive processes, but with a slight difference. Real time processes will belong to all the groups, as the interactive processes do, but they will not have a shrunken time slice.

The kernel will not swap out Real time processes, because they belong to all the groups. In addition, Real time processes will have the same privilege Linux traditionally gives them. It should be noted that the scheduler has to calculate their memory needs in every group as the scheduler did for the interactive processes. This handling is identical for FIFO Real-Time processes and for RR Real-Time processes. This treatment has also been applied to the "init" process and the "Idle and Swapper" process of Linux, which cannot be suspended.

Priority

Another important issue of the bin packing scheduling discussion is the priority management. Hypothetically, it might happen that the highest priority processes belong to one group, whereas the lowest priority processes belong to another. Then, when Linux switches between the processes within the groups, the priority is not taken into account.

One solution can be finding out how many bins there should be, by calculating the total size of the memory needs and dividing by the size of the available physical memory (The size of the bin), just as the medium-term scheduler always does. Then, sorting the process list by priority, and finally, taking the processes from the sorted list and filling the bins in a Round-Robin manner. This solution cannot be implemented together with the shared pages solution, because the shared pages solution requires sorting by the number of the shared pages, rather than by the priority.

Another solution is assigning different time slice to each group, according to the average priority of the processes inside the group. For each group the average priority is calculated. A group having a high average priority will be awarded a longer time slice. This solution was chosen based on the results that are shown in section 5.4.

PERFORMANCE RESULTS

Actually, the best way to evaluate the medium term scheduler is by considering its performance results. In the following subsections, an extensive evaluation that has been made to the medium term scheduler is described.

TESTBED

We tested the performance of the kernel with the new scheduling approach using five different benchmarks to get the widest view we could:

1. SPEC – cpu2000 (SPEC, 2000). The SPEC manual explicitly notes that attempting to run the suite with less than 256Mbytes of memory will cause a measuring of the paging system speed instead of the CPU speed. This suits us well, because our aim is precisely to measure the paging system speed; hence, we used a machine with just 128MB of RAM. Using machine with a larger RAM would have been forced us not to use SPEC.

2. A synthetic benchmark that forks processes which demand a constant number of pages – 8MBytes. The processes use the memory in a random access; therefore they cause thrashing. This benchmark was tested within the range of 16MBytes-136MBytes. The parent process forks processes whose total size is the required one, and collects the information from the children. Let us denote this test by SYN8.

3. Matlab formal benchmark. This benchmark executes six different Matlab tasks described in (MATLAB, 2004).

4. Another synthetic benchmark using massive shared memory allocations. The test has two processes that share 16MBytes and has 2 more Mbytes for each one of the processes. The processes copy parts of their private memory into the shared memory and parts of the shared memory into their private memory in a random access. The benchmark consists of a number of such tests according to the desired size. Let us denote this test as SYNSHARED.

5. For interactive and real-time processes, we used the Xine MPEG viewer. It was used to show a short video clip in a loop.

The benchmarks were executed on a Pentium 2.4GHz with 128MB RAM and a cache of 1MB running Linux kernel 2.6.9 with Fedora core 2 distribution. The size of the page was 4KBytes. It should be noted that even though the platform machine had 128MBytes of physical memory, we should take into the bin size considerations that a certain portion of this memory is occupied by the daemons of Linux/RedHat and the X-windows, plus the kernel itself along with its threads. After

Figure 2. a. SYN8's Number of Swaps; b. SYN8's Execution Time

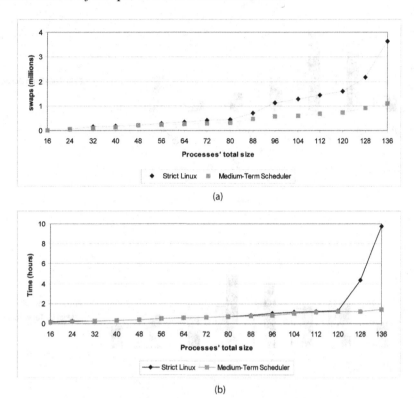

(a)

(b)

an evaluation of the extra size, we used bins of 96MBytes.

Execution Time

Figure 2a and Figure 2b show the performance of the synthetic benchmark SYN8. Figure 2a shows the number of swaps that were performed in both the schedulers as a function of the total size of the processes, whereas Figure 2b shows the execution time of SYN8 as a function of the same processes' total size. In these figures, the medium-term scheduler time slice was one second.

It can be seen that when the size of the processes is too large, Linux starts swapping in and out many more pages. From roughly 64MB Linux swaps more pages, but there is no noteworthy influence on the I/O time, because Linux lets other processes run while the I/O is performed. Roughly, from 128MB the I/O buffer is incapable

of responding to all the paging requests, and the thrashing becomes acute. The medium-term scheduler dramatically reduces the number of the page faults; thus, fewer swaps are performed and the execution time remains reasonable. Processes that require 144MB or more were sustainable for the medium-term scheduler, but not for the Linux scheduler.

We also employed Matlab formal benchmark. Matlab benchmark is a very memory consuming process. It takes about 290MB with Matlab 7.0.0.19901 (R14) running on our Linux 2.6.9 machine, but when memory pressure becomes high, Matlab will be able to continue working when just 28MB are resident in the physical memory, whereas 14MB of them are shared memory with other possible Matlab processes. When we executed several Matlab processes in parallel, the results were very similar to the synthetic benchmark. However, a significantly larger portion of

Figure 3. a. SPEC's Number of Swaps; b. SPEC's Execution Time

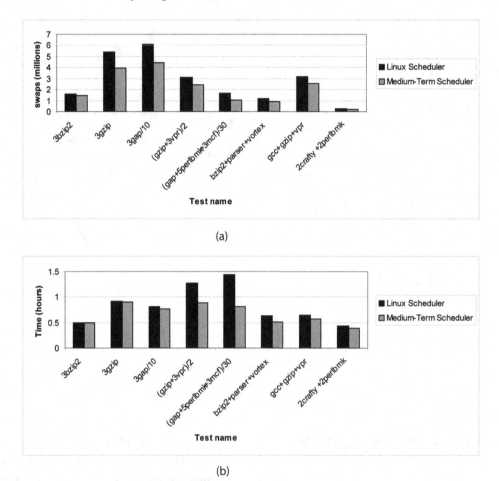

(a)

(b)

the swap area was necessary, because just 14MB out of each Matlab process was physically in the internal memory and the other memory allocations (except of the shared allocation) of the Matlab processes were in the swap area. We preferred no to reshow the results that are almost the same as Figure 2a and 2b and instead to show in the next figures different benchmarks results.

Figure 3a and Figure 3b show the performance of the medium-term scheduler vs. the Linux kernel using the tests of SPEC cpu2000 benchmarks. The prefix 3 (or 2) before the test name indicates that we iterated the test 3 (or 2) times. Sometimes we divided the numbers by some constants in order to fit the data to the scale of the diagram. These

constants are denoted as Test/Constant. When we used more than one test, we added a '+' sign between the names of the tests.

When each group contains just a few memory-consuming processes, the idle task might be invoked too often, even though there are other processes in other groups that can be executed. This can reduce the time saved by eliminating the thrashing effect. When a test has large memory allocations and is executed in a different group, the results will not as good as when executing several smaller SPEC tests concurrently in one group. A higher idle time will be emerged when the content of each group is just one process; thus the results of Figures 3a and 3b are not as good

Figure 4. a. Time Slice's Effect on Number of Swaps; b. Time Slice's Effect on Execution Time

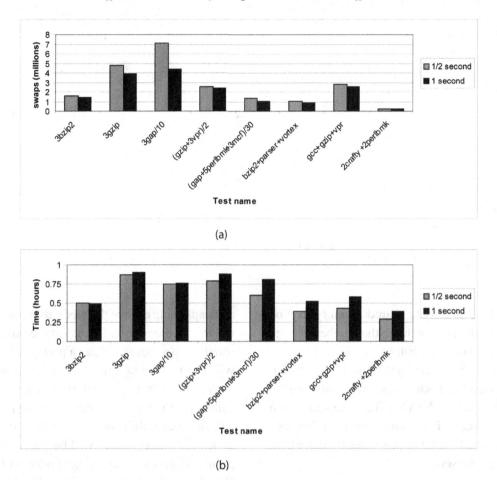

(a)

(b)

as the results of Figures 2a and 2b. However, the elimination of the thrashing saved more time than was wasted idling, and the medium-term scheduler still outperforms the traditional Linux scheduler.

Figure 4a and Figure 4b show the effect of the medium-term scheduler time slice on the process' execution time. The tests were conducted using SPEC. It can be seen that when the time slice exceeds a certain limit, the execution time might suffer. This damage is caused by the higher average idle time. When the number of processes per group is too small, it may happen that none of the processes in the current group is on the Ready queue. Such a case may happen due to many I/O operations. Clearly, this might turn out

with a lower group time slice as well, but it will not happen as often as with a higher time slice, because at the beginning of the time slice all the processes are usually ready to run and not waiting for an I/O.

When the time slice is higher, the cycle will be longer. An extremely high time slice will actually make the medium-term scheduler behave like a FIFO scheduler. On the other hand, the page faults rate is lower for the one-second scheduler, because of the longer time slice. Pages are usually swapped out when the group context is switched, so if all the pages are replaced on context switch, the half-a-second scheduler should have double number of pages faults comparing to the one-second scheduler. However, sometimes the bins

Figure 5. Execution Time as a Function of Processes' Total Size

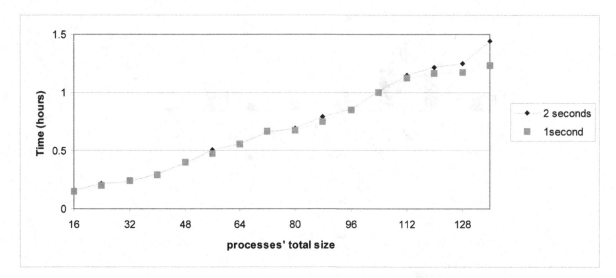

are not full, and some shared memory can be present, so the ratio between the number of page faults is actually less than two.

Figure 5 shows the same time slices but with more processes. This test was conducted using the synthetic benchmark SYN8. It can be clearly seen that the effect of increasing time slice damages the execution time when processes for more than one bin are present.

The Bin Packing Approximations

There are more than a few approximations for the Bin-Packing optimal solution. Some of them have been mentioned in section 3. Figure 6a and Figure 6b compare two of these approximations. The First-Fit Approximation (Also known as the greedy approximation) is described in section 4.1. The Best-Fit Approximation finds for each process the most unfilled bin and put the process in it.

When there is almost no shared memory, the performance of both of the methods will be almost the same. However, when a significant amount of shared memory is allocated, the First-Fit approach outperforms the Best-Fit approach. The benchmark that was used in Figures 6a and 6b is SYNSHARED. Figure 6a compares the number

of swaps using each of the methods. First Fit sorts the processes according to their shared size; hence usually processes that share a portion of memory will be in the same group. As was explained in section 4.3 processes that share memory typically have the same number of shared pages. As a result, they will be in adjacent positions in the sorted list and probably will be put in the same group. Therefore, less page faults will occur. Best-Fit cannot guarantee this quality; hence, the performance will not be as good as the First-Fit performance. The higher number of page faults causes a longer execution time as can be seen in Figure 6b.

Priority Implementation Evaluation

The priority can be implemented by another approximation which first determines how many bins should be. Next, it sorts the processes by their priority and finally, it fills the bins in a Round-Robin manner. This method can scatter the higher priority processes (and the lower priority processes) among the bins, more or less equally. However, the shared memory handling requires a sorting by the shared size; hence, if there are many processes with shared memory

Figure 6. a. Number of swaps using best fit or first fit; b. Execution time using best fit or first fit

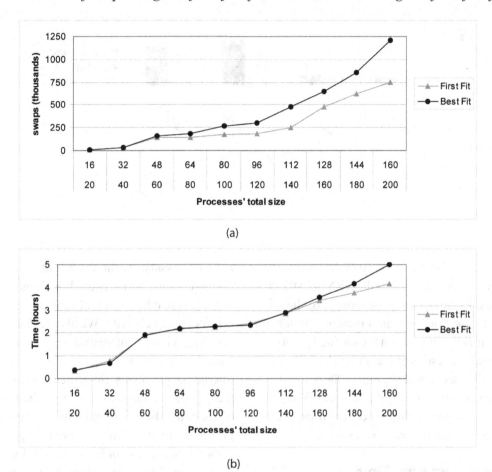

(a)

(b)

allocations, this approach can lengthen the execution time.

Another approach implements the priority by dynamically changing the time slice according to the average priority of the processes in the group. This approach sorts the processes by their shared memory sizes and builds bins using a First-Fit version that has been introduced above. Actually, this approach performs the same procedure of building the bins, but each group gets a dynamically different time slice, according to the average priority of the group. The medium-term scheduler calculates the global average priority of all the processes currently run and the average priority of the processes in each group. Next, it calculates the difference between the average of each group and the global average. Let us denote this vector of differences as D and the global average priorities of all the processes as P. Then, the medium-term scheduler gives each group $(D[i]+P)/P*TS$ where TS is the default group time slice and i is the index the group.

Figure 7 shows the differences between the approaches. We used the SPEC benchmark. We took in each test one process and we awarded it the highest priority: -20. We always took another process and demoted its priority to the lowest one: 19. The tests are written on the X-axis. The promoted test is written below. We did not change any other process' priority. The default group slice time was one second.

Figure 7. Different Sorting Strategies of the Medium Term Scheduler

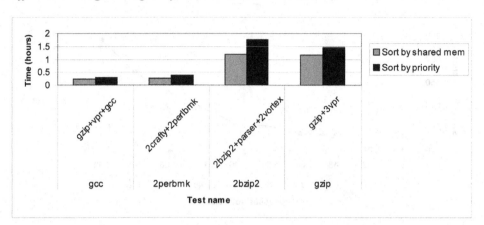

The differences between the two strategies can be clearly shown when using the SYNSHARED benchmark. Because of the massive use of shared memory, the sorting by shared memory strategy will dramatically outperform the sorting by priority strategy. The results of the SYNSHARED are shown in Figures 8a and 8b. Figure 8a shows the influence of the strategies on the number of swaps. This is quite a dramatic difference. The difference of the execution time is notable as well.

Interactive and Real Time Implementation Evaluation

The interactive and real time processes were checked using the Xine movie player. It is a well-known MPEG player on Linux machines. We configured Xine to play a short video clip in a loop. The memory needs of Xine are much lower than the physical RAM we had in our machine. In order to check that Xine will continue to respond even when the memory is overloaded, we deliberately overfilled the memory by executing many copies of SYN8. The results of this test can be found in Figure 9. When the movie player process is not handled as an interactive process, many frames are lost. When Xine's bin is not active, no CPU time is given and no frames can be displayed. Even when a CPU time is given, if the slice is

reduced because of the overall load, sometimes the given slice is not enough and just when the process is handled as a real-time process, a good result can be achieved. We also reniced Xine by -20. This yielded interesting results. The results were better than the interactive mode, because interactive processes' time slice is reduced when there are too many bins, whereas the reductions of the time slice of bins include a high priority process is smaller. On the other hand, a high priority process does not have the privileges Linux gives to real-time processes, so the results are worse than real-time mode.

CONCLUSION

The scheduling approach of the new proposed scheduler is built on the simple concept of adding another layer of scheduling. The experimental results are promising. Given a high memory pressure caused by some processes, the medium-term scheduler will be able to significantly reduce the thrashing overhead. In addition, no performance reduction has been generated when the memory load is low and no swapping is needed. The medium-term scheduler has been written as a kernel patch; therefore it can be easily installed on any Linux machine. If a user decides to install

Figure 8. a. SYNSHARED's number of swaps with different sorting methods; b. SYNSHARED's Execution time with different sorting methods

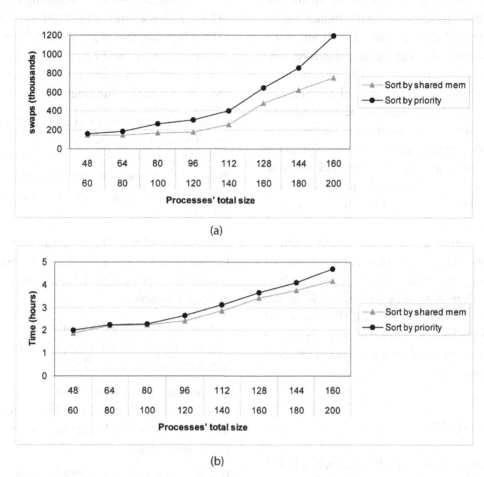

(a)

(b)

Figure 9. Frame loss as function of the number of bins

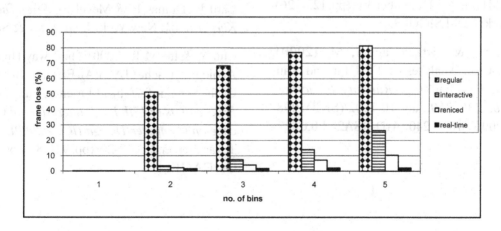

this patch, the patch can help the machine handling a massive paging in a thrashing situation in a more tolerant means than the traditional way of Linux that was killing processes. Moreover, the responsiveness of the machine keeps being reasonable for heavier memory load. The medium-term scheduler does not require special resources or extensive needs; therefore, it can be easily adapted by almost any Linux machines. Furthermore, there is no prevention from implementing the medium-term scheduler on a parallel machine or a cluster; hence, heavy load projects like the Human Genome Project can benefit from the new scheduling strategic.

In the future, we would like to find a pattern for memory usage reoccurrence. Such a pattern can improve the efficiency of the scheduling decisions. Some applications like (Wiseman et al., 2004), (Wiseman, 2001), (Wiseman and Klein, 2003) have a pattern of memory usage reoccurrence and the Operating System can take an advantage of it.

REFERENCES

Abrossimov, V., Rozier, M., & Shapiro, M. (1989). Virtual Memory Management for Operating System Kernels. In *Proceedings of the 12th ACM Symposium on Operating Systems Principles*, Litchfield Park, AZ, December 3-6, (pp. 123-126). New-York: ACM SIGOPS.

Albers, S., & Mitzenmacher, M. (2000). Average-Case Analyses of First Fit and Random Fit Bin Packing. *Random Structures Alg.*, *16*, 240–259. doi:10.1002/(SICI)1098-2418(200005)16:3<240::AID-RSA2>3.0.CO;2-V

Alverson, G., Kahan, S., Korry, R., McCann, C., & Smith, B. (1995). Scheduling on the Tera MTA. In *Proceedings of the 1st Workshop on Job Scheduling Strategies for Parallel Processing, In Conjunction with IPPS '95* Fess Parker's Red Lion Resort, Santa Barbara, California, April 25, (pp. 19-44). Berlin: Springer-Verlag.

Batat, A., & Feitelson, D. G. (2000). Gang scheduling with memory considerations. In *Proceedings of the 14th International Parallel and Distributed Processing Symposium (IPDPS'2000)*, Cancun, Mexico, May 1-5, (pp. 109-114). Los Alamitos, CA: IEEE.

Beck, M., Bohme, H., Dziadzka, M., Kunitz, U., Magnus, R., & Verworner, D. (1998). *Linux Kernel Internals* (2nd Ed.). Harlow, MA: Addison Wesley, Longman

Belady, L. A. (1966). A Study of Replacement Algorithms for Virtual Storage Computers. *IBM Systems Journal*, *5*(2), 78–101.

Benchmark, B. E. N. C. H.-M. A. T. L. A. B. (2004). *Matlab Performance Tests*. Natick, MA: The MathWorks, Inc. Retrieved from http://www.mathworks.com/

Bovet, D., & Cesati, M. (2003). *Undersatnding the Linux Kernel*, (2nd Ed.). Sebastopol, CA: O'Reilly Press.

Card, R., Dumas, E., & Mevel, F. (1998). *The Linux Kernel Book*. New York: John Wiley & Sons.

Chu, Y., & Ito, M. R. (2000). The 2-way Thrashing-Avoidance Cache (TAC): An Efficient Instruction Cache Scheme for Object-Oriented Languages. In *Proceedings of 17th IEEE International Conference on Computer Design (ICCD2000)*, Austin, Texas, September 17-20, (pp. 93-98). Los Alamitos, CA: IEEE.

Coffman, E. G., Jr., Garey, M. R., & Johnson, D. S. (1997). Approximation Algorithms for Bin Packing: A Survey. In D. Hochbaum (ed.), *Approximation Algorithms for NP-Hard Problems,* (pp. 46-93). Boston: PWS Publishing.

Denning, P. (1970). Virtual Memory. [CSUR]. *ACM Computing Surveys*, *2*(3), 153–189. doi:10.1145/356571.356573

Etsion, Y., Tsafrir, D., & Feitelson, D. G. (2004). Desktop Scheduling: How Can We Know What the User Wants? In *Proceedings of the 14th ACM International Workshop on Network & Operating Systems Support for Digital Audio & Video (NOSSDAV'2004)*, Cork, Ireland, June 16-18, (pp. 110-115). New York: ACM.

Fekete, S. P., & Schepers, J. (2001). New Classes of Fast Lower Bounds for Bin Packing Problems. *Mathematical Programming*, *91*(1), 11–31.

Galvin, P. B., & Silberschatz, A. (1998). *Operating System Concepts* (6th Ed.). Harlow, MA: Addison Wesley Longman.

Gent, I. (1998). Heuristic Solution of Open Bin Packing Problems. *Journal of Heuristics*, *3*, 299–304. doi:10.1023/A:1009678411503

Gonzalez, A., Valero, M., Topham, N., & Parcerisa, J. M. (1997). Eliminating Cache Conflict Misses through XOR-Based Placement Functions. In *Proceedings of the International Conference on Supercomputing*, Vienna, Austria, July 7-11, (pp. 76-83). New-York: ACM.

Gorman, M. (2004). *Understanding The Linux Virtual Memory Management* (Bruce Peren's Open Book Series).

Jiang, S., & Zhang, X. (2001). Adaptive Page Replacement to Protect Thrashing in Linux. In *Proceedings of the 5th USENIX Annual Linux Showcase and Conference, (ALS'01)*, Oakland, California, November 5-10, (pp. 143-151). Berkeley, CA: USENIX.

Jiang, S., & Zhang, X. (2002). TPF: a System Thrashing Protection Facility. *Software, Practice & Experience*, *32*(3), 295–318. doi:10.1002/spe.437

Jiang, S., & Zhang, X. (2005). Token-ordered LRU: An Effective Page Replacement Policy and Implementation in Linux systems. *Performance Evaluation*, *60*(1-4), 5–29. doi:10.1016/j.peva.2004.10.002

Karp, R. M. (1972). Reducibility Among Combinatorial Problems. In R.E. Miller & J.M. Thatcher, (Eds.) *Complexity of Computer Computations*, (pp. 85-103). New York: Plenum Press.

Klein, S. T., & Wiseman, Y. (2003). Parallel Huffman Decoding with Applications to JPEG Files. *The Computer Journal*, *46*(5), 487–497. doi:10.1093/comjnl/46.5.487

Komarinski, M. F., & Collett, C. (1998). *Linux System Administration Handbook*. Upper Saddle River, NJ: Prentice Hall.

Manber, U. (1989). *Introduction to Algorithms – A Creative Approach,* (pp.130-131). Harlow, MA: Addison-Wesley.

Martello, S., & Toth, P. (1990). Lower Bounds and Reduction Procedures for the Bin Packing Problem. *Discrete Applied Mathematics*, *28*, 59–70. doi:10.1016/0166-218X(90)90094-S

Marti, D. (2002). System Development Jump Start Class. *Linux Journal, 7*.

Nikolopoulos, D. S. (2003). Malleable Memory Mapping: User-Level Control of Memory Bounds for Effective Program Adaptation. In *Proceedings of the 17th International Parallel and Distributed Processing Symposium (IPDPS'2003)*, Nice, France, April 22-26, [CD-ROM]. Los Alamitos, CA: IEEE.

Reuven, M., & Wiseman, Y. (2005). *Reducing the Thrashing Effect Using Bin Packing, Proc. IASTED Modeling, Simulation, and Optimization Conference*, MSO-2005, Oranjestad, Aruba, (pp. 5-10).

Reuven, M., & Wiseman, Y. (2006). Medium-Term Scheduler as a Solution for the Thrashing Effect. *The Computer Journal*, *49*(3), 297–309. doi:10.1093/comjnl/bxl001

Scholl, A., Klein, R., & Jurgens, C. (1997). BISON: A Fast Hybrid Procedure for Exactly Solving the One-Dimensional Bin Packing Problem. *Computers & Operations Research*, *24*, 627–645. doi:10.1016/S0305-0548(96)00082-2

SPEC. (2000). CPU-2000. *Standard Performance Evaluation Corporation, Warrenton, VA*. Retrieved from http://www.spec.org/

Stallings, W. (1998). *Operating Systems Internals and Design Principles*, (3rd Ed., p. 383). Upper Saddle River, NJ: Prentice-Hall.

Vahalia, U. (1996). *UNIX Internals: The New Frontiers* (pp. 112-148). Upper Saddle River, NJ: Prentice Hall.

Wiseman, Y. (2001). A Pipeline Chip for Quasi Arithmetic Coding. *IEICE Journal - Trans. Fundamentals, Tokyo, Japan . E (Norwalk, Conn.)*, *84-A*(4), 1034–1041.

Wiseman, Y., & Feitelson, D. G. (2003). Paired Gang Scheduling. *IEEE Transactions on Parallel and Distributed Systems*, *14*(6), 581–592. doi:10.1109/TPDS.2003.1206505

Wiseman, Y., Schwan, K., & Widener, P. (2004). Efficient End to End Data Exchange Using Configurable Compression. In *Proc. The 24th IEEE Conference on Distributed Computing Systems (ICDCS 2004)*, Tokyo, Japan, (pp. 228-235).

Zahorjan, J., Lazowsk, E., & Eager, D. (1991). The Effect of Scheduling Discipline on Spin Overhead in Shared Memory Multiprocessors. *IEEE Transactions on Parallel and Distributed Systems*, *2*(2), 180–198. doi:10.1109/71.89064

Zhou, P., Pandey, V., Sundaresan, J., Raghuraman, A., Zhou, Y., & Kumar, S. (2004). Dynamically Tracking Miss-Ratio-Curve for Memory Management. In *Proceedings of the Eleventh International Conference on Architectural Support for Programming Languages and Operating Systems (ASPLOS'04)*, Boston, MA, October 7-13, (pp.177-188). New York: ACM.

Section 3
Systems Profiling

Chapter 8
The Exokernel Operating System and Active Networks

Timothy R. Leschke
University of Maryland, Baltimore County, USA

ABSTRACT

There are two forces that are demanding a change in the traditional design of operating systems. One force requires a more flexible operating system that can accommodate the evolving requirements of new hardware and new user applications. The other force requires an operating system that is fast enough to keep pace with faster hardware and faster communication speeds. If a radical change in operating system design is not implemented soon, the traditional operating system will become the performance bottle-neck for computers in the very near future. The Exokernel Operating System, developed at the Massachusetts Institute of Technology, is an operating system that meets the needs of increased speed and increased flexibility. The Exokernel is extensible, which means that it is easily modified. The Exokernel can be easily modified to meet the requirements of the latest hardware or user applications. Ease in modification also means the Exokernel's performance can be optimized to meet the speed requirements of faster hardware and faster communication. In this chapter, the author explores some details of the Exokernel Operating System. He also explores Active Networking, which is a technology that exploits the extensibility of the Exokernel. His investigation reveals the strengths of the Exokernel as well as some of its design concerns. He concludes his discussion by embracing the Exokernel Operating System and by encouraging more research into this approach to operating system design.

INTRODUCTION

The traditional operating system (OS) is seen as providing both management and protection of resources. As a manager, the OS controls how resources such as I/O devices, file-storage space, memory space, and CPU time get allocated. As a protector, the traditional OS controls how processes use these resources to avoid errors. Because the operating system's role is so important, it is the one

DOI: 10.4018/978-1-60566-850-5.ch008

program that is always running on a computer. The heart of the operating system is called the *kernel*.

Within a traditional computer system, the complexity of the hardware is masked behind the abstractions provided by the operating system. Although this abstraction prevents user programs from interacting with the hardware directly, user programs benefit by having a single interface that they can interact with. It is easier for a user program to interact with one operating system interface rather than developing software that must know how to interact with the different hardware components that could be present within a computer system at any one time. Because the operating system is the main interface between user programs and the raw hardware, the traditional operating system must be involved in every software-hardware interaction.

Although the traditional operating system is desirable because it provides a single interface for other software to interact with, it is ironic that this efficient interface should be the root cause of the modern computer system's performance bottleneck. By presenting a single interface to user applications, the traditional operating system is the middle-man between all user processes and the computer hardware. By being the middle-man, the operating system tries to be all-things to all-processes. This "all-things to all-processes" approach is precisely why the design of the traditional operating system is flawed. So long as the operating system is designed to meet the minimum of a broad spectrum of operational requirements, the optimization of any one process is very unlikely. Therefore, while every application might run on a traditional operating system, few applications run well (reaches it maximum performance level) on a traditional operating system.

A team of researchers at the Massachusetts Institute of Technology (MIT) has challenged the traditional operating system design with their experimental operating system - the Exokernel Operating System. Their new approach is to separate

management of resources from the protection of those resources. The Exokernel Operating System provides only protection and multiplexing of resources while allowing user processes themselves to provide the management and optimization of that resource. As Engler, Kaashoek, and O'Toole say "Applications know better than operating systems what the goal of their resource management decisions should be and therefore, they should be given as much control as possible over those decisions" (Engler, Kaashoek, & O'Toole, 1995). By separating management from protection, the abstraction provided by the traditional operating system has been eliminated. Likewise, the door to process optimization has been opened and great advances in operating system speed and flexibility have become possible.

As we investigate the Exokernel Operating System, we will discuss how it is possible to separate management from protection while still multiplexing resources within a secure environment. We will discuss select Exokernel functions such as downloading code into the kernel, reading and writing to disk memory, exception and interrupt handling, interprocess communication, tracking resource ownership, protecting and revoking resource usage, and resource management. Networking with an Exokernel will be discussed as we look at packet sending, packet receiving, the naming and routing of packets, and network error reporting. Lastly, as an example of other technologies that benefit from the Exokernel, we will briefly explore the emerging technology of Active Networking and see how the Exokernel is the ideal operating system upon which to build this new technology.

In response to the Exokernel, we will investigate why the Exokernel has not been widely accepted as the main-stream approach to Operating System design. We will investigate the potential issues with providing customer support to an extensible operating system like the Exokernel. We will argue against removing *all* management from the kernel. We will discuss code optimization and who is best suited for this task. We will concede that some processes - like multithreaded applications - perform worse in an Ekokernel environment. We will finally question if extensibility is even the solution to the growing problem of operating systems becoming the bottleneck of computer system performance. We will conclude that despite some of the issues that make the Exokernel commercially unacceptable at this time, the Exokernel's enhancements outweigh its shortcomings and therefore we encourage the reader to embrace its approach.

PROBLEM DESCRIPTION

The need for a new operating system design has been motivated by two forces - the need for speed and the need for flexibility. These two forces are explained next.

The Need for Flexibility

Trying to define the term "operating system" is an ongoing debate. Some say the operating system is simply that software program that sits between the hardware and the other user programs. It is that program that provides a simple interface that allows processes to interact with the hardware. Others say the operating system is the manager and protector of computer resources. It manages how every computer resource gets used and also protects the resources against improper use.

Some have argued that an operating system is defined by the manufacturer. As was stated previously, an operating system is "whatever comes in the box when it is purchased" (Leschke, 2004). This means that if a user-manual is included in the package, then the user-manual is a formal part of the operating system. Furthermore, whatever software is bundled-with or integrated-with the operating system is also a part of the operating system. For example, if a text editor or an entire suite of office application software is integrated

into the operating system, then these items must also be considered to be part of the definition of an operating system.

Regardless of which definition of an operating system you agree with, we must all agree that the traditional operating system is that program that abstracts the hardware and offers the user a single interface with which to interact with. It is this single interface approach that has the traditional operating system literally caught in the middle between two different forces. One force is the need for a more flexible operating system. As 64 bit processors replace 32 bit processors, the need for an operating system that can interact with this new hardware has grown. Larger memory devices - such as hard drives that are now measured in terrabytes - as well as fiber-optic networks, high-bandwidth networks, and new data storage devices, have also demanded a more flexible operating system.

In addition to the flexibility demands being made by hardware, software applications are also demanding a more flexible operating system to meet their needs. For example, realistic gaming programs are requiring access to hardware in non-traditional ways. Portable computing and communication devices are requiring the ability to up-load and down-load data more easily. Database systems want to be able to access memory in their own ways, and real-time systems demand a specific performance level that can be best achieved through a flexible operating system. All of these have combined into one force that is demanding the traditional operating system become more flexible to change.

The traditional operating system could be pulled-apart by these forces if it continues to remain rigid in its design. Therefore, the traditional operating system needs a more flexible design.

The Need for Speed

Gene Amdahl has provided us with "Amdahl's Law" - one of the fundamental laws of computer architecture. His law states that the increased speed that is gained by using an improved mode of execution is restricted by how much the new mode is actually used. For example, if an execution mode that is used 10% of the time is modified to be 100% faster, the entire efficiency of the system will only increase by about 5%. On the other hand, if a mode of execution that is used 90% of the time is modified to be 50% faster than it was before, the entire system will experience a 45% increase in efficiency. This means that a small improvement in a mode of execution that is used frequently will have a much larger impact on performance than a large improvement made in a mode of execution that is seldom used. If one wants to have the greatest impact on the efficiency of a system, one should try to improve those processes that account for the greatest share of the execution time. This means designers of computer systems must pay attention to changes in technology, identify those technologies that have had the greatest speed-up, and then make sure the old technologies that the new technology has to interact with do not impede the speed-up gained by the new technology.

As an example, the Central Processing Unit (CPU) is one of those technologies that enjoyed some great improvement in the recent past. Although the speed and capacity of the newest CPUs - as well as other key hardware components - have been increasing, if the rest of the computer system cannot keep pace with this increase, then the full benefit of the increase will not be realized. Just like the CPU, another part of the computer system that might not be keeping pace with the ever increasing speeds of hardware is the Operating System. As Engler, Kaashoek, and O'Toole explain, "Traditional operating systems limit the performance, flexibility, and functionality of applications by fixing the interface and implementation of operating system abstractions such as interprocess communication and virtual memory" (Engler, Kaashoek, & O'Toole, 1995). Furthermore, as another example, John Ousterhout

states "Operating systems derived from UNIX use caches to speed up reads, but they require synchronous disk I/O of operations that modify files. If this coupling isn't eliminated, a large class of file-intensive programs will receive little or no benefit form faster hardware" (Ousterhout, 1989). The new era of operating system design demands that operating systems keep pace with faster hardware or risk being the cause of computer system speeds being stagnant.

The Approach

As Lee Carver and others state, an operating system is a necessary evil (Carver, Chen, & Reyes, 1998). Therefore, computers will have an operating system of one sort or another. The growing requirements that operating systems become faster and more flexible have encouraged many researchers to consider operating systems with radical designs. One of the new designs is an extensible operating system.

An extensible operating system is simply an operating system that is flexible to change. The needs of the underlying hardware can be better met by an operating system that can be easily modified. The needs of the user applications can also be better met by an operating system that can be easily modified. Speed is achieved by an extensible operating system because the system can be easily changed and optimized. The speed and flexibility issue are both addressed by an extensible operating system. By providing the hope of increased speed and a more flexible implementation, the approach offered by an extensible operating system, at least momentarily, seems to be one way to prevent the increased speed of computer systems from becoming stagnant while also addressing the rapidly changing needs of user applications.

A group of researchers at the Massachusetts Institute of Technology have implemented their version of the extensible operating system in what they have called the Exokernel Operating System.

The main approach of the Exokernel is to attempt a very clear separation between management and protection of resources. Management is left to the user processes - because user processes themselves know how to better utilize the resources under their control. Protection of the resources is provided by the Exokernel, but in a very minimal amount so as not to interfere with any attempts to optimize the user processes. The end result is an operating system that is easily modified to meet the changing needs of user processes while also allowing real optimizations to occur - which result in major speed-ups in process execution times. We will be taking a closer look at the separation of management from protection as we investigate the Exokernel Operating System.

THE EXOKERNEL SOLUTION

Previously we stated the Exokernel only provides protection and proper sharing of resources. According to Dawson Engler, the process of protecting resources consists of three major tasks; 1) tracking ownership of resources, 2) ensuring protection by guarding all resource usage or binding points, and 3) revoking access to resources (Engler, 1998). Lesser tasks of the Exokernel include; protecting a processes ability to execute privileged instructions, protecting the processing of the central processing unit, and protecting physical memory - which includes writes to "special" memory locations that are used by devices, and protection of network devices. We stress that while the Exokernel is providing protection of these activities, it is not getting involved in the micro-management of these activities. The micro-management of these activities is provided by user-processes that are located in user-space rather than kernel space. In other words, the Exokernel will grant a user-process access to a resource, and it might revoke that access if necessary, however, it does not regulate how the resource is used. This means that a user-process could use a resource

improperly if it wanted to, but it also means the user-process has the freedom to optimize how the resource is utilized. This added freedom means software engineers need to develop computer programs that police themselves to ensure that the shared resources provided by an Exokernel are used properly.

Dawson Engler provides a better example of the separation of management from protection as he explains how the Exokernel protects physical memory. The accessing of physical memory through read and write requests are *privileged* instructions for a traditional operating system. The traditional kernel stands guard over the memory and verifies every read/write request to ensure each request has the proper access rights. Because the traditional operating system stands between the user-processes and the physical hardware, when a user-process wants to send a message to the hardware, it passes the message to the traditional operating system and the operating system then passes the message to the hardware on behalf of the user process. When a user-process passes a message to the operating system in this manner, it is called a system-call. One of the down-sides of the traditional system-call is that user-processes cannot directly execute privileged instructions. Because the traditional operating system is the constant middle-man that gets involved in every system-call, the overall efficiency within the entire computer system is greatly reduced.

In response to the issue of reduced global efficiency, Dawson Engler explains that the Exokernel's solution is "to make traditionally privileged code unprivileged by limiting the duties of the kernel to just these required for protection" (Engler, 1998). This means that the Exokernel allows user-processes to have much more direct access to memory. The Exokernel still gets involved a little, but only enough to ensure the memory access is "safe". Once safety is guaranteed, a user-process is allowed to directly access the hardware itself.

In the next pages, we continue to illuminate some of the unique aspects of the Exokernel Operating System. The aspects that we have chosen to look at are by no means a comprehensive list, but they are intended to leave the reader with a good understanding of the Exokernel's approach.

Tracking Ownership of Resources

The allocation of a resource is actually accomplished by what the research group calls the Library Operating System (LibOS). This LibOS is outside of the kernel; therefore the kernel is only minimally involved. The kernel gets involved just enough to record the ownership information associated with a resource. For example, when physical memory gets allocated, the kernel keeps track of which process the resource has been allocated to and which processes have 'read' and 'write' permissions (Engler, 1998). As a way to retain its minimal involvement, the Exokernel records resource allocations in what the research group calls an *open bookkeeping policy*. Through this open bookkeeping policy, as Engler explains, resource allocation records are made available to all user processes in read-only mode. This allows the user processes to look-up for themselves if the resource that they want is actually available. This means the kernel does not need to be interrupted by a process that keeps requesting a resource that is currently unavailable.

Ensuring Protection by Guarding all Resource Usage or Binding Points

It is very important for a process to retain use of a resource until it is done using it. For example, a process should be able to securely use a block of memory until the process decides to de-allocate it. The Exokernel uses what are called "secure-bindings" when binding a resource to a process.

A secure-binding separates the authorization to use a resource from the actual use of that resource. Authorization to use a resource is granted or denied when the resource is first requested. Once the process has the authority to use a resource, it

retains this authority until it gives it up (Engler, Kaashoek, & O'Toole, 1995). The Exokernel is only minimally involved in this process as it only provides the authorization to use the resource and it does not get involved in the ongoing management of the use of that resource.

Furthermore, the Exokernel can provide secure-bindings without any special knowledge of what it is binding. The semantics of binding a resource to application software can get very complex. However, the Exokernel does not get involved in the details of the binding. It only gets involved to the extent that it can provide the security associated with that binding. As Engler, Kaashoek, and O'Toole say, "a secure binding allows the kernel to protect resources without understanding them" (Engler, Kaashoek, & O'Toole, 1995).

Revoking Access to Resources

Although a secure-binding, in theory, allows a process to use a resource until it is done with it - in reality, there still must be a way for the operating system to force a revocation of the resource binding under certain conditions. Unlike the Exokernel, when a traditional operating system brakes a resource binding it does so by what is known as *invisible revocation*. With an invisible revocation, the resource binding is simply broken and the process has no knowledge of the circumstances that prompted the revocation. A disadvantage of using invisible revocation is that operating systems "cannot guide de-allocation and have no knowledge that resources are scarce" (Engler, Kaashoek, & O'Toole, 1995).

When an Exokernel breaks a secure binding, it uses a technique that the researchers have named *visible revocation*. With visible revocation, communication occurs between the kernel and the process. Because of this communication, the process is informed of the need to have the resource binding broken. By being warned of the resource revocation before the event, the process can prepare for it by saving any data that it needs and bring itself to a stable state. For example, a process may be asked to give up a page of memory and it may not matter which page of memory it de-allocates. Because the process is kept informed of the resource de-allocation, the process may be allowed to simply change a few pointers to reflect the change, or it may be allowed to choose which page of memory it gives up. It may also choose to write that page of memory to disk to free-up the memory requested by the kernel. In either case, the process cooperates with the kernel, and by doing so, the revocation of the resource is less intrusive for the process.

Just like in a traditional operating system, a process that is not cooperating with the kernel's request to de-allocate a resource must, on occasion, be forced to comply with the kernel's request. When a secure-binding has to be broken by force, it "simply breaks all existing secure bindings to the resource and informs the Library OS" (Engler, Kaashoek, & O'Toole, 1995).

Management by User Level Library

Previously we stated, the Exokernel Operating System's kernel is responsible for providing protection of resources while the management of those resources is left up to another entity. This other entity is known as the "user level library operating system", or "LibOS" for short. This LibOS lies outside the kernel where it is available to user processes.

The LibOS can be thought of as being very similar to a traditional operating system in that the LibOS is the middle-man between the user processes and the actual hardware. Like the traditional operating system, the LibOS provides the abstraction that user processes interact with when they want to communicate with the hardware. However, unlike a traditional operating system, a LibOS can be customized to fit the needs of the software applications. This customization leads directly to optimization, which in turn leads to a much more efficient operating system. Furthermore, since a LibOS is written with a specific user process in mind, a LibOS does not have to be all-things to all-processes as we stated was true of a traditional operating system. A LibOS can be simple and more specialized, primarily because "library operating systems need not multiplex a resource among competing applications with widely different demands" (Engler, Kaashoek, & O'Toole, 1995). So far as the LibOSs use standardized interfaces, these LibOSs allow for applications to be easily ported to different computing hardware. Because the LibOSs are so specialized, one may wonder if this leads to a lot of extra code in user space. One may also wonder if some of this code is also redundant. The Exokernel addresses this concern by what the researchers call "shared libraries".

Shared Libraries

Not all of the user level libraries have to be specialized code that is written for a specific process. Different processes can often reuse the same code that is written for another process. Therefore, the Exokernel allows processes to share code in what it calls a shared library. By sharing code, the amount of disk-space and memory-usage can be significantly reduced. The disadvantage of sharing code with a LibOS is what Douglas Wyatt calls a "bootstrapping problem" (Wyatt, 1997). The problem is that the code that is needed to load the LibOS from disk into memory is actually found in the LibOS itself (which cannot be accessed until the LibOS is actually loaded into memory). The solution to the bootstrapping issue will be explained when we discuss the shared library server (section 3.7).

Another of the key issues that Douglas Wyatt has identified with a shared library system is what he calls "symbol resolution" (Wyatt, 1997). The issue arises from the fact that when a program is run for the first time, it needs to know particular memory addresses in order to run correctly. One way to address this problem is to load a shared library into the same virtual address space so that the particular memory addresses will be known prior to program execution. Although this approach works, it is not the best approach to this issue.

The symbol resolution issue might be better solved by what Wyatt calls an "indirection table" (Wyatt, 1997). Rather than force a shared library to always be loaded into the same virtual memory space, the solution requires a table be used to record the required memory addresses. This table is then provided to each shared library which uses the data within the table to calculate the relative offset of the memory address that it is looking for. Using an indirection table allows the shared libraries enough flexibility to load themselves into any address space.

Implementing a Shared Library

Before a program loads a shared library, it checks the indirection table to see if the library is already loaded somewhere else. If it is loaded somewhere else, it simply updates its page table to include the location of the existing library. However, if a program checks the indirection table and does not find a reference to the library that it needs, it loads the library and updates the indirection table to reflect the change.

Using an indirection table solves the symbol resolution issue described by Wyatt, but it does come at a price. The price is the extra time that is now needed to check the indirection table for libraries that are already loaded. When one considers the benefits of using an indirection table, one can see that using an indirection table is an expense that pays for itself. One of the benefits of an indirection table is that it requires the system to use less memory, which translates into having fewer page faults. Fewer memory page faults mean programs can run faster. Shared libraries can be updated and improved, which makes the system more flexible to change. Furthermore, when a shared library is changed, it can be compiled

independently of the other programs that interact with it. This mechanism can be also implemented in a multi page size environment (Itshak & Wiseman, 2008).

The Shared Library Server

The bootstrapping problem mentioned previously is an issue that arises from trying to load a library operating system into memory when the code needed to do this is actually found within the library operating system itself. The researchers have addressed this issue with what they have called the "shared library server" or SLS.

The shared library server is started as soon as the Exokernel is booted. The shared library server is responsible for communicating with applications that want to communicate with a shared library. This communication includes the ability to 1) open, read, and write files, 2) map files from disk, 3) open and read directories, and 4) perform basic input and output operations. This basic functionality is just enough to help a shared library overcome the bootstrapping problem and load itself into memory.

Interprocess Communication (IPC)

The passing of messages between processes, or what is known as interprocess communication (IPC), is used so frequently within an operating system that it is a potential performance bottleneck it if is not accomplished efficiently. The Exokernel accomplishes interprocess communication by what Benjie Chen calls "protected control transfer" (Chen, 2000). The Exokernel implements IPC by using secure registers to pass data. Passing data by using secure registers allows the communication to be immediate, which means the data gets passed between the processes without any need for the kernel to get involved. This implementation allows the Exokernel to provide protection - in the form of a secure register. The Exokernel keeps itself out of the management details while still retaining the role of the protector of resources. Because this form of interprocess communication is immediate, the Exokernel enjoys a processing speed-up.

Exceptions and Interrupts

An exception or interrupt requires a traditional operating system to save register data to a more secure location in order to protect and preserve its current state of operation. The kernel also has to respond to the exception, which requires the exception to be decoded by the kernel and then specific code needs to be executed to handle the issue raised by the exception. Once the exception has been dealt with, the kernel has to restore the registers to their pre-exception state and start running the original program from a point where the program counter was just prior to the exception.

An Exokernel, on the other hand, handles exceptions and interrupts by getting less involved. For example, exceptions and interrupts that arise from hardware are handled directly by the applications themselves. The Exokernel only gets involved enough to save important register information to what Engler calls an agreed upon, user accessible, "save area" (Engler, 1998). The Exokernel saves the register data, loads the exception, then starts to execute at the memory address of the code that has been written specifically to handle the exception. This special code is understood to be located in what we have been calling the user level library.

The kernel's job is done as soon as the Library OS takes over the handling of the exception. As soon as the exception is handled, the original register data is written back to the registers from where they were stored in user-accessible memory. The normal program execution continues from where it left off just prior to the exception without any further assistance from the kernel. Therefore, the kernel gets involved just enough to provide protection of the current state of the registers, whereas the actual manage-

ment of the exception is handled in user space, by the Library OS.

Disk I/O

Disk I/O – reading and writing to memory locations – is accomplished asynchronously in order to minimize the involvement of the kernel. It is the Exokernel's "exodisk" that handles all read and write requests. When an application needs access to memory, the exodisk simply passes the request off to the disk driver. After the read or write request is made, the calling application immediately regains control. Since the request is asynchronous, the calling application has the option of waiting for the memory request to complete, or it can continue without waiting for a completion response from the exodisk.

When the memory read or write request completes, the Exokernel is notified of this event by the requesting application. However, very little more is required of the Exokernel. The Exokernel retains its minimal involvement by helping pass the disk I/O request to the exodisk and allowing all of the details of the disk I/O request to be handled by user-level code found in the Library OS.

Downloading Code into the Kernel

Since one of the goals of the Exokernel is to be optimally efficient, one of the ways the Exokernel attempts this is by downloading code into the kernel. Downloading code into the kernel is not unique to the Exokernel. It is a technique that other operating systems have used as a way to minimize the cost of a context switch.

One of the main advantages of downloading code into the kernel is that it eliminates the need for code to make what are called "kernel crossings", which can require an expensive context switch (Engler, Kaashoek, & O'Toole, 1995). Context switches are undesirable because they can severely impede an application's execution speed. By eliminating kernel crossings, context switches are reduced, and applications experience faster execution speeds.

A second benefit of downloading code into the kernel is that "the execution of downloaded code can be readily bounded" (Engler, Kaashoek, & O'Toole, 1995). They mean downloaded code can be executed at times when there are just a few microseconds of processing time available. This processing time-slice is too small to allow for a full context switch, so a traditional approach that requires a context switch would normally not be able to take advantage of such a small processing time-slice. Engler has stated that being able to process code during these small time-slices makes the Exokernel more powerful (Engler, 1998). The Exokernel is more powerful because it can optimize its processing of code by taking advantage of these small time-slices and increase the throughput of the applications. The freedom to optimize, as we stated previously, is a key part of being able to increase the processing speeds of operating systems.

Packet Sending and Receiving

Networking with an Exokernel is accomplished by what Ganger and others have called "application-level" networking (Ganger, Engler, Kaashoek, Briceño, Hunt, & Pinckney, 2002). The Exokernel's application-level networking allows an application to interact *almost* directly with the networking interface. Because the Exokernel provides much less of an abstraction for the application, the application-level code can provide more of its own management. This means the Exokernel is in a much better position to optimize its own operations, which can lead to an over-all higher performance level for the entire computer. The research documents are a little vague about the details of how networking is actually achieved, but it is clear that a first-in-first-out (FIFO) send queue is used. The documentation is also clear that the Exokernel also has a way of receiving packets and delivering them to the proper re-

ceiving application. Both of these processes are explained next.

The Exokernel sends a packet on a network through a system call referenced by "send_packet". When this function gets called, the packet gets added to a first-in-first-out queue and the kernel's involvement in the transmission ends at this point. The rest of the transmission gets handled by a network interface card or a device driver. The Exokernel gets involved minimally, but only to the extent that is needed to provide for a secure networking environment. The networking transmission management details are provided by the device driver code, which is located in user-space.

Packet receiving by the Exokernel is handled a little differently, but without much more involvement by the Exokernel. According to Ganger and others, the Exokernel receives packets by using two major processes; *packet demultiplexing* and *packet buffering*. Packet demultiplexing involves deciding which application a particular packet should be associated with. The information that the Exokernel uses to accomplish this is actually found within each packet which is located at a particular memory offset value. The process of actually delivering a packet to a particular application is called packet buffering by Ganger and others. Similar to the pre-arranged "save-area" mentioned in section 3.9 (Exceptions and Interrupts), the Exokernel copies the packet to a pre-registered memory area. Once the packet is successfully copied to the appropriate memory area, the Exokernel's involvement is complete. From this point, any further management or handling of the packet is accomplished by user-level code.

Naming and Routing of Packets

When a packet's high-level identifier gets translated into a low-level identifier, this is called "naming". Before a packet can be properly routed through a network, it must first be identified by a name. Therefore, naming of packets is an important component to routing packets. Naming is also how the Address Resolution Protocol (ARP) is able to assign a unique identifier to each computer within a network. Without a unique name for each computer on a network, it would be impossible to properly address packets. The Exokernel supports the naming and routing of packets by what Ganger and others call the "sharing model" (Ganger, Engler, Kaashoek, Briceño, Hunt, & Pinckney, 2002). The Exokernel implements the sharing model by publishing all of the Address Resolution Protocol information in a *translation table*. Because this translation table is made available to user code in a read-only format, an application can look-up the information that it requires without asking the kernel for assistance. When a process does not find the information that it needs in the translation table, it can then ask the network for the information. This is called the sharing model because all of the applications share the translation table.

Network Error Reporting

It is important to notify the sender of a packet when the addressee of a packet cannot be located. According to Granger and others, the Exokernel's "stray packet" daemon takes care of TCP segment errors and network packets that cannot be delivered to the correct location (Ganger, Engler, Kaashoek, Briceño, Hunt, & Pinckney, 2002). Although the exact details of how the daemon handles these issues is unclear, it is interesting to note that the kernel is very much involved in this service. The researchers justify the kernel's heavy involvement by noting that this service is most closely related to protection rather than management. Therefore, the Exokernel can still be thought of as providing mostly protection of resources and allowing the actual management to be provided by code found in user-space.

PERFORMANCE RESULTS

Perhaps the best way to evaluate the Exokernel is by considering its performance results. In the following paragraphs, we will look at five areas that show enhanced operating system performance due to the Exokernel's approach. These results suggest the Exokernel's extensible approach provides enough of an enhancement as to make this approach a desirable alternative to the traditional operating system design.

Common Applications Benefit from an Exokernel

When comparing the results of benchmark tests that were performed by Xok/ExOS (a version of the Exokernel) with FreeBSD and OpenBSD (two other operating systems), we see that Xok/ExOS was able to complete 11 tests in just 41 seconds - which is about 19 seconds faster than the operating systems it was compared with. On three benchmark tests, Xok/ExOS did behave slightly slower than the competition, but these results were expected because of how the benchmark test was weighted. The slightly slower results were also of such a small degree as to not be really significant. As an overall score, the researchers state the Xok/ExOS is about 32% more efficient than the other operating systems that it was tested against.

Exokernel's Flexibility is not Costly

Benchmark tests were also used to see if the Exokernel's flexibility added too much overhead and made its execution less efficient. In the test, Xok/ExOS was compared to OpenBSD/C-FFS. The Xok/ExOS completed the test in 41 seconds versus the 51 seconds of the competition. Thus, Xok/ExOS was about 20% faster than the other operating systems. It is results like this that prompted Engler to state that "an Exokernel's flexibility can be provided for free" (Engler, 1998). Part of the reason why the Exokernel is a little more efficient is because the Exokernel is leaner - largely because protection mechanisms that usually get duplicated in a traditional operating system are not present.

Aggressive Applications are Significantly Times Faster

One of the goals of the extensible approach of the Exokernel is that its performance can be optimized. In order to test this theory, researchers attempted to make optimizations to applications running on an Exokernel system. As an experiment, XCP and CP were tested against each other. Although XCP and CP are both file copy programs, XCP is a file copy program that is optimized to take advantage of the flexibility of the Exokernel Operating System. The test results show that the XCP file copy program can complete its tasks about three times faster than that of CP. Other experiments were also conducted to test the speed of a Cheetah web server. The Cheetah web server, when running on top of the Exokernel OS (Xok), was found to be four times faster, for small documents. These results support the claim that the Exokernel OS does allow the user to optimize application code to achieve significant speed-ups in processing speeds.

Local Control can Lead to Enhanced Global Performance

The Exokernel researchers wondered if only specific processes can be optimized, or if the global performance of an operating system can be optimized. The researchers tested the Exokernel as it ran multiple applications concurrently and compared the results with non-extensible operating systems. The results show the Exokernel is, at least, as efficient as the non-extensible operating systems. Furthermore, after an Exokernel Operating System is optimized – what the researchers have called "local optimizations" – the "global performance" of the Exokernel is also enhance.

Therefore, local optimizations do in fact support the global optimization of the Exokernel.

Exokernel's File Storage Scheme Enhances Run-Time

The researchers conducted experiments to test what Robert Grimm calls the Exokernel's "fine grained interleaving of disk storage" (Grimm, 1996). In the experiments, two applications were compared as they each accessed 1,000 10-KByte files. The Ekokernel's "fine grained interleaving" seems to account for a 45% faster file access time than that of an operating system that does not use this "fine grained interleaving" approach. The Exokernel's flexibility also seems to be responsible for allowing the Exokernel to conduct "file insert" operations about 6 times faster. These test results seem to support the conclusion that the Exokernel's file storage scheme does enhance the over-all run-time of the operating system.

ACTIVE NETWORKING

One of the technologies that has benefited from the Exokernel is Active Networking. The concept of an active network evolved from research being conducted at the Defense Advanced Research Projects Agency. This group is known for developing the "DARPA Internet", which is the foundation for our modern day Internet.

In a traditional network like the Internet, data is passively transported from a start point to an end point. Along its journey, the data passes through nodes that route the data packets based on header information while ignoring the actual data found in the packet contents. In the words of David L. Tennenhouse and others, the DARPA research community identified the following problems with networks;

1. "The difficulty of integrating new technologies and standards into the shared network

infrastructure."

2. "Poor performance due to redundant operations at several protocol layers."

3. "Difficulty accommodating new services in the existing architectural model."

(Tennenhouse, & Wetherall, 1996).

Tennenhouse and others state, in contrast to a passive network, an active network contains nodes that "can perform computations on, and modify, the packet contents." Furthermore, "this processing can be customized on a per user or per application basis" (Tennenhouse, & Wetherall, 1996). David Wetherall states well the benefit of active networks when he states that active networks "enable a range of new applications that leverage computation within the network; and it would accelerate the pace of innovation by decoupling services from the underlying infrastructure" (Wetherall, 1999).

A good example of an active network is provided by Parveen Patel. Patel states that active packets may encrypt themselves before entering an un-trusted portion of a network. The code to conduct the actual encryption could be carried by the active packets themselves, or the code could be resident on the node and simply be executed by the packets when they arrive. In either case, the data packets are *active* within the network, encrypting and decrypting themselves as necessary when passing through un-trusted sections of a network (Patel, 2002).

Hrishikesh Dandekar and others at NAI Labs (Network Associates, Inc. of Los Angeles, California) provide the link in our discussion that joins Active Networks and the Exokernel Operating System. Their research is named AMP. They state AMP is "a secure platform upon which the mobile code [of an active network] can be safely executed" (Dandekar, Purtell, & Schwab, 2002). The interesting part is that "AMP is layered on top of the MIT ExoPC (Exokernel) operating System's Xok kernel" (Dandekar, Purtell, & Schwab, 2002).

The Exokernel is a good foundation upon which to build AMP because the Exokernel offers AMP security, flexibility, and extensibility. Because the Exokernel's security mechanism "dovetails" nicely with the needs of AMP, Dandekar and others have stated AMPs "development time is reduced, modularity is enhanced, and security requirements can be addressed in a straightforward manner" (Dandekar, Purtell, & Schwab, 2002).

Flexibility with the Exokernel is reflected in its lack of abstractions. As Dandekar and others state, "an exokernel provides a minimal set of abstractions above the raw hardware. Only those mechanisms required in order to control access to physical resources and kernel abstractions are provided" (Dandekar, Purtell, & Schwab, 2002). As hardware gets abstracted by the operating system, the use of that hardware becomes less flexible. AMP's "NodeOS" provides a set of interfaces through which the code within an active network can request services of the underlying operating system. Abstracted by these interfaces are services such as networking channels, thread pools, memory pools, and domains. As Dandekar and others explain, "these abstractions provide the active application of platform-independent means for accessing a common set of resources which will be available across all of the heterogeneous network" (Dandekar, Purtell, & Schwab, 2002). It is precisely because the underlying Exokernel provides a minimal set of abstractions that the AMP NodeOS can utilize this functionality so easily.

Lastly, the Exokernel was designed to be extensible. The library operating system of the Exokernel matches up nicely with the libraries found in AMP (libAMP). An application like AMP can only be as extensible as the operating system that supports it. Thus, the superior extensibility of the Exokernel makes possible the superior flexibility of AMP.

In conclusion of our look at active networking, we see that the three "problems with networks" that were identified by DARPA are addressed by active networks. Active networks provide a means to 1) easily integrate new technologies into the network infrastructure, 2) optimize performance, and 3) easily accommodate new services. Because the Exokernel makes our example of active networking possible, the Exokernel must share in the credit of giving rise to a solution to the problems with networks as identified by DARPA.

ANALYSIS AND DISCUSSION

In the following paragraphs, we present some of the criticisms of the Exokernel Operating System that have been offered by some of her detractors. We address the criticisms and offer some of our own. We offer further comments and reactions as a way to stimulate more discussion about the Exokernel Operating System.

Customer-Support

We begin our commentary with a quote from Jeff Mogul of Compaq Western Research Laboratory. Mogul says, "Extensibility has its problems. For example, it makes the customer-support issues a lot more complicated, because you no longer know which OS each of your customers is running" (Milojicic, 1999).

What Jeff Mogul seems to be pointing out is that each extensible operating system can be modified to the point of being unique. If each extensible operating system is user-modified and user-configured, then the challenge becomes how to efficiently provide customer support for a group of users if each user is essentially using a different operating system. For example, if both the *file management system* and the *communication manager* are uniquely modified, then trying to solve the issues that arise from their interaction could be very difficult.

Although providing customer support for an extensible operating system might present new challenges, it does not mean the extensible ap-

proach has to be eliminated. Previously (section 3.4), we explained that it is not necessary to customize an entire operating system. In fact, many users may not even need to customize any of the operating system. They may simply rely on the services provided by the user level library. So, as long as users are using the standard code found in the user level library, they are all using the same version of the operating system and therefore the customer service issue becomes a non-issue. It is only those users that decide to modify and optimize the libraries that pose the problem to customer service.

Presumably, users that are savvy enough to optimize their own code are probably savvy enough to trouble-shoot the issues that may arise from working with such a flexible operating system. In reality, it might not even be individual users that are optimizing their own code but rather software manufacturers that customize a user-level library so their product works faster on the extensible operating system. If this were the case, then perhaps there is no additional customer support issue for users of the standard user level libraries, and perhaps customer support issues that arise from optimized user-level libraries should be handled by the creators of the optimized code. So, if the customer support issue is even an issue at all, it becomes and issue for the optimizers of the user-level libraries and not an issue for the engineers of the extensible operating system. Thus, perhaps an extensible operating system should be brought to market and second-party software manufacturers should accept the responsibility of customer support if they choose to modify the standard user libraries.

On the other hand, as was stated previously "extensibility could actually help the customer support issue" (Leschke, 2004). In so far as extensible operating systems are easier to fix, then it should be easier to eliminate bugs and offer the community a more solid, error-free operating system. Since user level libraries can be replaced independently of the kernel, providing updated and corrected libraries to the users of an extensible operating system should be straight forward. So, if extensibility means there might be fewer bugs or issues in the kernel, and also if extensibility means updated user level libraries might be easily added to an existing system, then perhaps an extensible operating system might lead to less of a customer support issue.

Furthermore, one might even argue that customer support will be easier to provide with an extensible operating system. Consider a customer support issue that arises from the use of a particular user level library. In so far as the issue is contained within that one user level library, then the customer support provider only needs to be an expert in that one library. This means customer support employees can be specialized. In so far as it is easier to train someone to be an expert in a limited number of user level libraries rather than an expert in the entire operating system, it seems that training customer support personnel will also be much easier with an extensible operating system.

Eliminating Management

One may argue that it is not necessary to eliminate *all* management from the operating system. Perhaps there are some operating system management functions that cannot be further optimized, and therefore, they should continue to be provided by the kernel. Or, perhaps the amount of optimization that is possible is so small as to not be worth the effort to move them outside the kernel. Perhaps the better approach is to allow the kernel to manage those processes that cannot be further optimized and to move into user-space that code that can be further optimized. A very logical question is - how will we know when code cannot be further optimized? Unfortunately, this is a question that cannot be answered without some further experience. On one hand, it seems that all processes will probably agree upon some common approaches to management, whereas on the other hand, if one

wants maximum flexibility then one must move all management out of the kernel and make the code available in user-space.

The point we are trying to argue is that maybe eliminating *all* management from the kernel is too strong of a position. Maybe some management should remain in the kernel while other management code should be moved to user-space where it can be modified and optimized. Further research into this issue may reveal that maximum optimization can be achieved even if the operating system kernel retains some of the management responsibility.

As an illustration of our point, we cite Riechmann and Kleinöder as they state "As multithreaded applications become common, scheduling inside applications play a very important role for efficiency and fairness" (Riechmann, & Kleinöder, 1996). They further state the Exokernel's design leads to inefficiency because the Exokernel's thread scheduling algorithm requires an additional thread switch during execution. Their solution is to separate the management policy from the management implementation. Their research demonstrates that if one places the thread switching mechanism inside the kernel while allowing user-level code to handle the scheduling algorithm, some efficiency is gained over the Exokernel's approach. The idea of two level scheduling was also used by (Reuven & Wiseman, 2006) even though they suggest to implement both of the scheduling level within the kernel, but their implementation will be activated only if thrashing occurs (Wiseman, 2009), (Jiang, 2009).

Riechmann and Kleinöder argue our point for us. Our point is that perhaps a clean division between implementing protection within the kernel and implementing management within user code is too extreme. The research conducted by Riechmann and Kleinöder suggests that a pure Exokernel approach might not be the best answer. The Exokernel's approach needs to be embraced, but just not tightly. In conclusion, perhaps the best design for an operating system is one in which there is a separation of mechanism from policy. Although the Exokernel has a policy of only allowing code in user-space to handle management of processes, perhaps on occasion the actual mechanism of management has to allow for some code to be executed within the kernel whenever it is more efficient to do so.

Optimizing Usage

When we talk about optimizing a computer, we are really talking about optimizing computer hardware rather than computer code. Admittedly, we do optimize computer code, but only as a way to optimize computer hardware. Thus, optimizing computer hardware is always the real goal. As such, who is the most qualified to optimize computer hardware? Software engineers? One might argue that hardware engineers – those that have an intimate understanding of the hardware components – are best suited for optimizing computer hardware. If the extensible approach becomes main-stream, we might see the line that separates computer engineering from software engineering becoming less distinct. Perhaps the engineers of the future will play two roles – one of hardware engineer and one of software engineer. The engineers of the future will surely need a strong understanding of computer code - since that is how we communicate with hardware - but they will also need an expert understanding of computer hardware, since that is what is actually being optimized. So, the extensible approach to operating system design might lead to a paradigm shift in how computers are optimized - but the final result will be a society of fully optimized computers.

The paradigm shift that will be caused by the extensible operating system will help put the *science* back into the Computer Science of the Information Technology Industry. Computer developers will be forced to make good Computer Science decisions from the ground up. Optimization will become the central focus of the computer industry.

Optimization will eliminate the design approach seen in the current monolithic operating systems and give birth to a new breed of operating system that can keep pace with advancing computer technology. The entire computer science industry will experience a tremendous speed-up once the extensible operating system design becomes fully embraced.

Is Extensibility the Answer?

Druschel and others have argued against the Exokernel by saying "it is unclear to what extent the performance gains are due to extensibility, rather than merely resulting from optimizations that could equally be applied to an operating system that is not extensible" (Druschel, Pai, & Zwaenepoel, 1997). Through their research, Druschel and others have shown that traditional monolithic operating systems can be optimized just like the Exokernel. They claim the key to the speed-up is the optimization, not extensibility.

The Druschel research group tempers their argument against the Exokernel by saying "the real value in extensible kernels lies in their ability to stimulate research by allowing rapid experimentation using general extensions" (Druschel, Pai, & Zwaenepoel, 1997). They seem to be saying that extensible operating systems provide a means to quickly engineer prototypes of operating systems. This fast prototyping has caused a speed-up in the research, which had lead to a quicker way to discover techniques for optimizing operating systems. Although the Druschel group would say extensibility is not *the* answer, they do support the extensible approach because it is a tool that can be used to speed-up research and help bring a solution to market faster.

The argument provided by the Druschel group is well founded. However, perhaps they are overstating their position. Although we will agree that any code can be optimized - even monolithic operating systems - we still hold strong to the point that it is extensibility that really makes optimization possible. In order to optimize an operating system, the system must first be flexible enough to be optimized. An operating system that is extensible is by its very nature open to changes and therefore easy to optimize. Although traditional operating systems can be optimized, they lack the flexibility required to make the changes easy. Because extensible operating systems are easy to change, they are perhaps the best design to work with when trying to optimize an operating system. Therefore, we still maintain that it is extensibility that is the foundation of being able to optimize operating systems.

CONCLUSION

As we bring our discussion to a close, we recall the two forces that are stretching the capabilities of the modern monolithic operating system. On one side there is the need for the operating system to be more flexible to accommodate new technologies. On the other side is the need for the operating system to become faster so it can keep pace with faster hardware and faster communication speeds. Our discussion showed how an extensible operating system like the Exokernel might fulfill both needs. Extensibility allows an operating system to be flexible enough to meet the changing demands of new technologies, while also making optimization easier, which translates into faster operating systems that can keep pace with faster computing environments.

In conclusion, there is a need for a faster and more flexible operating system, and the extensible approach of the Exokernel seems to meet this need. The speed and flexibility offered by the Exokernel will help operating systems avoid being the performance bottleneck in computer systems for years to come. Although extensible operating system technology is still in its infancy, the initial findings are encouraging to researchers. If contemporary operating systems are to keep pace with the forces that are being placed upon

them, then modern operating system designers need to embrace the extensible approach found in the Exokernel.

REFERENCES

Chen, B. (2000). *Multiprocessing with the Exokernel Operating System*. Unpublished.

Dandekar, H., Purtell, A., & Schwab, S. (2002). AMP: Experiences with Building and Exokernel-based Platform for Active Networking. In *Proceedings: DARPA Active Networks Conference and Exposition*, (pp. 77-91).

Druschel, P., Pai, V., & Zwaenepoel, W. (1997). Extensible Kernels and Leading the OS Research Astray. In *Operating Systems*, (pp. 38-42).

Engler, D. R., Kaashoek, M. F., & O'Toole, J. (1995). Exokernel: an Operating System Architecture for Application-level Resource Management. In *15th ACM Symposium on Operating Systems Principles* (pp. 251-266).

Ganger, G., Engler, D., Kaashoek, M. F., Briceño, H., Hunt, R., & Pinckney, T. (2002). Fast and Flexible Application-level Networking on Exokernel Systems. *ACM Transactions on Computer Science*, *20*(1), 49–83. doi:10.1145/505452.505455

Grimm, R. (1996). *Exodisk: Maximizing Application Control Over Storage Management*. Unpublished.

Itshak, M., & Wiseman, Y. (2008). AMSQM: Adaptive Multiple SuperPage Queue Management. In *Proc. IEEE Conference on Information Reuse and Integration (IEEE IRI-2008)*, Las Vegas, Nevada, (pp. 52-57).

Leschke, T. R. (2004). Achieving Speed and Flexibility by Separating Management From Protection: Embracing the Exokernel Operating System. *Operating Systems Review*, *38*(4), 5–19. doi:10.1145/1031154.1031155

Milojicic, D. (1999). Operating Systems - Now and in the Future. *IEEE Concurrency*, 7(1), 12–21. doi:10.1109/MCC.1999.749132

Ousterhout, J. (1989). *Why Aren't Operating Systems Getting Faster as Fast as Hardware*. Unpublished. Carver, L., Chen, B., & Reyes, B. (1998). *Practice and Technique in Extensible Operating Systems*. Manuscript submitted for publication. Engler, D. R. (1998). *The Exokernel Operating System Architecture*. Unpublished.

Patel, P. (2002). An Introduction to Active Network Node Operating Systems. *Crossroads*, 9(2), 21–26. doi:10.1145/904067.904072

Reuven, M., & Wiseman, Y. (2006). Medium-Term Scheduler as a Solution for the Thrashing Effect. *The Computer Journal*, 49(3), 297–309. doi:10.1093/comjnl/bxl001

Riechmann, T., & Kleinöder, J. (1996). *User-Level Scheduling with Kernel Threads*. Unpublished.

Tennenhouse, D. L., Smith, J. M., Sincoskie, W. D., Wetherall, D. J., & Minden, G. J. (1997). A Survey of Active Network Research. *IEEE Communications Magazine*, 35(1), 80–86. doi:10.1109/35.568214

Tennenhouse, D. L., & Wetherall, D. J. (1996). Towards an Active Network Architecture. *Computer Communications Review*, 26 (2).

Wetherall, D. (1999). Active Network Vision and Reality: Lessons From a Capsule-based System. *Operating Systems Review*, 34(5), 64–79. doi:10.1145/319344.319156

Wyatt, D. (1997). *Shared Libraries in an Exokernel Operating System*. Unpublished.

Chapter 9
Dynamic Analysis and Profiling of Multithreaded Systems

Daniel G. Waddington
Lockheed Martin, USA

Nilabja Roy
Vanderbilt University, USA

Douglas C. Schmidt
Vanderbilt University, USA

ABSTRACT

As software-intensive systems become larger, more parallel, and more unpredictable the ability to analyze their behavior is increasingly important. There are two basic approaches to behavioral analysis: static and dynamic. Although static analysis techniques, such as model checking, provide valuable information to software developers and testers, they cannot capture and predict a complete, precise, image of behavior for large-scale systems due to scalability limitations and the inability to model complex external stimuli. This chapter explores four approaches to analyzing the behavior of software systems via dynamic analysis: compiler-based instrumentation, operating system and middleware profiling, virtual machine profiling, and hardware-based profiling. We highlight the advantages and disadvantages of each approach with respect to measuring the performance of multithreaded systems and demonstrate how these approaches can be applied in practice.

INTRODUCTION

Microprocessors execute code as a sequential flow of instructions. Most contemporary operating systems support multitasking, which allows more than one program to execute simultaneously. Multitasking is achieved by dynamically scheduling different executions to the available processors over time (sometimes referred to as time slicing).

The unit of logical flow within a running program is a thread. Although the exact definition of a thread can vary, threads are typically defined as a lightweight representation of execution state. The underlying kernel data structure for a thread includes the address of the run-time stacks, priority information, and scheduling status. Each thread belongs to a single process (a process requires at least one thread). Processes define initial code and data, a private virtual address space, and state relevant to active system resources (e.g., files and semaphores). Threads that belong to the same process share the same virtual address space and other system resources. There is no memory protection between threads in the same process, which makes it easy to exchange data efficiently between threads. At the same time, however, threads can write to many parts of the process' memory. Data integrity can be quickly lost, therefore, if access to shared data by individual threads is not controlled carefully.

Threads have traditionally been used on single processor systems to help programmers implement logically concurrent tasks and manage multiple activities within the same program (Rinard, 2001). For example, a program that handles both GUI events and performs network I/O could be implemented with two separate threads that run within the same process. Here the use of threads avoids the need to "poll" for GUI and packet I/O events. It also avoids the need to adjust priorities and preempt running tasks, which is instead performed by the operating system's scheduler.

With the recent advent of multicore and symmetric multiprocessor (SMP) systems, threads represent logically concurrent program functions that can be mapped to physically parallel processing hardware. For example, a program deployed on a four-way multicore processor must provide at least four independent tasks to fully exploit the available resources (of course it may not get a chance to use all of the processing cores if they are occupied by higher priority tasks). As parallel processing capabilities in commodity hardware

grow, the need for multithreaded programming has increased because explicit design of parallelism in software is now key to exploiting performance capabilities in next-generation processors (Sutter, 2005).

This chapter reviews key techniques and methodologies that can be used to collect thread-behavior information from running systems. We highlight the strengths and weaknesses of each technique and lend insight into how they can be applied from a practical perspective.

Understanding Multithreaded System Behavior

Building large-scale software systems is both an art and an engineering discipline. Software construction is an inherently iterative process, where system architects and developers iterate between problem understanding and realization of the solution. A superficial understanding of behavior is often insufficient for production systems, particularly mission-critical systems where performance is tightly coupled to variations in the execution environment, such as load on shared resources and hardware clock speeds. Such variations are common in multithreaded systems where execution is affected directly by resource contention arising from other programs executing at the same time on the same platform. To build predictable and optimized large-scale multithreaded systems, therefore, we need tools that can help improve understanding of software subsystems and help avoid potential chaotic effects that may arise from their broader integration into systems.

Multithreaded programs are inherently complex for several reasons (Lee, 2006; Sutter & Larus, 2005), including: (1) the use of nondeterministic thread scheduling and pre-emption; and (2) control and data dependencies across threads. Most commercial-off-the-shelf (COTS) operating systems use priority queue-based, preemptive thread scheduling. The time and space resources a thread needs to execute on an operating system are thus affected by:

- Thread priority, which determines the order in which threads run;
- Processor affinity, which defines the processors that the thread may run on;
- Execution state, which defines whether the thread is ready, waiting, or stopped; and
- Starvation time, which is caused by system delay during peak load periods.

Switching execution context between multiple threads results in an execution "interleaving" for each processor in the system. In a single-processor system, there is only one stage of scheduling: the choice of deciding which runnable thread to execute next. Systems that have multiple cores or SMP processors require an additional stage that maps the threads ready to run on to one of many possibly available cores, as shown in Figure 1.

Even if we know exactly how long each thread will have access to the processor (which ignores any form of priority-driven pre-emption and interthread dependency), the number of feasible interleavings that can occur in the system are staggering. For example, using the criteria in Figure 1, which has only four independent threads, each with eight execution quanta, there are 10^{17} possible interleavings for just one processor! Server-based systems with hundreds of threads and tens of processors are now common. Over the next decade we expect tera-scale systems will have hundreds of cores (Intel Corporation, 2006b).

Approaches to Extracting Multithreaded Behavioral Characteristics

There are two basic approaches to behavioral analysis: static and dynamic. Static analysis inspects the underlying constituents of a system without executing any program (Jackson & Rinard, 2000). It therefore requires some "model" of the system or implementation artifact that is correlated directly with expected behavior. For example, analysis of program source code is considered a form of static analysis. This type of analysis has the advantage that it can be performed without running the system. In particular, it can explore dimensions of behavior that are hard to stimulate through manipulation of program input.

Static analysis tools typically construct program execution models, potentially through

Figure 1. Interleavings caused by 1-stage and 2-stage scheduling

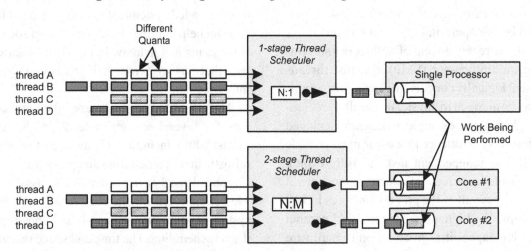

reverse engineering. These models can then be analyzed to derive and ensure behavioral characteristics. Model checking (Clarke, Grumberg, & Peled, 2000) is a static analysis technique that is often applied to multithreaded programs to explore all feasible interleavings exhaustively to ensure correctness properties, such as absence of deadlock and livelock (Rinard, 2001). This approach can check all feasible paths of execution (and interleavings) and thus avoid leaving any behavior unchecked.

In practice, model checking is computationally expensive and limited in its applicability, due to the vast number of feasible interleavings a large multithreaded system may exhibit. Other forms of static analysis, such as automated checking of design intent (Greenhouse, 2003) and program analysis driven theorem proving (Freund & Qadeer, 2003), have also been applied to multithreaded systems to ensure correct behavior. Each approach trades off analytical thoroughness and computational cost. Static-analysis techniques typically do a good job of modeling relative time and temporal ordering. They do not, however, model—and thus cannot reason about—absolute (wall-clock) time.

The only practical approach to behavioral analysis that can incorporate aspects of absolute time is dynamic analysis, also known as profiling. Profiling is inspection of behavior of a running system. An advantage of this approach is that it can measure aspects of the system and know that they are exactly representative of the system. Approaches to profiling can be classed as either active or passive. Active profiling requires that the application or system being measured explicitly generates information about its execution. An example of active profiling is the user of compiler-based probe insertion, where the application makes callbacks to the trace collection engine to record execution behavior. Conversely, passive profiling relies on explicit inspection of control flow and execution state through an external entity, such as a probe or modified runtime environment.

Passive profiling typically does not require any modification of the measured system, but is harder to implement and may require specialized tracing hardware.

Profiling (whether active or passive) collects precise and fine-grained behavioral data from a running multithreaded systems, which can be coupled with off-line analysis to help summarize and reason about observed results. The collected data is thus accurate and representative of system execution, as long as the overhead of the measurement has not unduly influenced the results. Profiling can also only provide behavioral data for control paths that actually execute, so successfully applying profiling tools depends largely on analyzing multiple runs of the program that test all relevant paths in the system. This coverage can be achieved through careful selection of stimuli (e.g., input data) to the system, as well as through artificial fault injection.

Profiling is limited, however, to the inspection of behavior that can be made to run by appropriate stimulation of the system, for example, through selection of input. This limitation means that profiling is more useful for behavior analysis in circumstances where a sampling of behavior is sufficient. For example, profiling is useful for optimizations that aim to improve performance on statistically frequent paths of execution. Profiling is thus not well suited to ensure correct behavior in a system when only one execution in a million can lead to system failure.

Both static analysis and dynamic analysis have their advantages and disadvantages. Advanced behavioral analysis solutions (Nimmer & Ernst, 2001; Waddington, Amduka, DaCosta, Foster, & Sprinkle, 2006) commonly use a combination of static and dynamic analysis to provide a more complete picture of system behavior. The remainder of this chapter presents and evaluates general approaches to profiling within the context of multithreaded systems. We examine the type and scale of behavioral data that can be collected dynamically from running systems and review state-of-the-art profiling tools and methodologies available today that operate at various levels of abstraction, including the operating system, virtual machine, and middleware levels.

BACKGROUND

Behavioral analysis is the examination and understanding of a system's behavior. Within the context of computing systems, behavioral analysis can be applied throughout the software lifecycle. The role of behavioral analysis—and the benefits it brings—vary according to how it is applied and the point in the life cycle to which it is applied. At a broad level, behavioral analysis supports assurance, optimization, diagnosis and prediction of software-system execution. Table 1 shows the relationship between these roles and different stages of software development.

Nondeterministic Behavior in Multithreaded Systems

Systems that behave according to classical physics, including electronic computers that are based on the von Neumann architecture, are deterministic in a strict sense. Actually predicting the behavior of a computing system, however, is fundamentally connected with the ability to gather all necessary information about the start state of the system. In most cases this is impractical, primarily due to very long causal chains (sequences of interrelated effects) and environmental interactions (i.e., input) that are hard to model and predict. In this chapter, we define determinism as the ability to predict the future state of a system. We therefore consider computer systems as generally being nondeterministic because we cannot practically predict the future state of the system. Accurate predictions would require a complete understanding of the start state, as well as prediction of environmental variables, such as user interaction and environmental effects (e.g., temperature sensitivity).

Most enterprise-style computing systems today demonstrate nondeterministic behavior. Key sources of nondeterminism in these systems include distributed communications (e.g., interaction across a network to machines with unknown state), user input (e.g., mouse/keyboard), and dynamic scheduling (e.g., priority-based with dynamic priority queues). These activities and actions typically result in a system whose execution behavior is hard to predict a priori.

A prominent cause of nondeterminism in multithreaded systems stems from the operating system's scheduler. The choice of which logical thread to execute on which physical processor is

Table 1. Roles of behavioral analysis in software-systems development

Role	Lifecycle Stage	Purpose
Assurance	Design, Implementation, Testing	Ensuring correct functionality and performance
Optimization	Implementation	Ensuring optimal use of computing resources
Diagnosis	Integration, Testing	Determining the conditions that lead to unexpected behavior
Prediction	Maintenance	Assessing how program modifications and integration will affect system behavior

derived from a number of factors, including thread readiness, current system load (e.g., other threads waiting to be run), priority, and starvation time (i.e., how long a thread has been waiting to be run). Many COTS operating systems use complex scheduling algorithms to maintain appropriate timeliness for time-sensitive tasks and also to achieve optimal use of processing resources. From the perspective of behavior analysis, however, these types of scheduling algorithms make static prediction of scheduling outcome infeasible in practice. Certain properties, such as absence of deadlock, can be checked effectively using static analysis because all possibilities can be explored explicitly. However, other properties, such as the absolute time taken to execute given functionality, can only be assessed practically using runtime profiling.

Behavioral Characteristics Relevant to Multithreaded Programs

Certain elements of behavior result from, and are thus pertinent to, the use of multithreaded programming. Table 2 describes some different characteristics that are commonly specified and measured in real-time and safety-critical systems. These are the types of characteristics that can be analyzed using the profiling tools and technologies discussed in this chapter.

To provide a sense of the necessary sampling scale (i.e., frequency of events) in today's COTS-based systems, we performed a number of simple experiments to gather some system measures. Understanding the expected sampling rates is useful to understanding the viability

Table 2. Common characteristics of multithreaded systems

Behavioral Characteristic	Description
Synchronization overhead	The additional processing time incurred by the use of synchronization mechanisms, such as mutexes, semaphores, and condition variables. Different mechanisms and topologies (e.g., inter- and intra-processor) typically have different overhead.
Task latency and jitter	The time between a thread being released (e.g., by a lock being freed) and regaining access to the processor. The task jitter is the observed variation in latency.
Task execution quanta	The length of time a thread executes for before either yielding access explicitly, or by being pre-empted by the operating system scheduler.
Unsafe memory access	Data that is being shared between threads must be controlled carefully to avoid data corruption due to the inability to modify data in one atomic action. To ensure the integrity of shared data is maintained, appropriate synchronization mechanisms must be used.
Priority inversion	Priority inversion occurs when a lower priority task is preventing a higher priority task from executing by being unable to execute and thus release a resource required by the higher priority task. A common solution to the priority inversion problem is for the lower priority to temporarily inherit the higher (waiting) priority so that it can release the resource.
Deadlock and livelock	Deadlock is a cyclic dependency between two or more threads. For example, thread A is waiting for a resource R1 from thread B before it will give up R2, and thread B is waiting for resource R2 from thread A before it will give up R1. In this condition both threads are blocked and cannot progress. Livelock is a similar condition to deadlock, except that the interdependent threads cause each other to perform an infinite amount of work before becoming free.
Effective parallelism	Effective parallelism is a measure of the ability of threads to perform work over time. For example, threads that do not have data interdependencies have a very high effective parallelism, whereas threads that are "lock-stepped" by a single shared resource have a low effective parallelism.
Worst-case execution time	Worst-case execution time (WCET) relates to task latency and jitter caused by load on the system. WCET is the maximum time a given thread or set of threads takes to perform some function. This measure is invaluable in building real-time systems that must adhere to strict deadlines.

and impact of different profiling techniques. Our experimentation is based on measurements taken from Microsoft Windows XP, running on a dual-processor, hyper-threaded (Intel Xeon 2.8 GHz) system, executing a stress-test Web client/server application. The measurements were taken using both Windows performance counters and the on-chip Intel performance counters. Table 3 shows the results.

The data listed in Table 3 is comprised primarily of finer-grained metrics that occur at very high frequencies in the lower levels of the system. Of course, less frequent "application-level" events are also of interest in understanding the behavior of a system. For example, rare error conditions are often of importance. The data in Table 3 shows that the frequency (and therefore quantity) of measurable events can vary significantly by up to nine orders of magnitude. Because the impact of measurement is scaled proportionally, analysis methodologies that work well for low-frequency events may not do so for higher-frequency events.

Challenges of Multithreaded System Profiling

The remainder of this chapter focuses on the realization and application of runtime profiling on multithreaded systems. Profiling multithreaded systems involves addressing the following key challenges:

*   Measurement of events at high frequencies—Events of interest typically occur at high frequency. The overhead and effect of measurement on the system being measured must be controlled carefully. Without careful control of overhead, results become skewed as the process of measurement directly alters the system's behavior.

*   Mapping across multilevel concepts—Threads can be used at multiple levels of a system. For example, threads can exist in the operating system, virtual machine, middleware, and in the application (lightweight threads and fibers). Virtual machine and application-layer threads can map to underlying operating system threads. Extracting

Table 3. Example metric ranges

Category	Metric	Range
Processor	Clock Rate	2,793,000,000 Hz *
	Micro-ops Queued	630,000,000 uops/second *
	Instructions Per Second	344,000,000 instructions/second *
	L2 Cache Reads	65,000,000 reads/second *
Thread Scheduling	Number of Threads	500 total count
	Context Switch Rate	800-170,000 switches/sec
	Thread Queue Length	0-15 total count
	Scheduling Quanta	20-120 ms
System Resources	System Calls	400-240,000 calls/sec
	Hardware Interrupts	300-1000 interrupts/sec
	Synchronization Objects	400-2200 total count

* per logical processor

the mapping between thread representations is inherently hard because in many cases the mappings are not one-to-one and are even adjusted dynamically.

- Extraction of complex interactions— Threads represent the fundamental unit of execution in a software system and are inherently interdependent. Their interactions are facilitated through the sharing of system resources, such as memory, file, and devices. Determining which resources are the medium of thread interaction is inherently hard because measuring events on all of the resources in the system is not feasible due to excessive instrumentation overhead.

- Interpolation between raw events and broader properties—Deriving the behavior of a system requires more than simple collection of event data. Raw event data (i.e., data collected directly from low-level execution activities) must be used to build

a composition of behavior that can be more readily analyzed by engineers. Abstraction and collation of data is a key requirement in deriving properties of synchronization that exist in multithreaded systems.

Research in the area of multithreaded software profiling and analysis has made some inroads into these challenges. In this chapter, we review the state-of-the-art in tools and techniques, some of which are commercial products and others that are research prototypes, and discuss how they try to address some of the challenges described above.

COMPILER-BASED INSTRUMENTATION TECHNIQUES

The most common approach to runtime profiling is to modify the code that executes so it explicitly generates trace information. A wide

Figure 2. Different points of code modification

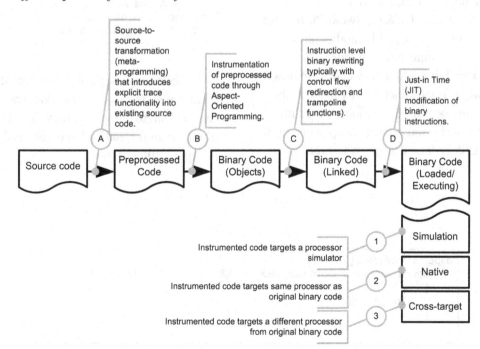

array of techniques can be used to generate this information, applied at different stages of the program code lifecycle, as shown in call-outs A to D in Figure 2.

Source-Code Instrumentation

Instrumenting source code manually is impractical in large systems. Instrumentation can be automated, however, through source-to-source transformation. Metaprogramming frameworks, such as Proteus (Waddington & Yao, 2005), TXL (Cordy, Halpern, & Promislow, 1991), Stratego (Visser, 2001) and DMS (Baxter, 2004), enable modifications to source code before it is compiled or preprocessed (Figure 2, label A). These metaprogramming frameworks provide a programming language that can be used to define context-sensitive modifications to source code. Transformation programs are compiled into applications that perform rewriting and instrumentation of source, which is given as input. Source code can also be instrumented just before it is compiled in a form of preprocessing (Figure 2, label B). Aspect-oriented programming (Spinczyk, Lohmann, & Urban, 2005; Kiczale, Hilsdale, Hugunin, Kersten, Palm, & Griswold, 2001) is an example of preprocessed code modification.

Applying instrumentation to source code—as opposed to applying it to binary code—makes it easier to align trace functionality with higher-level, domain-specific abstractions, which minimizes instrumentation because the placement of additional code is limited to only what is necessary.

For example, to measure the wait times of threads that are processing HTTP packets received from a network in a given application, developers could instrument only those wait calls that exist in a particular function, as opposed to all wait calls across the complete program. Definition of the context (function and condition) is straightforward in a metaprogramming or aspect-programming language. The following excerpt illustrates an AspectC++ (Spinczyk et al., 2005) rule for such an example.

Given the original code:

```
#include <stdio.h>
#include <pthread.h>

pthread_mutex_t * mute;
int count = 0;

int main() {
    pthread_mutex_init(mute, NULL);
    pthread_mutex_lock(mute);
    count = 1;
    pthread_mutex_unlock(mute);

    ReadPacket();
    return 0;
}

void ReadPacket() {
    /* code that we wish to instrument */
    pthread_mutex_lock(mute);
    pthread_mutex_unlock(mute);
}
```

The following AspectC++ aspect defines a rule that inserts calls to function TraceEvent() after each call to pthread_mutex_lock that exists within function ReadPacket (expressed through a join-point filter). (Box 1)

Box 1.

```
aspect TraceAspect {
    advice call("% pthread_mutex_lock(...)") && within("% ReadPacket(...)") : after()
    {
        TraceEvent();
    }
};
```

The result of "weaving" (i.e., performing source-to-source transformation) the above source code is the following. The weaving process has defined additional classes and inline functions to support the specified trace functionality. It has also redirected control flow according to the trace requirement (after call to function). (Box 2)

Aspect-oriented programming and other forms of source-to-source transformation are useful for selective and precise instrumentation of source code. Modification of source code is portable with respect to different processor architectures. The performance impact of the measurement is often minimal because instrumentation is customized

Box 2.

```
#ifndef __ac_fwd_TraceAspect__
#define __ac_fwd_TraceAspect__
class TraceAspect;
namespace AC {
    inline void invoke_TraceAspect_TraceAspect_a0_after();
}
#endif

...

#line 1 "main.cc"
#include <stdio.h>
#include <pthread.h>

pthread_mutex_t * mute;

int main()
{
    pthread_mutex_init(mute, NULL);
    pthread_mutex_lock(mute);
    pthread_mutex_unlock(mute);

    return 0;
}

/* Function generated by aspect weaver to call the "trace" aspect
    after calls to pthread_mutex_lock */

inline int __call__ZN10ReadPacketEv_0_0 (::pthread_mutex_t * arg0) {
    AC::ResultBuffer< int > result;
    ::new (&result) int (::pthread_mutex_lock(arg0));
    AC::invoke_TraceAspect_TraceAspect_a0_after ();
    return (int)result;
    }

void ReadPacket()
{
    __call__ZN10ReadPacketEv_0_0 (mute);
    pthread_mutex_unlock(mute);

}
...
```

continued on following page

Box 2. continued

```
class TraceAspect {

    public:
        static TraceAspect *aspectof () {
            static TraceAspect __instance;
            return &__instance;
        }
        static TraceAspect *aspectOf () {
            return aspectof ();
        }

    public:
        void __a0_after()
        {
        printf("TRACE");
        }
};

namespace AC {
    inline void invoke_TraceAspect_TraceAspect_
a0_after () {
    ::TraceAspect::aspectof()->__a0_after ();
    }
}
```

and only inserted where absolutely necessary. Instrumentation can be performed in the same order of time that is needed to compile the code. Source-code instrumentation is ideal for coarse-grained event tracing, particularly where the trace criteria must be related to application-level abstract events that are hard, if not impossible, to detect at the instruction level. Nevertheless, source-code instrumentation is target language dependent and can also be problematic when dealing with language idiosyncrasies, such as language preprocessing and syntactic variations.

Static Binary-Code Instrumentation

An alternative approach to adding event-tracing functionality to source code is to modify compiled binary code directly. Many compilers, such as GNU GCC, and profiling tools, such as Rational Purify and Quantify (IBM Corporation, 2003),

can compile code with additional profiling instrumentation and also to link with pre-instrumented runtime libraries. For example, applying the command line options -pg, -ftrace-arcs, and -ftest-coverage, to the GNU GCC compiler produces binary code that is instrumented with additional functionality that traces the count of function calls and basic blocks executed in the program. The following excerpts show the basic profiling instrumentation produced by the GNU GCC compiler for this example C source code:

```
void foo(){
    if(i<10)
        i++;
    else
        i=0;
    return;
}
```

The generated assembly code (x86) without instrumentation is shown in Box 3.

Box 3.

```
08048373 <foo>:
 8048373:  55                           push   %ebp
 8048374:  89  e5                       mov    %esp,%ebp
 8048376:  83  3d  78  95  04  08  09   cmpl   $0x9,0x8049578
 804837d:  7f  08                       jg     8048387 <foo+0x14>
 804837f:  ff  05  78  95  04  08       incl   0x8049578
 8048385:  eb  0a                       jmp    8048391 <foo+0x1e>
 8048387:  c7  05  78  95  04  08  00   movl   $0x0,0x8049578
 804838e:  00  00  00
 8048391:  c9                           leave
 8048392:  c3                           ret
 8048393:  90                           nop
```

Box 4.

```
080488da <foo>:
 80488da:  55                           push   %ebp
 80488db:  89  e5                       mov    %esp,%ebp
 80488dd:  e8  62  fd  ff  ff           call   8048644 <mcount@plt>
 80488e2:  83  3d  00  a2  04  08  09   cmpl   $0x9,0x804a200
 80488e9:  7f  16                       jg     8048901 <foo+0x27>
 80488eb:  ff  05  00  a2  04  08       incl   0x804a200
 80488f1:  83  05  38  a2  04  08  01   addl   $0x1,0x804a238
 80488f8:  83  15  3c  a2  04  08  00   adcl   $0x0,0x804a23c
 80488ff:  eb  18                       jmp    8048919 <foo+0x3f>
 8048901:  c7  05  00  a2  04  08  00   movl   $0x0,0x804a200
 8048908:  00  00  00
 804890b:  83  05  40  a2  04  08  01   addl   $0x1,0x804a240
 8048912:  83  15  44  a2  04  08  00   adcl   $0x0,0x804a244
 8048919:  c9                           leave
 804891a:  c3                           ret
```

The generated assembly code (x86) with instrumentation is shown in Box 4.

The first highlighted (80488dd) block represents a call to the profiling library's mcount() function. The mcount() function is called by every function and records in an in-memory call graph table a mapping between the current function (given by the current program counter) and the function's parent (given by return address). This mapping is typically derived by inspecting the stack. The second highlighted block (80488f1) contains instructions that increment counters for each of the basic blocks (triggered by the -ftrace-arcs option).

Profiling data that is collected through the profiling counters is written to a data file (gmon. out). This data can be inspected later using the GNU gprof tool. Summarized data includes basic control flow graph information and timing information between measure points in code. The overhead incurred through this type of profiling can be significant (over 60%) primarily because the instrumentation works on an "all or nothing" basis. Table 4 shows experimental results measuring the performance impact of the GNU GCC profiling features. Tests were performed by running the BYTEmark benchmark program (Grehan, 1995) on a 3.00 GHz Intel Pentium-D running Redhat Enterprise Linux v4.0. It is possible, however, to

Table 4. Slow-down incurred by GNU GCC profiling

Test	No profiling	With profiling	% Slow Down
Numeric Sort	812.32	498.2	38.67
String Sort	103.24	76.499	25.90
Bitfield	4.35E+08	1.65E+08	62.11
FP Emulation	73.76	52.96	28.20
Fourier	15366	15245	0.79
Assignment	24.292	9.77	59.78
Huffman	1412.7	1088.7	22.93
Neural Net	18.091	12.734	29.61
LU Decomp	909.76	421.48	53.67

enable profiling on selected compilation units, thereby minimizing instrumentation costs.

This type of code instrumentation is termed static because the code is modified before execution of the program (Figure 2, label C). COTS compiler-based instrumentation for profiling is generally limited to function calls and iteration counts. Another more powerful form of static binary instrumentation involves the use of a set of libraries and APIs that enable users to quickly write applications that perform binary rewriting (Hunt & Brubacher, 1999; Larus & Schnarr, 1995; Srivastava & Eustace, 1994; Romer, et al., 1997; Hollingsworth, Miller, & Cargille, 1994). The following capabilities are typical of binary rewriting libraries:

- Redirection of function calls and insertion of trampoline functions that execute the originally called function;
- Insertion of additional code and data; and
- Control and data-flow analysis to guide instrumentation.

The following code illustrates the use of control-flow analysis and insertion of additional code through the Editing Executable Library (EEL) (Larus & Schnarr, 1995), machine-independent, executable editing API: (Box 5)

EEL code "snippets" encapsulate of pieces of code that can be inserted into existing binary code. They are either written directly in assembly language (which makes the instrumentation machine dependent) or written using a higher-level language that is compiled into assembly. To graft snippet code into existing code, each snippet identifies registers used in the snippet that must be assigned to unused registers.

Dynamic Binary-Code Instrumentation

An alternative to static binary instrumentation is dynamic instrumentation. Dynamic instrumentation, implemented as Just-in Time (JIT) compilation, is performed after a program has been loaded into memory and immediately prior to execution (Figure 2, label D). Dynamic instrumentation has the advantage that profiling functionality can be selectively added or removed from the program without the need to recompile: Trace functionality is only present when needed. Moreover, dynamic instrumentation can be applied reactively, for example, in response to some event in the system, such as processor slow down. Dynamic instrumentation is particularly useful for facilitating conditional breakpoints in code, for example, Buck and Hollingsworth (2000) show that this approach is 600 times more efficient than conventional trap-based debug breakpoints.

Box 5.

```
nt main(int argc, char* argv[])
{
 executable* exec = new executable(argv[1]);
 exec->read_contents();
 routine* r;

 FOREACH_ROUTINE (r, exec->routines())
     {
     instrument(r);
     while(!exec->hidden_routines()->is_empty())
         {
         r = exec->hidden_routines()->first();
         exec->hidden_routines()->remove(r);
         instrument(r);
         exec->routines()->add(r);
         }
     }

 addr x = exec->edited_addr(exec->start_address());
 exec->write_edited_executable(st_cat(argv[1], ".count"), x);
 return (0);
}

void instrument(routine* r)
{
 static long num = 0;
 cfg* g = r->control_flow_graph();
 bb* b;

 FOREACH_BB(b, g->blocks())
     {
     if (1 < b->succ()->size())
         {
          edge* e;

         FOREACH_EDGE (e, b->succ())
             {
             // incr_count is the user-defined code snippet
             e->add_code_along(incr_count(num));
             num += 1;
             }
         }
     }
 r->produce_edited_routine();
 r->delete_control_flow_graph();
}
```

The Paradyn work from the University of Wisconsin, Madison (Miller, Callaghan, Cargille, Hollingsworth, Irvin, & Karavanic, 1995) was designed specifically for measuring the performance of parallel programs. Paradyn uses dynamic instrumentation to apply trace functionality according to a set of resource hierarchies, as shown in Figure 3 (shaded nodes represent an example focus, all spin locks in CPU#1, in any procedure). Entities within the resource hierarchies effectively represent the scope of the current tracing functionality.

Buck and Hollingsworth expanded the dynamic instrumentation element of Paradyn in their Dyninst work (Buck & Hollingsworth, 2000). Dyninst provides a C++ API and a set of run-time libraries that allow users to build tools for modifying dynamic binary code. It attaches to loaded binaries that are either already running or that are explicitly loaded by the Dyninst run-time. Once attached to an executable, tools written using the Dyninst API (termed mutators) can be used to modify the binary image directly in memory.

Dyninst works by adding "trampolines" into the target binary at selected positions, shown in D. Branch instructions are inserted into the target program, at user-defined positions, to redirect control flow into the base trampoline. Base trampolines are instantiated for each instrumentation point in the target code. Each contains pre- and post- branching to global primitives (called for all processes) and local instrumentation primitives (called only for the specific instrumentation point). Base trampolines also include the original code that was displaced from the target, which is also executed.

Dyninst's thread abstraction allows developers to associate instrumentation with specific threads that are running in the system, which is a necessary part of their selective profiling scheme. With this approach the overhead of instrumentation is incurred up-front in modifying the binary image. After the image has been modified, the only overhead is the cost of trampolining and the additional instructions imposed by the instrumented primitives.

Snippet code (the code which is being added to the target image) is created using the DyninstAPI to dynamically assemble variable declarations, expressions, and so forth. The following excerpt illustrates how the Dyninst API can be used to create a global counter variable and an expression that increments it. (Box 6)

Dyninst is designed to target the native processor; the modified instructions target the actual underlying hardware. Other work, such as Pin (Luk et al., 2005), Dixie (Fernandez, Ramirez, Cernuda, & Espasa, 1999), DynamoRIO (Bruening, 2004), and Valgrind (Nethercote, 2004), have pursued the use of JIT cross-compilation so that the modified binary code can be executed on an emulated (i.e., virtual) machine architecture. Targeting a virtual machine provides more control and the ability to inspect low-level details of behavior, such as register and cache activity. It also does not necessarily imply translation across different instruction set architectures (ISA). In most instances, the virtual machine uses the same ISA as the underlying host, so that while hooks and interceptors can be put in place, the bulk of the code can simply be passed through and executed by the host.

The Pin program analysis system (Luk et al. 2005) is an example of dynamic compilation targeting a virtual machine architecture using

Box 6.

```
// create a global int variable in the address space of the application
//
BPatch_variableExpr * intCounter = appThread->malloc(*appImage->findType("int"));

// create an expression that increments counter variable
//
BPatch_arithExpr addOne(BPatch_assign, *intCounter, BPatch_constExpr(1));
```

the same ISA as the underlying host. As shown in Figure 5, the Pin system consists of:

- Instrumentation API, which is used to write programs that perform dynamic interception and replacement;
- JIT Compiler, which compiles and instruments the bytecode immediately before execution;
- Code cache, which caches translations between the target binary and the JIT compiled code;
- Emulation unit, which interprets instructions that cannot be executed directly; and
- Dispatcher, which retrieves and executes code from the code cache.

To analyze a program's behavior (multithreaded or not), Pin users must write a program that performs dynamic instrumentation. Pin provides an API based on the ATOM API (Srivastava & Eustace, 1994) that shields programmers from idiosyncrasies of the underlying instruction set and allows passing of context information, such as register contents, to the injected code as parameters. Pin programs typically consist of analysis and instrumentation elements. The basic building blocks for defining instrumentation points are machine instructions, basic blocks, procedures, images, and applications. For example, the C++ code below shows the use of the Pin API to instrument the target code with trace functions each time `sleep()` is invoked.

First, a replacement function is defined with the same signature as the function that is being replaced (in this example `sleep()`). (Box 7)

A callback function `ImageLoad()` is used to intercept binary-image loads that are executed by the target application. The Pin API can then be used to obtain the function that will be replaced with the new tracing/trampoline function. (Box 8)

The instrumentation function is "hooked" onto image loads through `IMG _ AddInstrument-Function()` as follows:

Figure 5. The Pin software architecture

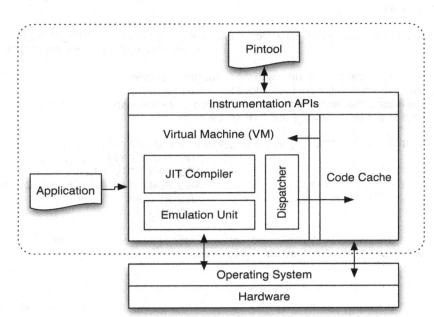

Box 7.

```
typedef VOID * ( *FP_SLEEP )( unsigned int );

// This is the replacement routine.
VOID * NewSleep( FP_SLEEP orgFuncptr, UINT32 arg0, ADDRINT returnIp ) {
    // Normally one would do something more interesting with this data.
    //
    cout << "NewSleep ("
        << hex << ADDRINT ( orgFuncptr ) << ", "
        << dec << arg0 << ", "
        << hex << returnIp << ")"
        << endl << flush;

    // Call the relocated entry point of the original (replaced) routine.
    //
    VOID * v = orgFuncptr( arg0 );
    return v;
}
```

Box 8.

```
// Pin calls this function every time a new image is loaded. It is best to do probe
// replacement when the image is loaded,because only one thread knows about the image at
// this time.
VOID ImageLoad( IMG image, VOID *v )
{
    // See if sleep() is present in the image. If so, replace it.
    //
    RTN rtn = RTN_FindByName( image, "sleep" );

    if (RTN_Valid(rtn))
    {
        cout << "Replacing sleep in " << IMG_Name(image) << endl;

        // Define a function prototype that describes the application routine
        // that will be replaced.
        //
        PROTO proto_sleep = PROTO_Allocate( PIN_PARG(void *), CALLINGSTD_DEFAULT,
                                            "sleep", PIN_PARG(int), PIN_PARG_END() );

        // Replace the application routine with the replacement function.
        // Additional arguments have been added to the replacement routine.
        // The return value and the argument passed into the replacement
        // function with IARG_ORIG_FUNCPTR are the same.
        //
        AFUNPTR origptr = RTN_ReplaceSignatureProbed(rtn, AFUNPTR(NewSleep),
                                IARG_PROTOTYPE, proto_sleep,
                                IARG_ORIG_FUNCPTR,
                                IARG_FUNCARG_ENTRYPOINT_VALUE, 0,
                                IARG_RETURN_IP,
                                IARG_END);

        cout << "The original entry point to the replaced function has been moved to 0x";
        cout << hex << ( ADDRINT ) origptr << dec << endl;
```

continued on following page

Box 8. continued

```
            // Free the function prototype.
            PROTO_Free( proto_sleep );
    }
    else {
            cout << "Could not find routine in image\n";
    }
}
```

```
int main( INT32 argc, CHAR *argv[] ) {
  // Initialize symbol processing
  //
  PIN_InitSymbols();

  // Initialize pin
  //
  PIN_Init( argc, argv );

  // Register ImageLoad to be called when an image is
loaded
  //
  IMG_AddInstrumentFunction( ImageLoad, 0 );

  // Start the program in probe mode, never returns
  //
  PIN_StartProgramProbed();

  return 0;
}
```

The target program is run until completion through PIN _ StartProgramProbed(). Pin also supports the ability to dynamically attach and detach from a long-running process if transient tracing is needed.

Dynamic compilation and virtual machine execution incur overhead. With respect to Pin, overhead primarily stems from performing JIT-compilation, helped by the use of a code-translation cache.

Figure 6 shows Pin performance data taken from Luk et al. (2005). These results show that the slowdown incurred by Pin is approximately four times slower than the original code without instrumentation. Even though this slowdown is significant, the Pin approach is one of the fastest JIT-based profiling solutions available today.

Summary of Compiler-Based Instrumentation Techniques

Instrumenting program code with tracing functionality is a powerful means of understanding system behavior. Modifying source code provides a straightforward means to collect trace information that must relate to application-level program functionality. It therefore enables the customization of trace insertion according to the program "features" of interest.

Alternatively, binary instrumentation is well equipped to handle complex software where the executed code cannot be identified until runtime. Binary-level modifications and execution on virtual machine architectures allow straightforward inspection of machine-level registers and data, such as the stack and caches. Conversely, because binary modification operates at such a low level, it is sometimes hard to specify what to instrument when semantics cannot be easily linked to program-level functions and basic blocks. Binary instrumentation is primarily supportive of active profiling, although the use of a virtual machine to execute code also provides a means to profile passively.

From the perspective of profiling multithreaded programs specifically, binary-code instrumentation can provide an effective means to intercept and instrument synchronization functions where source code is not available or when there is a need for very fine-grained information, such as access to cache state. Binary-code instrumentation also

Figure 6. Pin performance test results (Luk et al., 2005)

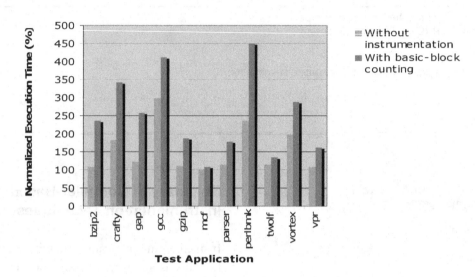

provides detailed access to memory and thus access to thread and process-control blocks useful in profiling multithreaded applications.

OPERATING SYSTEM AND MIDDLEWARE PROFILING TECHNIQUES

All applications rely upon services provided by the underlying operating system. These services are primarily used to coordinate access to shared resources within the system. To measure service "requests" probes can be placed directly within the operating system code that can record individual application access to provided services. Many COTS operating systems also provide a number of performance counters that explicitly track usage of shared resources. Data generated from these counters—along with data from embedded probes—can be combined to form a more complete picture of application behavior.

Another common form of shared processing infrastructure is distributed computing middleware, such as OMG's CORBA and Microsoft's

.NET, which provide common services, such as location transparency and concurrency management. Distributed computing middleware often provides a number of "hook points," such as interceptors and smart proxies that are accessible to users. These hooks provide placeholders for adding probe functionality that can be used to measure events typically hidden deeper within the middleware.

This section first discusses techniques that can be used to place probes into operating system services and how this information can be combined with data generated from operating system-level performance counters. We then discuss two approaches to profiling distribute middleware applications deployed on the CORBA platform.

Profiling System Call Interception

A typical process contains one or more threads and a shared memory space. Application code that is executed by threads within a process is free to access various operating system resources and services, such as virtual memory, files, and network devices. Access to these resources and services is facilitated through APIs that are provided by system libraries. Each thread in the system executes in either user space or kernel space, depending upon the work it is doing at that given time.

Whenever a thread makes a system call, it transitions (e.g., via a trap) from user space to kernel space (Soloman, 1998; Beck et al., 1999). Invoking system calls for thread management (e.g., thread creation, suspension, or termination) and synchronization (e.g., mutex or semaphore acquisition) often require such a transition. System call transitioning code therefore provides a useful interception point at which process activity can be monitored and a profile of system resource use can be extracted on a per-thread basis.

Figure 7 shows the use of the interpositioning technique, where libraries are built to mimic the system API. These libraries contain code that record a call event and then forward the call to the underlying system library.

The threadmon (Cantrill & Doeppner, 1997) tool uses interpositioning to insert trace code between the user-level threads library and the application by redefining many of the functions that the library uses internally to change thread state. This technique is also used by Broberg's Visualization of Parallel Program Behavior (VPPB) tool (Broberg, Lundberg, & Grahn, 1999) to gather user-level thread information. In both approaches,

data obtained by user library interpositioning is integrated with data collected from other operating system services, such as the UNIX /proc file system or kstat utility. The threadmon and VPPB tools both target the Solaris operating system and therefore rely upon Solaris-specific system utilities, such as memory mapping of /dev/kmem to access the kernel.

Cantrill and Doeppner (1997) and Broberg et al. (1999) have also used another tool known as Trace Normal Form (TNF) (Murayama, 2001). This tool generates execution event traces from the Solaris kernel and user processes. Solaris provides an API for inserting TNF probes into the source code of any C/C++ program. A TNF probe is a parameterized macro that records argument values. The code excerpt below shows how C macroprobes can be inserted at the beginning and end of critical code to record the absolute (wall-clock) time required for the code to execute.

```
#include <tnf/probe.h>
.

.
extern mutex_t list_mutex;

.

.
TNF_PROBE_1(critical_start, "critical section start",
"mutex acquire", tnf_opaque, list_lock, &list_mutex)

mutex_lock(&list_mutex);
.
```

Figure 7. Systems calls intercepted by system trap profiling library

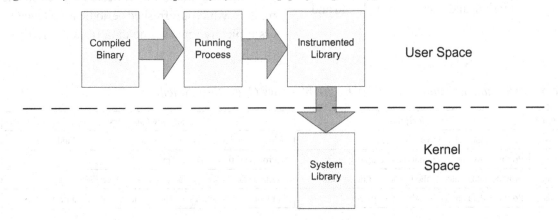

```
.
/* critical section code */
.
.
mutex_unlock(&list_mutex);

TNF_PROBE_1(critical_end, «critical section end»,
«mutex release»,
tnf_opaque, list_lock, &list_mutex)
```

These probes can be selectively activated dynamically at run time. Events are recorded each time a probe is executed. Each probe automatically records thread-specific information, such as the thread identifier, but it may also record other data related to the state of the application at the time the event was triggered. Event records are written to a binary file that is subsequently parsed and analyzed by an offline process. The Solaris kernel also contains a number of TNF probes that can record kernel activity, such as system calls, I/O operations, and thread state change. These probes can be enabled/disabled using a command-line utility known as prex (Murayama, 2001). Data records from the probes are accumulated within a contiguous portion of the kernel's virtual address space and cannot be viewed directly. Another utility that runs with administrator privileges can be used to extract the data and write it to a user file. This data can then be correlated with other user-level data to provide a clear understanding of the behavior of the application run.

The probe-based technique described above provides a detailed view of the running state of the application. Behavioral data details call counts, timing information, and resource use (thread and system state). There are some drawbacks to this approach, however, including:

- The solution is not portable because it depends on Solaris features that are not available on other operating systems.
- It requires a considerable amount of development effort because thread libraries must be modified.
- Applications must be separately built and linked for profiling.
- Tools that are used to collect the data like TNF or kstat may require lengthy setup and configuration.

Microsoft Windows Performance Counters

- Other operating systems have comparable probe-based features that can be used to get comparable data-defining application behavior. For example, Microsoft Windows provides performance counters (Microsoft, 2007a) that contain data associated to the running system. Windows provides a console that can be used to select certain specific counters related to specific processes. Once selected, the values of these counters will be displayed on the console at regular intervals. Table 5 shows example counters that are available.

Windows stores the collected values in the registry, which is refreshed periodically. Developers typically retrieve the data from the registry

Table 5. Performance counters provided by the Windows Operating System

Category	Description	Sample Counters
Process	Provides data related to each process	% Processor Time, % User Time, IO activity, Page Faults etc.
Processor	Provides information about the overall machine	% Processor time, % User Time, %Idle Time etc.
Memory	Provide data related to the memory of the system	Available Bytes, #Page Faults/sec, #Page Reads/sec etc.
Threads	Provides data on the threads in the system	# of Context Switches/sec, Thread State, Thread Wait Reason etc.

directly or use an API known as Performance Data Helper (Microsoft, 2007c; Pietrik, 1998). Alternatively, the Microsoft .NET framework provides the `System.Diagnostics` namespace that facilitates access to all the counters from within a .NET application.

Windows performance counters can be used to acquire data related to the running system, which can be correlated with a particular application run. These counters give an external view of the application, however, and there is no straightforward method of mapping counter values to logical application events. To more closely inspect a running application, therefore, instrumentation is needed within the application itself to record logical events and combine them with data generated through performance counters.

Distributed System Profiling

A distributed system consists of applications whose components are spread over a network of hosts that work together to provide the overarching functionality. The complexity of distributed applications is often considerably greater than a stand-alone application. In particular, distributed applications must address inherent complexities, such as latency, causal ordering, reliability, load balancing, and optimal component placement, that are either absent from (or less complicated in) stand-alone applications (Schmidt, Stal, Rohnert, & Buschmann, 2000). The analysis and profiling of distributed applications involves monitoring key interactions and their characteristics along with localized functionality occurring within each component. Below we examine two approaches to profiling distributed system behavior. One approach modifies generated stubs and skeletons, whereas the other uses profiling extensibility features available in the middleware.

Monitoring of Component-Based Systems (MCBS)

MCBS (Li, 2002) is a CORBA middleware-based monitoring framework that can be used to capture application semantics, timing latency, and shared resource usage. Although the MCBS prototype is CORBA-based the solution can be extended to any distributed object architecture that generates stubs and skeletons. The MCBS approach recreates call sequences across remote interfaces. Probes are

Figure 8. MCBS probe instrumentation

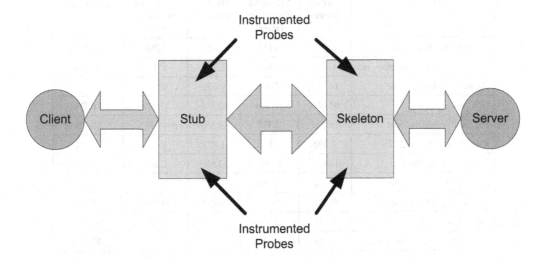

instrumented automatically through a specialized Interface Description Language (IDL) compiler, which directly modifies the generated stubs and skeletons with code that records call entry and return events, as shown in Figure 8.

Along with calls and returns, the MCBS-modified stubs and skeletons can also profile higher-level transactions (as aggregated calls), as well as parameters and return values. Event data is recorded to a log and a unique identifier assigned so that the scenario/call chain can be identified later. This identifier is generated at the start probe and is propagated through the calling sequence via thread-local storage (Schmidt et al., 2000), which is global data that is only available to the owning thread. When each new interface is invoked, the stub receives the identifier from the thread-specific storage, creates a record with it, and stores a number identifying its position in the call chain. After control returns to the caller stub, the last record is generated and the call chain record completed.

Whenever a new thread is created by the application, the parent thread identifier is stored along with the new thread identifier to help identify the logical call chain in cases where threads are spawned by user-application code. Event data is stored in a memory buffer during application execution and is dumped to a file regularly as the buffer becomes full. An off-line data collector picks up the different files for the different processes and loads them into a database. The analyzer component processes the data and constructs entire call graphs. The end-to-end timing latency of call scenarios is calculated from the timestamps and latencies calculated from their deltas.

MCBS also allows the comparison of measurement overhead against normal (uninstrumented) operation. This comparison measures the instrumented execution timing with timings collected from the original application that has been manually instrumented. The manual instrumentation is restricted to a single function at a time to minimize overhead. Table 6 shows performance data for a sample application. The sample scenarios are known to have deterministic functionality, that is, they perform the same set of actions every time.

MCBS can reduce measurement overhead by profiling only specific components of the application. Component selection can be achieved in two ways:

Table 6. Overhead of instrumentation due to probes inserted in stubs and skeletons

Function	Average (msec)	Standard Deviation (msec)	Average (msec)	Standard Deviation (msec)	Interference
EngineController::print	1.535	0.158	1.484	1.288	3.4%
DeviceChannel::is_supplier_set	1.865	0.054	1.236	0.025	50.9%
IO::retrieve_from_queue	10.155	0.094	9.636	0.094	5.4%
GDI::draw_circle	95.066	10.206	85.866	11.342	10.7%
RIP::notify_downstream	13.831	2.377	11.557	0.381	19.7%
RIP::Insert_Obj_To_DL	2.502	0.141	1.879	0.127	33.2%
IO::push_to_queue	13.626	0.298	13.580	2.887	0.3%
UserApplication::notified	0.418	0.04	0.282	0.099	48.3%
Render::deposit_to_queue	0.529	0.097	0.358	0.010	47.8%
Render::render_object	7.138	2.104	6.280	0.074	13.6%
Render::retrieve_from_queue	0.501	0.040	0.318	0.010	57.6%

- Statically prior to executing, where monitored components are selected and the application is then run. The application must be stopped and restarted if the selected set of components changes.
- Dynamically while the application is running, where the monitored components can be selected at runtime. Dynamic selection helps developers focus on problem area and analyze it without incurring overhead due to measurement of other components.

Li (2002) has implemented both approaches and suggests that static selection is more straightforward (in terms of instrumentation effort) than dynamic selection. Dynamic selection is more complicated because it must avoid data inconsistency that can arise if a component process receives an off event, where monitoring is forced to stop during a run. Modifying instrumentation dynamically thus relies on the system reaching a steady state.

The current MCBS prototype is restricted to synchronous remote procedure calls. It does not support dynamic function invocations (e.g., through CORBA DII) nor does it support stubless colocated objects.

OVATION

OVATION (Object Computing Incorporated, 2006; Gontla, Drury, & Stanley, 2003) is a distributed monitoring framework that uses similar concepts as the MCBS framework. It is, however, specifically targeted to CORBA middleware and has been tested on both TAO (Schmidt, Natarajan, Gokhale, Wang, & Gill, 2002) and JacORB (Brose, 1997).

The OVATION tool uses CORBA Portable Interceptors (OMG, 2002) to insert probes. Portable Interceptors are based on the Interceptor pattern (Schmidt et al., 2000), which allows transparent addition of services to a framework and automatic triggering of these services when

certain events occur. Whenever a CORBA client calls a server component client stub and server skeleton interceptors are invoked. Each interceptor can perform any arbitrary function, such as timestamping an event or recording information about a call to a log file.

OVATION provides a number of predefined probes, including:

- **Snooper Probe,** which captures CORBA operation information, such as request name, arguments, request start time, end time and the threads and the processes to which an operation belongs;
- **Milestone Probe,** which permits the manual demarcation of specific events in the application code; and
- **Trace Probe,** which is used to capture information about the other non-CORBA, C++ or Java object method calls.

OVATION also allows users to add their own custom probes to the monitoring framework. This feature allows developers to profile application-specific characteristic without changing their source code. Moreover, custom probes can be dynamically enabled and disabled at run time.

Call graphs among components, along with latency measurements, are reconstructed for each scenario. OVATION generates log files during program execution that contain information detailing processes, threads, and objects involved in the interaction. The OVATION visualizer transforms the log file into a graphical representation of the recorded remote object interactions. An example screenshot from the visualizer showing measured call sequences is illustrated in Figure 9.

Summary of Operating System and Middleware Profiling Techniques

All applications interact with the operating system and many interact with middleware services for distributed communication, fault tolerance,

Figure 9. Screenshot of the OVATION visualization tool

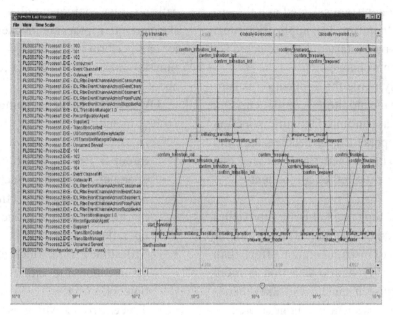

security, resource management, and so forth. Measuring behavior in the layers that supports application execution is crucial to gaining a complete understanding of the broader system because applications share resources (e.g., memory, files and devices) via these layers. Complex interactions and dependencies are often hidden and not obviously understood by the systems engineer. As large-scale systems are integrated together, these hidden dependencies result in resource conflicts and "causal chains" that lead to unexpected, and often undesirable, behavior. The tools described in this section allow profiling of execution that passes through the operating system and middleware layers. One challenge faced by these tools and their users is mapping these behaviors to higher-level application and distributed events.

VIRTUAL MACHINE PROFILING TECHNIQUES

The use of virtual machine, such as the Java Virtual Machine and the Microsoft Common Runtime Language (CLR), is becoming increasingly common in enterprise applications where portability and security are key requirements. Figure 10 illustrates a typical VM-based application architecture where each user application is independently layered above the VM.

The use of VMs to run "managed programs" lends itself to more portable profiling. For example, dynamic instrumentation of complete binaries for VM platforms is more straightforward because the bytecode represents a hardware agnostic, and more abstract representation, of the binary code (Gosling, 1995).

In general, profiling strategies for VMs, such as sampling and instrumentation, are comparable to their native counterparts; the main factors that determine effectiveness of a given approach include (1) implementation complexity, (2) incurred time/space overhead, and (3) level of detail in the output. This section describes different methods used for VM profiling and evaluates the advantages and disadvantages of each.

Figure 10. Applications running on virtual machine

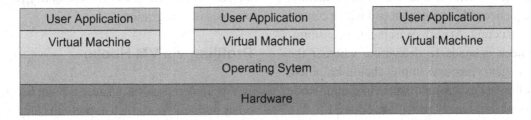

Sampling-Based VM Profiling

One approach to profiling applications that execute in a VM environment is to sample the execution state (i.e., program counter value and call stack) at periodic timer-driven intervals. Whaley (2000) demonstrates the use of such timer-driven sampling via a "samping profiler" that examines threads within the JVM process corresponding to the Java application being profiled. The profiler then periodic traverses the operating system's thread queues, and for each active Java thread, retrieves the register state (program counter and stack pointer) as well as the current time. In effect, this is a combination of operating system level profiling with the restriction on VM processes (i.e., crossing the OS-VM boundary).

Although sampling-based profiling methods are relatively lightweight, they are susceptible to certain problems (Subramaniam & Thazhuthaveetil, 1994), including:

- **Straddling effect of counters:** the initial analysis to segregate the bytecode for different methods will be approximate, causing inconsistent results;
- **Short submethods:** short-lived calls that take less time than the sampling frequency may not be recorded at all; and
- **Resonance effects:** the time to complete a single iteration of a loop can coincide with the sampling period, which may sample the same point each time, while other sections are never measured.

These problems can be avoided by using techniques described in Subramaniam and Thazhuthaveetil (1994). To obtain a consistent picture of application behavior, however, a significant number of runs must be performed. This number will vary from application to application, so the sampling period may also require configuration for each application.

Bytecode Counting

Another instance of VM sampling-based profiling is Komorium (Binder, 2005). Komorium does not check the program counter at regular intervals. Instead, a snapshot of the call stack is recorded by each thread after a certain number of bytecodes are executed. The motivation for this approach is that bytecode counting is a platform-independent metric that does not depend upon VM-specific profiling services. Bytecode counting can also be done without on the need for low-level platform-dependent utilities to acquire resource usage data, thus making it more portable and easier to maintain.

Komorium relies on the periodic activation of a user-defined profiling agent to process samples of the call stack. Bytecode rewriting is used to pass the current call stack of the caller into the profiling function. To schedule regular activation of the custom profiling function, each thread maintains an activation counter (ac) that represents the upper bound of the number of executed bytecodes since the last invocation. The active count is decremented at given points in the code. The default behavior is to update the active count at the beginning of each basic block, which is defined as a sequence of bytecode that end with a control flow instruction. At each decrement, a consumption check is made to determine whether the custom agent (processSample) should be called. The following excerpt illustrates in pseudo-code the Komorium binary rewriting: (Box 7)

Binder, Hulaas, and Villaz (2001) evaluated the Komorium approach through experimentation. They showed that their approach could sample at an accuracy of 91% using an overlapping percentage metric (Arnold & Ryder, 2001). The best results were obtained from a profiling granularity of 5,000-10,000 bytecodes per sample, resulting in an average overhead of 47-56% for a 10,000 bytecode granularity.

VM sampling-based profiling provides an effective method of collecting temporal information relating to program control. These techniques are can be used to determine task latency, jitter, and execution quanta, as well as to identify patterns of processor migration.

Profiling via VM Hooks

A VM hook represents an access point to a previously defined event, such as method entry/exit or thread start/stop, that can occur within the context of a running application. The profiling agent implements callback methods on the profiling interface and registers them with the appropriate VM hooks. The VM then detects the events and invokes the corresponding callback method when these events occur in the application. It is straightforward to develop profilers based on VM hooks because profiler developers need only implement an interface provided by the VM, without worrying about the complications that can arise from modifying the application directly.

Box 7.

```
// Pseudo Java code illustrating Komorium re-writing. Bold represents additional
// code added by Komorium.
//
// ac = per-thread activation counter representing the upper bound of the
// number of executed bytecodes
//
// mids, sp = represents reifed method ids, stack pointer pair
//
class Foo {
    private static final MID mid_sum;
    static {
        String cl = Class.forName("Foo").getName();
        mid_sum = createMID(c1, "sum", "(II)I");
    }

    static int sum(int from, int to, AC ac, MID[] mids, int sp) {

        mids[sp++] = mid_sum;
        decrementAC(2);
        if(getValue(ac) <= 0)
            setValue(ac, processSample(mids, sp));

        int result = 0;

        while(true) {
```

continued on following page

Box 7. continued

```
            decrementAC(3);
            if(getValue(ac) <= 0)
                setValue(ac, processSample(mids, sp));
            if(from > to) {
                decrementAC(2);
                if(getValue(ac) <= 0)
                    setValue(ac, processSample(mids, sp));
                return result;
            }
            decrementAC(7);
            if(getValue(ac) <= 0)
                setValue(ac, processSample(mids, sp));

            result += f(from, ac, mids, sp);
            ++from;
        }
    }

    static int sum(int from, int to) {
        Thread t = Thread.currentThread();
        return sum(from, to, ac, new MID[STACKSIZE], 0);
    }
}
```

Although the VM and profiling agent provide the monitoring infrastructure, profiler developers are responsible for certain tasks, such as synchronization. For example, multithreaded applications can spawn multiple instances of the same event simultaneously, which will invoke the same callback method on the same instance of the profiling agent. Callbacks must therefore be made reentrant via synchronization mechanisms, such as mutexes, to avoid compromising profiler internal state.

The Microsoft Common Language Runtime (CLR) profiler and the Java Virtual Machine Tool Interface (JVMTI) are two examples of VM profilers that that support VM hooks, as described below.

CLR Profiler

The CLR Profiler (Hilyard, 2005) interface allows the integration of custom profiling functionality provided in the form of a pluggable dynamic link library, written in a native language like C or C++. The plug-in module, termed the agent, accesses profiling services of the CLR via the `ICorProfilerInfo2` interface. The agent must also implement the `ICorProfilerCallback2` interface so the CLR can call the agent back to indicate the occurrence of events in the context of the profiled application.

At startup, the CLR initializes the agent and sets the events of interest. When an event occurs, the CLR calls the corresponding method on the `ICorProfilerCallback2` interface. The agent can then inspect the execution state of the application by calling methods back on the CLR (`ICorProfilerInfo2`).

Figure 11 shows the series of communications triggered by each function entered in the CLR execution. In this example, in between processing function enter/exit call-backs, the profiling agent requests a stack snapshot so it can identify the

Figure 11. Messaging sequence of CLR profiling

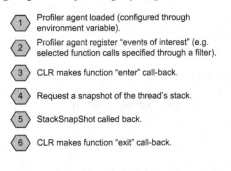

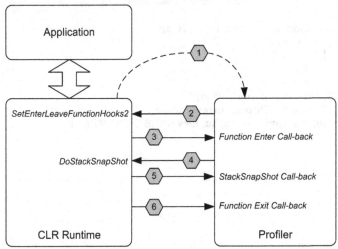

fully qualified method name and also the call's parent, that is, the method from which the method being traced was called.

Inspecting the stack to determine parental methods (and ultimately the call-chain) is a useful technique for disambiguating system calls. For example, this approach can be used to disambiguate different lock calls so that per-lock information (e.g., hold and wait times) can be correlated with different call sites in the source code.

JVMTI Profiler

The JVMTI (Sun Microsystems Corporation, 2004) is similar to the CLR Profiler Interface in that it requires a plug-in, which is implemented as a dynamic link library using a native language that supports C. The JVM interacts with the agent

through JVMTI functions, such as `Agent_OnLoad()` and `Agent_OnUnload()`, which are exported by the agent. The JVM supplies a pointer, via the `Agent_Onload()` call, that the agent can use to get an instance of the JVMTI environment. The agent can then use this pointer to access JVMTI features, such as reading the state of a thread, stopping/interrupting threads, obtaining a stack trace of a thread, or reading local variable information. The agent uses the `SetEventCallbacks()` method to pass a set of function pointers for different events it is interested. When events occur, the corresponding function is called by the JVM, which allows the agent to record the state of the application.

Although the CLR and JVMTI profilers share many common features, such as events related to methods or threads and stack tracing ability, there are differences. For example, the JVMTI provides application-specific details, such as the method name, object name, class name, and parameters, from the calls, whereas the CLR interface provides them in a metadata format and details can only be extracted using the metadata API, which is tedious. The JVMTI also provides additional features compared to the CLR, including monitor wait and monitor waited, which provide information related to thread blocking on critical sections of code.

Research (Reiss, 2003, 2005) has shown that the JVMTI interface incurs significant runtime overhead because the profiling agent is written in a native language, so JNI calls (Sun Microsystems Corporation, 2002) are needed to call this agent. JNI calls can incur significant overhead because they perform actions such as saving registers, marshaling arguments, and wrapping objects in JNI handles (Dmitriev, 2002). This overhead may not be acceptable for some applications, so the explicit bytecode instrumentation approach described in the next section may be a less costly solution because it does not use JNI.

Application Code Instrumentation

Although sampling- and hook-based instrumentation can be performed with relatively little overhead, the breadth of the information collected is limited and often insufficient to build application-level detail. An alternative is to instrument the application's bytecode directly. Bytecode instrumentation inserts functionality (in the form of additional bytecodes) that performs application profiling within compiled code. The Komorium work discussed previously is a form of byte code instrumentation. However, we differentiate the discussion in this section by instrumentation that is driven directly by the application logic.

As a general approach, bytecode instrumentation involves redefining classes that are going to be profiled by replacing the original bytecode with instrumented code that contains logging ac-

tions triggered by specific events. This approach enables the use of application-specific events for profiling, such as transaction completion or data regarding critical sections of the application. Bytecode instrumentation has in most instances less overhead and greater flexibility than using VM-provided profiling interfaces. Nevertheless, the responsibility of implementing measurement functionality lies with the profiler user.

There are several approaches to bytecode instrumentation, including:

- Static instrumentation, which involves changing the compiled code off-line before execution that is, creating a copy of the instrumented intermediate code. Many commercial profilers, such as OptimizeIt (Borland Software Corporation, 2006), work this way. Static instrumentation has also been implemented by Reiss (2003) and later extended in Reiss (2005).
- Load-time instrumentation, which calls the agent before loading each class, and passes it the bytecode for the class that can be changed by the agent and returned. The JVMTI/CLR profiler interfaces are examples of load-time instrumentation.
- Dynamic instrumentation, which works when the application is already running and also uses a profiler interface (Dmitriev, 2002). The agent makes a call to the VM passing it the new definitions of the classes that are installed by the VM at runtime.

Like other forms of code modification, dynamic instrumentation supports "fix and continue" debugging, which avoids lengthy exit, recompile, and restart cycles. It also helps reduce application overhead by enabling developers to (1) pinpoint specific regions of code that are experiencing performance problems at runtime and (2) instrument the classes' involved, rather than instrumenting the entire application. Instrumented classes can be replaced with the original ones after sufficient data is collected.

Dynamic instrumentation of bytecode is typically more straightforward than dynamic instrumentation of low-level machine instructions because of the higher level of abstraction. Moreover, modifying bytecode provides a more portable solution that is largely agnostic to the underlying operating system and hardware platform.

Within the context of Java, the JVMTI provides a method known as RedefineClasses() that a profiler agent can use to insert "new" bytecode into an existing class. When this method is invoked, the JVM performs all the steps needed to load a class, parse the class code, create objects of the class, and initializes them. After these steps are complete, the JVM performs hot-swapping by suspending all threads and replacing the class, while ensuring that all pointers are updated to point to the new object (Dmitriev, 2001).

These dynamic instrumentation activities can incur significant overhead in production environments and thus must be accounted for accordingly. Some research is investigating techniques to minimize the overhead incurred by dynamic instrumentation. For example, work by Dmitriev (2002) is investigating the use of "method swapping" so that bytecode replacement can be done at a finer granularity than class-level replacement. Similar techniques are also being explored within the context of the .NET platform (Vaswani & Srikant, 2003).

A number of tools have been developed to help instrument bytecode, much like the Pin API described earlier. Examples include BIT (Lee, 1997) and IBM's Jikes Bytecode Toolkit (IBM Corporation, 2000). These tools shield application developers from the complexity of bytecode by providing an API that can be used to parse and modify it.

- The three bytecode instrument techniques (i.e., static, load-time, and dynamic) incur similar overhead. Dynamic bytecode instrumentation is more powerful, but is generally more complex and error-prone than static

and load time instrumentation. Dynamic instrumentation also requires creating "new" objects of the "new" classes corresponding to all "old" objects in the application, initializing their state to the state of the old object, suspend the running threads, and switching all pointers to the "old" objects to the "new" objects. This replacement process is complicated, so application state may be inconsistent after the operation, which can cause incorrect behavior.

- Static and load-time instrumentation are generally easier to implement than dynamic instrumentation because they need not worry about the consistency of a running application. Dynamic instrumentation has a broader range of applicability, however, if done efficiently. Current research (Dmitriev, 2002, 2004) is focusing on how to make dynamic instrumentation more efficient and less complicated.

Aspect-Oriented Techniques Used for Instrumentation

Although explicit bytecode instrumentation is more flexible and incurs less overhead than VM hooks, the implementation complexity is higher because developers must be highly skilled in bytecode syntax to instrument it effectively without corrupting application code. Aspect-oriented Programming (AOP) helps remove this complexity and enables bytecode instrumenting at a higher level of abstraction. Developers can therefore focus on the logic of the code snippets and the appropriate insertion points, rather than wrestling with low-level implementation details (Davies, Huismans, Slaney, Whiting, & Webster, 2003). Relevant AOP concepts include (1) join-points, which define placeholders for instrumentation within application code, (2) point-cuts, which identify a selection of join-points to instrument, and (3) advice, which specifies the code to insert at the corresponding join-point.

AspectWerkz (Boner, 2004) is a framework that uses AOP to support static, load-time, and dynamic (runtime) instrumentation of bytecode. The advantages and disadvantages of the various techniques are largely similar to those discussed earlier. There are also aspects to consider when using an AOP-based approach, however, which we discuss below.

The AOP paradigm makes it easier for developers to insert profiling to an existing application by defining a profiler aspect consisting of point-cuts and advice. The following excerpt illustrates the use of AspectWerkz to define join-points before, after, and around the execution of the method `HelloWorld.greet()`. The annotations in the comments section of the Aspect class express the semantics, for example, "`@Before execution (* <package_name>.<class_name>.<method_name>)`" means the method will be called before the execution of the `<method_name>` mentioned.

```
//////////////////////////////////////////////////
//
package testAOP;

import org.codehaus.aspectwerkz.joinpoint.JoinPoint;

public class HelloWorldAspect {
    /**
     * @Before execution(* testAOP.HelloWorld.greet(..))
     */
    public void beforeGreeting(JoinPoint joinPoint) {
        System.out.println("before greeting...");
    }

    /**
     * @After execution(* testAOP.HelloWorld.greet(..))
     */
    public void afterGreeting(JoinPoint joinPoint) {
        System.out.println("after greeting...");
    }

/**
     * @Around execution(* testAOP.HelloWorld2.greet(..))
     */
    public Object around_greet (JoinPoint joinPoint) {
        Object greeting = joinPoint.proceed();
        return "<yell>" + greeting + "</yell>";
    }
}
```

Advice code can be written in the managed language, so there is no need to learn the low-level syntax of bytecode because the AOP framework can handle these details. The bulk of the effort therefore shifts to learning the framework rather than bytecode/IL syntax, which is advantageous because these frameworks are similar even if the target application language changes, for example, from Java to C#. Another advantage is the increased reliability and stability provided by a proven framework with dedicated support. For example, developers need not worry about problems arising with hot-swap or multiple threads being profiled because these are handled by the framework.

Some problems encountered by AOP approaches are the design and deployment overhead of using the framework. AOP frameworks are generally extensive and contain a gamut of configuration and deployment options, which may take time to master. Moreover, developers must also master another framework on top of the actual application, which may make it hard to use profiling extensively. Another potential drawback is that profiling can only occur at the join-points provided by the framework, which is often restricted to the methods of each class, that is, before a method is called or after a method returns. Application-specific events occurring within a method call therefore cannot be profiled, which means that nondeterministic events cannot be captured by AOP profilers.

Summary of Virtual Machine Profiling Techniques

Java and C# are two prominent VM-based languages that are becoming increasingly dominant in the development of enterprise-style systems. The advantage of ease-of-use, security and portability is driving their success. Nevertheless, from a run-time analysis and profiling perspective, they do pose additional challenges by executing programs in a "hidden" VM. The tools in this section can be used to extend profiling capabilities into a VM environment.

The decision to choose a particular profiling technique depends upon application requirements. The following criteria are useful to decide which approach is appropriate for a given application.

- Sampling is most effective when there is a need to minimize runtime overhead and use profiling in production deployments, though application-specific logical events may not be tracked properly.
- The simplest way to implement profiling is by using the JVMTI/CLR profiling interface, which has the shortest development time and is easy to master. Detailed logical events may not be captured, however, and the overhead incurred may be heavier than bytecode/IL instrumentation.
- Bytecode/IL instrumentation is harder to implement, but gives unlimited freedom to the profiler to record any event in the application. Implementing a profiler is harder than using the JVMTI/CLR profiling interface, however, and a detailed knowledge of bytecode/IL is required. Among the different bytecode/IL instrumentation ways, complexity of implementation increases from static-time instrumentation to load-time to dynamic instrumentation. Dynamic instrumentation provides powerful features, such as "fix and continue" and runtime problem tracking.
- The use of an AOP framework can reduce the development complexity and increase reliability because bytecode/IL need not be manipulated directly. Conversely, AOP can increase design and deployment overhead, which may make it unsuitable for profiling. Moreover, application-level events may be hard to capture using AOP if join-points locations are limited.

HARDWARE-BASED PROFILING TECHNIQUES

Previous sections have concentrated on modifications to program code (e.g., via instrumentation) or code that implements the execution environment (e.g., VM profiling). This section describes hardware profiling techniques that collect behavioral information in multithreaded systems, focusing on two main categories of hardware-based profiling solutions: on-chip performance counters and on-chip debugging/in-circuit emulation interfaces.

On-Chip Performance Counters

On-chip debugging/profiling interfaces are specialized circuitries that are added to a microprocessor to collect events and measure time. Modern COTS processors provide on-chip performance monitoring and debugging support. On-chip, performance-monitoring support includes selectable counting registers and time stamping clocks. The Intel Pentium/Xeon family of processors and the IBM PowerPC family of processors both provide these performance monitoring features (Intel Corporation, 2006a; IBM Corporation, 1998).

For example, the Intel Xeon processor provides one 64-bit timestamp counter and eighteen 40-bit-wide Model Specific Registers (MSR) as counters (different processor models have a different number of performance counters available). Each core (in a multicore configuration) has its own timestamp counter and counter registers. The timestamp counter is incremented at the processor's clock speed and is constant (at least in later versions of the processors) across multiple cores and processors in an SMP environment. Timestamp counters are initially synchronized because each is started on the processor RESET signal. Timestamp counters can be written to later, however, potentially get them out of sync. Counters must be carefully synchronized when accessing them from different threads that potentially execute on different cores.

The performance counters and timestamp MSRs are accessed through specialized machine instructions (i.e., RDMSR, WRMSR, and RDTSC) or through higher-level APIs such as the Performance Application Programming Interface (PAPI) (London, Moore, Mucci, Seymour, & Luczak, 2001). A set of control registers are also provided to select which of the available performance monitoring events should be maintained in the available counter set. The advantages of using on-chip performance counters are: (1) they do not cost anything in addition to the off-the-shelf processor and (2) they can be used with a very low overhead. For instance, copying the current 64-bit timestamp counter into memory (user or kernel) through the Intel RDTSC instruction costs less than 100 cycles.

Countable events on the Intel Xeon processor include branch predictions, prediction misses, misaligned memory references, cache misses and transfers, I/O bus transactions, memory bus transactions, instruction decoding, micro-op execution, and floating-point assistance. These events are counted on a per-logical core basis, that is, the Intel performance counter features do not provide any means of differentiating event counts across different threads or processes. Certain architectures, however, such as the IBM PowerPC 604e (IBM Corporation, 1998), do provide the ability to trigger an interrupt when performance counters negate or wrap-around. This interrupt can be filtered on a per processor basis and used to support a crude means of thread-association for infrequent events.

On-chip performance counters have limited use in profiling characteristics specific to multithreaded programming. Nevertheless, on-chip timestamp collection can be useful for measuring execution time intervals (Wolf, 2003). For example, measurement of context switch times of the operating systems can be easily done through the insertion of RDTSC into the operating system-kernel switching code. Coupling timestamp features with compiler-based instrumentation can be an effective way to measure lock wait and hold times.

On-Chip Debugging Interfaces and In-Circuit Emulators (ICE)

Performance counters are only useful for counting global events in the system. Additional functionality is therefore needed to perform more powerful inspection of execution and register/memory state. One way to provide this functionality is by augmenting the "normal" target processor with additional functionality. The term in-circuit emulator (ICE) refers to the use of a substitute processor module that "emulates" the target microprocessor and provides additional debugging functionality (Collins 1997).

ICE modules are usually plugged directly into the microprocessor socket using a specialized adapter, as shown in Figure 12. Many modern microprocessors, however, provide explicit support for ICE, including most x86 and PowerPC-based CPUs. A special debug connector on the motherboard normally provides access to the on-chip ICE features.

Two key standards define debugging functionality adopted by most ICE solutions: JTAG (IEEE, 2001) and the more recent Nexus (IEEE-ISTO, 2003). The Nexus debugging interface is a superset of JTAG and consists of between 25 and 100 auxiliary message-based channels that connect directly to the target processor. The Nexus specification defines a number of different "classes" of support that represent different capability sets composed from the following sets:

- Ownership trace messaging (OTM), which facilitates ownership tracing by providing visibility of which process identity (ID) or operating system task is activated. An OTM is transmitted to indicate when a new process/task is activated, thereby allowing development tools to trace ownership flow. For embedded processors that implement

Figure 12. Example ICE adapter and ICE module

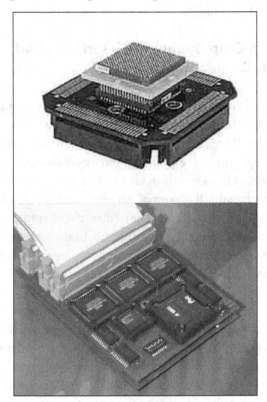

virtual addressing or address translation, moreover, an OTM is also transmitted periodically during runtime at a minimum frequency of every 256 Program/Trace messages.

- Program trace via branch trace messaging (BTM), where messages are triggered for each change in program flow discontinuity as a result of either a branch decision or an exception. Control flow can be correlated to program code, where the code is static. BTM messages include timestamp information and the full target-branch address. Thread/task ownership can be correlated from the last received OTM message.

- Data trace messaging (DTM), where a minimum of two trace windows define the start and end memory addresses that should be monitored. DTM messages are dispatched on each read and write of memory in the defined range. Depending on the type of DTM message, a timestamp, the data value read/written, the address of memory access, the current mapped page, and a control flow association are included.

- Runtime system memory substitution via memory substitution messaging (MSM), which has the ability to substitute portions of memory with new code passed from the debugging host via the Nexus interface. Triggers for substitution are exit, reset, and watchpoints.

- Signal watchpoint and breakpoint events, which are used to indicate that specific instruction addresses or data addresses (conditional) have been accessed. Watchpoints are a variation of breakpoints that do not halt the target processor. Both watchpoints and breakpoints can be set to operating system and runtime library functions of interest, such as thread control and synchronization.

Nexus and JTAG-compatible devices can be chained together and read from the same debugging host, which is particularly useful for SMP and multi-core environments, where the profiling needs to collate events from different processors.

On-chip debugging interfaces and ICE solutions provide a primitive means for extracting low-level behavior of a program. They are particularly useful at collecting "raw" low-level details of execution, such as control flow and memory activity, that in turn can be used to assure absence of race conditions, deadlock, and so forth. For example, the following approach might be used to ensure that a program is free of race-conditions:

- Identify address ranges for memory that are shared across one or more threads.
- Identify addresses for synchronization locks and/or functions.

- Establish data-write triggers for identified memory addresses and record triggered events over the execution of the program in a test run.
- Ensure that the appropriate sequence of take lock, access memory (N times), release lock, is followed.

Of course, because this type of profiling is dynamic, the properties can only be ensured for the states the program entered during the test.

Summary of Hardware-Based Profiling Techniques

Hardware profiling is typically reserved for embedded and safety-critical system where understanding and ensuring system behavior is of utmost importance. Although hardware profiling can be relatively costly, it offers the following advantages over software profiling solutions:

- Nonintrusive data collection. Behavioral data can be collected with little or no impact on normal execution of the target system.
- Support for fine-grained data collection. High frequency data can be precisely collected at speeds commensurate with processor/bus clock speeds.
- Off-chip inspection capability. Elements of behavior, such as bus and cache interconnect activity, that do not propagate directly into a general-purpose CPU, can be inspected.

Hardware profiling is particularly advantageous for analyzing certain types of system behavior (such as memory cache hits/misses) that are not easily inspected through software means. Nevertheless, while hardware profiling excels at inspection of fine-grained system events, deriving higher-level measures can be harder. For example, using a hardware profiler to determine the level of concurrency in a system would be hard.

FUTURE TRENDS

This section discusses emerging and future technological trends in the behavioral analysis of systems.

Increased Focus on Synergies Between Static and Dynamic Analysis Techniques and Tools

Since there is no single approach to system profiling that addresses every need, we believe that the most effective approach is to use a combination of static and dynamic analysis to provide a more complete picture of system behavior. Static analysis can be used to explore all possible paths of execution and statistically proportion their execution likelihood. Likewise, dynamic analysis can be used to collect more precise information for concrete instances of a program execution.

New tools and techniques are needed, however, that strategically combine static and dynamic analysis, and that partition the system into well-defined "behavioral containers." As an example of such tools, work by Artho and Biere (2005) has developed generic analysis algorithms that can be applied in either a static or dynamic context. This solution has been demonstrated within the context of software fault detection, whereby faults identified through static analysis are subsequently verified by actual execution and dynamic analysis.

Greater Emphasis on Probabilistic Assurance of Dynamic System Behavior

Even when static and dynamic analysis techniques are combined, certain behavioral properties of large-scale dynamic software systems are still hard to measure and assure precisely, including absence of deadlock and livelock conditions, effective parallelism, and worst-case execution time. These properties can often be assured to a given statistical probability, though both dynamic and static analyses are unable to provide absolute assurance in all cases. Even techniques like explicit-state model checking can only provide assurance in very small systems, where interaction with the external environment is well understood and controlled.

A key reason these properties are hard to measure accurately stems from sources of (apparent) nondeterminism in today's software systems. Deep causal chains, multiple levels of caching, and unpredictable interactions between threads and their environment lead to an incomprehensible number of behavior patterns. The openness of operating systems in their external interactions, such as networks, devices, and other processors, and the use of throughput-efficient-scheduling strategies, such as dynamic priority queues and task preemption, are the principal cause of such behavioral uncertainty. Although real-time and safety-critical operating systems try to ensure higher levels of determinism by applying constraints on execution, such as off-line scheduling, resource reservation, and cache disabling, these solutions are often not applicable for general-purpose systems.

New tools and techniques are needed, therefore, that can assure behaviors of dynamic systems with greater probability. Examples include system execution modeling (SEM) tools (Hill, Schmidt, & Slaby, 2007) that enable software architects, developers, and systems engineers to explore design alternatives from multiple computational and valuation perspectives at multiple lifecycle phases using multiple quality criteria with multiple stakeholders and suppliers. In addition to validating design rules and checking for design conformance, SEM tools facilitate "what if" analysis of alternative designs to quantify the costs of certain design choices on end-to-end system performance. For example, SEM tools can help empirically determine the maximum number of components a host can handle before performance degrades, the average and worse response time for various

workloads, and the ability of alternative system configurations and deployments to meet end-to-end QoS requirements for a particular workload. Although the results of SEM tool analysis are probabilistic—rather than absolute—they still provide valuable information to users.

Implicit Support for Measurement of Infrastructure Software and Processors

Infrastructure software (such as operating systems, virtual machines, and middleware) and processors increasingly provide measurement logic that collects behavioral information during multithreaded system execution. Although these capabilities are useful, they are often provided as add-ons, rather than being integrated seamlessly into the infrastructure software and processors. As a result, the measurement hooks are often not available when needed or undue effort is required to configure and optimize them.

New tools and techniques are needed, therefore, to provide implicit support for measuring of infrastructure software and processors. In particular, the ability to measure and monitor behavior of the system should be a first class concern.

Total-System Measurement that Relates and Combines Microscopic Measurements Together to Give a Unified View of System Behavior

The nondeterministic nature of today's large-scale systems is exacerbated by the lack of integration between various microscopic measurement techniques—both in hardware and in software—and the need for a broader perspective in reasoning about and analyzing end-to-end system behavior. This problem is particularly acute in distributed real-time and embedded (DRE) systems that must combine hardware and software components to meet the following challenging requirements:

As distributed systems, DRE systems require capabilities to measure the quantity/quality of connections and message transfer between separate machines,

As real-time systems, DRE systems require predictable and efficient control over end-to-end system resources, such as memory, networks, and processors, and

As embedded systems, DRE systems have weight, cost, and power constraints that limit their computing and memory resources.

Microscopic measurements of such DRE systems often fail to provide a unified view of system behavior, which makes it hard to assure that the systems meet their functional and QoS requirements.

New tools and techniques are needed, therefore, to provide total-system measurement that provides a unified view of system behavior. An example of such a tool is Intel's VTune Performance Analyzer (REF). This tool combines behavioral information from the microprocessor (measuring on-chip counters), the operating system (OS-level context switching etc.) and the application (application-level function profiling) to provide an effective approach to application tuning.

CONCLUDING REMARKS

This chapter reviewed four approaches to analyzing the behavior of software systems via dynamic analysis: compiler-based instrumentation, operating system and middleware profiling, virtual machine profiling and hardware-based profiling. We highlighted the advantages and disadvantages of each approach with respect to measuring the performance of multithreaded and SMP systems, and demonstrated how these approaches can be applied in practice.

Table 7 summarizes our assessment of the utility of each approach with respect to key problems that arise in developing large-scale, multithreaded systems. The number of dots in each category indicates how effective the approach is for measuring the corresponding characteristics (defined previously in Table 2).

The results in Table 7 show that dynamic profil-

Table 7. Summary of dynamic profiling capabilities

	Compiler-based Instrumentation	Operating System & Middleware Profiling	Virtual Machine Profiling	Hardware-based Profiling
Synchronization overhead	●●●	●●●	●●●	●●●
Task latency & jitter	●●●	●●●	●●●	●●
Task execution quanta		●●●	●●●	●●●
Unsafe memory access	●●●		●	●●●
Processor migration		●●●		●●●
Priority inversion		●●	●●	
Deadlock and livelock		●	●	●
Effective parallelism		●	●	
Worst-case execution time				●

●●●:   *Well suited to analysis of property*
●●:   *Able to partially analyze property or is typically difficult to engineer*
●:   *Approach can be used to collect relevant data, but requires additional processing/analysis capability*
No dots: *Unable to analyze property effectively*

ing is particularly useful where fine-grained event data can be collected and used to derive characteristics of a running system. Dynamic analysis is weaker and less capable, when the behavioral characteristic depends on system-wide analysis, such as the global thread state. It is therefore clear that runtime profiling alone is insufficient to capture and predict a complete image of system behavior due to the "as observed" syndrome, that is, dynamic analysis can only assure statistical certainty of behavior because it just collects behavioral data for a given execution trace.

The alternative to dynamic analysis is static analysis, such as program analysis and model checking. The benefits of static analysis are its ability to (1) perform analysis without running the system (useful for pre-integration testing), and (2) allow the inspection of all theoretically possible (albeit less frequent) conditions. Although static analysis is promising in some areas, it also cannot capture and predict a complete image of behavior for large-scale systems. In particular, static-analysis techniques are limited in their practical applicability (e.g., scalability) and in their ability to relate to wall-clock time.

Behavioral analysis technology will be increasingly important as the systems we build become larger, more parallel, and more unpredictable. New tools and techniques that strategically combine static and dynamic analysis—and that partition the system into well-defined "behavioral containers"—will be critical to the progression along this path.

REFERENCES

Arnold, M., & Ryder, B. G. (2001). A framework for reducing the cost of instrumented code. In *Proceedings of the SIGPLAN Conference on Programming Language Design and Implementation*, (pp. 168-179).

Artho, C., & Biere, A. (2005). Combined static and dynamic analysis. In *Proceedings of the 1ˢᵗ International Workshop on Abstract Interpretation of Object-oriented Language (AIOOL 2005)*, ENTCS, Paris. Elsevier Science Publishing.

Baxter, I. (2004). DMS: Program transformations for practical scalable software evolution. In *Proceedings of the 26ᵗʰ International Conference on Software Engineering*, (pp. 625-634).

Beck, M., Bohme, H., Dziadzka, M., Kunitz, U., Magnus, R., & Verworner, D. (1999). *Linux Kernel internals (2nd ed.)*. Addison Wesley Longman.

Binder, W. (2005). A portable and customizable profiling framework for Java based on bytecode instruction counting. In *Proceedings of the Third Asian Symposium on Programming Languages and Systems (APLAS 2005)*, (LNCS 3780, pp. 178-194).

Binder, W., & Hulaas, J. (2004, October). A portable CPU-management framework for Java. *IEEE Internet Computing, 8*(5), 74-83.

Binder, W., Hulaas J., &Villaz A. (2001). Portable resource control in Java. In *Proceedings of the 2001 ACM SIGPLAN Conference on Object Oriented Programming, Systems, Languages and Applications*, (Vol. 36, No. 11, pp. 139-155).

Boner, J. (2004, March). AspectWerkz—Dynamic AOP for Java. In *Proceedings of the 3ʳᵈ International Conference on Aspect-oriented development (AOSD 2004)*. Lancaster, UK.

Borland Software Corporation. (2006). *Borland Optimize-it Enterprise Suite* (Computer software). Retrieved March 11, 2008, from http://www.borland.com/us/products/optimizeit/index.html

Broberg, M., Lundberg, L., & Grahn, H. (1999, April). Visualization and performance prediction of multithreaded solaris programs by tracing kernel threads. In *Proceedings of the 13th International Parallel Processing Symposium*, (pp. 407-413).

Brose, G. (1997, September). JacORB: Implementation and design of a Java ORB. In *Proceedings of IFIP DAIS'97*, (pp. 143-154).

Bruening, D. L. (2004). *Efficient, transparent, and comprehensive runtime code manipulation.* Unpublished doctoral dissertation, Massachusetts Institute of Technology.

Buck, B., & Hollingsworth, J. K. (2000). An API for runtime code patching. *International Journal of High Performance Computing Applications*, 317-329.

Cantrill, B., & Doeppner, T. W. (1997, January). Threadmon: A tool for monitoring multithreaded program performance. In *Proceedings of the 30th Hawaii International Conference on Systems Sciences*, (pp. 253-265).

Clarke, E. M., Grumberg, O., & Peled, D. A. (2000). *Model checking. Massachusetts Institute of Technology.* Cambridge, MA: The MIT Press.

Clauss, P., Kenmei, B., & Beyler, J.C. (2005, September). The periodic-linear model of program behavior capture. In *Proceedings of Euro-Par 2005* (LNCS 3648, pp. 325-335).

Collins, R. (1997, September). In-circuit emulation: How the microprocessor evolved over time. *Dr. Dobbs Journal.* Retrieved March 11, 2008, from http://www.rcollins.org/ddj/Sep97

Cordy, R., Halpern C., & Promislow, E. (1991). TXL: A rapid prototyping system for programming language dialects. In *Proceedings of the International Conference on Computer Languages* (Vol. 16, No. 1, pp. 97-107).

Davies, J., Huismans, N., Slaney, R., Whiting, S., & Webster, M. (2003). *An aspect-oriented performance analysis environment.* AOSD'03 Practitioner Report, 2003.

Dmitriev, M. (2001a). *Safe evolution of large and long-lived Java applications.* Unpublished doctoral dissertation, Department of Computing Science, University of Glasgow, Glasgow G12 8QQ, Scotland.

Dmitriev, M. (2001b). Towards flexible and safe technology for runtime evolution of Java language applications. In *Proceedings of the Workshop on Engineering Complex Object-Oriented Systems for Evolution* (pp. 14-18). In Association with OOPSLA 2001 International Conference, Tampa Bay, FL, USA.

Dmitriev, M. (2002). Application of the HotSwap technology to advanced profiling. In *Proceedings of the First Workshop on Unanticipated Software Evolution,* held at ECOOP 2002 International Conference, Malaga, Spain.

Dmitriev, M. (2004). Profiling Java applications using code hotswapping and dynamic call graph revelation. In *Proceedings of the 4th International Workshop on Software and Performance*, Redwood Shores, CA, (pp. 139-150).

Fernandez, M., & Espasa, R. (1999). Dixie: A retargetable binary instrumentation tool. In *Proceedings of the Workshop on Binary Translation, held in conjunction with the International Conference on Parallel Architectures and Compilation Techniques.*

Freund, S. N., & Qadeer, S. (2003). *Checking concise specifications of multithreaded software.* Technical Note 01-2002, Williams College.

Gontla, P., Drury, H., & Stanley, K. (2003, May 2003). An introduction to OVATION—Object viewing and analysis tool for integrated object networks. *CORBA News Brief, Object Computing Inc.* [Electronic media]. Retrieved March 11, 2008, from http://www.ociweb.com/cnb/CORBANews-Brief-200305.html

Gosling J. (1995, January 23). Java intermediate bytecodes. In *Proceedings of the ACM SIGPLAN Workshop on Intermediate Representations (IR'95).* (pp. 111-118), San Francisco, CA, USA.

Greenhouse, A. (2003). *A programmer-oriented approach to safe concurrency.* Unpublished doctoral dissertation, Carnegie Mellon University School of Computer Science.

Grehan, R. (1995). *BYTEmark Native Mode Benchmark,* Release 2.0, [Computer software]. BYTE Magazine.

Hollingsworth, J. K., Miller, B. P., & Cargille, J. (1994). Dynamic program instrumentation for scalable performance tools. In *Proceedings of the Scalable High-Performance Computing Conference, Knoxville, TN,* (pp. 841-850).

Hill, J., Schmidt, D.C., & Slaby, J. (2007). *System execution modeling tools for evaluating the quality of service of enterprise distributed real-time and embedded systems.* In P. F. Tiako (Ed.). *Designing software-intensive systems: Methods and principles.* Langston University, OK.

Hilyard, J. (2005, January). No code can hide from the profiling API in the .NET framework 2.0. *MSDN Magazine.* Retrieved March 11, 2008, from http://msdn.microsoft.com/msdnmag/issues/05/01/CLRProfiler/

Hunt, G., & Brubacher, D. (1999). Detours: Binary interception of Win32 functions. In *Proceedings of the 3rd USENIX Windows NT Symposium,* (pp. 135-144).

IBM Corporation. (1998). *PowerPC 604e RISC microprocessor user's manual with supplement for PowerPC 604 microprocessor* (Publication No. G522-0330-00) [Electronic media]. Retrieved March 11, 2008, from http://www-3.ibm.com/chips/techlib/

IBM Corporation. (2000). *Jikes Bytecode toolkit* [Computer Software]. Retrieved March 11, 2008, from http://www-128.ibm.com/developerworks/opensource/

IBM Corporation. (2003). *Develop fast, reliable code with IBM rational PurifyPlus.* Whitepaper. Retrieved March 11, 2008, from ftp://ftp.software.ibm.com/software/rational/web/whitepapers/2003/PurifyPlusPDF.pdf

IEEE. (2001). *IEEE standard test access port and boundary-scan architecture.* IEEE Std. 1149.1-2001.

IEEE-ISTO. (2003). *The Nexus 5001 forum standard for global embedded processor debug interface, version 2.0* [Electronic media]. Retrieved March 11, 2008, from http://www.ieee-isto.org

Intel Corporation. (2006a). *Intel 64 and IA-32 architectures software developer's manual (Vol. 3B, System Programming Guide, Part 2).* Retrieved March 11, 2008, from www.intel.com/design/processor/manuals/253669.pdf

Intel Corporation. (2006b). Intel's tera-scale research prepares for tens, hundreds of cores. *Technology@Intel Magazine.* Retrieved March 11, 2008, from http://www.intel.com/technology/magazine/computing/tera-scale-0606.htm

Jackson, D., & Rinard, M. (2000). Software analysis: A roadmap. In *Proceedings of the IEEE International Conference on Software Engineering,* (pp. 133-145).

Kiczale, G., Hilsdale, E., Hugunin, J., Kersten, M., Palm, J., & Griswold, W. G. (2001). *An overview of AspectJ.* (LNCS, 2072, pp. 327-355).

Larus, J., & Schnarr, E. (1995). EEL: Machine-independent executable editing. In *Proceedings of the ACM SIGPLAN Conference on Programming Language Designes and Implementation,* (pp. 291-300).

Lee, H. B. (1997, July). *BIT: Bytecode instrumenting tool.* Unpublished master's thesis, University of Colorado, Boulder, CO.

Lee, E. A. (2006). The problem with threads. *IEEE Computer, 39*(11), 33-42.

Li, J. (2002). *Monitoring of component-based systems* (Tech. Rep. No. HPL-2002-25R1. HP). Laboratories, Palo Alto, CA, USA.

London, K., Moore, S., Mucci, P., Seymour, K., & Luczak, R. (2001, June 18-21). The PAPI cross-platform interface to hardware performance counters. In *Proceedings of the Department of Defense Users' Group Conference.*

Luk, C., Cohn, R., Muth, R., Patil, H., Klauser, A., Lowney, G., et al. (2005). Pin: Building customized program analysis tools with dynamic instrumentation. In *Proceedings of the ACM SIGPLAN Conference on Programming Language Design and Implementation,* (pp. 190-200).

Microsoft Corporation. (2007a). *Windows server 2003 performance counters reference.* Microsoft TechNet [Electronic media]. Retrieved March 11, 2008, from http://technet2.microsoft.com/ WindowsServer/en/library/3fb01419-b1ab-4f52-a9f8-09d5ebeb9ef21033.mspx?mfr=true

Microsoft Corporation. (2007b). *Using the registry functions to consume counter data.* Microsoft Developer Network [Electronic media]. Retrieved March 11, 2008, from http://msdn2.microsoft. com/en-us/library/aa373219.aspx

Microsoft Corporation. (2007c). *Using the PDH functions to consume counter data.* Microsoft Developer Network [Electronic media]. Retrieved March 11, 2008, from http://msdn2.microsoft. com/en-us/library/aa373214.aspx

Miller, B.P., Callaghan, M.D., Cargille, J.M., Hollingsworth, J.K., Irvin, R.B., & Karavanic, K.L. (1995, December). The Paradyn parallel performance measurement tool. *IEEE Computer, 28*(11), 37-46.

Mock, M. (2003). Dynamic analysis from the bottom up. In *Proceedings of the ICSE 2003 Workshop on Dynamic Analysis (WODA 2003).*

Murayama, J. (2001, July). *Performance profiling using TNF. Sun Developer Network.* Retrieved March 11, 2008, from http://developers.sun.com/ solaris/articles/tnf.html

Nethercote, N. (2004). *Dynamic binary analysis and instrumentation.* Unpublished doctoral dissertation, University of Cambridge, UK.

Nimmer, J., & Ernst, M. D. (2001). Static verification of dynamically detected program invariants: Integrating Daikon and ESC/Java. In *Proceedings of the 1st International Workshop on Runtime Verification.*

Object Computing Incorporated. (2006). *A window into your systems* [Electronic media]. Retrieved March 11, 2008, from http://www.ociweb.com/ products/OVATION

OMG. (2002). *Object Management Group: the common object request broker: Architecture and specification, revision 3.0.* OMG Technical Documents, 02-06-33 [Electronic media]. Retrieved March 11, 2008, from http://www.omg.org/cgi-bin/doc?formal/04-03-01

Pietrik, M. (1998, May). Under the hood. *Microsoft Systems Journal.* Retrieved March 11, 2008, from http://www.microsoft.com/msj/0598/ hood0598.aspx

Reiss, S. P. (2003). Visualizing Java in action. In *Proceedings of the 2003 ACM Symposium on Software Visualization,* (p. 57).

Reiss, S. P. (2005). Efficient monitoring and display of thread state in java. In *Proceedings of the IEEE International Workshop on Program Comprehension* (pp. 247-256). St. Louis, MO.

Rinard, M. (2001). *Analysis of multithreaded programs.* (LNCS 2126, pp. 1-19).

Romer, T., Voelker, G., Lee, D., Wolman, A., Wong, W., Levy, H., et al. (1997). Instrumentation and optimization of Win32/Intel executables using Etch. In *Proceedings of the USENIX Windows NT Workshop.*

Schmidt, D. C., Natarajan, B., Gokhale, G., Wang, N., & Gill, C. (2002, February). TAO: A pattern-oriented object request broker for distributed real-time and embedded systems. *IEEE Distributed Systems Online, 3*(2).

Schmidt, D. C., Stal, M., Rohnert, H., & Buschmann, F. (2000). *Pattern-oriented software architecture patterns for concurrent and networked objects.* John Wiley & Sons.

Soloman, D. A. (1998). *Inside Windows NT (2nd ed).* Redmond: Microsoft Press.

Spinczyk, O., Lohmann, D., & Urban, M. (2005). Aspect C++: An AOP extension for C++. *Software Developer's Journal,* 68-76.

Srivastava, A., & Eustace A. (1994). *ATOM: A system for building customized program analysis tools* (Tech. Rep. No. 94/2). Western Research Lab, Compaq Corporation.

Subramaniam, K., & Thazhuthaveetil, M. (1994). Effectiveness of sampling based software profilers. In *Proceedings of the 1st International Conference on Reliability and Quality Assurance,* (pp. 1-5).

Sun Microsystems Corporation. (2002). *The Java native interface programmer's guide and specification* [Electronic media]. Retrieved March 11, 2008, from http://java.sun.com/docs/books/jni/html/jniTOC.html

Sun Microsystems Corporation. (2004). *JVM tool interface* [Computer software]. Retrieved March 11, 2008, from http://java.sun.com/j2se/1.5.0/docs/guide/jvmti/

Sutter, H. (2005). The free lunch is over: A fundamental turn towards concurrency in software. *Dr. Dobb's Journal, 30*(3).

Sutter, H., & Larus J. (2005). Software and the concurrency revolution. *ACM Queue Magazine, 3*(7).

Vaswani, K., & Srikant, Y. N. (2003), Dynamic recompilation and profile-guided optimizations for a .NET JIT compiler. In *Proceedings of the*

IEEE Software Special on Rotor .NET, (Vol. 150, pp. 296-302). IEEE Publishing.

Visser, E. (2001). *Stratego: A language for program transformation based on rewriting strategies.* (LNCS 2051, pp. 357).

Waddington, D. G., Amduka, M., DaCosta, D., Foster, P., & Sprinkle, J. (2006, February). *EASEL: Model centric design tools for effective design and implementation of multi-threaded concurrent applications* (Technical Document). Lockheed Martin ATL.

Waddington, D. G., & Yao, B. (2005). High fidelity C++ code transformation. In *Proceedings of the 5th Workshop on Language Descriptions, Tools and Applications.*

Whaley, J. (2000). A portable sampling-based profiler for Java virtual machines. In *Proceedings of ACM Java Grand* (pp. 78-87).

Wolf, F., & Mohr, B. (2003). Hardware-counter based automatic performance analysis of parallel programs. In *Proceedings of the Mini-symposium on Performance Analysis, Conference on Parallel Computing (PARCO).* Dreseden, Germany.

ADDITIONAL READING

In addition to the references made in this chapter, we recommend the following particular reading on this subject.

"Dynamic Analysis from the bottom up" (Mock, 2003) stresses the increasing importance of dynamic analysis in view of modern software development and deployment. It discusses three main directions of research: (i) exploiting run-time information to optimize programs, (ii) applying dynamic analysis to understand, maintain and evolve software and (iii) efficient collection of run-time information.

"Static and Dynamic Analysis: synergy and duality" (Ernst, 2003) discusses the synergy between static and dynamic analysis techniques. The paper describes ways to use both these techniques in a complementary manner. It proposes the development of a hybrid analysis method and argues that static and dynamic analyses are not as different as they seem and in fact have much in common.

"The Periodic-Linear Model of Program Behavior Capture" (Clauss, Kenmei, & Beyler, 2005) presents an analysis and modeling strategy of program behavior characteristics. The approach focuses on the use of traces that are generated from instrumented code.

"Aspect C++: *An* AOP Extension for C++" (Spinczyk, Lohmann, & Urban, 2005) discusses the fundamental concepts of aspect-oriented programming. It specifically provides details of AOP within the context of C++ source code instrumentation.

"An Overview of AspectJ" (Kiczale, Hilsdale, Hugunin, Kersten, Palm, & Griswold, 2001) examines aspect-oriented programming for the Java programming language.

"An API for Runtime Code Patching" (Buck & Hollingsworth, 2000) presents the concepts behind the DynInst tool, which is a technique for dynamic binary-code instrumentation. This paper discusses the basic architecture and the use of trampoline functions to implant modifications to existing code.

"Windows Server 2003 Performance Counters Reference" (Microsoft, 2007a) contains a detailed description of the Windows Performance counters that can be used to profile applications. This reference includes a listing of available performance counters and a description of the APIs used to access them.

"JVM Tool Interface (JVM TI)" (Sun Microsystems Corporation, 2004) is an online resource describing the API provided by the JVM. It first explains the basic concept and architecture of the JVMTI before going into the details on the interface. In each section, there are small examples to help implement a profiler.

Section 4
I/O Prefetching

Chapter 10
Exploiting Disk Layout and Block Access History for I/O Prefetch

Feng Chen
The Ohio State University, USA

Xiaoning Ding
The Ohio State University, USA

Song Jiang
Wayne State University, USA

ABSTRACT

As the major secondary storage device, the hard disk plays a critical role in modern computer system. In order to improve disk performance, most operating systems conduct data prefetch policies by tracking I/O access pattern, mostly at the level of file abstractions. Though such a solution is useful to exploit application-level access patterns, file-level prefetching has many constraints that limit the capability of fully exploiting disk performance. The reasons are twofold. First, certain prefetch opportunities can only be detected by knowing the data layout on the hard disk, such as metadata blocks. Second, due to the non-uniform access cost on the hard disk, the penalty of mis-prefetching a random block is much more costly than mis-prefetching a sequential block. In order to address the intrinsic limitations of file-level prefetching, we propose to prefetch data blocks directly at the disk level in a portable way. Our proposed scheme, called DiskSeen, is designed to supplement file-level prefetching. DiskSeen observes the workload access pattern by tracking the locations and access times of disk blocks. Based on analysis of the temporal and spatial relationships of disk data blocks, DiskSeen can significantly increase the sequentiality of disk accesses and improve disk performance in turn. We implemented the DiskSeen scheme in the Linux 2.6 kernel and we show that it can significantly improve the effectiveness of file-level prefetching and reduce execution times by 20-53% for various types of applications, including grep, CVS, and TPC-H.

DOI: 10.4018/978-1-60566-850-5.ch010

Figure 1. Performance gap between processors and disks.

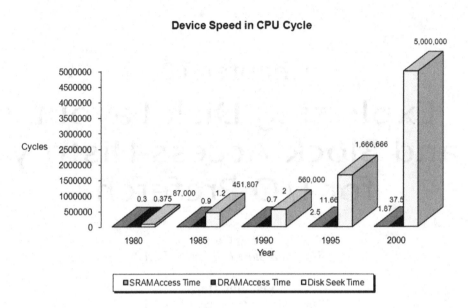

INTRODUCTION

As the Moore's law states, over the last three decades the processor speed doubles every 18 months, which brings a steady performance improvement at an exponential rate. In contrast, the access time of the hard disk, an electro-mechanical device, has been improved at a much slower pace, only around 8% per year (Gray & Shenoy, 2000). As a result, the performance gap between processors and hard disks is increasingly widening and this trend will continue in the future. As shown in Figure 1, in 1980 each disk access costs around 87,000 CPU cycles only, while this number grows to 5,000,000 cycles in 2000 (Bryant and O'Hallaron 2003). In other words, relative to the processor speed, the hard disk is becoming 57 times slower during the twenty years. Such an ever-growing performance gap between the processor and the hard disk strongly indicates that, the disk performance is becoming the key bottleneck of overall system performance.

The excessively high access latency of the hard disk essentially stems from its mechanic nature. Hard disk drives store data on the surface of rotating disk platters. These data can be read or written through the disk head attached on the moving disk arms. In general, accessing one data block involves three major operations, each of which causes a delay accordingly. When the hard disk receives a request (read/write) to data on a certain location, the disk arm must first position to the correct disk track where the data is located. This operation results in a *seek latency*. Then the disk head has to wait until the disk platters rotate to the correct position where the target data block is right beneath the disk head, which causes a *rotational latency*. Finally, data transfer can be started from or to the disk platter surface, depending on the operation type (read/write), which leads to a *transfer latency*. These three types of latency together form the aggregate latency of servicing a disk request. Since *seek* and *rotational* latencies are essentially determined by the speed of mechanic parts, the first two operations usually account for a large portion of the aggregate service latency to complete a disk access and should be minimized.

The performance of the hard disk is highly dependent on the workload access pattern, i.e.

the order of incoming requests to the hard disk. In specific, *sequential* disk accesses are much more efficient than *random* disk accesses, often in orders of magnitude. The reason is that, when sequentially accessing disk data that are continuously located on the disk track, only one disk head movement (seek and rotation) is needed to read a large amount of data. In contrast, randomly accessing disk data that are dispersed over the disk platters, each data access requires a costly disk seek and/or rotation, which is extremely inefficient. In order to optimize disk performance, many research works have been done to organize *large* and *sequential* disk accesses, and *prefetching* is an important technique to achieve this objective. In this chapter, we will present an efficient disk-level prefetch scheme, called DiskSeen, which can effectively improve the disk performance by creating large and sequential disk accesses.

BACKGROUND

Prefetching

Prefetching, speculatively reading data from the hard disk by predicting future requests, is an effective technique to improve overall system performance. This is due to two reasons. First, since the execution of an application is usually interleaved by *computation* and *data access*, by performing disk accesses in parallel with computation, the high disk access latency can be effectively hidden behind computations. Second, prefetching usually attempts to organize large sequential data accesses on the hard disk, thus each time a large number of data blocks can be read into the memory with only one disk access. As a result, the long disk head seek and rotation latency can be amortized over a large amount of data blocks, and the average access cost per block is reduced. As a critical optimization technique, prefetching is widely adopted in most existing operating systems as a standard component.

The effectiveness of prefetch policies is determined by two factors, accurate prediction on future data accesses and actual time cost of individual accesses. Many previous research works are focused on improving the accuracy of prediction on data accesses (e.g. Li, Chen, Srinivasan, & Zhou, 2004). However, two factors make the later factor increasingly more important. First, the hard disk is a non-uniform-access device, as described previously. Since sequential data accesses without disk head movement is at least one order of magnitude faster than random data accesses, prefetching data blocks in a random pattern would be much less efficient than prefetching data blocks in a sequential pattern. Accordingly, the penalty of mis-prefetching for sequential data accesses is much lower than that for random accesses. Second, as the processors are becoming increasingly more powerful, computation during an application's execution would account for a decreasing percentage. In other words, applications are becoming increasingly I/O bound, and less opportunity would be left to hide long disk access latency behind computations. As a result, the importance of efficient sequential prefetching is more pronouncing relative to that of prefetching randomly located data blocks.

It's also worth pointing out here, although many sophisticated prefetching algorithms have been proposed (e.g. Griffioen & Appleton, 1994; Kroeger & Long, 2001), general-purpose operating systems only provide sequential prefetching, which predicts and prefetches sequentially accessed data blocks, or similar variants. This design is a rational choice in practical systems, due to two reasons. First, extra overhead may be introduced in these complicated prefetch policies, and potential implementation difficulty has to be avoided in practice. Imposing excessive overhead in a general system is undesirable. Second, the relative penalties for incorrectly prefetching a sequential block are much lower, compared to prefetching a random block, which involves more disk I/O. In this chapter, the prefetch policies are specific to that used in general-purpose operating systems.

Prefetching at Logic File Level

Most practical prefetch policies usually detect access patterns and issue prefetch requests at the logical file level (Pai, Pulavarty, & Cao, 2004). Such a design is based on the fact that applications usually make I/O requests through logic files, such as reading a file via system call read (), so their discernable access patterns can be identified in terms of logic files. For example, in the Linux kernel, when a file is opened, the logic offset in the file of each access is tracked. If the application sequentially accesses data in the file, prefetching (called *readahead* mechanism in the Linux kernel) is activated to speculatively read data in advance. If the sequential access pattern changes, prefetching is slowed down or stopped to avoid loading useless data blocks into memory. Such a file-level prefetching is widely adopted in most general-purpose operating systems, such as FreeBSD and Linux.

Prefetching at logic file level is simple and portable. For example, the same prefetch policy can be applied to different file systems and benefit most applications transparently. However, because disk data layout information cannot be exploited at the logic file level, the disk-specific knowledge, such as where the next prefetched block would be relative to the currently fetched block, is unknown, which makes estimating prefetching cost infeasible. Thus, in file-level prefetching, the effectiveness of prefetching, which is needed as a feedback to adjust prefetching aggressiveness, has to be presented in terms of the *number* of mis-prefetched blocks rather than a more relevant metric, the *penalty* of mis-prefetching. Here we summarize the limitations of file-level prefetching as follows.

- ***Blocks continuously located in a file may not be continuous on disk*** – Though file

systems generally attempt to map data blocks that are logically continuous in one file also physically continuous on the hard disk, as the file system ages or becomes full, this correspondence may deteriorate inevitably. This further worsens the penalty for mis-prediction.

- ***Small files cannot benefit from prefetching*** – Since prefetching detects sequential data accesses within each individual file, prefetching for a small file barely has a chance to be activated before reaching the end of the file. Thus, data blocks in small files cannot be prefetched.

- ***Inter-file sequentiality cannot not be exploited*** – As prefetching cannot across the boundary of files, sequential data accesses in multiple files cannot be detected, even if the data blocks of these files are actually located on the hard disk continuously.

- ***File system metadata blocks cannot be prefetched*** – File system metadata blocks, such as inode blocks, are usually placed separately from the file content data blocks and transparent for applications. Prefetching at file level is only effective for the file content data blocks.

Prefetching in Disk Firmware

Modern hard disks are usually equipped with a large RAM buffer (e.g. 16MB), and the disk firmware can also apply some simple prefetching policies to preload data into the disk buffer. For example, when waiting for disk platters to rotate to the target position, disk firmware would read the data blocks beneath the disk head into the disk buffer with no extra cost. In some cases, as many as a full track of data blocks can be prefetched. Such a firmware-level prefetching has many limitations. First, since this readahead is usually carried out on each individual track, it cannot take into consideration the relatively *long-term* temporal and spatial locality of blocks across the entire disk working set. Second, the performance potential of firmware-level readahead is further constrained by the thin disk interface, which significantly limits the communication between the disk and operating systems. For example, since the disk firmware is unaware of the status of the buffer cache (main memory), data blocks would be unnecessarily prefetched into the disk buffer even when they are already resident in buffer cache (main memory). Without sophisticated policies, prefetching at disk firmware is far from sufficient to exploit the disk performance potential.

A Disk-Level Prefetch Policy – DiskSeen

In this chapter, we present a disk-level prefetching scheme, called *DiskSeen*, to address the aforesaid limitations of existing prefetch policies. In DiskSeen, current and historical information of disk data blocks is used to achieve *efficient* and *effective* prefetching. Working in OS kernel, DiskSeen monitors the accesses to disk blocks and observes the access pattern directly on the disk level. By analyzing the disk blocks' access history, DiskSeen is able to quickly identify the relationship between data blocks being accessed and accurately predicts the disk blocks to be accessed in the future.

Compared to the file-level prefetching, DiskSeen can effectively exploit prefetching opportunities that cannot be leveraged by the file-level prefetching. For example, DiskSeen can prefetch data blocks across boundaries of files, if these data blocks are continuously located on the hard disk. Moreover, the file system metadata blocks, which are transparent to file-level prefetchers, can be prefetched as well. Compared to prefetching in disk firmware, DiskSeen has much richer knowledge about the status and history of data blocks being accessed during a long history, thus more sophisticated prefetch policy can be conducted with a long-term view. It is worth pointing out here that, the purpose of DiskSeen is not to replace the existing prefetching policies, at file level or firmware level. Instead, DiskSeen can be well complementary to the existing prefetching schemes and correct some inappropriate prefetching decisions. In our experiments, the prototype of DiskSeen shows that substantial performance improvement can be achieved by applying such a disk-level prefetching in existing storage systems.

TRACKING DISK ACCESSES

In order to conduct prefetching at disk level, two questions must be answered first, (1) what information about disk accesses is needed by the disk-level prefetch policy, and (2) how to efficiently manage the huge amount of history information with small overhead.

Disk Layout Information

Effective disk-level prefetching relies on detailed information about disk layout. Generally speaking, the more specific the information available for a particular disk, the more accurate an estimate a disk-aware policy can make about access costs. For example, if we know that the requested blocks span a track boundary, we would predict that the request would incur a track crossing penalty (Schindler, Griffin, Lumb, & Ganger, 2002). Unfortunately, such detailed knowledge about physical disk geometry is often not disclosed by disk manufacturers. Extracting such information about disk is challenging (Schindler and Ganger, 2000) and often works with certain types of disk drives (such as SCSI disks) only.

In practice, hard disk firmware usually exposes the logical disk geometry as an array of logic blocks, which are labeled by *logical block numbers* (LBNs). This is a generic interface to communicate between disk drives and operating systems. Although the LBN does not disclose precise disk-specific information, it can be used to represent disk layout sufficiently well. This is because disk manufacturers usually attempt to carefully map logical blocks to physical blocks with minimal disk head positioning cost, so that accessing blocks with consecutive LBNs has performance close to that of accessing blocks physically contiguous on disk (Schlosser, Schindler, Papadomanolakis, Shao, Ailamaki, Faloutsos, & Ganger, 2005). Such a standard logic interface is used by operating systems and upper-level components to access disk data, thus it is available and portable across various computing platforms. In practice, we find that using this logical disk layout is sufficient to exploit disk-side information in prefetch policies.

In DiskSeen, the LBNs are used to track the access times of recently accessed disk blocks for analyzing the associations of access times among adjacent blocks. In other words, we use LBNs as abstraction of physical disk blocks and analyze the access pattern of blocks.

The Block Table

In order to analyze workload access pattern, the access history of all data blocks in the storage space, which is often as large as multiple Terabytes, has to be maintained. It is challenging to efficiently manage such a huge amount of information with low overhead. First, the data structure holding this information must support efficient access of block entries and their neighboring blocks via LBNs. Second, addition, removal, and lookup of block entries must be efficient to avoid high runtime overhead. Finally, maintaining the history information should require low memory space. In DiskSeen, we use a data structure called *block table* to achieve these requirements.

The *block table* is inspired by the multi-level page table used for a process's memory address translation, which is widely used in nearly all operating systems. Different from the page table, the block table is used to manage the storage space, instead of memory space. As shown in

Figure 2, the block table has three levels, *Block Global Directory* (BGD), *Block Middle Directory* (BMD), and *Block Table Entry* (BTE). Each level consists of multiple 4KB pages, each of which is further divided into multiple entries. A block's LBN is correspondingly broken into three segments, each of which is used as an offset to locate an entry in the page of the corresponding level. The BTE entries in the block table are used to maintain data access information (e.g. block access times). Different from BTE entries, BGD and BMD entries also maintain a *pointer* field, which is the address of a memory page in the next level. In this way, the block table is organized as a tree structure with three levels. For a given LBN, at most three memory accesses are needed to reach the BTE entry. As an example shown in Figure 2, suppose one page can hold 512 entries, the access times of a block with LBN 2,631,710 $(10 \times 512^2 + 20 \times 512 + 30)$ can be efficiently reached via BGD entry (10), BMD entry (20), and BTE entry (30).

In DiskSeen, block access times are needed to identify the relationship between data blocks. However, knowing the physical wall clock time is unnecessary. Instead, we use the logic block access time. Suppose the entire sequence of accessed disk blocks is referred to as a *block access stream*. The nth block in the stream has access index n. We maintain a global access counter, which is incremented with each block reference. Upon a data access, the value of the access counter is read as the *access index* for the accessed block. The access index is recorded in the corresponding BTE entry to represent its logic access time. In our prototype, each BTE entry can record up to four access indices as its access history.

As time elapses, the block table may grow and occupy an excessively large amount of memory space, thus we need to remove the out-of-date history information to reduce spatial overhead. To facilitate an efficient removal of old BTEs, each directory entry (BGD and BMD entry) records the largest access index of all of the blocks under

Figure 2. The structure of block bable with three levels (BGD, BMD, and BTE)

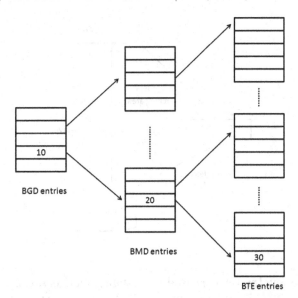

that entry. Purging the table of old blocks involves removing all blocks with access indices smaller than some given index. This operation entails traversing the table, top level first, identifying access indices smaller than the given index, removing the corresponding sub-trees, and reclaiming the memory. Since such an operation is only needed to be performed occasionally, the incurred overhead is very small.

THE DESIGN OF DISKSEEN

As a disk-level prefetch policy, DiskSeen sits between the file system and the disk drive. Disk-Seen intercepts the requests issued from upper-level components, tracks the disk access history, and maintains the information in the block table. By analyzing the history access information, DiskSeen identifies the relationship between data blocks and predicts the blocks to be accessed in the future. Finally, DiskSeen prefetches data blocks into memory to achieve performance improvement.

Overview

In DiskSeen, the buffer cache (main memory) is divided into two areas, *prefetching* and *caching* areas. The caching area corresponds to the traditional buffer cache and it is managed by the existing OS kernel policies (e.g. the 2Q algorithm in Linux). The prefetching area is used to maintain prefetched data blocks in DiskSeen. A block could be prefetched into the prefetching area based on access information recorded in the block table, or as directed by file-level prefetching. If a block resident in the prefetching area is accessed by an on-demand request, it is moved into the caching area. DiskSeen distinguishes on-demand requests from file-level prefetch requests and makes prefetch decision based on on-demand accesses, because only on-demand requests reflect applications' actual access patterns.

In DiskSeen, file-level prefetching is still enabled. However, the low level prefetching is conducted concurrently to mitigate the inadequacies of file-level prefetching. DiskSeen generally respects the decisions made by a file-level prefetcher, but it also attempts to identify and correct inaccurate

Figure 3. Architecture of DiskSeen.

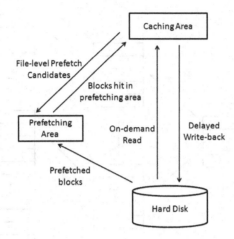

predictions made by the file-level prefetcher based on its knowledge of the deep access history. To this end, the requests from file-level prefetchers are dispatched to DiskSeen, instead of directly to the disk drive, and DiskSeen decides how to handle these requests. On-demand requests are forwarded directly to disk driver by DiskSeen. We refer to disk requests from 'above' DiskSeen (e.g., application or file-level prefetchers) as *high-level requests* and the data blocks requested by file-level prefetcher as *prefetch candidates*.

Recording Access Indices

As mentioned previously, DiskSeen uses the block access indices as virtual access times. Block access indices are read from a counter that increments whenever a block is read into the caching area on demand. When a request is completed, either via a hit in the prefetching area or via the completion of a disk I/O operation, the current reading of the counter, the *access index*, is used as the access time of the block to be recorded in the corresponding BTE in the block table. Each BTE holds the most recent access indices, to a maximum of four. In our prototype, the size of a BTE is 128 bits. Each access index takes 31 bits and the other 4 bits are used to indicate block

status, such as *resident* bit. With a block size of 4K Bytes, the 31-bit access index can distinguish accesses to 8 TBytes of disk data.

As time elapses, the counter approaches to its maximum value. To handle this situation, when the range for used access index exceeds 7/8 of the maximum index range, we remove the indices whose values are in the first half of the used range in the block table, such that the values can be gradually updated. This progressive *index clearing* takes place very infrequently and incurs minimal overhead in practice.

Coordinating with File-Level Prefetching

As mentioned previously, traditional file-level prefetching may perform ineffectively due to lack of low-level knowledge. By tracking the actual use of blocks prefetched by file-level prefetcher, DiskSeen can measure the effectiveness of high-level prefetchers and correct inaccurate prefetching decisions.

When a prefetch candidate block is read into the prefetching area, we set the status of the block as *prefetched* in its BTE. This status bit is unset only when an on-demand access of the block occurs. When the file-level prefetcher requests a prefetch candidate that is not yet resident in memory, DiskSeen checks its prefetched status bit, if it is set, DiskSeen would drop the prefetch request, because this block has been previously prefetched by the file-level prefetcher but not been accessed by any on-demand request, which suggests an inaccurate prefetch decision. In this way, DiskSeen can identify and correct some of the mis-prefetchings made by file-level prefetch policies.

In order to coordinate multiple requests for the same block, we designate a *resident* bit and a *busy* bit in each BTE. When a block enters buffer cache, the resident bit is set to 1, and it is reset to 0 when it leaves the cache. Before a request is sent to the disk scheduler, we check the blocks demanded in the request against the corresponding BTEs to determine whether the blocks are already in the prefetching area. If true, which means the blocks are hit in the prefetching area, we move them to the caching area. The *busy* bit in each BTE serves as a lock to coordinate simultaneous requests for a particular block. A set busy bit indicates that a disk service on the corresponding block is under way, and succeeding requests for the block must wait on the lock. In this way, we can avoid the consistence problem caused by the situation that multiple I/O requests are issued to the disk drive for the same data block.

Sequence-Based Prefetching

Based on the data access history recorded in the block table, DiskSeen identifies sequential data accesses at disk level and prefetches data blocks by predicting the data blocks to be accessed in advance. The sequence detection and prefetching in DiskSeen is similar in principle to that used by the file-level prefetchers in Linux.

Sequence Detection

In DiskSeen, prefetching is activated when accesses of K contiguous blocks are detected, where K is set 8. The sequence detection is conducted based on the current access information maintained in the block table. For a block in a high-level request, we examine the most recent access indices of blocks physically *preceding* the block to see whether it is the Kth block in a sequence. For example, for a block with LBN N, we will examine the blocks with LBNs of $N-1$, $N-2$, …, etc. Compared to disk service time, this back-tracking operation in the block table is an efficient operation. Since accesses of a sequence can be interleaved with accesses in other sequences, the most recent access indices of the blocks in the sequence are not necessarily consecutive. We only require that access indices of the blocks be *monotonically* decreasing during back-tracking. However, if a very large gap of the access indices exists between two contiguous blocks, it indicates that one of the two blocks might not be accessed before being evicted from the prefetching area, if they were prefetched together as a sequence. Thus these two blocks should not belong to the same sequence. The access index gap threshold, T, is set as 1/64 of the size of the system memory, measured in blocks.

Sequence-Based Prefetching

Once we detect a sequence, we create two windows, called the *current window* and the *readahead window*, whose initial sizes are set 8 blocks. We prefetch 8 blocks immediately ahead of the sequence into the current window, and the following 8 blocks into the readahead window. We then track the number f of blocks that are hit in the current window by high-level requests, and f serves as a feedback to determine the prefetching aggressiveness. When the blocks in the readahead window start to be requested, a new readahead window is created with size of $2f$, and the existing readahead window becomes the new current window. We set minimal and maximum window sizes, *min* and *max*, respectively. If $2f < min$, the prefetching is stopped, because requesting a small number of blocks cannot effectively amortize a disk head repositioning cost and so is inefficient. If $2f > max$, the prefetching window size is set as max. This is because too aggressive prefetching imposes a high risk of mis-prefetching and increases memory pressure on the prefetching area. In our prototype, *min* is 8 blocks and *max* is 32 blocks, which is also the default maximum prefetch window size in Linux. In this way, we can gradually increase the aggressiveness of prefetching, if previously prefetched data blocks are being accessed by on-demand requests, and quickly reduce the aggressiveness of prefetching, if otherwise.

Also note that the actual number of blocks that are read into memory can be less than the specified prefetch size, because blocks that are already resident in memory are excluded from prefetching. If many blocks in the prefetch scope are already resident in memory, the window size turns small, which in turn slows down or even stops the prefetching.

Managing Prefetched Blocks

For file-level prefetch policies, the data structure for managing prefetched blocks is naturally affiliated to logic files. In the DiskSeen scheme, which views the whole storage space as a single sequence of blocks, each on-going prefetch is represented using a data structure called the *prefetch stream*. The prefetch stream is a pseudo-FIFO queue, and the prefetched blocks in the two windows are placed in the order of their LBNs. In DiskSeen, multiple prefetch streams may exist concurrently.

In order to manage blocks in the prefetching area, we also maintain a global FIFO queue called the *reclamation queue*. The length of reclamation queue is determined by the size of prefetching area. All prefetched blocks, which may belong to various prefetch streams, are placed at the queue tail in the order of their arrival. Thus, blocks in the prefetch windows stay in both prefetch streams

and the reclamation queue. When a block reaches the head of the reclamation queue, it is evicted from memory. When a block is requested by an on-demand request, it is moved to the caching area.

History-Aware Prefetching

Sequence-based prefetching is based on currently observed disk accesses and only works for sequential disk accesses. By exploiting deep history information of disk accesses in the block table, we can further conduct more comprehensive prefetching for disk accesses. In this section, we present a history-aware prefetching for non-sequential disk accesses.

Disk Access Trails

The basic idea of history-aware prefetching is to match the current disk access sequence with the history access sequence, if a match is found, we can use the history accesses to predict the data blocks to be accessed in the future. To this end, we first present a data structure to describe the access history.

We use *trail* to describe a sequence of blocks that have been accessed with a small time gap between each pair of adjacent blocks in the sequence and are located in a small region on disk. Suppose blocks $(B_1, B_2, \ldots, B_n)$ are a trail, where $0 < access\_index(B_i) - access\_index(B_{i-1}) < T$, and $|LBN(B_i) - LBN(B_1)| < S$, $(i = 2, 3, \ldots, n)$, where T is the access index gap threshold. T is the same as the one used in the sequence detection for the sequence-based prefetching. Each data block maintains up to four access indices in the corresponding BTE entry. Any access index can be used to satisfy the given condition. This means that, in a trail $(B_1, B_2, \ldots, B_n)$ and B_1 is the start block, all of the following blocks must be on either side of B_1 within distance S, and any two consecutive blocks must have an access in-

Figure 4. An Example of Access Trails

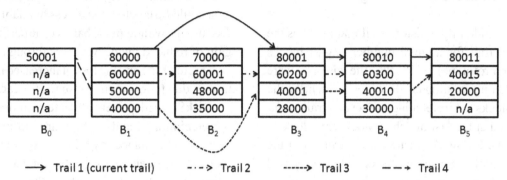

dex gap smaller than T. We refer to the window of $2S$ blocks, centered at the start block, as the *trail extent*. Actually the sequence detected in the sequence-based prefetching can be viewed as a special trail in which all blocks are on the same side of start block and have contiguous LBNs.

The limited window size, S, enforces to search for a trail in a small area on disk, so that prefetching such a trail is efficient and the penalty for a mis-prefetching would be small. In our prototype, S is set 128. If a program accesses data over a large area, multiple trails would be formed to track each set of proximate accesses, rather than forming an extended trail, to avoid expensive disk head movements. Also note that the trail detection brings low cost because, for a given access index of one block in a trail, at most one access index of its following block is likely to be within T. This is because, due to the existence of buffer cache, a block would not need to be reloaded from disk until it is evicted from memory, which only happens after a large amount of other data blocks are read from disk into memory. Thus, two consecutive disk accesses to the same block would normally have a large gap, in terms of access indices.

Figure 4 illustrates an example of access trails. Access index threshold T is assumed to be 256. There are four trails starting from block B_1, one current trail and three history trails. Trail 1 (B_1, B_3, B_4, B_5) corresponds to the on-going continuous block accesses. Sequence-based prefetch would not be activated because B_2 is skipped over. Trail 1

is overlapped with two history trails, Trails 2 and 3. Note that Trail 4 runs in the reverse direction.

Matching Trails

Unlike sequence-based prefetching, which predicts sequential disk access based on current on-going tail, history-aware prefetching predicts disk accesses based on access history, which is unnecessary to be strictly sequential. In DiskSeen, when the sequence-based prefetching cannot detect a pure sequence for activating prefetching, history-aware prefetching can take advantage of history information, if available, and prefetch more accurately. The general idea is to use the current trail to match history trails, so that we can identify blocks for prefetching by following the matched history trails.

When there is an on-demand access of a disk block that is not in any current trail extent, we start tracking a new trail from that block. In the meantime, we examine the history trails consisting of blocks visited by the current trail in the same order. As shown in Figure 4, when the current trail extends from B_1(80000) to B_3(80001), two history trails are identified: Trail 2 (B_1(60000), B_3(60200)) and Trail 3 (B_1(40000), B_3(40001)). However, when Trail 1 extends to B5, only Trail 3 can match the current trail. In this way, we can identify the repeated disk accesses by matching the current trail with the history trails.

History-Aware Prefetching

After we identify a history trail that matches the current trail for a small number (e.g. 4 blocks in our prototype) of blocks, the history-aware prefetching is initiated. In order to identify the data blocks for prefetching, we set up a trail extent centered at the last matched block, say block B. Then we follow the history trails from B in the extent to obtain a set of blocks that are accessed in the matched history trails. Suppose t is an access index of block B that is used in forming a matched history trail, and T is access index gap threshold. We then search the extent for the blocks with an access index between t and $t+T$, and we can get a set of blocks for prefetch. We prefetch the non-resident blocks in the order of their LBNs to minimize the disk positioning overhead.

Similar to the sequence-based prefetching, we also adopt two windows for history-aware prefetching. These prefetched blocks are placed in the current window first. Starting from the last prefetched block, we further prefetch blocks into a readahead window. The initial sizes of two windows are 8 blocks. The prefetching is stopped, if the window size is less than *min* (8 blocks). When the window size is larger than *max* (64 blocks), only the first *max* blocks are prefetched into memory. There must be at least one matched history trail; otherwise, history-aware prefetching is aborted. Sometimes multiple matched history trails may be found, we only prefetch the intersection of these trails. The two history-aware windows are shifted forward in the same way as in the sequence-based prefetching. If the history-aware prefetching aborts, sequence-based prefetching is attempted.

Balancing Memory Allocation

The memory allocation between the prefetching and caching area can affect system performance. Obviously, the larger the prefetching area is, the more prefetched data block can be held, but mean-while, the more likely the blocks in the caching area could be evicted due to less available space. Essentially, we attempt to balance the performance gain of reduced memory misses through aggressive prefetching and the loss of increased memory misses due to less memory space for caching.

DiskSeen adaptively allocate memory for the prefetching area and caching area to maximize system performance, as follows. We extend the reclamation queue in the prefetching area with a segment of 2048 blocks to hold the metadata of blocks evicted from the queue. We also set up a FIFO queue, of the same size as the segment for the caching area to hold the metadata of blocks evicted from the caching area. The runtime is divided into epochs, during which $N_{p\text{-}area}$ disk blocks are requested, where $N_{p\text{-}area}$ is a sample of current sizes of the prefetching area in blocks. In each epoch we monitor the numbers of hits to these two segments, suppose they are $H_{prefetch}$ and H_{cache}, respectively. If $|(H_{prefetch} - H_{cache})|/ N_{p\text{-}area}$ is larger than 10%, we move 128 blocks of memory from the area with fewer hits to the other area to balance the misses between the two. The intuition behind this design is that, by tracking the hits to the blocks evicted from both areas, we can know increasing the size for which area can remove more memory misses. So we always attempt to allocate more memory space to the area that can save more memory misses.

IMPLEMENTATION ISSUES

In order to evaluate the performance of DiskSeen in a mainstream operating system, we implemented a prototype of DiskSeen in the Linux 2.6.11 kernel. The current Linux kernel conducts a file-level prefetching at generic file system level. Similar to the sequence-based prefetching in DiskSeen, two windows are maintained to track the access pattern for each opened file. When a sequential access pattern is detected, the logic data blocks in the file are prefetched.

Unlike the existing file-level prefetch policies, DiskSeen directly accesses disk blocks via LBNs, including both file content data blocks and meta-data blocks, such as inode and indirect blocks. The challenge is that, being prefetched at disk level, these blocks' semantic information is unknown, except their LBNs. In other words, we would not know which file a block belongs to, or what type a block is. Meanwhile, back-translating LBNs to files/offset is cumbersome too. In order to make the LBN-based prefetched blocks usable by high-level I/O routines, we treat a disk partition as a raw device file to read blocks and place them in the prefetching area. Only when a high-level I/O request is issued, we check the LBNs of requested blocks against those of prefetched blocks resident in the prefetching area. If a match is found, the prefetched block is moved into the caching area to satisfy the I/O request. This design significantly simplifies the implementation complexity.

PERFORMANCE EVALUATION

Our experimental system is a machine with a 3.0GHz Intel Pentium 4 processor, 512MB memory, and a Western Digital WD1600JB 160GB 7200RPM hard drive. The hard drive has an 8MB cache. The OS is Redhat Linux WS4 with the Linux 2.6.11 kernel using the Ext3 file system. For configuration in DiskSeen, T, the access index gap threshold, is set as 2048, and S, which is used to determine the trail extent, is set as 128. The other system configurations are set using default values.

Workloads

In order to analyze the performance of DiskSeen in different scenarios, we carefully select six representative data intensive benchmarks with different access patterns to measure their execution times. The six benchmarks include two synthetic workloads, *strided* and *reversed*, and another four

real-life applications. We briefly introduce the six workloads as follows.

- *strided* – a synthetic program reading a 1GB file in a strided fashion by reading every other 4KB of data from the beginning to the end of the file. There is a small amount of compute time after each read.
- *reversed* – a synthetic program sequentially reading one 1GB file from its end to its beginning.
- *CVS* – a version control utility widely used in software development environment. We use command (cvs –q diff) to compare a user working directory to the CVS repository. Two identical set of data are stored on disk with 50GB space in between.
- *diff* – a Linux tool that compares files character by character. Similar to CVS, it accesses two data sets.
- *grep* – a textual search tool that scans a collection of files for lines containing a match for a keyword in given expression.
- *TPC-H* – a widely used decision support benchmark that handles business-oriented queries against a database system. We use PostgreSQL 7.3.18 as the database server, and the data set is generated using scale factor 1. Query 4 is used in the experiments.

For analysis of experimental results across different benchmarks, we use the source code tree of Linux kernel 2.6.11 as the data set, whose size is about 236MB, in benchmarks *CVS*, *diff*, and *grep*.

Experimental Results

In order to examine the performance of sequence-based prefetching and history-aware prefetching in DiskSeen, we show the execution times of the benchmarks on the stock Linux kernel, and the times for their first and second runs on the kernel with the DiskSeen scheme in Table 1. Note that,

Table 1.Execution Times (seconds) of workloads on the stock Linux kernel and kernel with DiskSeen

Workload name	Linux 2.6.11	DiskSeen – 1st Run	DiskSeen – 2nd Run
strided	33.99	33.69	24.93
reversed	99.98	100.26	49.17
CVS	81.57	68.22	55.50
diff	98.36	81.14	46.12
grep	17.24	14.02	13.83
TPC-H (Q4)	93.85	88.22	69.43

since there is no history information stored in the block table, only sequence-based prefetching is available for the first run with DiskSeen. Between any two consecutive runs, the buffer cache is emptied by un-mounting the file system to ensure all blocks are accessed from disk in the next run.

Strided and Reversed

As synthetic workloads, *strided* and *reversed* represent two different I/O access patterns to examine the effectiveness of DiskSeen in extreme cases. Obviously, with a non-sequential access pattern, *strided* and *reversed* cannot benefit from sequence-based prefetching either at the file level or at disk level. As shown in Table 1, the execution times of their first runs with DiskSeen are not reduced. However, the execution times are not increased either, which indicates that DiskSeen introduces negligible overhead.

When the history information is available, the history-aware prefetching is activated during the second runs of the two benchmarks. As a result, DiskSeen shows significant reductions of execution times, in specific, 27% for *stride* and 51% for *reversed*. This is because history trails lead us to identify the prefetchable blocks. In the stock Linux kernel, reversed accesses can cause a full disk rotation to service each request, and disk scheduler has little chance to improve such synchronous disk accesses. In contrast, DiskSeen can identifies the prefetchable blocks and requests a large amount of blocks in ascending order of

their LBNs, such that these data blocks can be prefetched in one disk rotation. This also explains performance improvement observed for *strided*.

It is worth pointing out here that, reverse sequential and forward/backward strided accesses are not rare in real-life systems, especially in high-performance computing environment. For example, both the GPFS file system from IBM (Schmuck & Haskin, 2002) and the MPI-IO standards (MPI forum, 1997) provide special mechanism for identifying and handling these cases. In DiskSeen, such access patterns can be well handled without extra efforts to change file systems.

CVS and Diff

CVS and *diff* have a similar data access pattern. In both workloads, two sets of the Linux source code tree are compared file by file. Such a disk access pattern represents a very inefficient pattern – a long seek distance exists between two consecutive disk accesses, thus each disk access would raise a long disk head seek and rotation latency.

As shown in Table 1, DiskSeen significantly improves the performance of both *CVS* and *diff* on the first runs and further on the second runs. This is because the Linux source code tree accessed in both workloads mostly consists of small files, which are laid out on the disk sequentially. However, the file-level prefetching in the stock Linux kernel cannot detect sequential disk accesses across files and most of these files are of small size, so prefetching is only occasionally

Table 2. Request Size (blocks) of workloads on the stock Linux kernel and kernel with DiskSeen

Workload name	Linux 2.6.11	DiskSeeen – 1st Run	DiskSeen – 2nd Run
strided	2	2	59.54
reversed	1	1	29.79
CVS	2.73	5.98	8.42
diff	2.88	3.94	5.4
grep	2.86	82.26	97.41
TPC-H (Q4)	6.49	6.89	10.37

activated. In contrast, with DiskSeen, sequential disk accesses across file boundary can be detected at the disk level by the sequence-based prefetching during the first runs. As a result, *CVS* and *diff* have a reduction of execution times by 16% and 18%, respectively. The second runs of them can further reduce the times by another 19% and 43%, because accesses to non-continuous data blocks are identified and prefetched as well.

Grep

Different from *CVS* and *diff*, which gains significant performance improvement due to alternate accesses of two remote disk regions, *grep* only searches a local directory but also exhibits substantial performance improvement, a 20% reduction in its execution time.

In EXT2/EXT2, disk is segmented into multiple 128MB cylinder groups. In each cylinder group, inode blocks are grouped at the beginning and followed by file data blocks. Before a file is accessed, its inode must be inspected first, so accessing a large number of small files causes the disk head to wildly move between disk regions containing file content blocks and regions containing metadata blocks. Since the inode blocks in one cylinder group are laid out continuously at the beginning, sequence-based prefetching in DiskSeen can effectively prefetch these inode blocks into memory, thus most of the disk head movements are removed, which explains the 20% performance improvement.

TPC-H

In TPC-H workloads, Query 4 performs a merge-join against table *orders* and table *lineitem*. It sequentially searches table *orders* for orders placed in a specific time frame. For each record, the query searches for the matched records in table *lineitem* by referring to an index file.

During the first run, DiskSeen can identify sequences for accesses to table *lineitem*, which is created by appending records in the order time. In the second run, history-aware prefetching can further exploit history trails for disk accesses to the *index* file, and DiskSeen achieve a 26% reduction of execution time compared to the stock Linux kernel.

Disk Request Size

The hard disk performance is directly affected by the size of requests received on the disk. Generally speaking, the larger disk requests are, the more efficient disk performance is. Thus, we also examined the size of disk requests for each workload. To obtain the request sizes, we modify the Linux kernel to monitor READ/WRITE commands issued to the disk driver and trace the sizes of disk requests. Table 2 shows the average size of all the requests during the executions of benchmarks.

As shown in the table, DiskSeen significantly increases the average request sizes in most cases, which explains their respective execution reductions shown in Table 1. For example, the first run of *grep* with DiskSeen increases the request size by 28 times, compared to the stock Linux kernel. We can also see that, with more aggressive prefetching in the second run, the request size is also effectively increased further. Also note that, the increases of request size are not proportional to their respective reductions in execution time. This is due to many factors, such as the percentage of computation and data accesses in a program. However, this figure clearly shows that DiskSeen effectively improves the efficiency of disk accesses by increasing request sizes, as expected.

CONCLUSION

For improving disk performance, prefetching plays an important role in operating systems. Unfortunately, the widely adopted file-level prefetching has many intrinsic limitations, which cannot be addressed at the logic file level. In this chapter, we present a disk-level prefetching scheme, called DiskSeen, to exploit the disk-specific information and complement the traditional file-level prefetch policies. By directly observing data accesses at disk level, DiskSeen can identify sequential disk accesses and perform more accurate sequence-based prefetching. By exploiting block access history, DiskSeen can effectively identify non-sequential disk accesses that are repeated in history and perform efficient block prefetching with low overhead. Working at disk level, Disk-Seen overcomes barriers imposed by file-level prefetching such as prefetching data blocks across file boundaries or across lifetimes of open files. At the same time, DiskSeen complements rather than replaces high-level prefetching schemes, which help preserve the effectiveness of existing file-level prefetching and correct its inaccurate prefetch decision. The DiskSeen prototype implemented in the Linux 2.6 kernel shows that such a disk-level prefetching can significantly improve the effectiveness of file-level prefetching, by reducing execution times by 20%-53% for both

synthetic workloads and real applications such as *grep, CVS, TPC-H*.

REFERENCES

Bryant, R. E., & O'Hallaron, D. R. (2003). Computer Systems: A Programmer's Perspective. Prentice Hall, pp.294.

Forum, M. P. I. (1997). MPI-2: Extensions to the Message-Passing Interface, URL: http://www.mpi-forum.org/docs/mpi-20-html/mpi2-report.html

Gray, J., & Shenoy, P. J. (2000). Rules of Thumb in Data Engineering. *Proceedings of International Conference on Data Engineering, 2000*, 3–12.

Griffioen, J., & Appleton, R. (1994). Reducing file system latency using a predictive approach. Proceedings of the USENIX Summer Conference, June 1994, pp. 197-208.

Kroeger, T. M., & Long, D. D. E. (2001). Design and implementation of a predictive file prefetching algorithm. Proceedings of the 2001 USENIX Annual Technical Conference, January 2001.

Li, Z., Chen, Z., Srinivasan, S., & Zhou, Y. (2004). C-Miner: Mining Block Correlations in Storage Systems. Proceedings of 3rd USENIX Conference on File and Storage Technologies (FAST04), March 2004.

Pai, R., Pulavarty, B., & Cao, M. (2004). Linux 2.6 Performance Improvement through Readahead Optimization. Proceedings of the Linux Symposium, July 2004.

Papathanasiou, A. E., & Scott, M. L. (2005). Aggressive Prefetching: An Idea Whose Time Has Come. Proceedings of the Tenth Workshop on Hot Topics in Operating Systems, June 2005.

Schindler, J., & Ganger, G. R. (2000). Automated Disk Drive Characterization. Proceeding of 2000 ACM SIGMETRICS Conference, June 2000.

Schindler, J., Griffin, J. L., Lumb, C. R., & Ganger, G. R. (2002). Track-Aligned Extents: Matching Access Patterns to Disk Drive Characteristics. Proceedings of USENIX Conference on File and Storage Technologies, January 2002.

Schlosser, S. W., Schindler, J., Papadomanolakis, S., Shao, M., Ailamaki, A., Faloutsos, C., & Ganger, G. R. (2005). On Multidimensional Data and Modern Disks. Proceedings of the 4th USENIX Conference on File and Storage Technology, December 2005.

Schmuck, F., & Haskin, R. (2002). GPFS: A Shared-Disk File System for Large Computing Clusters. Proceedings of USENIX Conference on File and Storage Technologies, January 2002.

Chapter 11
Sequential File Prefetching in Linux

Fengguang Wu
Intel Corporation, China

ABSTRACT

Sequential prefetching is a well established technique for improving I/O performance. As Linux runs an increasing variety of workloads, its in-kernel prefetching algorithm has been challenged by many unexpected and subtle problems; As computer hardware evolves, the design goals should also be adapted. To meet the new challenges and demands, a prefetching algorithm that is aggressive yet safe, flexible yet simple, scalable yet efficient is desired. In this chapter, the author explores the principles of I/O prefetching and present a demand readahead algorithm for Linux. He demonstrates how it handles common readahead issues by a host of case studies. Both static, logic and dynamic behaviors of the readahead algorithm are covered, so as to help readers building both theoretical and practical views of sequential prefetching.

INTRODUCTION

Sequential prefetching, also known as readahead in Linux, is a widely deployed technique to bridge the huge gap between the characteristics of storage devices and their inefficient ways of usage by applications. At one end, disk drives and disk arrays are better utilized by large accesses. At the other, applications tend to do lots of tiny sequential reads. To make the two ends meet, operating systems do prefetching: to bring in data blocks for the upcoming requests, and do so in large chunks.

The Linux kernel does sequential file prefetching in a generic readahead framework that dates back to 2002. It actively intercepts file read requests in the VFS layer and transforms the sequential ones into large and asynchronous readahead requests. This seemingly simple task turns out to be rather tricky in practice (Pai, Pulavarty, and Cao, 2004; Wu, Xi, Li, and Zou, 2007). The wide deployment of Linux --- from embedded devices to supercom-

DOI: 10.4018/978-1-60566-850-5.ch011

puters --- confronts its readahead algorithm with an incredible variety of workloads.

In the mean while, there are two trends that bring new demands and challenges to prefetching. Firstly, the relative cost of disk seeks has been growing steadily. In the past 15 years, the disk bandwidth improved by 90 times, while the disk access latency only saw 3-4 times speedup(Schmid, 2006). As an effective technique for reducing seeks, prefetching is thus growing more and more important. However the traditional readahead algorithm was designed in a day when memory and bandwidth resources are scare and precious. It was optimized for high readahead hit ratio and may be too conservative for today's hardware configuration. We need a readahead algorithm that put more emphasis on "avoiding seeks".

Secondly, I/O parallelism keeps growing. As it becomes more and more hard to increase single-thread performance, the parallel execution of a pool of threads raises to be a new focus. The deserialize of hardware and software means the parallelization of I/O. Prefetching helps parallel I/O performance. In turn it is also challenged by the forms and degree of I/O concurrency: How to detect and keep track of states for multiple I/O streams that are interleaved together? How to maintain good readahead behavior for a sequential stream that is concurrently served by a pool of cooperative threads? How to achieve low time and space overheads in the cases of single thread I/O as well as highly concurrent I/O?

The questions will be answered in the following sections. We will start by the introduction to prefetching with its values for storage devices and roles in I/O optimization. We will give a reference to basic forms of prefetching, discuss the design tradeoffs and argue for more aggressive prefetching policies. We then proceed to introduce the demand readahead algorithm in Linux and explain the differences to the legacy one. At last we demonstrate its dynamic behaviors and advantages by a host of case studies and benchmarks.

PRINCIPLES OF I/O PREFETCHING

Bandwidth and latency are the two major aspects of I/O performance. For both metrics, there have been huge and growing performance gaps between disk, memory and processor. For example, the Intel[R] QuickPath[TM] Interconnect (QPI) can provide 12.8GB/s bandwidth per direction for processor-to-processor and processor-to-io data transfers. Today's DDR3-1333 memory has a theoretical bandwidth of 10666MB/s and response time of 12 nanoseconds, while a Seagate[R] 7200.11 SATA disk has a maximum sustained transfer rate of 105MB/s and average seek time of 8.5ms. Hence the performance gap as of 2009 is about 10 times for bandwidth and 7e5 times for latency. In this section, we demonstrate how I/O prefetching can help fill the performance gaps.

Storage Devices

The I/O latency is such a dominant factor in disk I/O operations that it can be approximated by a simple I/O model. A typical disk I/O takes two steps: Firstly, the disk head moves to the data track and waits for the data sector to rotate under it; Secondly, data read and transfer start. Correspondingly there are two operational times: the average access time, whose typical value is 8ms; the data transfer time, which roughly equals to the multiplication of I/O size and the disk's sustained transfer rate, which averages to 80MB/s for commodity disks today.

In a full I/O period, only the data transfer time makes real utilization of the disk data channel. The larger I/O size, the more time will be spent in data transfer and less time wasted in seeking, hence the more we can harvest disk utilization ratio and I/O bandwidth. Figure 1 reflects this correlation given the above disk I/O model and representative parameter values. One major function of I/O prefetching is to shift a disk's working point from left to right in the graph, so as to achieve better disk utilization and I/O bandwidth.

Figure 1. Disks can be better utilized with larger I/O sizes

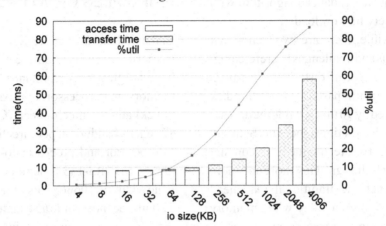

Two exciting advances about cache media are the great abundance of dynamic memory and the general availability of flash memory. One might expect them to bring negative impacts to the relevance of prefetching techniques. When more data can be cached in the two types of memories, there would be less disk I/Os and readahead invocations. However, in this era of information explosion, data set and disk size grow rapidly at the same time. There are increasing I/O intensive applications and I/O parallelism that demand more flexible, robust and aggressive prefetching. Another consequence of the larger memory is, aggressive prefetching becomes a practical consideration for modern desktop systems. A well known example is boot time prefetching for fast system boot and application startup(Esfahbod, 2006).

Flash memory and its caching algorithms fit nicely in one big arena where magnetic disk and its prefetching algorithms are not good at: small random accesses. The Intel[R] turbo memory and hybrid hard drive are two widely recognized ways to utilize the flash memory as a complementary cache for magnetic disks. And apparently the solid-state disk(SSD) is the future for mobile computing. However, the huge capacity gap isn't closing any time soon. Hard disks and storage networks are still the main choice in the foreseeable future to meet the unprecedented storage demand created

by the explosion of digital information, where readahead algorithms will continue to play an important role.

The solid-state disks greatly reduced the costly seek time, however there are still non-trivial access delays. In particular, SSD storage is basically comprised of a number of chips operating in parallel, and the larger prefetching I/O will be able to take advantage of the parallel chips. The optimal I/O size required to get full performance from the SSD storage will be different from spinning media, and vary from device to device. So I/O prefetching with larger and tunable size is key even on SSD.

In summary, where there is sequential access patterns, there's arena for I/O prefetching. Whether it be platter-based disk or solid state disk.

2.2 I/O Optimization and Prefetching

According to (Russel, 1997), there are four basic I/O optimization strategies:

Avoidance. The best option is to avoid the costly disk accesses totally or to reduce disk access frequency. This can achieved by file caching. Prefetching is also good at converting small read requests into large ones, which effectively reduces the number of disk accesses and therefore the costly seeks. Another concrete example is the well known

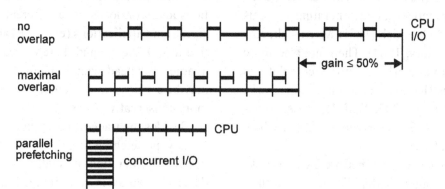

Figure 2. Prefetching helps achieve I/O asynchrony and parallelism

Linux VFS (Virtual File System) mount options noatime and relatime for eliminating undesirable writes triggered by mtime updates.

Sequentiality. Sequential accesses enable sequential prefetching and maximize disk utilization. For concurrent sequential accesses, prefetching plays an essential role in aggregating interleaved tiny I/Os into larger ones. For non-sequential accesses, it still benefits to minimize seek and rotational delays by employing techniques such as smart disk layout management, informed prefetching, I/O queuing and scheduling. To name a few real world examples: the deadline, anticipatory and CFQ (Complete Fairness Queuing) I/O elevators in Linux; the TCQ (Tagged Command Queuing) for SCSI disks and NCQ (Native Command Queuing) for SATA disks; the delayed allocation and pre-allocation features of ext4/xfs; the writeback clustering in xfs; etc.

Asynchrony. Asynchronous accesses improve I/O computing efficiency by pipelining processor and disk activities, and hiding I/O latencies to the application. AIO, non-blocking I/O, writeback and readahead are common facilities for asynchronous I/O.

Parallelism. Disk arrays have been a standard practice for aggregating multiple disks' capacity as well as bandwidth. Beyond the traditional RAID layer, the emerging file systems exemplified by zfs and btrfs target to manage large pool of disks on their own. For large scale cloud computing and high performance computing, large pools of storage servers can be organized with the Google file system, Lustre, pNFS or other cluster file systems. On the other hand, device level parallelism are being employed inside SSD. For example, Intel[R] pioneered 10 parallel NAND flash channels in its SATA solid-state drives to deliver up to 250MB/s read bandwidth and 35,000 IOPS. Concurrent I/O requesting and parallel data transfer are the keys to I/O throughput of the above parallel systems. Aggressive prefetching plays a vital role in this arena: they typically need large and asynchronous prefetching I/O to fill the parallel data channels.

It is obvious that prefetching plays an important role in each of the four I/O optimization strategies. Prefetching brings benefits to applications, storage devices and storage pools, and even processing resources(Shriver, Small, and Smith, 1999). Applications can run smoother and faster by masking the low level I/O delays. Disks can be better utilized by large I/O size. Storage pools can be better parallelized. The larger I/O unit also helps amortize processing overheads in the whole I/O path.

Basic Approaches to Prefetching

Prefetching algorithms can be either heuristic or informed. The heuristic algorithms try to predict I/O blocks to be accessed in the near future based on the past ones. The most successful one is sequential readahead, which has long been a standard practice among operating systems (Feiertag and Organick, 1971; McKusick, Joy, Leffler, and Fabry, 1984). There are also more comprehensive works to mine correlations between files (Kroeger and Long, 2001; Paris, Amer, and Long, 2003; Whittle, Paris, Amer, Long, and Burns, 2003) or data blocks (Li, Chen, and Zhou, 2005).

On the other hand, informed prefetching works with hints from individual applications about their future I/O operations. The hints could either be explicitly controlled by application (Cao, Felten, Karlin, and Li, 1996; Patterson, Gibson, Ginting, Stodolsky, and Zelenka, 1995; Patterson, Gibson, and Satyanarayanan, 1993) or be automatically generated (Brown, Mowry, and Krieger, 2001).

Caching is another ubiquitous performance optimization technique. It is a common practice to share prefetching memory with cache memory, this opens the door to interactions between prefetching and caching. Besides the basic defensive support for readahead thrashing discussed in this chapter, there are also comprehensive works dealing with integrated prefetching and caching (Butt, Gniady, and Hu, 2005; Cao, Felten, Karlin, and Li, 1995; Cao, Felten, Karlin, and Li, 1996; Dini, Lettieri, and Lopriore, 2006; Gill and Modha, 2005; Patterson, Gibson, Ginting, Stodolsky, and Zelenka, 1995; Itshak and Wiseman, 2008) and schemes to dynamically adapt the prefetching memory (Li and Shen, 2005) or prefetch depth (Gill and Bathen, 2007; Li, Shen, and Papathanasiou, 2007; Liang, Jiang, and Zhang, 2007).

Design Tradeoffs of Prefetching

The prefetching size can greatly impact I/O performance and is considered as the main I/O parameter. One must tradeoff between throughput and latency on determining its value. The general guideline is: prefetching size should be large enough to deliver good I/O throughput and small enough to prevent undesirable long I/O latencies.

Different storage devices, disk array configurations and workloads have different optimal I/O size. Some applications (e.g. FTP) are not sensitive to I/O latency and therefore can safely use a large readahead size; Some others (e.g. VOD) may be sensitive to I/O latency and should use a more conservative I/O size.

Besides the tradeoff between throughput and latency, prefetching hit ratio is another common design consideration. It is defined as: for all the data pages faulted in by the prefetching algorithm, how much of them are actually accessed before being reclaimed. To keep prefetching hit ratio high, adaptive readahead size shall be employed. This is because even we are sure that an application is doing sequential reads, we have no idea how long the read sequence will last. For example, it is possible that an application scans one file from beginning to end, while only accesses the first two pages in another file.

Fortunately, the common I/O behaviors are somehow inferable. Firstly, the number of pages to be read (not considering the end-of-file case) and the number of pages have been accessed are normally positively correlated. Secondly, the larger read size, the more possibility it will be repeated. Because the large read size implies an optimization made by the developer for an expected long run of reads. Based on the above two empirical rules, the possibility of the current access pattern being repeated can be estimated, upon which an adaptive prefetching size can be calculated.

The prefetching hit ratio has served as one major goal in the design of prefetching algorithms. A low hit ratio means waste of memory and disk I/O resources. The cost was high and unacceptable in a day when these resources are scare and precious. So traditional prefetching algorithms tend to do prefetching for only strictly sequential reads. They employ conservative policies on prefetching size as well as sequential detection, seeking for a high prefetching hit ratio. For example, Linux 2.6 has been using a conservative 128KB readahead size since its infancy.

However, with the rapid evolvement of computer hardware, we are now facing new constraints and demands. The bandwidth and capacity of memory and disk both improved greatly, while the disk access times remain slow and become more and more an I/O bottleneck. As a consequence, the benefit of readahead hits goes up. It not only adds importance to prefetching, but also favors aggressive prefetching.

The cost of prefetching misses has been much lowered, reducing the performance relevance of prefetching hit ratio. There are two major costs of prefetching miss: Firstly, wasted memory cache. When more memory is taken by prefetching, less is available for caching. This may lower the cache hit ratio and increase number of I/O. However, in the context of memory abundance, the impact of cache size on cache hit ratio should be limited. Secondly, wasted disk bandwidth. It is relatively easy to estimate the impact of prefetching misses on I/O bandwidth. For an I/O intensive application, if a page being asynchronously prefetched is accessed later, it typically means one less I/O operation, assume that the saved disk seek time is 5ms; on the other hand, a prefetching miss page costs about 4KB/80MBps=0.05ms extra disk transfer time. From these two numbers alone, we could say that a prefetching hit ratio larger than 1% would be beneficial if not optimal.

So it deserves to use more aggressive prefetching polices. It can improve overall I/O performance even when sacrificing the hit ratio. The prefetching hit ratio of a workload depends on its accuracy of pattern recognition and pattern run length estimation. For sequential workloads, loosing the pattern recognition accuracy means that the strict page-after-page pattern matching for read requests is no longer necessary, which will allow the detection of more interleaved and semi-sequential patterns; loosing the run length estimation accuracy means larger prefetching size.

It is argued in (Papathanasiou and Scott, 2005) that more aggressive prefetching policies be employed to take advantage of new hardware and fulfill increasing I/O demands. Our experiences are backing it: there are risks of regression in extending the sequential detection logic to cover more semi-sequential access patterns, however we received no single negative feedback since the wide deployment of the new policies in Linux 2.6.23. It's all about performance gains in practice, including the tricky retry based AIO reads(Bhattacharya, Tran, Sullivan, and Mason, 2004) and locally disordered NFS reads(Ellard, Ledlie, Malkani, and Seltzer, 2003; Ellard and Seltzer, 2003), which will be discussed in this chapter.

READAHEAD IN LINUX

Linux 2.6 does autonomous file level prefetching in two ways: read-around for memory mapped file accesses, and read-ahead for general buffered reads. The read-around logic is mainly designed for executables and libraries, which are perhaps the most prevalent mmap file users. They typically do a lot of random reads that exhibit strong locality of reference. So a simple read-around policy is employed for mmap files: on every mmap cache miss, try to pre-fault some more pages around the faulting page. This policy also does a reasonable good job for sequential accesses in either forward or backward directions.

The readahead logic for buffered reads, including read(), pread(), readv(), sendfile(), aio_read() and the Linux specific splice() system calls, is designed to be a general purpose one and hence is more comprehensive. It watches those read requests and tries to discover predictable patterns in them, so that it can prefetch data in a more I/O efficient way. Due to the highly diversity of access patterns and wide range of system dynamics, it has been hard to get right, and only the sequential access patterns are supported for now.

The read-around and read-ahead algorithms are either dumb or heuristic, in various cases these in-kernel logics can be aided with some kind of user/

Figure 3. Page cache oriented read and readahead: when an empty page cache file is asked for the first 4KB data, a 16KB readahead I/O will be triggered

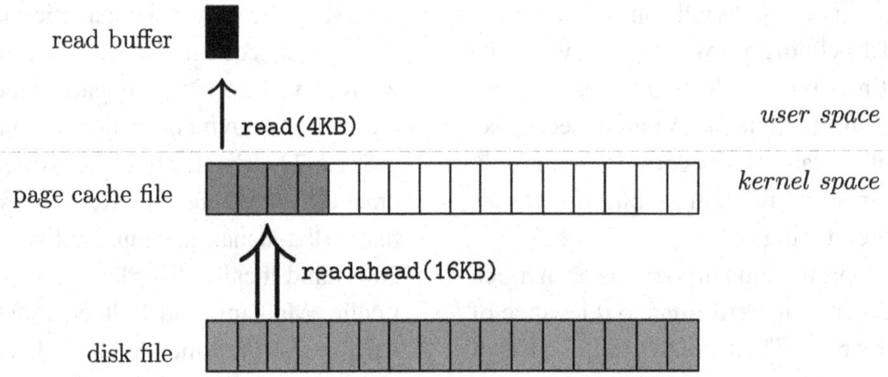

application provided I/O hints. Linux provides a per-device tunable max_readahead parameter that can be queried and modified with command blockdev. As for now it defaults to 128KB for hard disks and may be increased in the future. To better parallelize I/O for disk arrays, it defaults to 2*stripe_width for software RAID.

Linux also provides madvise(), posix_fadvise() and the non-portable readahead() system calls. The first two calls allow applications to indicate their future access patterns as normal, random or sequential, which correspondingly set the read-around and read-ahead policies to be default, disabled or aggressive. The APIs also make application controlled prefetching possible by allowing the application to specify the exact time and location to do readahead. Mysql is a good example to make use of this facility in carrying out its random queries.

The Page Cache

Figure 3 shows how Linux transforms a regular read() system call into an internal readahead request. Here the page cache plays a central role: user space data consumers do read()s which transfer data from page cache, while the in-kernel readahead routine populates page cache with data from the storage device. The read requests are thus decoupled from real disk I/Os.

This layer of indirection enables the kernel to reshape "silly" I/O requests from applications: a huge sendfile(1GB) request will be served in smaller max_readahead sized I/O chunks; while a sequence of tiny 1KB reads will be aggregated into up to max_readahead sized readahead I/Os.

The readahead algorithm does not manage a standalone readahead buffer. Prefetched pages are put into page cache together with cached pages. It also does not take care of the in-LRU-queue life time of the prefetched pages in general. Every prefetched page will be inserted not only into the per-file radix tree based page cache for ease of reference, but also to one of the system wide LRU queues managed by the page replacement algorithm.

This design is simple and elegant in general; however when memory pressure goes high, the memory will thrash (Wiseman, 2009), (Jiang, 2009) and the interactions between prefetching and caching algorithms will become visible. On the one hand, readahead blurs the correlation between a page's position in the LRU queue with its first reference time. Such correlation is relied on by the page replacement algorithm to do proper page aging and eviction. On the other hand, in a memory hungry system, the page replacement algorithm may evict readahead pages before they are accessed by the application, leading to readahead thrashings. The latter issue will be revisited in section 5.3.

Readahead Windows and Pipelining

Each time a readahead I/O decision is made, it is recorded as a "readahead window". A readahead window takes the form of (start, size), where start is the first page index and size is the number of pages. The readahead window produced from this run of readahead will be saved for reference in the next run.

Pipelining is an old technique to enhance the utilization of the computer components (Wiseman, 2001). Readahead pipelining is a technique to parallelize CPU and disk activities for better resource utilization and I/O computing performance. The legacy readahead algorithm adopts dual windows to do pipelining: while the application is walking in the current_window, I/O is underway asynchronously in the ahead_window. Whenever the read request is crossing into ahead_window, it becomes current_window, and a readahead I/O will be triggered to make the new ahead_window.

Readahead pipelining is all about doing asynchronous readahead. The key question is how early should the next readahead be started asynchronously? The dual window scheme cannot provide an exact answer, since both read request and ahead_window are wide ranges. As a result it is not able to control the "degree of asynchrony".

Our solution is to introduce it as an explicit parameter async_size: as soon as the number of not-yet-consumed readahead pages falls under this threshold, it is time to start next readahead. async_size can be freely tuned in the range [0, size]: async_size = 0 disables pipelining, whereas async_size = size opens full pipelining. It avoids maintaining two readahead windows and decouples async_size from size.

Figure 4 shows the data structures. Note that we also tag the page at start + size - async_size with PG_readahead. This newly introduced page flag is one fundamental facility in our proposed readahead framework. It was originally intended to help support the interleaved reads: It is more stable than the per-file-descriptor readahead states, and can tell if the readahead states are still valid and dependable in the case of multiple readers in one file descriptor. Then we quickly find it a handy tool for handling other cases, as an integral part of the following readahead call convention.

Call Convention

The traditional practice is to feed every read request to the readahead algorithm, and let it handle all possible system states in the process of sorting out the access patterns and making readahead decisions. The handling everything in one interception routine approach leads to unnecessary invocations of readahead logic and makes it unnecessarily complex.

There are also fundamental issues with read requests. They may be too small(less than 1 page) or too large(more than max_readahead pages) that require special handling. What's more, they are unreliable and confusing: the same pages may be requested more than one times in the case of readahead thrashing and retried sequential reads.

The above observations lead us to two new principles: Firstly, trap into the readahead heuristics only when it is the right time to do readahead; Secondly, judge by the page status instead of the read requests and readahead windows whenever feasible. These principles yield a modular readahead framework that separates the following readahead trigger conditions with the main readahead logic. When these two types of pages are read, it is time to do readahead:

1. *cache miss page*: it's time for synchronous readahead. An I/O is required to fault in the current page. The I/O size could be inflated to piggy back more pages.

2. *PG_readaheadpage*: it's time for asynchronous readahead. The PG_readahead tag is set by a previous readahead to indicate the time to do next readahead.

Figure 4. The readahead windows

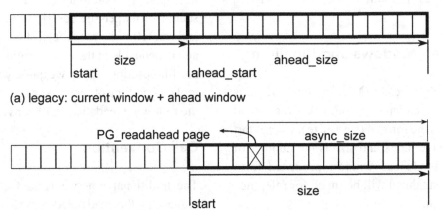

(a) legacy: current window + ahead window

(b) new: readahead window + async_size

Sequentiality

Table 1 shows the common sequentiality criteria. The most fundamental one among them is the "consecutive criterion" in the last line, where page access offsets are incremented one by one. The legacy readahead algorithm enforces the sequentiality criteria on each and every read request, so one single seek will immediately shutdown the readahead windows. Such rigid policy guarantees high readahead hit ratio. However it was found to be too conservative to be useful for many important real life workloads.

Instead of demanding a rigorous sequentiality, we propose to do readahead for reads that have good probability to be sequential. In particular, the following rules are adopted:

1. Check sequentiality only for synchronous readahead triggered by a missing page. This ensures that random reads will be recognized as the random pattern, while a random read in between a sequential stream wont interrupt the stream's readahead sequence.

2. Assume sequentiality for the asynchronous readahead triggered by a PG_readahead page. Even if the page was hit by a true random read, it indicates two random reads that are close enough both spatially and temporally. Hence it may well be a hot accessed area that deserves to be readahead.

Concurrent Streams

The consecutive criterion in table 1 demands both time and space continuity. However when multiple threads do sequential reads on the same file in parallel, the read requests may appear interleaved in time but still continuous in their respective access spaces. Such kind of interleaved pattern used to

Table. 1. Common sequentiality criterions

criterion	case
read_size > max_readahead	oversize read, common in sendfile() calls
offset == 0 && prev_offset == -1	first read on start of file
offset == prev_offset	unaligned consecutive reads
offset == prev_offset + 1	trivial consecutive reads

Figure 5. For a typical readahead window, async_size equals to size, and PG_readahead lies in the first page

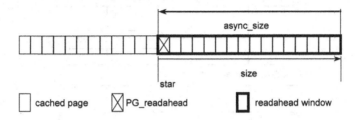

be a great challenge to the readahead algorithm. The interleaving of several sequential streams may be perceived as random reads.

In theory, it is possible to track the state of each and every stream. However the cost would be unacceptable: since each read request may start a new stream, we will end up remembering every read in the case of random reads. ZFS takes this approach but limits the number of streams it can track to a small value. The implementation also has to deal with the complexity to dynamically allocate, lookup, age and free the stream objects.

Linux takes a simple and stupid approach: to statically allocate one readahead data structure for each file descriptor. This is handy in serving the common case of one stream per file descriptor, however it leaves the support for multiple interleaved streams an open question.

When there are multiple streams per file descriptor, the streams will contend the single space slot for read offset and readahead window, and end up overwriting each other's state. This gives rise to two problems. Firstly, given an unreliable prev_offset, how do we know the current read request is a sequential one and therefore should be prefetched? Secondly, given an unreliable readahead window, how do we know it is valid for the current stream and if not, how can we recover it? The first problem has in fact been addressed in the previous subsection. It is also straightforward to validate the ownership of a readahead window: if it contains the current PG_readahead page, then

it is the readhead window for the current stream. Otherwise we have to seek alternative ways for finding out the lost information about readahead window.

Fortunately, we found that the lost readahead window information can be inferred from the page cache. Figure 5 shows the typical status of a page cache. The application hits the PG_readahead page and is triggering an interleaved readahead. To recover the readahead window information, we scan forward in the page cache from the current page to the first missing page. The number of pages in between is exactly async_size. As we know that async_size equals to size for all subsequent readaheads and at least size/2 for the initial readahead, we can safely take async_size as size, and calculate the next readahead size from it.

Readahead Sequence

Assume the sequence of readahead for a sequential read stream to be A0, A1, A2, ... We call A0 the "initial readahead" and A1, A2, ... the "subsequent readaheads". The initial readahead is typically synchronous in that it contains the currently requested page and the reader have to stop and wait for the readahead I/O. The subsequent readaheads can normally be asynchronous in that the readahead pages are not immediately needed by the application.

A typical readahead sequence starts with a small initial readahead size, which is inferred

Figure 6. The readahead framework in Linux 2.6.24

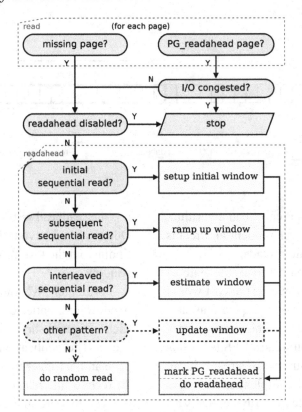

from the read size, and then ramps up exponentially to max_readahead. However in the case of a large sendfile() call, the readahead window can immediately expand to its full size. The resulting readahead size is adaptive to the current read size as well as the accumulated sequential read sizes.

We conclude this section with the block diagram of the demand readahead in Linux 2.6.24.

CASE STUDY

A Typical Readahead Stream

Take the "cp" command as an example, it does 4KB page sized sequential reads covering the whole file. Table 2 and figure 7 demonstrates the first three readahead invocations. The initial read triggers a readahead that is four times the read size,

whose initial async_size is such that the second sequential read request will immediately trigger the next readahead asynchronously. The goal of the rules is to start asynchronous readahead as soon as possible, while trying to avoid useless readahead for applications that only examine the file head.

Readahead Cache Hits

Linux manages kernel level "page cache" to keep frequently accessed file pages in memory. A read request for an already cached page is called a "cache hit", otherwise it is a "cache miss". If a readahead request is made for an already cached page, it makes a "readahead cache hit". Cache hits are good whereas readahead cache hits are evil: they are undesirable and normally avoidable overheads. Since cache hits can far outweigh

Figure 7. Readahead I/O triggered by "cp"

cache misses in a typical system, it is important to shutdown readahead on large ranges of cached pages to avoid excessive readahead cache hits.

The classical way to disable readahead for cached page ranges is to set a RA_FLAG_IN-CACHE flag after 256 back-to-back readahead cache hits and to clear it after the first cache miss. Although this scheme works, it is not ideal. Firstly, the threshold does not apply to cached files that are smaller than 1MB, which is a common case; Secondly, during the in-cache-no-readahead mode, the readahead algorithm will be invoked for *every page* instead of every read request or max_readahead pages, to ensure on time resume of readahead(yet it still misses readahead for the first cache miss page), so it's converting one type of overhead into another hopefully smaller one.

Our proposed readahead trigger scheme can handle readahead cache hits automatically. This is achieved by taking care that PG_readahead be only set on a newly allocated readahead page and get cleared on the first read hit. So when the new readahead window lies inside a range of cached pages, PG_readahead won't be set, disabling further readaheads. As soon as the reader steps out of the cached range, there will be a cache miss which immediately restarts readahead. If the whole file is cached, there will be no missing or PG_readahead pages at all to trigger an

undesired readahead. Another merit is that the in-kernel readahead will automatically stop when the user space is carrying out accurate application controlled readahead.

Readahead Thrashing

We call a page the "readahead page" if it was populated by the readahead algorithm and is waiting to be accessed by some reader. Once being referenced, it is turned into a "cached page". Linux manages readahead pages in inactive_list together with cached pages. For the readahead pages, inactive_list can be viewed as a simple FIFO queue. It may be rotated quickly in a loaded and memory tight server. Readahead thrashing happens when some readahead pages are shifted out of inactive_list and reclaimed, before a slow reader is able to access them in time.

Readahead thrashing can be easily detected. If a cache miss occurs inside the readahead windows, a thrashing happened. In this case, the legacy readahead algorithm will decrease the next readahead size by 2. By doing so it hopes to adapt readahead size to the "thrashing threshold", which is defined as the largest possible thrashing safe readahead size. As the readahead size steps slowly off to the thrashing threshold, the thrashings will fade away.

Table. 2. Readahead invocations triggered by "cp"

offset	trigger condition	readahead type	size	async_size
0	missing page	initial/sync readahead	4*read_size = 4	size-read_size = 3
1	PG_readahead	subsequent/async	2*prev_size = 8	size = 8
4	page	readahead	2*prev_size = 16	size = 16

Figure 8. The trivial, unaligned, and retried sequential reads

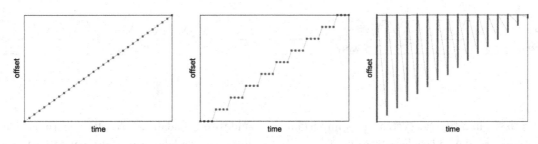

However, once the thrashings stop, the readahead algorithm immediately reverts back to the normal behavior of ramping up the window size by 2 or 4, leading to a new round of thrashings. On average, about half of the readahead pages will be lost and re-read from disk.

Besides the wastage of memory and bandwidth resources, there are much more destructive disk seeks. When thrashing is detected, the legacy readahead takes no action to recover the lost pages inside the readahead windows. The VFS read routine then has to fault them in one by one, generating a lot of tiny 4KB I/Os and hence disk seeks. Overall, up to half pages will be faulted in this destructive way.

Our proposed framework has basic safeguards against readahead thrashing. Firstly, the first read after thrashing makes a cache miss, which will automatically restart readahead from the current position. Therefore it avoids the catastrophic 1-page tiny I/Os suffered by the legacy readahead. Secondly, the size ramp up process may be starting from a small initial value and keep growing exponentially until thrashing again, which effectively keeps the average readahead size above half of the thrashing threshold. If necessary, more fine grained control can be practiced after thrashing.

Non-Trivial Sequential Reads

Interestingly, sequential reads may not look like sequential. Figure 8 shows three different forms of sequential reads that have been discovered in the Linux readahead practices. For the following two cases, the consecutive test offset == prev_offset + 1 can fail even when an application is visiting data consecutively.

Unaligned Reads. File reads work on byte ranges, while readahead algorithm works on pages. When a read request does not start or stop at page boundaries, it becomes an "unaligned read". Sequential unaligned reads can access the same page more than once. For example, 1KB sized unaligned reads will present the readahead algorithm with a page series of {0, 0, 0, 0, 1, 1, 1, 1, ...} To cover such cases, this sequentiality criterion has been added: offset == prev_offset.

Retried Reads. In many cases --- such as non-blocking I/O, the retry based Linux AIO, or an interrupted system call --- the kernel may interrupt a read that has only transferred partial amounts of data. A typical application will issue "retried read" requests for the remaining data. The possible requested page ranges could be: {[0, 1000], [4, 1000], [8, 1000], ...}. Such pattern confuses the legacy readahead totally. They will be taken as oversize reads and trigger the following readahead requests: {(0, 64), (4, 64), (8, 64), ...}. Which are overlapped with each other, leading to a lot of readahead cache hits and tiny 4-page I/Os. The new call convention can mask off the retried parts perfectly, in which readahead is triggered by the real accessed pages instead of spurious read requests. So the readahead heuristics won't even be aware of the existence of retried reads.

Figure 9. Sequential accesses over NFS can be out of order when reaching the readahead routine

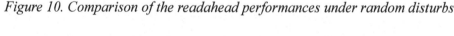

Locally Disordered Reads

Access patterns in real world workloads can deviate from the sequential model in many ways. One common case is the reordered NFS reads. The pages may not be served at NFS server in the same order they are requested by a client side application. They may get reordered in the process of being sent out, arriving at the server, and finally hitting the readahead logic. Figure 9 shows a trace of NFS reads observed by the readahead logic.

The in-depth discussion for such complex kind of workload is beyond the scope of this book. However the readahead framework does offer clean and basic support for semi-sequential reads.

Its call convention and sequential detection logics can help a readahead sequence to start and go on in the face of random disturbances:

Startup. It's easy to start an initial readahead window. It will be opened as soon as two consecutive cache misses occur. Since semi-sequential reads are mostly consecutive, it happens very quickly.

Continuation. It's guaranteed that one readahead window will lead to another in the absence of cache hits. So a readahead sequence won't be interrupted by some wild random reads. A PG_ readahead tag will be set for each new readahead window. It will be hit by a subsequent read and unconditionally trigger the next readahead. It does not matter if that read is a non-consecutive one.

Figure 10. Comparison of the readahead performances under random disturbs

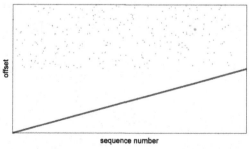

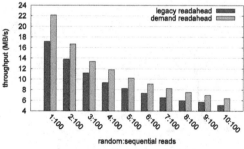

(a) mixed random/sequential access pattern   (b) throughput of the readahead algorithms

PERFORMANCE EVALUATION

In this section we explore the readahead performances of Linux 2.6.24 and 2.6.22 side by side, which implements the new and legacy readahead algorithms respectively. The max readahead size is set to 1MB for better I/O performance. The testing platform is a single Hitachi[R] Deskstar[TM] T7K250 160GB 7200RPM 8MB hard disk and Intel[R] Core[TM]2 E6800 2.93GHz CPU. The selected comparison experiments illustrate how much impact readahead algorithms can have on single disk I/O performance. One can expect much larger differences for disk arrays.

Intermixed Random and Sequential Reads

We created a 200MB file to carry out the intermixed 4KB random and sequential reads. The sequential stream begins at start of file and stops at middle of file, while the random reads land randomly in the second half of the file. We created ten access patterns where the amount of sequential reads are fixed at 100MB and the amount of random reads increase from 1MB to 10MB. Figure 10(a) describes the first access pattern. Figure 10(b) shows the I/O throughputs for each of the 10 ac-

cess patterns. The in-disk readahead function is disabled to highlight the performance impact of OS readahead.

Not surprisingly the I/O throughput decreases with more and more random reads. Also notably, the new readahead algorithm maintains a stable lead over the legacy one. In the case of 1:100 random:sequential bytes ratio, the throughputs are 17.18MB/s and 22.15MB/s respectively, with the new readahead showing an edge of 28.9% over the legacy one. When the ratio goes up to 10:100, the throughputs decrease to 5.10MB/s and 6.39MB/s, but still keeps a performance edge of 25.4%.

The performance edges originate from the different readahead behaviors under random disturbs. Figure 11 demonstrates the readahead sequences submitted for the first 1600 pages by the two readahead algorithms. Figure 11(a) shows vividly how the legacy readahead sequences are interrupted by random reads. On each and every random read, the readahead window will be shutdown. And then followed by a new readahead size ramp up process. Due to the existence of async readahead pages, the new readahead sequence will be overlapping with the old one, leading to series of readahead cache hits. In contrast, the demand readahead algorithm ramps up and pushes forward the

Figure 11. Comparison of readahead sequences under random disturbs

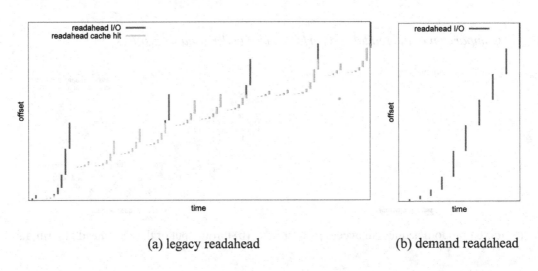

(a) legacy readahead   (b) demand readahead

Figure 12. Five interleaved sequential streams

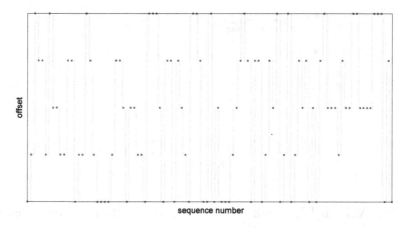

readahead window steadily and is not disturbed by the random reads.

Interleaved Sequential Streams

To validate readahead performance on concurrent streams, we created 10 sequential streams S_i, i=1,2,...,10, where S_i is a sequence of 4KB reads that start from byte (i-1)*100MB and stop at i*100MB. By interleaving the first n streams, we get C_n=interleave($S_1,S_2,...,S_n$), n=1,2,...,10. Where $C_1=S_1$ is a time and space consecutive read stream, and C_n, n=2,3,...,10 is an interleaved access pattern that has n sequential streams. Figure 12 shows a segment of C_5.

Figure 13 plots the I/O throughputs for C_1-C_{10}. The single stream throughputs are close, with 24.95MB/s for legacy readahead and 28.32MB/s for demand readahead. When there are 2 and 3 interleaved streams, the legacy readahead quickly slows down to 7.05MB/s and 3.15MB/s, while the new one is not affected. When there are 10 interleaved streams, the legacy readahead throughput crawls along at 0.81MB/s, while the demand readahead still maintains a high throughput of 21.78MB/s, which is 26.9 times the former one.

We also measured performance with disk readahead enabled. As showed in figure 13(b), the in-disk readahead have very positive effects on the performance. However due to limited disk cache and capability, it can only support a limited number of streams. As the number of streams increase, the influence of the in-disk readahead decreases. When there are 10 streams, the through-

Figure 13 Comparison of readahead performances on interleaved reads

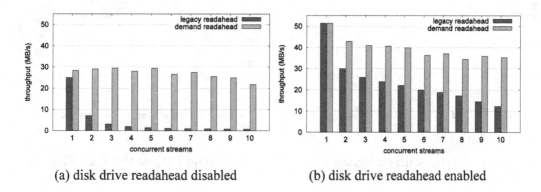

(a) disk drive readahead disabled   (b) disk drive readahead enabled

Figure 14. Application visible I/O delays on 100MB interleaved reads

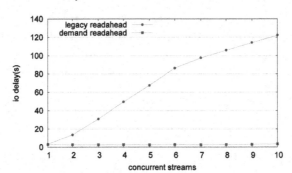

puts decrease to 12.29MB/s and 35.30MB/s, in which the demand readahead is 2.87 times fast. When it comes to hundreds of concurrent clients, which is commonplace for production file servers, it effectively renders the in-disk readahead useless. So figure 13(a) may be a more realistic measurement of the readahead performance at high concurrency.

Figure 14 plots the total application visible I/O delays in each benchmark. When the number of streams increases, the legacy readahead delays increase rapidly from 3.36s for single stream to 122.35s for 10 streams, while the demand readahead delays increase slowly from 2.89s to 3.44s. There is a huge gap of 35.56 times for the 10 streams case. This stems from the fact that the

legacy readahead windows can hardly ramp up to the ideal size, leading to smaller I/O and more seeks, increasing the total disk I/O latencies. Because the async readahead size will also be reset and limited to small values, it can hardly hide I/O latencies to the upper layer.

Readahead Thrashing

We boot the kernel with mem=128m single, and start one new 100KB/s stream on every second. Various statistics are collected and showed in figure 15. The thrashing begins at 20 second. The legacy readahead starts to overload the disk at 50 second, and eventually achieved 5MB/s maximum network throughput. With the new framework,

Figure 15. I/O performance on readahead thrashing

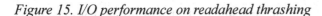

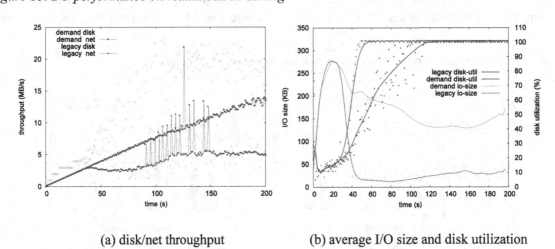

(a) disk/net throughput   (b) average I/O size and disk utilization

throughput keeps growing and the trend is going up to 15MB/s. That's three times better. The average I/O size also improves a lot. It used to drop sharply to about 5KB, while the new behavior is to slowly go down to 40KB under increasing loads. Correspondingly, the disk quickly goes 100% utilization for legacy readahead. It is actually overloaded by the storm of seeks as a result of the tiny 1-page I/Os.

CONCLUSION

Sequential prefetching is a standard function of modern operating systems. It tries to discover application I/O access pattern and prefetch data pages for them. Its two major ways of improving I/O performance are: increasing I/O size for better throughput; facilitating async I/O to mask I/O latency.

The diversity of application behaviors and system dynamics sets high standards to the adaptability of prefetching algorithms. Concurrent and interleaved streams are also big challenges for their capabilities. These challenges became more imminent by two trends: the increasing relative cost of disk seeks and the prevalence of multi-core processors and parallel computing.

Based upon experiences and lessons gained in the Linux readahead practices, we designed a demand readahead algorithm with flexible heuristics that can cover varied sequential access patterns and support interleaved streams. It also enjoys great simplicity by handling most abnormal cases in an implicit way. Its power stems from the relaxed criteria on sequential pattern recognition and the exploitation of page and page cache states. The new design guidelines seem to work well in practice. Since its wide deployment with Linux 2.6.23, we have not received any regression reports.

REFERENCES

Bhattacharya, S., Tran, J., Sullivan, M., & Mason, C. (2004). Linux AIO Performance and Robustness for Enterprise Workloads. In . *Proceedings of the Linux Symposium, 1*, 63–78.

Brown, A. D., Mowry, T. C., & Krieger, O. (2001). Compiler-based i/o prefetching for out-of-core applications. *ACM Transactions on Computer Systems, 19*, 111–170. doi:10.1145/377769.377774

Butt, A. R., Gniady, C., & Hu, Y. C. (2007). The Performance Impact of Kernel Prefetching on Buffer Cache Replacement Algorithms. *IEEE Transactions on Computers, 56*(7), 889–908. doi:10.1109/TC.2007.1029

Cao, P., Felten, E. W., Karlin, A. R., & Li, K. (1995). A study of integrated prefetching and caching strategies. In *Proceedings of the 1995 ACM SIGMETRICS joint international conference on Measurement and modeling of computer systems,* (pp. 188-197).

Cao, P., Felten, E. W., Karlin, A. R., & Li, K. (1996). Implementation and performance of integrated application-controlled file caching, prefetching, and disk scheduling. *ACM Transactions on Computer Systems, 14*, 311–343. doi:10.1145/235543.235544

Dini, G., Lettieri, G., & Lopriore, L. (2006). Caching and prefetching algorithms for programs with looping reference patterns. *The Computer Journal, 49*, 42–61. doi:10.1093/comjnl/bxh140

Ellard, D., Ledlie, J., Malkani, P., & Seltzer, M. (2003). Passive NFS Tracing of Email and Research Workloads. In *Proceedings of the Second USENIX Conference on File and Storage Technologies (FAST'03),* (pp. 203-216).

Ellard, D., & Seltzer, M. (2003). NFS Tricks and Benchmarking Traps. In *Proceedings of the FREENIX 2003 Technical Conference,* (pp. 101-114).

Esfahbod, B. (2006). *Preload - An Adaptive Prefetching Daemon*. PhD thesis. Graduate Department of Computer Science, University of Toronto, Canada.

Feiertag, R. J., & Organick, E. I. (1971). The multics input/output system. In *Proceedings of the third ACM symposium on Operating systems principles*, (pp. 35-41).

Gill, B. S., & Bathen, L. A. D. (2007). Optimal multistream sequential prefetching in a shared cache. *ACM Transactions on Storage, 3*(3), 10. doi:10.1145/1288783.1288789

Gill, B. S., & Modha, D. S. (2005). Sarc: sequential prefetching in adaptive replacement cache. *Proceedings of the USENIX Annual Technical Conference 2005 on USENIX Annual Technical Conference*, (pp. 33-33).

Itshak, M., & Wiseman, Y. (2008). AMSQM: Adaptive Multiple SuperPage Queue Management. In *Proc. IEEE Conference on Information Reuse and Integration (IEEE IRI-2008)*, Las Vegas, NV, (pp. 52-57).

Kroeger, T. M., & Long, D. D. E. (2001). Design and implementation of a predictive file prefetching algorithm. In *Proceedings of the General Track: 2002 USENIX Annual Technical Conference*, (pp. 105-118).

Li, C., & Shen, K. (2005). Managing prefetch memory for data-intensive online servers. In *Proceedings of the 4th conference on USENIX Conference on File and Storage Technologies*, (pp. 19).

Li, C., Shen, K., & Papathanasiou, A. E. (2007). Competitive prefetching for concurrent sequential i/o. In *Proceedings of the ACM SIGOPS/EuroSys European Conference on Computer Systems 2007*, (pp. 189-202).

Li, Z., Chen, Z., & Zhou, Y. (2005). Mining block correlations to improve storage performance. *ACM Transactions on Storage, 1*, 213–245. doi:10.1145/1063786.1063790

Liang, S., Jiang, S., & Zhang, X. (2007). STEP: Sequentiality and Thrashing Detection Based Prefetching to Improve Performance of Networked Storage Servers. *27th International Conference on Distributed Computing Systems (ICDCS'07)*, (p. 64).

McKusick, M. K., Joy, W. N., Leffler, S. J., & Fabry, R. S. (1984). A fast file system for unix. *ACM Transactions on Computer Systems, 2*(3), 181–197. doi:10.1145/989.990

Pai, R., Pulavarty, B., & Cao, M. (2004). Linux 2.6 performance improvement through readahead optimization. In . *Proceedings of the Linux Symposium, 2*, 391–402.

Papathanasiou, A. E., & Scott, M. L. (2005). Aggressive prefetching: An idea whose time has come. In *Proceedings of the 10th Workshop on Hot Topics in Operating Systems (HotOS)*.

Paris, J.-F. Amer, A. & Long, D. D. E. (2003). A stochastic approach to file access prediction. In *Proceedings of the international workshop on Storage network architecture and parallel I/Os*, (pp. 36-40).

Patterson, R. H., Gibson, G. A., Ginting, E., Stodolsky, D., & Zelenka, J. (1995). Informed prefetching and caching. In *Proceedings of the fifteenth ACM symposium on Operating systems principles*, (pp. 79-95).

Patterson, R. H., Gibson, G. A., & Satyanarayanan, M. (1993). A status report on research in transparent informed prefetching. *SIGOPS Operating Systems Review, 27*(2), 21–34. doi:10.1145/155848.155855

Patterson III Russel. H. (1997). *Informed Prefetching and Caching*. PhD thesis, School of Computer Science, Carnegie Mellon University, Pittsburgh, PA.

Schmid, P. (2006). *15 years of hard drive history: Capacities outran performance*. Retrieved from http://www.tomshardware.com/reviews/15-years-of-hard-drive-history,1368.html

Shriver, E., Small, C., & Smith, K. A. (1999). Why does file system prefetching work? In *Proceedings of the Annual Technical Conference on 1999 USENIX Annual Technical Conference*, (pp. 71-84).

Whittle, G. A. S., Paris, J.-F., Amer, A., Long, D. D. E., & Burns, R. (2003). Using multiple predictors to improve the accuracy of file access predictions. In *Proceedings of the 20th IEEE/11th NASA Goddard Conference on Mass Storage Systems and Technologies (MSS'03)*, (pp. 230).

Wu, F., Xi, H., Li, J., & Zou, N. (2007). Linux readahead: less tricks for more. In . *Proceedings of the Linux Symposium*, *2*, 273–284.

Wu, F., Xi, H., & Xu, C. (2008). On the design of a new linux readahead framework. *ACM SIGOPS Operating Systems Review*, *42*(5), 75–84. doi:10.1145/1400097.1400106

Chapter 12
Peer–Based Collaborative Caching and Prefetching in Mobile Broadcast

Wei Wu
Singapore-MIT Alliance, and School of Computing, National University of Singapore, Singapore

Kian-Lee Tan
Singapore-MIT Alliance, and School of Computing, National University of Singapore, Singapore

ABSTRACT

Caching and prefetching are two effective ways for mobile peers to improve access latency in mobile environments. With short-range communication such as IEEE 802.11 and Bluetooth, a mobile peer can communicate with neighboring peers and share cached or prefetched data objects. This kind of cooperation improves data availability and access latency. In this chapter the authors review several cooperative caching and prefetching schemes in a mobile environment that supports broadcasting. They present two schemes in detail: CPIX (Cooperative PIX) and ACP (Announcement-based Cooperative Prefetching). CPIX is suitable for mobile peers that have limited power and access the broadcast channel in a demand-driven fashion. ACP is designed for mobile peers that have sufficient power and prefetch from the broadcast channel. They both consider the data availability in local cache, neighbors' cache, and on the broadcast channel. Moreover, these schemes are simple enough so that they do not incur much information exchange among peers and each peer can make autonomous caching and prefetching decisions.

INTRODUCTION

Mobile broadcast is a scalable data dissemination model for mobile computing (Acharya & Alonso, 1995; Imielinski, 1997; Tan, 2000). In mobile broadcast, a server broadcasts data objects on a wireless channel and (a large number of) mobile peers get their required data objects by tuning into the broadcast channel and retrieving the data objects when they appear. Data broadcast differs from traditional point-to-point access in that the broadcast channel is open to all mobile clients and one transmission of a data object on the broadcast channel can satisfy the needs of potentially many clients. Mobile broadcast is especially suitable for data dissemination in asymmetric communication environments where the client to server ratio is large and there is a high degree of commonality among client interests. Information interesting to the majority of the clients is more suitable for broadcast. Many projects and systems are based on the data broadcast technology (Acharya & Franklin, 1995; Acharya, 1997; Acharya, 1998; Altinel, 1999; Hughes, 2008; Gifford, 1990; Imielinski, 1997; Microsoft, 2008; Zheng, 2005). They are sometimes referred to in the literature as Dissemination-Based Information Systems (DBIS) (Franklin, 1996).

Mobile peers in broadcast environments sometimes suffer from long access latency (the time elapsed from the moment a client has a query for a data object to the point when the client gets the data object), especially when the broadcast cycle is long due to large volume of data or limited broadcast channel. When the broadcast cycle is long, a mobile peer has to wait a long time before their required data objects appear on the broadcast channel.

Caching and prefetching are two effective ways to improve response time. They both store copies of data objects locally for future use. The difference is that caching happens after data access while prefetching stores data objects that are not currently under demand but believed to be useful in the future. In other words, caching is driven by data accesses, and prefetching is driven by anticipation of future accesses. In the environments of mobile broadcast, caching is the mechanism used to store a data object after it is taken from the broadcast channel to fulfill a pending request, and prefetching is to actively listen to the broadcast channel to grab objects that are anticipated to be useful. Thus in prefetching the mobile peer listens to the broadcast channel

even when there is no pending request and stores interesting objects locally. A carefully designed prefetching scheme results in better access latency than a caching scheme does, while consuming more energy (Acharya, 1996).

The fact that the mobile peers have small local storage space limits the effectiveness of caching and prefetching. Local storage constraint makes it impossible to hold all interesting data objects that may be accessed.

With short-range wireless communication technologies, such as IEEE802.11 and Bluetooth, a mobile peer is able to communicate with other mobile peers in its communication range. Figure 1 is an illustration of cooperative mobile peers in a mobile broadcast environment. A line between two mobile peers means they can communicate directly and share contents in a simple peer-to-peer fashion. This enables the mobile peers to share cached or prefetched data objects: when a mobile peer needs a data object, it can request it from its neighbors (we define a mobile peer's neighbors as the mobile peers within its communication range, i.e. one hop away). Such cooperation improves applications' response time, because a mobile peer now can probably get its required data object from its neighbors before getting it on the broadcast channel. This may even reduce energy consumption because getting a data object from

Figure 1. Cooperation among mobile peers. A line between two peers means they can communicate directly and share contents in a simple peer-to-peer fashion

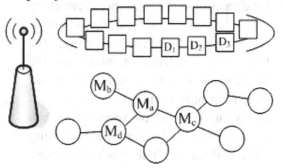

a neighbor may be cheaper than getting from the broadcast channel if the mobile peer has to monitor the broadcast channel for a long time before the data object appears.

A cooperative caching (or prefetching) strategy that takes the sharing between peers into account is more effective than an individual caching (or prefetching) scheme. For example, a simple cooperative strategy could be: a peer caches locally only the data objects that its neighbors do not have. In this way, the overall data availability among the neighborhood is improved, and then the response time is improved.

We believe that a good cooperative cache (or prefetching) management scheme for mobile peers in a broadcast environment should meet two requirements.

• First, mobile peers should retain their autonomy. By autonomy we mean that a mobile peer can make a caching (or prefetching) decision based on its own knowledge (about itself, its neighborhood, and the broadcast channel) and does not require a leader (or super-peer) to make central decisions. Because the peers are moving and their cache contents change with time, to have accurate and real-time knowledge of neighbors' cache content is very expensive. In such a highly dynamic environment leader selection and information synchronization will incur a very high communication (and battery energy) cost.

• Second, it should consider not only the data availability from the neighbors, but also the data availability on the broadcast channel. A data object can be available in three places: local cache, neighbor's cache, and the broadcast channel. In a non-uniform mobile broadcast, popular data objects are broadcast more frequently and they have a high availability on the broadcast channel. A mobile peer should consider both the availability from neighbors and from broadcast channels

when making local caching decisions.

In this chapter, we discuss both cooperative caching and cooperative prefetching in a broadcast environment. For cooperative caching, we discuss in detail a scheme called CPIX (Cooperative PIX). CPIX is a modified version of GCM (Wu, 2006). CPIX extends the well-known PIX caching scheme (designed for broadcast environment) (Acharya, 1995) to the cooperative scenario. CPIX considers two important factors: local access frequency and the *global availability* of data objects. Access frequency helps to identify critical objects that should be locally cached to improve *local cache hits* (and hence reduce waiting time and energy consumption). Global data availability is used to identify the data objects that are neither widely cached by other mobile peers nor are frequently broadcast by the server. Note that here data availability not only means whether the data is available globally, but also means how long it takes for a mobile peer to get the data. For cooperative prefetching, we discuss in detail a scheme called ACP (Announcement-based Cooperative Prefetching) (Wu, 2005). The basic idea of ACP is to let a mobile peer make prefetching decisions based on its neighbors' prefetching decisions while keeping them autonomous. The objective is to help peers avoid prefetching the same data objects, and to improve data availability. Both CPIX and ACP are designed for push-based broadcast environments where the mobile peers can move freely. The schemes consider not only a mobile peer's local access pattern, but also the data availability from other mobile peers and from the broadcast channel.

In the remainder of the chapter, we give the background knowledge on mobile broadcast and individual caching and prefetching schemes, review briefly some cooperative caching and prefetching schemes, and present in detail CPIX and ACP and a performance study of their effectiveness.

BACKGROUND

Mobile Broadcast

According to the mechanism used for scheduling data objects on the broadcast channel, data broadcast can be classified into three categories: push-based, pull-based, and hybrid. In push-based broadcast (Acharya, 1995), the clients do not interact with the server: the server broadcasts data objects based on its knowledge of the mobile peers' overall data access requirements, and the mobile peers get their required data objects when they appear on the broadcast channel. In pull-based broadcast (Aksoy, 1998), which is also called on-demand broadcast, the mobile peers submit their requests through an uplink channel to the server, then the server broadcasts data objects based on the received requests (pull-based broadcast is different from point-to-point access in that the object requested by a query is delivered on a broadcast channel such that all the pending queries for that data object are answered with one transmission). Hybrid broadcast (Acharya, 1997) combines push-based broadcast and pull-based broadcast (or even point-to-point access) to complement each other: popular data objects are pushed, and infrequently accessed data objects are retrieved on demand (by pulling or point-to-point access).

Data objects are typically scheduled for broadcasting according to the overall access interests of the mobile peers in the system. The basic idea is to broadcast hot data objects more frequently than the others. Many algorithms have been proposed for scheduling the broadcast in different environments (Acharya, 1998; Guo, 2001; Hameed, 1997; Liu, 2003; Zheng, 2005).

To facilitate mobile peers saving energy, index of data objects is introduced into the broadcast. Basically, a broadcast index tells the mobile peers what data objects will be available when. The broadcast index itself is also broadcast intermittently on the broadcast channel. Once a mobile peer knows when its interested data object will be broadcast, it can operate in sleep mode and

wake up before that time. Many researches on mobile broadcast focus on designing broadcast index (Hu, 1999; Imielinski, 1994; Lee, 2003; Lo, 2000; Shivakumar, 1996; Tan, 2000).

System Model

In this chapter, we assume a broadcast environment where:

- The mobile broadcast is push-based. A server broadcasts data objects repeatedly to many mobile peers through a broadcast channel and there is no uplink for the mobile peers to send requests to the server.
- The broadcast is non-uniform. Data objects are broadcast with different frequencies. Popular data objects are broadcast more frequently than the others.
- Broadcast index is available so that mobile peers know the broadcast frequencies of data objects.
- All mobile peers are in the broadcast server's transmission range. They get their required data objects by tuning into the broadcast channel.
- All data objects are of the same size and they are not updated. This assumption lets us ignore the factor of object size and the problem of cache invalidation so that we focus on the cooperative strategies for cache management.
- The mobile peers are equipped with short range communication devices. A mobile peer can communicate with the mobile peers within its communication range.
- There is no super peer in the mobile peers. Peers have the same levels of computational ability and battery power.

Sample Applications

Many interesting applications follow the system model that we described before. In such applications, multimedia information needs to be disseminated to (potentially) a large number of audiences. Here we list two sample applications.

In an academic **conference**, people are often interested in paper abstracts, presenters' profiles, and short introduction (such as name, a small photo, university, and research interests) of each researcher who is attending the conference. Each piece of these introduction (in the form of a web page) information can be seen as a data object. These data objects can be broadcast at the conference site. Notice that paper abstracts and presenters' profiles should be broadcast more frequently than the attendees' information. Also notice that a paper abstract, a presenter's profile, and an attendee's profile are of similar sizes and they normally do not change during the conference.

In **museums**, short video clips about the items on display can be broadcast to the visitors. Each video clip is a data object. The clips are of about the same size and available throughout the exhibition. People are more interested in masterpieces; therefore clips about the masterpieces should be broadcast more frequently than the clips about other art works. Each visitor to the museum gets a mobile device that retrieves the information he/she wants (the device obtains introduction clips from the broadcast channel or a nearby device if the neighboring device happens to have cached the required clip locally).

Data Access Process

When a mobile peer wants to access a data object, it first looks for it in its own local cache. If the data object is not found in the local cache, the mobile peer requests for it from its neighbors. If none of its neighbors has the data object, the mobile peer tunes into the broadcast channel and waits for the data object to appear.

To facilitate the discussion, we define a few terms to describe the situations of cache miss and cache hit. Let M_q be a mobile peer and D_k be the data object that M_q wants to access.

Local Cache Hit: M_q's local cache has D_k.

Local Cache Miss: M_q's local cache does not contain D_k.

Neighbor Cache Hit: at least one of M_q's neighbors has D_k in its local cache.

Neighbor Cache Miss: none of M_q's neighbors has D_k in its local cache.

Broadcast Hit: M_q gets D_k from the broadcast channel.

When M_q asks for D_k from its neighbors, several types of messages are exchanged. The mobile peer first sends a **Request** message for D_k to its neighbors. M_q's neighbors having D_k in their cache send back a **Reply** message to M_q. Upon receiving the *reply* message(s), M_q sends a **Retrieve** message to the neighbor who replied first, then the target mobile peer transmits D_k to M_q.

KR: Keep Requesting

In some cooperative cache management schemes for mobile peers in broadcast systems, when a *neighbor cache miss* happens, the mobile peer simply tunes into the broadcast channel and waits for the required data object to appear. In these schemes, a *neighbor cache miss* always results in a *broadcast hit*. However, a *neighbor cache miss* only means that the **current** neighbors do not have the required data object, but not necessarily the **future** neighbors. Since a mobile peer's neighbors may be changing all the time (especially in a highly dynamic environment), a neighbor having the required data object may come by before the object appears on the broadcast channel.

In the schemes that we will discuss in detail, an enhancement called Keep Request (KR) (Wu, 2006) is used. In the KR mode, a mobile peer continues to send out *request* messages repeatedly to its neighborhood even though a *neighbor cache miss* has happened. There are two situations in which the query may be answered before the required data object is broadcast by the server. The first is after certain time the mobile peer has a new neighbor who caches the data object, because the mobile peers are moving. The second is after certain time an existing neighbor has the required data object, because it has, during the time, requested and obtained the object from its neighbors. By repeatedly sending out *request* messages, the response time will improve as some queries may be answered before *broadcast hits*. A mobile peer should control the frequency of sending out request message and avoid sending the *request* message too frequently, because broadcasting message consumes energy and increases chances of wireless signal collision. KR is independent of the cooperative cache management scheme; therefore it can be applied on any cooperative cache management scheme.

With Keep Requesting, the process of data access becomes the one shown in Figure 2. Notice that the states of *local cache miss* and *neighbor cache miss* are omitted in the figure.

Caching and Prefetching

In a broadcast system, a mobile peer's data access from broadcast channel can be demand-driven or proactive. The data access is demand-driven if the mobile peer retrieves data objects from broadcast channel only when it has local cache miss. On the contrary, if a mobile peer continuously monitors broadcast channel and stores locally the data

objects that are potentially useful to it, the mobile peer is prefetching data from the broadcast channel and its data access is proactive. Prefetching from broadcast channel improves response time, but incurs more energy consumption (Acharya, 1996; Grassi, 2000; Hu, 2003). Generally speaking, mobile peers with limited energy tend to access the broadcast channel only when there are pending requests, and mobile peers with enough energy (such as devices on vehicles) may access the broadcast channel proactively.

We assume that the mobile peers in a system are with the same type and they have the same data access fashion, i.e. they are either all demand-driven or all proactive.

In both demand-driven access and proactive access, when a mobile peer gets a data object, it faces the problem of deciding whether to store the data object locally. A caching scheme helps a mobile peer to make such decision under demand-driven access, and a prefetching scheme helps it to make such decision under proactive access.

Caching and prefetching schemes for individual mobile peer in broadcast environments have been studied extensively. Here "individual" means that the caching (or prefetching) scheme does not take the possible collaboration among the mobile peers into account. With the advance of short-range communication and mobile peer-to-peer networks, researchers have begun to study

Figure 2. Data access process

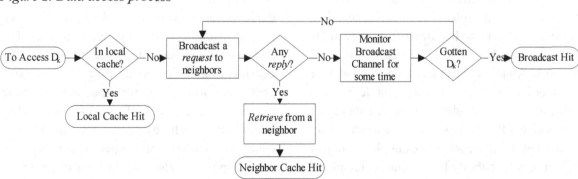

cooperative caching and cooperative prefetching for mobile peers.

Individual Caching

We refer to the caching schemes that do not consider the collaboration among mobile peers as *individual caching* schemes.

Classic caching algorithms (like LRU) designed for client-server environments may result in poor performance in a broadcast system. In a client-server environment, accessing different data objects from the server takes similar amount of time. That being the case, caching the hottest data objects is a good idea. However, in a non-uniform broadcast environment where data objects are broadcast with different frequencies, the latencies for accessing different objects from the broadcast channel may vary greatly. This difference makes the idea of caching the most accessed data object not the best choice.

Caching strategies for mobile broadcast environments were proposed in (Acharya, 1995; Su, 1998; Xu, 2000; Xu, 2004). Here we briefly review the main idea of a scheme called PIX (Acharya, 1995). Knowing PIX will be helpful for understanding CPIX, which is the cooperative caching scheme that we will discuss in detail later.

PIX. PIX is specifically designed for non-uniform broadcast environments. The basic idea is for mobile peers to store those data objects for which the local probability of access is significantly greater than the object's frequency of broadcast. PIX (P Inverse X) uses the ratio P_i / X_i, where P_i is the probability of access to a data object D_i and X_i is the broadcast frequency of D_i, to decide whether D_i should be cached in local memory. A mobile client estimates the value of P_i using its data access history, and derives the value of X_i from broadcast index. A data object with a higher PIX score will replace a data object with a lower PIX score. For example, let object D_a's access probability be 5% and its broadcast frequency be 1%, and let object D_b's access prob-

ability be 3% and its broadcast frequency be 0.5%. The PIX score of D_a is 5, and the PIX score of D_b is 6. Object D_b may cause longer access latency, so D_b will be cached if only one object can be cached. PIX is an optimal individual caching scheme for non-uniform broadcast because an object's PIX score is the expectation of the object's access latency.

Individual Prefetching

As in individual caching, we refer to the prefetching schemes that do not consider the collaboration among mobile peers as *individual prefetching* schemes.

Prefetching from broadcast channel is very different from prefetching from a server in traditional client-server systems or prefetching from hard disk to main memory. The most important characteristic of prefetching from broadcast channel is that the prefetching (and the related cache management scheme) is driven by broadcast program: each time a data object appears on the broadcast channel, the mobile peer needs to decide whether to prefetch the data object locally. This is also the fundamental difference between prefetching and demand-driven caching in broadcast environments. Recall that in demand-driven caching, the caching scheme is triggered only when there is an access and the needed data object is received.

The advantage of prefetching from broadcast channel is that it improves response time and does not add any extra workload and overhead to the broadcast server—the mobile peers prefetch by just listening to the broadcast channel. The disadvantage is that it incurs additional energy consumption at the mobile peer, as the mobile peer needs to be in active mode and listens to the broadcast channel when prefetching. Thus in applications where response time is the major concern and where mobile peer has enough energy supply (e.g., computing device on vehicles), prefetching will be preferable.

Prefetching schemes in broadcast environments were studied in (Acharya, 1996; Cao, 2002; Grassi, 2000; Hu, 2003). Prefetching data from broadcast channel improves response time by avoiding costly cache misses. Let us take the well-known *PT* prefetching heuristic (Acharya, 1996) as an example to show how prefetching from broadcast channel works. PT is used in ACP, the cooperative prefetching scheme that we will discuss in detail, to make an individual decision before negotiating with peers.

PT. In *PT*, *PT* values are used to make cache admission and replacement decisions. The *PT* value of a data object D_i at time t is defined as P_i*T_i, where P_i is the mobile peer's access probability to D_i, and T_i is the time that will elapse from t until D_i appears on the broadcast channel. As in PIX, the value of P_i is estimated from local access history, and T_i is derived from the broadcast index. The *PT* prefetching scheme works like this: each time when a data object is broadcast, the mobile peer finds the data object in cache with the lowest *PT* value and replaces it with the currently broadcast data object if the latter has a higher *PT* value. The rationale behind the *PT* heuristic is to prefetch data objects whose expectation of waiting time (P_i*T_i) is long. As a result, using *PT*, data objects that were just broadcast are more likely to be kept in cache and the data object that are closer to being re-broadcast, are more likely to be replaced.

Note that PT score (P_i*T_i) is not the same as the PIX score (P_i/X_i) which is used in the PIX demand-driven caching scheme, because Ti is not the same as $1/X_i$. For a data object with a fixed broadcast frequency, $1/X_i$ is fixed, but the value T_i changes with time. Remember that T_i is the time remaining from the current time to the nearest moment when the object will be broadcast. For example, if object D_a is going to be broadcast every 100 time units, T_i of D_a changes in the range from 100 to 0 when time goes on, and T_i becomes 100 after 0. If D_a's next broadcast time is t_{500}, and current time is t_{450}, then at this time T_i =50.

Cooperative Caching

In recent years, cooperative data management in mobile environments are gaining more attention (Papadopouli, 2001; Xu, 2004) and people begin to study the cooperative cache management problem for mobile peers (Chow, 2004; Chow, 2005; Hara, 2002; Lau, 2002; Shen, 2005; Wu, 2005; Wu, 2006; Yin, 2004).

(Chow et. al., 2004) proposed a cooperative caching scheme called GroCoca (GROup-based COoperative CAching) for mobile peers in a pull-based mobile environment. In GroCoca, mobile peers report their locations to a central server and access data objects from the server by sending requests to it. The central server uses a clustering algorithm to find tightly-coupled groups of mobile peers. A set of peers are said to be tightly-coupled if they have similar movement pattern and data access interest. The server informs mobile peers about the groups they are in, and then peers in the same tightly-coupled group manage data objects cooperatively. GroCoca is a centralized solution, because a central server collects mobile peers' location information and access interests and clusters the peers into groups.

(Chow et. al., 2005) further proposed a distributed solution called DGCoca (Distributed Group-based Cooperative caching) for mobile peers in push-based broadcast environments. In the DGCoca scheme, a mobile peer exchanges summary of its cached objects with its stable neighbors (a stable neighbor is defined as a neighbor who has been nearby for certain amount of time) and makes cache replacement decisions with respect to its own access frequency to the data objects and whether the data objects are available at its stable neighbors.

Cooperative Prefetching

(Hara, 2002; Wu et al., 2005) study the problem of cooperative caching management in the scenario where mobile peers prefetch from broadcast channel. As in (Wu, 2005), we call this kind of schemes *cooperative prefetching* schemes.

In (Hara, 2002), the author proposed two cooperative schemes for mobile peers in push-based broadcast systems, namely GOP (Global OPtimal) and SOP (Stable group OPtimal). The author calls them *cooperative caching* schemes. They are classified as *cooperative prefetching* schemes in this chapter because their behaviors of caching are triggered by the broadcast rather than data accesses. In GOP, the mobile peers construct an ad-hoc network and cooperate through multi-hop communication. The idea is to exchange information of access interests and cached objects among all connected mobile peers each time when a data object is broadcast, and then one of the mobile peers collects this information and decides globally which mobile peer(s) should cache the data object according to the network topology. Finally the decision is flooded to all mobile peers and every one conducts a behavior according to the decision. GOP is not practical when the number of mobile peers is large, because large amount of control information and long computational time are needed for every caching decision. In SOP (Stable group OPtimal), data objects are cooperatively cached in stable groups of mobile peers. SOP works better than GOP because limiting the cooperation in a stable group guarantees data availability and reduces communication overhead.

ISSUES, CONTROVERSIES, PROBLEMS

The aforementioned cooperative schemes have several common drawbacks. First, they all try to find stable groups of mobile peers (i.e. group of peers that are within each other's communication range for certain amount of time). Because of this, they are only suitable for environments where groups of mobile peers do exist, and cannot be applied to scenarios where the mobile peers are

highly dynamic. Second, they consider the data availability from neighbors but fail to consider the data availability on the broadcast channel. Third, they require synchronization of a lot of information in a group, such as cache summary and access interests. This will incur high communication cost (and power consumption), because the cache summary of neighbors need to be updated quite frequently.

We identify two challenges for the mobile peers to manage caching cooperatively in a broadcast environment. The first is to handle the dynamics of the neighborhoods (topology). The second is to consider data objects' multiple availabilities in the system.

The dynamics of peer's neighborhood is due to the movement of the peers. The changes of neighborhoods make it infeasible to take the cache spaces of the mobile peers in a neighborhood as a whole and manage it for the benefit of all the involved mobile peers. Managing cache space in a neighborhood as a whole imposes several requirements: 1) a clear division of peers to neighborhoods (or groups); 2) synchronization of access interests in a neighborhood; 3) agreement on which peer should cache what data objects. The movement of peers makes these requirements very difficult and expensive to achieve, because

- There is no agreement on which neighborhood(s) a mobile peer belongs to-- a mobile peer has one neighborhood but belongs to many neighborhoods at the same time. Take the mobile peers in Figure-1 as an example. M_a belongs to the neighborhoods of M_b, M_c, and M_d. Which neighborhood shall it participate in? And who shall coordinate the neighborhood?

- Even though methods are used to divide the mobile peers into neighborhoods and to select a leader, the neighborhoods are changing frequently. This may incur a lot of information exchange, because each time a neighbor leaves or a new neighbor is encountered, the overall access pattern of the neighborhood may change.

For a mobile peer that can request for data object from its neighbors and can access data from a broadcast channel, data objects can be available in three ways: local cache, neighbors' cache, and broadcast channel. A data object's availabilities in local cache and neighbors' cache are not guaranteed, while its availability on the broadcast channel is assured. The cooperative cache management scheme in fact determines which peer to cache what data objects, and as a result it determines where to access a data object. Getting data object from different places have different costs in terms of both access latency and power consumption. In this situation, when doing caching management, a mobile peer not only needs to consider its own access interest, but also needs to take into account what its neighbors have in cache and the data objects' broadcast frequencies on the broadcast channel.

We believe that an effective cooperative cache management scheme should deal with both the aforementioned challenges. In the remainder of this chapter, we discuss two such schemes. One is a cooperative caching scheme called CPIX designed for mobile peers whose access to the broadcast channel is demand-driven. The other is a cooperative prefetching scheme called ACP designed for mobile peers whose access to the broadcast channel is proactive. CPIX could be used on mobile peers with limited power, while ACP could be applied on mobile peers for whom battery is not a problem.

CPIX and ACP share several common desirable properties that distinguish them from other schemes: 1) the mobile peers using the schemes are autonomous; 2) they consider the data availability from both the neighbors and the broadcast channel; 3) they are adaptable to the broadcast program; 4) they require very few message exchanges between mobile peers.

EFFECTIVE COLLABORATIVE CACHING AND PREFETCHING SCHEMES

CPIX: Cooperative Caching

PIX (Acharya, 1995) is a well-known individual caching scheme for mobile peers in broadcast environment (refer to the Background section for a brief review of PIX). CPIX (Cooperative PIX) is an extension of the PIX scheme for the mobile peers where they can communicate with each other in a Peer-to-Peer fashion.

The approach CPIX takes is to view the data availability at other mobile peers (not only the current neighbors) together with the data availability on the broadcast channel as the *global data availability*, and every mobile peer manages its own cache space according to its own access interest and its estimate of global data availability. The following observation leads to this idea. When a local cache miss happens, a mobile peer can request the data object from its neighbors and tune into the broadcast channel to wait for the data object. These two can be done in parallel. The mobile peer is happy as long as it can get the data object in a short period of time, and there is no need to distinguish whether the data object is from a neighboring peer or it is from the broadcast channel.

It is important to point out that here data availability does not mean whether the data is available, since (in the worst case) the data object is always available from the broadcast channel. It rather means how long it takes for a mobile peer to get the data.

Intuitively (as in PIX), data objects that are frequently accessed and are not readily available should get the highest priority to be cached locally, otherwise, many *local cache miss*es will happen due to its high access frequency and these *local cache miss*es will result in long waiting time since it is not easy to get them from the neighbors or broadcast channel.

CPIX considers two important factors: local access frequency and the *global availability* of data objects. Access frequency helps to identify critical objects that should be locally cached to improve *local cache hits* (and hence reduce waiting time and energy consumption). Global data availability is used to identify the data objects that are difficult to get from outside, i.e. they are neither widely cached by other mobile peers nor frequently broadcast by the server.

Although CPIX considers local access interest rather than neighborhood's access interest, in fact it benefits the whole peer community when every mobile peer is doing this. When every mobile peer is caching the data objects that are hard to get from external sources (including neighbors and broadcast channel), the global data availability is improved.

Both the information of access frequency and the information of global data availability are estimated from local statistics. A mobile peer may estimate its access frequency to the data objects by counting historical accesses. The global data availability of its interested data objects can be estimated from the waiting time it experienced for the local cache misses. To do so, each mobile peer keeps the following statistics for every data object D_i it has accessed:

- *NumAccess$_i$*: number of access.
- *NumLCM$_i$*: number of *local cache miss*.
- *SumWaitingTime$_i$*: the sum of waiting time the mobile peer experienced due to the local cache misses of D_i.

Notice that the idea of global data availability (viewing the data availability at other mobile peers and the data availability on the broadcast channel as a whole) simplifies the caching scheme. In CPIX a mobile peer does not need to get the knowledge of data objects' global availability by exchanging summary of cache content with neighbors and by analyzing the broadcast index.

The CPIX scheme works as follows. Each time when a query for data object D_i arise:

1. The mobile peer increases *NumAccess$_i$* by one.

2. If the query results in a *local cache miss*, the mobile peer increases *NumLCM$_i$* by one, records the time point when the *local cache miss* happens, and broadcasts a *request* message to neighbors. If KR (Keep Requesting, see the Background section) is enabled, in this step the mobile peer will keep sending out request message every certain time interval if *neighbor cache miss* for D_i happens, until the mobile peer gets D_i.

3. When the mobile peer gets D_i from either a neighbor or the broadcast channel,

    a. The mobile peer records the time point and calculates the waiting time for this local cache miss of D_i, and add the waiting time to *SumWaitingTime$_i$*.

    b. The mobile peer decides whether to cache the data locally. If there is free cache space available, the mobile peer caches D_i using the free space. If its cache space is full, a score for D_i is calculated. If D_i's score is not the smallest among the scores of cached data objects, the mobile peer caches D_i by replacing the data object with the smallest score. The score of a data object D_i is calculated using the formula as follows.

$$Score_i = NumAccess_i * \frac{SumWaitingTime_i}{NumLCM_i}$$

The rationale behind the score formula is that $Score_i$ tells the expectation of waiting time caused by a *local cache miss* of data object D_i.

We use $\frac{NumAccess_i}{\sum NumAccess}$ as the estimation of the access probability to data object D_i. Since every score has the same component $\sum NumAccess$ and we use the scores for comparison purpose only, we use $NumAccess_i$ to represent $\frac{NumAccess_i}{\sum NumAccess}$. $\frac{SumWaitingTime_i}{NumLCM_i}$ denotes the length of time it *takes on average fo*r the mobile peer to wait for each *local cache miss of Di, and gives a hint of* the global data availability of D_i.

If we consider $\frac{NumAccess_i}{\sum NumAccess}$ as P_i and $\frac{SumWaitingTime_i}{NumLCM_i}$ as $1/X_i$, CPIX can be seen as a cooperative version of the PIX scheme where P_i / X_i is used to make caching decisions. The important idea here is to use $\frac{SumWaitingTime_i}{NumLCM_i}$ to encapsulate the non-local availability, which includes both neighbors' cache and the broadcast channel.

With CPIX, the data objects that are frequently accessed (with high $NumAccess_i$ values) and difficult to get (with high $\frac{SumWaitingTime_i}{NumLCM_i}$ values) will be cached locally. Essentially, CPIX tries to reduce the number of local cache misses and to avoid costly *local cache misses*.

Note that in CPIX, $NumAccess_i$, $NumLCM_i$ and $SumWaitingTime_i$ are all cumulative. The side effect is that the estimation will be less accurate when access pattern or broadcast program changes at certain time. This problem can be resolved by using only the recent statistics.

ACP: Cooperative Prefetching

A mobile peer prefetches data objects from broadcast channel by continuously monitoring the broadcast channel and putting the data objects that are potentially useful to local cache. (Acharya, 1996) has shown that the PT prefetching scheme performs better (in terms of response time) than demand-driven caching schemes such as PIX. If the mobile peers collaborate when prefetching, then the resultant cooperative prefetching can further improve the performance. In this section, we discuss a solution called ACP, which stands for Announcement-based Cooperative Prefetching. ACP enables the mobile peers to prefetch cooperatively to improve data availability, while keeping the mobile peers autonomous.

Prefetching imposes a special challenge to cooperative caching management. The important property of prefetching is that it is driven by broadcast ticks. A consequence is that in prefetching mobile peers tend to cache the data objects that were just broadcast. For example, if the PT (refer to Background section for an introduction of PT) prefetching scheme is used, the *PT* values of objects that were just broadcast are high because their *T* values are high at this moment. As a (bad) result, the mobile peers may be caching the same set of data objects, especially when their access probabilities to the data objects are similar. In this situation, sharing cache contents with neighbors does not improve data availability much, and few queries can be answered with neighbors' cache.

The objective of ACP is to overcome the problem by avoiding prefetching multiple copies of the same data objects in a neighborhood.

The basic idea of the ACP strategy is: in deciding whether to prefetch an object D, if a mobile peer knows whether its neighbors will prefetch D, it can make a wiser prefetching decision for D. For example, if a mobile peer M_a knows that its neighbors M_b and M_c are prefetching D, then M_a may choose not to prefetch D if D is not very important to it, since it has a chance to get D from its neighbors. The benefits of this are: 1) M_a saves its cache space for another valuable data object; 2) it avoids the problem that M_a and its neighbors are prefetching the same data objects; and thus 3) the overall data availability is improved, and the mobile peer can have more queries answered by neighbors.

A simple application of this idea can be dangerous. First, a prefetched data object may be replaced by a more valuable data object soon after it was prefetched. Telling neighbors that it will prefetch data object D does not tell how long D will be kept in its cache. Accordingly, simply knowing that some neighbors will prefetch D, a mobile peer does not know the extent of reliance it can put on its neighbors. Second, if all mobile peers choose not to prefetch a data object because they think that their neighbors are prefetching it, no one prefetches the data object. They both result in a situation where some neighbors claimed to prefetch a data object but it is not available when someone wants to access the data object.

These problems are solved by enforcing the following two rules in the cooperation scheme: 1) a mobile peer informs its neighbors that it will prefetch a data object only when it will keep the data object in cache for certain time; 2) randomization is applied to let at least one of the mobile peers (that showed intention to prefetch the data object) prefetch the data object.

Considering these factors, ACP strategy is designed as follows:

- **Before** a data object D is broadcast (we assume broadcast index is available so that the mobile peers know when each data objects will be broadcast), every mobile peer decides whether to prefetch D based on the *PT* heuristic, and we call this **the first decision**.
  - If the first decision is "yes" then the mobile peer further predicts how long D will be in cache.
    - If it predicts that D will be in its cache for a long time, then the mobile peer broadcasts an **announcement** message to its neighbors.
- Each mobile peer whose first decision is "yes" counts the number of announcement messages for D it receives.
- **When** D appears on the channel, every mo-

bile peer makes its **final decision** on whether to prefetch D according to the importance of D to it, the number of announcement messages it received, and some random factor. If the final decision is still "yes", the mobile peer prefetches D; otherwise, the mobile peer does not prefetch it.

That is, when a mobile peer decides to prefetch D and believes it will cache D for a quite long time, it sends out an announcement message to its neighbors; a mobile peer's final prefetching decision for D is based on both the importance of D and the number of neighbors who will prefetch D. The objective of the announcement is to affect the neighbors' prefetching decisions. Note that the announcement should be made *before* the broadcast of D, but the mobile peers need not make announcement at the same time. To reduce the chance that a peer makes an announcement but moves away from its neighbors, a peer should send out the announcement close to the time the associated object will be broadcast.

There are two details of ACP to be addressed: 1) How to predict the time D will be in cache and whether it deserves an announcement? 2) How should the neighbors' announcements for D, if any, affect a mobile peer's final prefetching decision for D?

Deciding Whether to Send Out Announcement

Each mobile peer makes its first decision for D with the *PT* individual prefetching scheme. If there is empty cache space, the first decision is "yes"; if the cache space is full, the mobile peer checks the cached objects and see whether there is a cached object whose *PT* value is lower than the *PT* value of D, if so, the first decision is "yes", otherwise, the first decision is "no".

In ACP, every mobile peer records how long a data object was kept in its cache the last time: when a data object is prefetched, the mobile peer records the timestamp, and when the data object is replaced, it calculates the time the object is in cache and records it. The recorded **keeping time** of D is used to predict how long D will be in cache this time.

If the first decision is "yes", the mobile peer decides whether to send out an announcement by checking the following inequality.

$$\frac{keeping\ time}{Tinterval} \geq \delta$$

Here δ is a threshold parameter greater than zero, and *Tinterval* is the time between two consecutive broadcasts of the data object. If the inequality is satisfied, the mobile peer sends out an announcement, otherwise it does not. The intuition is: when an announcement for D is made, the neighbors know that the mobile peer may keep D longer than *Tinterval*$*\delta$, so they may have confidence to rely on the mobile peer for D.

Note that δ is a parameter that can be tuned. Also note that a mobile peer whose first decision for D is "yes" should count the number of the announcement messages for D it receives.

Making Final Decision

In ACP, a mobile peer's final prefetching decision for D is determined by the following factors:

1. PT_d, the PT value of D;
2. PT_c, the PT value of the replace candidate (the cached object with the lowest PT value);
3. γ, the reliance parameter;
4. n, the number of announcement messages for D the mobile peer received.

Here $\gamma(0 < \gamma \leq 1)$ is a parameter modeling the extent of reliance a mobile peer can put on a neighbor who sent out an announcement for D. In other words, γ models the probability that when the mobile peer has a query for D the neighbor still has D and is within the mobile peer's communication range.

A mobile peer that receives more announcement messages for D means it can rely more on its neighbors for D, since the chance that all of them move beyond the mobile peer's communication range is lower and it is more possible for the mobile peer to get D from its neighbors. Thus in our scheme, the total reliance the mobile peer can put on its neighbors for D is $\gamma*n$.

When D is broadcast, each mobile peer makes its final prefetching decision for D as follows.

- If the first decision is "no", the final decision is "no".
- If the first decision is "yes" and the mobile peer did not send out announcement for D, then check whether the following inequality is satisfied.

$$PT_d(1 - \gamma*n) > PT_c$$

- If the inequality is satisfied, the final decision is "yes", otherwise it is "no".
- If the first decision is "yes" and the mobile peer has sent out an announcement for D, then if $\gamma*n$ is smaller than 1, the final decision is "no", else ($\gamma*n$ is greater than 1) the mobile peer generates a random number p between 0 and 1, if p is bigger than $1/(\gamma*n)$, the final decision is "no", else the final decision is "yes".

The intuition of the final decision process is: a) If the first decision is "no", D is not important for the mobile peer, so the mobile peer should not prefetch D. b) If the first decision is "yes" but the mobile peer did not send out an announcement, D is not very important to the mobile peer, and the mobile peer's neighbors will not rely on the mobile peer for D, so the mobile peer is free to decide whether to prefetch D based on the total reliance it can put on its neighbors. It checks whether it is still beneficial to prefetch D after considering the possibility that it can get D from its neighbors. c)

If the mobile peer sent an announcement for D, D is very important for the mobile peer, and its neighbors may rely on it for D, thus the mobile peer is not free to put reliance on its neighbors and give up prefetching D. However, if it received enough announcements from neighbors ($\gamma * n > 1$), which means it is possible that the mobile peers share common access interests for D and too many mobile peers will prefetch D and the neighborhood is wasting cache space, then it is good that one or several (but not all) of them finally choose not to prefetch D. This decision is made by tossing a coin. Even though some mobile peers having made announcement may choose not to prefetch D after the coin flip, the overall availability of D is guaranteed by the process of coin flips, with a high probability.

Discussion on Relying on Neighbors

ACP and CPIX are quite different on the problem of whether to rely on current neighbors for caching some data objects. In CPIX, a peer's neighborhood does not directly participate when the peer makes a caching decision. In ACP, a peer's prefetching decision is partially based on neighbors' intensions on prefetching.

ACP's approach of relying on current neighbors may seem to be inconsistent with the analysis and arguments we made in the background section that a mobile peer should not make caching decisions based on the cache contents of its *current* neighbors, but in fact this is not a conflict because prefetching is very different from demand-driven caching. Let's use an example to show the difference.

Suppose the current time is t and data object D_l appears on the broadcast channel, and D_l will be broadcast again at time $t + t'$ (D_l is broadcast every t' time units). Mobile peer M_a gets D_l at time t. M_a has neighbors M_b, M_c and M_d. M_b and M_c will move out of M_a 's communication range at time $t + t'/2$.

Suppose the mobile peers are doing demand-driven caching, and M_b and M_c have data object D_l at time t; M_a decides not to cache D_l because its neighbors M_b and M_c have it; M_a has a query for D_l at time $t + t'/2 + \Delta t$. Notice that when M_a wants to access D_l, its neighbors with D_l have moved away. The latency of the access is the time duration from time $t + t'/2 + \Delta t$ to the time when D_l is broadcast. The latency can be represented as:

$$\begin{cases} \dfrac{t'}{2} - \Delta t, & \text{if } \Delta t \leq \dfrac{t'}{2} \\ t' - ((\Delta t - \dfrac{t'}{2})\%(t')), & \text{if } \Delta t > \dfrac{t'}{2} \end{cases}$$

In the expression, "%" is the *remainder* operation.

However, if the mobile peers are prefetching, and M_b and M_c will prefetch D_l, and M_a decides not to prefetch D_l because its neighbors M_b and M_c will prefetch it, then when M_a has a query for D_l at time $t + t'/2 + \Delta t$, its access latency will be:

$$\begin{cases} \dfrac{t'}{2} - \Delta t, & \text{if } \Delta t \leq \dfrac{t'}{2} \\ 0, & \text{if } \Delta t > \dfrac{t'}{2} \end{cases}$$

The difference is in the second case where $\Delta t > \dfrac{t'}{2}$. In prefetching, the access latency could be 0 because at time $t + t'$ (which is before $t + t'/2 + \Delta t$), M_a will make prefetching decision for D_l again and may cache it locally if this time no neighbors will prefetch it. Recall that D_l is broadcast every t' and prefetching is driven by broadcast program.

The point is that in ACP, a peer will notice the move-away of neighbors (who prefetched an interesting object) when the data object is broadcast again. In the example, when D_l is broadcast again, M_a will make a new prefetching decision on D_l. If at this time M_b and M_c are not around, then M_a

will not receive any announcement on prefetching of D_j so it will decide to prefetch D_j.

From this example, we see that in cooperative prefetching a mobile peer may rely on its neighbors for a data object, because the mobile peer is monitoring the broadcast channel continuously and once the data object is not available at its neighbors the mobile peer may prefetch it when it appears again, so that costly cache misses are avoided.

Nevertheless, CPIX and ACP share one important point in common: they keep the mobile peers autonomous even though each peer takes the data availability at its neighbors' into account when making caching and prefetching decisions. This ensures that small change in neighborhood will not affect CPIX and ACP. This is achieved by not relying on specific neighbors when making caching and prefetching decisions. Rather, a peer makes a decision based on its whole impression of its neighbors. In CPIX, a mobile peer makes caching decision totally based on local statistics, and it tolerates the changes of neighbors. In ACP, a mobile peer makes prefetching decision based on the number of announcements it receives. If a peer M_a makes a prefetching announcement for a data object but moves away soon, it will not have a significant effect on its neighbors because they do not rely on M_a specifically.

EVALUATION OF COLLABORATIVE CACHING AND PREFETCHING SCHEMES

To study the performance of CPIX and ACP, we conducted detailed simulation experiments. We report representative results here. The reader may find more details of the experiments and results in (Wu, 2005; Wu, 2006).

In the experiments, we compare CPIX, ACP with DGCoca (Chow, 2005), a cooperative caching scheme designed for push-based broadcast environment. We did not study the performance

of GOP and SOP because they are designed for mobile peers that form stable groups while we are interested in scenarios where each mobile peer follows its own trajectory.

Simulation Model

The simulated mobile environment is an X*Y (m^2) area where there are a broadcast server and n mobile peers. The server broadcasts data objects to the mobile peers through a wireless channel. The bandwidth of the broadcast channel is bb Mbps. All mobile peers can receive data objects that the server broadcasts. A mobile peer can communicate with another peer if they are in each other's communication range. Their transmission range is *TransRange* meters. The bandwidth of the short-range communication is sb Mbps. At the beginning, the mobile peers are randomly scattered in the area. The mobile peers then move in the area following a variant of the "random waypoint" mobility model.

In the model (and experimental results), we use a time unit called *broadcast unit*. A broadcast unit is the time the server takes to broadcast one data object.

Broadcast Server

We adopt *broadcast disk*s (Acharya & Alonso, 1995) to model the server's non-uniform broadcast. The server has m broadcast disks, and they are $Disk_i$ where $1 \leq i \leq m$. $Disk_i$ stores $DiskSize_i$ data objects and spins at a speed of $DiskSpeed_i$. All data objects are read-only and of the same size which is $DataSize$ KB. As in (Acharya & Alonso, 1995), we use a parameter Δ to capture the relative speeds of the disks: $DiskSpeed_i = ((m-i)*\Delta +1)$. For example, if the server has 3 broadcast disks and Δ is 2, then the rotation speed of the disks will be 5, 3 and 1. Δ is used to model the nonuniformity of the broadcast. When Δ is 0, the broadcast is uniform. The bigger the Δ is, the more non-uniform the broadcast is.

Mobile Peers

A variant of the "random waypoint" is used as the mobile peers' movement pattern. A mobile peer first randomly chooses a destination in the modeled area and a speed which is around *MoveSpeed* m/s. Then the mobile peer moves to the destination with that speed. After arriving at the destination, the mobile peer pauses for *PauseTime* seconds. The mobile peer repeats the aforementioned steps.

We call the set of data objects that a mobile peer is interested in as its access range. Access range consists of access regions (an access region is used to model a cluster of data objects related to one interest topic) that the mobile peer is interested in. The size of a mobile peer's access range is *AccessRange*, and the size of an access region is *RegionSize*, thus the number of access regions for each mobile peer is *AccessRange/RegionSize*. We assign a Zipf distribution with a skewness parameter θ to each mobile peer's access regions. The data objects within an access region have the same probability to be accessed. When assigning access distributions to the access regions, the access regions from faster disks get higher access probabilities.

A mobile peer's queries are generated according to its access distributions. A query is simply an access request for a data object. The time interval between a mobile peer's two consecutive queries is *ThinkTime* broadcast units. Each mobile peer generates *NumQuery* queries during the simulation.

The size of each mobile peer's cache space is *CacheSize*, which is a fraction of the size of the peer's *AccessRange*. For example, if the size of *AccessRange* is 1000 and the *CacheSize* is 20%, then the peer's cache space can hold 200 data objects.

List of Parameters

The parameters for the simulation model and their values are summarized in Table 1.

Among the parameters, δ and γ are parameters for ACP. To find the optimal values for δ and γ, we conducted detailed experiments to learn the effects of them on ACP's performance. We find that ACP performs best when δ and γ are set to values between 0.3 and 0.6. In the experiments presented as follows, we use 0.3 and 0.5 as optimal values of δ and γ. The parameters of DGCoca are not listed here. We follow (Chow, 2005) to assign values to DGCoca's parameters.

Table 1. Simulation model parameters

Parameter	Default Value	Range	Unit
System Parameters			
Area (X*Y)	1500*1500		m²
bb (broadcast bandwidth)	10		Mbps
sb (short-range bandwidth)	2		Mbps
n (num of clients)	100		
Server			
m (num of disks)	3		
DiskSizes	[500,1500,3000]		Data objects
Δ	3	[0-4]	
DataSize	10	[10-100]	KB
Mobile Peer			
TransRange	250	[0-250]	m
AccessRange	1000		Data objects
RegionSize	50		Data objects
CacheSize	20%	[1%-50%]	
MoveSpeed	2	[0-20]	m/s
PauseTime	30		s
NumQuery	3000		
θ (Zipf)	0.5	[0-1.0]	
ThinkTime	10		Broadcast Unit
ACP specific			
δ	0.3	[0-1.0]	
γ	0.5	[0-1.0]	

Experimental Results

The performance metric used in the experimental study is the average response time (access latency) measured in broadcast unit. We first study the performance of the schemes under the default parameter setting. Then we investigate the effects of some system parameters on the schemes.

Basic Performance Study

Here we investigate the performance of the schemes under the default parameter settings. The objectives are twofold: one is to compare individual schemes with cooperative schemes; the other is to study the performance differences of the cooperative schemes and to find the reasons behind the differences.

Figure 3(a) compares the response times of the five caching management schemes, namely PIX, DGCoca, CPIX, PT, and ACP. Recall that PIX is an individual caching scheme, PT is an individual prefetching scheme, DGCoca and CPIX are two cooperative caching schemes, and ACP is a cooperative prefetching scheme. From the figure, we first confirm that prefetching schemes perform better than demand-driven caching schemes: PT performs better than PIX, and ACP performs better than both DGCoca and CPIX. We also confirm that cooperative schemes perform better than individual schemes: DGCoca and CPIX perform better than PIX, and ACP performs better than PT.

Among the cooperative schemes, CPIX performs better than DGCoca, and ACP has the best performance. Figure 3(b) and Figure 3(c) reveal the underlying reasons.

Figure 3(b) shows the breakdown of query hits in each scheme. We observe that among the three cooperative cache management schemes DGCoca has the largest number of local cache hits and neighbor cache hits, and the smallest number of broadcast hits. This shows that DGCoca utilizes the local cache and neighbors' cache very well.

ACP has the largest number of broadcast hits: most of the queries are answered using the broadcast channel rather than local cache or neighbors' cache. CPIX is between them.

The interesting finding here is that the number (or the ratio) of local cache hits and neighbor cache hits is not the key factor that determines the schemes' performance (average response time). Figure 3(c) shows the key factor, the average response time of *broadcast hit*s. We see that DGCoca experiences the longest average waiting time for the broadcast hits (neighbor cache misses), and ACP experiences the shortest average waiting time for the broadcast hits. This is why DGCoca has the longest average response time although it has the largest number of local cache hits and neighbor cache hits, whereas ACP has the best response time although it has the largest number of broadcast hits.

Since the response times for local cache hits and neighbor cache hits are really short, the access latency caused by *neighbor cache misses* (i.e. the requested data object is in neither local cache nor neighbors' cache) -- the product of the number of broadcast hits and the average waiting time for a broadcast hit -- determines the average waiting time of a scheme. Although DGCoca has fewer broadcast hits, it takes a longer time to get a broadcast hit if a query is not answered by local cache or neighbors' cache. On the contrary, in ACP, although more queries are answered after broadcast hits, a mobile peer waits a shorter time before the required data object appears on the broadcast channel.

Recall that DGCoca does not consider the data availability on broadcast channel, CPIX considers the data availability on broadcast channel, and ACP further exploits the dynamics of data availability on broadcast channel. The key idea we have in CPIX and ACP is that both the data availability from neighborhood and the data availability on broadcast channel are important for making caching or prefetching decisions. For data objects with similar access probability, the

Figure 3. Performance under default setting

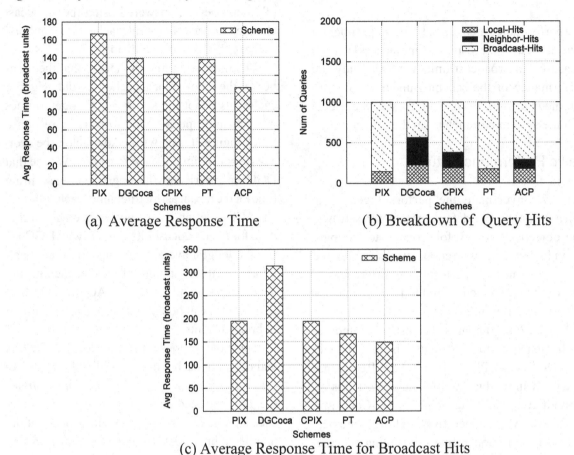

(a) Average Response Time

(b) Breakdown of Query Hits

(c) Average Response Time for Broadcast Hits

ones that are difficult to get from both neighbors and broadcast channel should be cached locally, thus long time waiting is avoided. In prefetching, the peers' cache space is refreshed with the most valuable objects at each broadcast tick.

The performance of individual cache management schemes PIX and PT are depicted in this set of experiments to show that cooperative cache management do help improve access latency. In the remainder of this section, we only compare the cooperative cache management schemes.

Adaptability to Non-Uniform Broadcast

In this set of experiments, we study their adaptability to non-uniform broadcast by varying Δ

to see the performance of the schemes under different extent of non-uniform broadcast. In the experiments the access pattern of the mobile peers does not change.

The results are depicted in Figure 4. It shows that CPIX and ACP adapt to the non-uniform broadcast better than DGCoca does: with the increase of Δ, the response times of the schemes all increase, but CPIX and ACP degrade slower than DGCoca does. The length of the broadcast cycle is $\sum(DiskSize_i*DiskSpeed_i)$ where $DiskSpeed_i=((m-i)*\Delta)+1$, m is the number of *broadcast disks*, and $1\leq i\leq m$. During a broadcast circle the data objects on $Disk_i$ are broadcast $DiskSpeed_i$ times. When Δ increases, data objects on the faster disk are broadcast more frequently, and it becomes harder

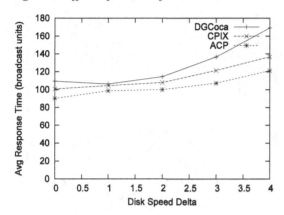

Figure 4. Effect of non-uniform broadcast

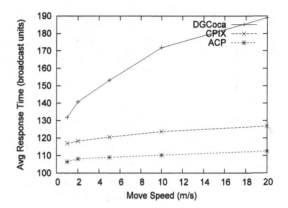

Figure 5. Effect of move Speed

to get the data objects that are on the slower disks. CPIX and ACP adapt to the change of broadcast better because they both consider the data availability on the broadcast channel. DGCoca makes cache decision based on access distribution thus it is not adaptive to the broadcast program.

Effect of Moving Speed

The effect of the mobile peers' move speed on the schemes' performance is studied by varying the mobile peers' speed from 1 to 20m/s. Figure 5 shows the results.

We observe that when the mobile peers move with a faster speed: (1) the response time of DGCoca increases dramatically, (2) the response times of CPIX and ACP increase very slowly. The reason for (1) is that the mobile peer groups that DGCoca tries to form are not stable when mobile peers move fast; a mobile peer may not even be able to find stable neighbors. Recall that in DG-Coca, information about current neighbors' cache contents is used to make local caching decisions. When the mobile peers move fast, the reliance on current neighbors have negative effect. The reason for (2) is that in CPIX and ACP a mobile peer does not rely on a specific set of neighbors, but rather consider the overall availability from the external sources (include neighbors and the broadcast channel).

Effect of Transmission Range

The aim of this set of experiments is to study the effect of mobile peers' transmission range on the schemes' performance. As shown in Figure 6, all schemes' performance improves with longer transmission range. This is due to the fact that a mobile peer may contact with more neighbors with longer transmission range.

One interesting observation here is that the performance gap between the schemes decreases with the increase of transmission range. When a mobile peer can communicate with more peers, the data availability in its neighborhood improves significantly. In this case, sharing of cache contents leads to performance improvement, and gain from clever cooperative cache management will be less obvious. Increasing the density of mobile peers or introducing multi-hop communication will have a similar effect.

Effect of Cache Size

The effect of cache size is studied by varying a mobile peer's cache size from 1 data object to half of its access range. Figure 7 shows that with the increase of cache size, the schemes all have better response time. This is as expected because increasing the cache size effectively improves the data availability. With larger cache space more

Figure 6. *Effect of communication range*

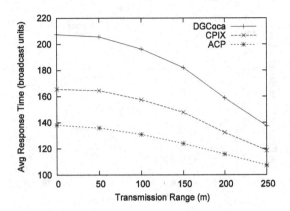

Figure 7. *Effect of cache size*

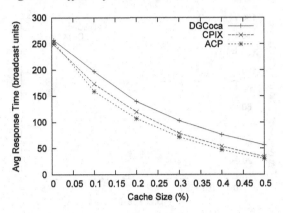

data objects are cached locally and shared in the neighborhood. The figure also shows that even when the mobile peers have large cache size (e.g. more than 40% of its access range), CPIX and ACP still outperform DGCoca and the performance difference is fairly stable.

CONCLUSION

In this chapter, we have reviewed the problem of cooperative cache management in mobile environments that support data broadcast. We discussed the difference between access-driven caching and proactive prefetching (from the broadcast channel), and presented our view of the challenges for cooperative caching and cooperative prefetching in such environments. After reviewing some solutions based on group-based cooperative cache management, we presented two schemes in detail, namely CPIX and ACP. CPIX is a cooperative caching scheme and ACP is a cooperative prefetching scheme. They differ from other schemes mainly in two ways. First, they do not require a mobile peer to have stable neighbors. This enables a mobile peer to make caching (or prefetching) decision autonomously, and does not impose high information synchronization overhead. Second, they consider both

the data availability on other peers and the data availability on the broadcast channel. While ACP is superior to CPIX in most cases, it consumes more energy. We believe that CPIX and ACP are two representative cooperative cache management schemes designed for highly dynamic mobile peers in broadcast environments.

Recently, many routing protocols have been designed to facilitate the multi-hop communication among mobile peers in the form of a MANET (Mobile Ad-Hoc Networks). Researchers are also working on P2P overlays for mobile peers. It will be interesting to investigate whether it is feasible and how to use multi-hop communication to further improve the performance of collaborative caching and prefetching in a highly dynamic environment. We believe the challenges are keeping the mobile peers autonomous and limiting the overhead (traffic) of information synchronization.

REFERENCES

Acharya, S., Alonso, R., et al. (1995). Broadcast disks: Data management for asymmetric communication environments. In *Proceedings of the ACM SIGMOD International Conference on Management of Data*.

Acharya, S., Franklin, M. J., et al. (1995). Dissemination-based data delivery using broadcast disks. IEEE *Personal Communications, 2*(6), 50-60.

Acharya, S., Franklin, M. J., et al. (1996). Prefetching from broadcast disks. In *Proceedings of the International Conference on Data Engineering.*

Acharya, S., Franklin, M. J., et al. (1997). Balancing push and pull for data broadcast. In *Proceedings of the ACM SIGMOD International Conference on Management of Data.*

Acharya, S., & Muthukrishnan, S. (1998). Scheduling on-demand broadcasts: New metrics and algorithms. In *Proceedings of the International Conference on Mobile Computing and Networking*, Dallas, Texas, USA.

Aksoy, D., & Franklin, M. J. (1998). Scheduling for large-scale on-demand data broadcasting. In *Proceedings of the IEEE Conference on Computer Communications.*

Altinel, M., Aksoy, D., et al. (1999). DBIS-toolkit: Adaptable middleware for large scale data delivery. In *Proceedings of the ACM SIGMOD International Conference on Management of Data*, Philadelphia, Pennsylvania, USA.

Cao, G. (2002). Proactive power-aware cache management for mobile computing systems. *IEEE Transactions on Computers, 51*(6), 608-621.

Chow, C.-Y., Leong, H. V., et al. (2004). Group-based cooperative cache management for mobile clients in a mobile environment. In *Proceedings of the International Conference on Parallel Processing (ICPP).*

Chow, C.-Y., Leong, H. V., et al. (2005). Distributed group-based cooperative caching in a mobile broadcast environment. In *Proceedings of the International Conference on Mobile Data Management.*

Hughes Network Systems, LLC. (2008). DIRECWAY. Retrieved May 25, 2008, from http://www.direcway.com/

Franklin, M., & Zdonik, S. (1996). Dissemination-based information systems. *IEEE Data Engineering Bulletin, 19*(3), 20-30.

Gifford, D. K. (1990). Polychannel systems for mass digital communications. *Communications of ACM, 33*(2), 141-151.

Grassi, V. (2000). Prefetching policies for energy saving and latency reduction in a wireless broadcast data delivery system. In *Proceedings of the International Workshop on Modeling Analysis and Simulation of Wireless and Mobile Systems.*

Guo, Y., Pinotti, M. C., et al. (2001). A new hybrid broadcast scheduling algorithm for asymmetric communication systems. *SIGMOBILE Mobile Computing and Communications Review, 5*(3), 39-54.

Hameed, S. & Vaidya, N. H. (1997). Log-time algorithms for scheduling single and multiple channel data broadcast. In *Proceedings of the International Conference on Mobile Computing and Networking.*

Hara, T. (2002). Cooperative caching by mobile clients in push-based information systems. In *Proceedings of the Conference on Information and Knowledge Management.*

Hu, Q., Lee, W. C., et al. (1999). Indexing techniques for wireless data broadcast under data clustering and scheduling. In *Proceedings of the Eighth International Conference on Information and Knowledge Management*, Kansas City, Missouri, USA.

Hu, H., Xu, J., et al. (2003). Adaptive power-aware prefetching schemes for mobile broadcast environments. In *Proceedings of the International Conference on Mobile Data Management.*

Imielinski, T., Viswanathan, S., et al. (1994). Energy efficient indexing on air. In *Proceedings of the ACM SIGMOD International Conference on Management of Data.*

Imielinski, T., Viswanathan, S., et al. (1997). Data on air: Organization and access. *IEEE Transactions on Knowledge and Data Engineering, 9*(3), 353-372.

Lau, W. H. O., Kumar, M., et al. (2002). A cooperative cache architecture in support of caching multimedia objects in MANETs. In *Proceedings of the International Symposium on a World of Wireless, Mobile and Multimedia Networks.*

Lee, S., Carney, D., et al. (2003). Index hint for on-demand broadcasting. In *Proceedings of the International Conference on Data Engineering.*

Liu, Y., & Knightly, E. (2003). Opportunistic fair scheduling over multiple wireless channels. In *Proceedings of the IEEE Conference on Computer Communications.*

Lo, S.-C., & Chen, A. L. P. (2000). Optimal index and data allocation in multiple broadcast channels. In *Proceedings of the 16th International Conference on Data Engineering.*

Microsoft. (2008). MSN Direct. Retrieved May 25, 2008, from http://www.msndirect.com/

Papadopouli, M., & Schulzrinne, H. (2001). Effects of power conservation, wireless coverage and cooperation on data dissemination among mobile devices. In *Proceedings of the International Symposium on Mobile Ad Hoc Networking and Computing.*

Shen, H., Joseph, M. S., et al. (2005). PReCinCt: A scheme for cooperative caching in mobile peer-to-peer systems. In *Proceedings of the International Parallel and Distributed Processing Symposium.*

Shivakumar, N., & Venkatasubramanian, S. (1996). Efficient indexing for broadcast based wireless systems. Mobile *Networks and Applications, 1*(4), 433-446.

Su, C.-J., & Tassiulas, L. (1998). Joint broadcast scheduling and user's cache management for efficient information delivery. In *Proceedings of the International Conference on Mobile Computing and Networking.*

Tan, K.-L., & Ooi, B. C. (2000). D*ata dissemination in wireless computing environments.* Norwell, MA. USA: Kluwer Academic Publishers.

Wu, W., & Tan, K.-L. (2005). Cooperative prefetching strategies for mobile peers in a broadcast wnvironment. In *Proceedings of the International Workshop on Databases, Information Systems and Peer-to-Peer Computing.*

Wu, W., & Tan, K.-L. (2006). Global cache management in non-uniform mobile broadcast. In *Proceedings of the International Conference on Mobile Data Management*, Nara, Japan.

Xu, J., Hu, Q., et al. (2000). SAIU: An efficient cache replacement policy for wireless on-demand broadcasts. In *Proceedings of the Conference on Information and Knowledge Management.*

Xu, J., Hu, Q., et al. (2004). Performance evaluation of an optimal cache replacement policy for wireless data dissemination. IEEE *Transactions on Knowledge and Data Engineering, 16*(1), 125-139.

Xu, B., & Wolfson, O. (2004). Data management in mobile peer-to-peer networks. In *Proceedings of the International Workshop on Databases, Information Systems and Peer-to-Peer Computing.*

Yin, L., & Cao, G. (2004). Supporting cooperative caching in ad hoc networks. In *Proceedings of the IEEE Conference on Computer Communications.*

Zheng, B., & Lee, D. L. (2005). Information dissemination via wireless broadcast. *Communications of ACM, 48*(5), 105-110.

Zheng, B., Wu, X., et al. (2005). TOSA: A near-optimal scheduling algorithm for multi-channel data broadcast. In *Proceedings of the 6th International Conference on Mobile Data Management*, Ayia Napa, Cyprus.

Section 5
Page Replacement Algorithms

Chapter 13
Adaptive Replacement Algorithm Templates and EELRU

Yannis Smaragdakis
University of Massachusetts, Amherst, USA

Scott Kaplan
Amherst College, USA

ABSTRACT

Replacement algorithms are a major component of operating system design. Every replacement algorithm, however, is pathologically bad for some scenarios, and often these scenarios correspond to common program patterns. This has prompted the design of adaptive replacement algorithms: algorithms that emulate two (or more) basic algorithms and pick the decision of the best one based on recent past behavior. The authors are interested in a special case of adaptive replacement algorithms, which are instances of adaptive replacement templates (ARTs). An ART is a template that can be applied to any two algorithms and yield a combination with some guarantees on the properties of the combination, relative to the properties of the component algorithm. For instance, they show ARTs that for any two algorithms A and B produce a combined algorithm AB that is guaranteed to emulate within a factor of 2 the better of A and B on the current input. They call this guarantee a robustness property. This performance guarantee of ARTs makes them effective but a naïve implementation may not be practically efficient—e.g., because it requires significant space to emulate both component algorithms at the same time. In practice, instantiations of an ART can be specialized to be highly efficient. The authors demonstrate this through a case study. They present the EELRU adaptive replacement algorithm, which pre-dates ARTs but is truly a highly optimized multiple ART instantiation. EELRU is well-known in the research literature and outperforms the well-known LRU algorithm when there is benefit to be gained, while emulating LRU otherwise.

DOI: 10.4018/978-1-60566-850-5.ch013

INTRODUCTION

An Operating System is an arbiter of hardware resources: it decides how to allocate low-level resources to user-level entities. One of the most important resources in a modern system is main memory. The OS typically uses main memory as a cache for the data of all OS processes. The question that arises is how to decide which data stay in main memory vs. which data get placed on disk, for maximum execution efficiency. This decision is equivalent to picking a *replacement algorithm*: an algorithm to compute which data get evicted (i.e., "replaced" with other data), when main memory is full and room needs to be made. Most traditional replacement algorithms are approximations of an LRU (Least Recently Used) policy, where the data not used the longest get evicted.

It is a well-known theoretical result, however, that all replacement algorithms can be lured into performing highly sub-optimally. Even worse, most replacement algorithms have failure scenarios that correspond to common program behavior. For instance, a recency-based policy, like LRU, fails badly for loops slightly larger than main memory and can cause Thrashing (Wiseman, 2009), (Jiang, 2009). A frequency-based policy, like LFU, can be fooled when different data have different usage patterns. This has given rise to the idea of adaptively combining replacement algorithms and emulating the better algorithm for the workload at hand.

Many past adaptive replacement algorithms have been ad hoc: they are designed as combinations of two (or more) specific algorithms. (E.g., see ARC (Megiddo & Modha, 2003), LRFU (Lee et al., 2001), LIRS (Jiang & Zhang, 2002).) We next describe a more general approach, which is based on adaptive replacement templates (ARTs). An ART is a template that can be applied to any two algorithms and yield a combination with some guarantees, relative to the properties of the component algorithms. In this way, an ART can be used to fix the failure mode of any particular replacement algorithm, by combining it with a different algorithm and adaptively switching between the two.

Specifically, given two replacement algorithms A and B, we show that we can produce an adaptive algorithm AB that will never incur more than a small multiplicative constant (e.g., 2 times) as many faults as either A or B. (The term "faults" refers to the number of replacements that need to take place overall and is the standard quality measure for replacement algorithms: A good algorithm prevents future replacements, and thus suffers fewer faults, by keeping in memory the data that are likely to be needed in the future.) Application of an ART can be generalized to more than 2 algorithms by adapting between the result of a previous ART instantiation, AB, and a third algorithm C, etc. The bound of 2x in the number of faults is usefully low because it is a *worst-case* guarantee. Therefore, even if algorithm A incurs many times (e.g., tens or hundreds) as many faults as B for some inputs, while B incurs many times as many faults as A for others, the combined algorithm AB will never be much worse than either A or B, drawing the best of both worlds. In practice, we find that good adaptive algorithms emulate the better of their two component algorithms very closely (within a few percent of total faults).

ARTs give the designer of a replacement algorithm significant ammunition. Even when the behavior of a workload is known (e.g., the workload has many small loops and one large one) it is hard to combine all the information and design a near-optimal replacement algorithm. For example, it is hard to design a good replacement policy that a) behaves comparably to LRU in replacing data that were not recently accessed; b) eagerly replaces data that are accessed only once, similarly to LFU; and c) behaves optimally for large linear loops. In contrast, ARTs make it easy to combine simple policies (LRU, LFU, loop detection) that do well for a single behavioral pattern each. The result has guaranteed effectiveness relative to the original algorithms.

An ART instantiation may be effective, yet it may not be a good candidate for straightforward applied implementation. For instance, the ART may be specifying that the combined algorithm needs to maintain the memory contents of its component algorithms. This is inefficient and wasteful when the memory contents of the two algorithms have few differences. The problem is exacerbated when more than two algorithms are being adapted over. For instance, when adapting over 8 algorithms, as has been the case in past experiments (Smaragdakis, 2004), a straightforward application of an ART will require over 8 times the memory space kept for the data structures of a single replacement algorithm. (This is not to be confused with the memory space used to store the actual data. The data structures used by the replacement algorithm are typically much smaller—asymptotically logarithmic—than the overall main memory that the algorithm manages.) Furthermore, the ART performance guarantees (i.e., the 2x bound in the number of faults) are significantly weakened when more algorithms are being adapted over. If, for instance, we combine 3 algorithms with an ART guaranteeing a 2x bound per combination, then the naïve application of the theory just yields a 4x bound. If we adapt over 4 algorithms, we get an 8x bound, etc.

These drawbacks are largely artifacts of the simplistic realization of the combinations, however. In practice, for specific algorithms being adapted over we can specialize the ART instantiation so that the overheads are nearly eliminated. We demonstrate this with a case study. We analyze EELRU: a well-known adaptive replacement algorithm that pre-dates (and to some extent inspired) the ART idea. EELRU can be seen as a specific instantiation of an ART. The configuration of EELRU in past experiments (Smaragdakis, Kaplan, & Wilson, 2003) is adapting over several hundred component algorithms! Nevertheless, we show that, with appropriate specialization, the space overhead of EELRU is a small (2.5x) increment over the space required for LRU—EELRU's main

component algorithm. Furthermore, EELRU can be proven to always perform within a small bound (3x) of LRU. This reveals the potential of specializing ARTs to get practical algorithms instead of just good policies.

ADAPTIVE REPLACEMENT TEMPLATES

Consider an adaptive replacement algorithm that dynamically (i.e., during execution) switches between algorithms A and B so that it uses A (resp. B) whenever recent behavior indicates that A (resp. B) outperforms B (resp. A). How can we define a general adaptive replacement template that is independent of A and B, yet has bounded worst-case behavior with respect to either A or B? We first discuss a very simple ART, which is not expected to work well in practice. Nevertheless, the simple template is very useful because it makes it trivial to prove desirable worst-case behavior properties.

We first introduce some terminology.

DEFINITION 1. *Robustness*: A replacement algorithm R1 is c-robust with respect to replacement algorithm R2 if R1 can never incur more than c times (plus possibly a constant, independent of the number of references) as many faults as R2 for any input and memory size.

All the ARTs we define have a common structure. They produce an adaptive replacement algorithm, AB, that simulates both component algorithms A and B in memory. AB has full knowledge of the memory contents under algorithms A and B in the given point of the execution. Thus, AB can tell whether a given reference to a memory page (the unit of data storage in virtual memory) would be a hit (i.e., would be in main memory) or a miss (i.e., a fault) for algorithms A and B, as well as what each algorithm would do in that point in the execution. Based on past behavior, memory contents, and what A and B would do, the adaptive algorithm decides on its own action.

Let us see this pattern in action, by defining a simple ART, which will produce adaptive algorithms that are 2-robust with respect to their component algorithms. The ART will adapt based on the behavior of A and B during the current reference, with no memory of how well A and B did in the past.

DEFINITION 2. $ART_0(A,B)$. On every reference to a page that is not in memory (i.e., on every miss) algorithm $ART_0(A,B)$ uses the following logic:

- if the reference is a miss for A but not for B, then evict one of the memory pages that are not in B's memory. (I.e., imitate B.)

(There have to be such pages, since the memories of $ART_0(A,B)$ and B have the same size, otherwise the contents of the real memory and those of the memory of B would be the same and the current reference would have been a miss for B, since it is a miss for $ART_0(A,B)$.)

- otherwise imitate A:
  - if the memory contains pages that are not in A's memory, then evict one of those pages.
  - otherwise evict whichever page A evicts.

To prove the 2-robustness of $ART_0(A,B)$ with respect to A and B, we need a simple lemma:

LEMMA 1. Consider the same reference sequence processed by replacement policies A, B and $ART_0(A,B)$. If at a certain point a page is both in the memory managed by A and in the memory managed by B then it is also in the memory managed by $ART_0(A,B)$.

Proof: The property holds initially and if it holds up to a point in the reference sequence, then consider the next fault for either algorithm A or B. If it is not a fault for $ART_0(A,B)$, then the property will hold after the replacement (because the new page is already in $ART_0(A,B)$'s memory). If it is

also a fault for algorithm $ART_0(A,B)$, then there are 3 cases in the $ART_0(A,B)$ eviction logic:

- $ART_0(A,B)$ evicts a page not in B's memory.
- $ART_0(A,B)$ evicts a page not in A's memory.
- $ART_0(A,B)$ evicts the same page as A.

In each of the above cases, the page evicted by $ART_0(A,B)$ could not have been present in both A's and B's memory before the eviction or will be evicted from one of them at the same time. Thus, if the property held before the current fault, it will hold after the eviction. □

The lemma means that the set of pages held in $ART_0(A,B)$'s memory is a superset of the intersection of the sets of pages in A's and B's memories at all points in time.

We can now prove our robustness result.

THEOREM 1. The adaptive replacement algorithm $ART_0(A,B)$ is 2-robust with respect to both A and B. That is, $ART_0(A,B)$, as defined above, never incurs more than twice as many faults as either A or B.

Proof: We define two "potential" quantities and examine how their values change on every fault for either algorithm A or B.

Let d_A be the number of pages currently in $ART_0(A,B)$'s memory that are not in A's memory at the same point in the execution.

Let d_B be the number of pages currently in $ART_0(A,B)$'s memory that are not in B's memory at the same point in the execution. The above values of d_A, and d_B change as follows on every fault (we denote the new values d'_A and d'_B):

(Note that according to Lemma 1 a hit for both A and B implies a hit for $ART_0(A,B)$ and none of the potentials changes.)

1 fault for B, hit for A, hit for $ART_0(A,B)$:
$d'_A = d_A$, $d'_B \leq d_B$
2 fault for B, hit for A, fault for $ART_0(A,B)$:
$d'_A < d_A$, $d'_B \leq d_B + 1$

3 fault for B, fault for A, fault for $ART_0(A,B)$: $d'_A \leq d_A$, $d'_B \leq d_B + 1$

4 fault for B, fault for A, hit for $ART_0(A,B)$: $d'_A \leq d_A$, $d'_B \leq d_B$

5 hit for B, fault for A, hit for $ART_0(A,B)$: $d'_A \leq d_A$, $d'_B = d_B$

6 hit for B, fault for A, fault for $ART_0(A,B)$: $d'_A \leq d_A + 1$, $d'_B < d_B$

We do not show all the case-by-case reasoning needed to derive the above values since the derivation is tedious but straightforward. As a single example, consider case 2. In this case, there is a fault for B and $ART_0(A,B)$ but a hit for A. Thus $ART_0(A,B)$ is imitating A and furthermore $ART_0(A,B)$'s memory contains pages not in A's memory (otherwise A would have suffered a fault as well). Then, the newly referenced page is already in A's memory and $ART_0(A,B)$ will replace a page not in A's memory. Thus, the difference of the two memories will strictly decrease: $d'_A < d_A$. At the same time, $ART_0(A,B)$ and B will fault-in the same page, but they may pick two different pages to evict and these pages could have been common to both their memories before. Thus d_B (the number of pages in $ART_0(A,B)$'s memory that are not in B's memory) may increase but at most by one (hence the $d'_B \leq d_B + 1$).

Now we can show that $ART_0(A,B)$ is 2-robust relative to A. To see this, consider that for each fault of $ART_0(A,B)$ that is not a fault of A (case 2) d_A is strictly decreasing (by 1). But d_A is originally 0, has to stay nonnegative, and increases only in the case where both A and $ART_0(A,B)$ incur a fault (case 6). Thus, for every fault of $ART_0(A,B)$ that is not a fault of A, A and $ART_0(A,B)$ must have suffered a common fault earlier. That is, $ART_0(A,B)$ can only incur up to twice as many faults as A.

Similarly, we can show that $ART_0(A,B)$ is 2-robust with respect to B. If $ART_0(A,B)$ suffers a fault that is not a fault of B (case 6) then d_B is strictly decreasing. But d_B is originally 0, has to stay non-negative, and increases only in cases 2 and 3, where both B and $ART_0(A,B)$ incur faults. Thus, for every fault of $ART_0(A,B)$ that is not a fault of B, B and $ART_0(A,B)$ must have suffered a common fault earlier. That is, $ART_0(A,B)$ can only incur up to twice as many faults as B. $\square$

ART_0 produces algorithms that are not too realistic because they only check the performance of algorithms A and B for the very last memory reference. A more realistic algorithm would remember what A and B have done over a longer timeframe and imitate the better algorithm. Indeed, a simple but powerful ART would be one that remembers how well A and B have done in the current execution, i.e., it uses two counters misses(A) and misses(B) that reflect the total number of misses so far. We call this template ART_∞.

DEFINITION 3. $ART_\infty(A,B)$. On every reference to a page that is not in memory (i.e., on every miss) algorithm $ART_\infty(A,B)$ uses the following logic:

- if (misses(A) > misses(B)) then imitate B:
   - if B missed AND the page B would evict is in memory, evict that page
   - otherwise evict one of the memory pages that are not in B's memory. (By same reasoning as in Def. 2, there have to be such pages.)
- otherwise imitate A (same as above with B replaced by A).

It is easy to show, with similar reasoning as in Lemma 1, that the set of pages held in $ART_\infty(A,B)$'s memory is a superset of the intersection of the sets of pages in A's and B's memories at all points in time.

We can prove relatively easily a robustness result for $ART_\infty(A,B)$.

THEOREM 2. The adaptive replacement algorithm $ART_\infty(A,B)$ is 2-robust with respect to both A and B. That is, $ART_\infty(A,B)$, as defined above, never incurs more than $2x + m$ faults, where x is the minimum number of faults of algorithms A and B, and m is the memory size.

Proof: Let C_A and C_B be the counts of total faults so far for algorithms A and B, respectively. We again define two "potential" quantities and examine how their values change on every fault for either algorithm A or B.

Let d_A be the number of pages currently in $ART_\infty(A,B)$'s memory that are not in A's memory at the same point in the execution. Let d_B be the number of pages currently in $ART_\infty(A,B)$'s memory that are not in B's memory at the same point in the execution. The values of C_A, C_B, d_A, and d_B change as follows on every fault (we denote the new values C'_A, C'_B, d'_A and d'_B):

(As discussed above, there is no possibility of a hit for A and B, but a miss for $ART_\infty(A,B)$.)

1. if $C_A > C_B$ (in which case $ART_\infty(A,B)$ imitates algorithm B)
    a. fault for B, hit for A, hit for $ART_\infty(A,B)$: $C'_A = C_A$, $C'_B = C_B + 1$, $d'_A = d_A$, $d'_B \leq d_B$
    b. fault for B, hit for A, fault for $ART_\infty(A,B)$: $C'_A = C_A$, $C'_B = C_B + 1$, $d'_A \leq d_A$, $d'_B \leq d_B$
    c. fault for B, fault for A, fault for $ART_\infty(A,B)$: $C'_A = C_A + 1$, $C'_B = C_B + 1$, $d'_A \leq d_A + 1$, $d'_B \leq d_B$
    d. fault for B, fault for A, hit for $ART_\infty(A,B)$: $C'_A = C_A + 1$, $C'_B = C_B + 1$, $d'_A \leq d_A$, $d'_B \leq d_B$
    e. hit for B, fault for A, hit for $ART_\infty(A,B)$: $C'_A = C_A + 1$, $C'_B = C_B$, $d'_A \leq d_A$, $d'_B = d_B$
    f. hit for B, fault for A, fault for $ART_\infty(A,B)$: $C'_A = C_A + 1$, $C'_B = C_B$, $d'_A \leq d_A + 1$, $d'_B < d_B$
2. if $C_A \leq C_B$ (in which case $ART_\infty(A,B)$ imitates algorithm A)
    a. fault for B, hit for A, hit for $ART_\infty(A,B)$: $C'_A = C_A$, $C'_B = C_B + 1$, $d'_A = d_A$, $d'_B \leq d_B$
    b. fault for B, hit for A, fault for $ART_\infty(A,B)$: $C'_A = C_A$, $C'_B = C_B + 1$, $d'_A < d_A$, $d'_B \leq d_B + 1$
    c. fault for B, fault for A, fault for $ART_\infty(A,B)$: $C'_A = C_A + 1$, $C'_B = C_B + 1$, $d'_A \leq d_A$, $d'_B \leq d_B + 1$
    d. fault for B, fault for A, hit for $ART_\infty(A,B)$: $C'_A = C_A + 1$, $C'_B = C_B + 1$, $d'_A \leq d_A$, $d'_B \leq d_B$
    e. hit for B, fault for A, hit for $ART_\infty(A,B)$: $C'_A = C_A + 1$, $C'_B = C_B$, $d'_A \leq d_A$, $d'_B = d_B$
    f. hit for B, fault for A, fault for $ART_\infty(A,B)$: $C'_A = C_A + 1$, $C'_B = C_B$, $d'_A \leq d_A$, $d'_B \leq d_B$

To see how the inequalities are derived, consider, for instance, case 1.e. In this case, there is a miss for A but not for B, which is reflected in the update of miss counts. Since the reference is a hit for $ART_\infty(A,B)$, one extra common page will exist in both memories (for A and for adaptive) after this reference is processed. At the same time, however, A can evict a page that is in the current system memory, so d_A (the number of pages kept in memory by ART_∞ that would not be in A's memory) may decrease or stay the same (hence the $d'_A \leq d_A$). d_B stays the same since the reference was a hit both for $ART_\infty(A,B)$ and for B.

Using the information on the potential quantities we can show our result. Assume, without loss of generality, that the algorithm with the fewest total faults is B. (The case of A is virtually identical.) Consider the point in the execution when C_A was last equal to C_B—we will call this the "turning point". This was the last time ART_∞ emulated algorithm A. (This point, of course, could be the very beginning of the execution.) The main theorem will be broken up in two parts: first we show that $ART_\infty(A,B)$ cannot have suffered more than twice as many misses as B until the turning point, and then we show that $ART_\infty(A,B)$ cannot have suffered more than m more misses than B after the turning point. The two bounds have a total of $2x + m$.

We can establish that $ART_\infty(A,B)$ never suffered more than twice as many misses as B until the turning point: $ART_\infty(A,B)$ suffers a miss that is not a miss for B only in cases 1.f and 2.f, above. But each of these cases increases the metric $C_A - C_B$. Since $C_A - C_B$ is zero initially and also zero at the turning point (by definition), the number of times cases 1.f and 2.f could have occurred is at most as many as the number of times the difference $C_A - C_B$ has decreased. But this only occurs in cases 1.a, 1.b, 2.a, and 2.b, and in all of those algorithm B suffers a miss. In other words, the number of misses for $ART_\infty(A,B)$ that are not misses for algorithm B are at most as many as the misses of B. That is, $ART_\infty(A,B)$ can only suffer up to twice the misses of B up until the turning point.

At the turning point (and, actually, any other point as well) the value of quantity d_B is at most equal to the memory size, m—since d_B reflects how many pages in the set are different between the memories of $ART_\infty(A,B)$ and B. After the turning point, $ART_\infty(A,B)$ imitates algorithm B. Thus, the only case where $ART_\infty(A,B)$ suffers a miss that is not a miss for B is case 1.f. But in this case, d_B gets decremented and it can never drop below zero. Thus, ART_∞ suffers at most d_B misses over those of B after the turning point, which is at most equal to m.

Hence, overall, $ART_\infty(A,B)$ never incurs more than $2x + m$ faults, where x is the number of faults of the better of the two algorithms A and B and m is the memory size. □

The above results demonstrate the generality and value of ARTs. Without any knowledge concerning algorithms A and B, and with no assumptions on the behavior of the workload, we can prove worst-case bounds on the performance of an adaptive algorithm relative to the performance of the better of A and B. The generality of the results for these ARTs means that they can be applied to various caching domains, even beyond operating systems (e.g., processor level-2 caching (Subramanian, Smaragdakis, & Loh, 2006)). Following similar reasoning as above, other robustness results for adaptive algorithms can

be proven (Smaragdakis, 2004). Most notably, an adaptive algorithm can base its decisions on a window of k recent misses, as opposed to just the last miss (as in ART_0) or all the misses that occurred in the past (as in ART_∞). This would produce a template ART_k, which has interesting practical instantiations, as seen next.

IMPLEMENTING ADAPTIVE REPLACEMENT ALGORITHMS— THE EELRU ALGORITHM

An adaptive replacement template can be used to produce effective policies, but it does not directly result in efficient algorithms. For instance, it is not clear how to combine a large number of existing algorithms without needing to keep a record of the memory contents of each one. For a single algorithm, keeping a record of the pages it would hold in memory is typically a small storage cost in a modern OS. For instance, keeping a record of which 8KB pages are resident in memory can typically be done with a data structure storing a few tens of bytes per page—an overhead of less than 0.5%. Nevertheless, when an adaptive algorithm wants to adapt over N distinct other algorithms, the overhead would be multiplied by N and would soon end up being prohibitive. Furthermore, it is not clear what is a tight bound for the robustness of an adaptive algorithm when it adapts over more than two basic algorithms. A simplistic application of our earlier theorems suggests that when N policies are being composed pair-wise, the resulting adaptive algorithm is only 2^{N-1}-robust with respect to two of them (the first in the composition). This bound can be likely tightened with further theoretical work, but the worst-case behavior of the general case (for arbitrary algorithms being adapted over) is not likely to be the worst-case behavior for specific algorithms that are useful in practice.

The space constraints and worst-case bounds of adaptive algorithms can be significantly alleviated in practice with a bit of work when creating specialized algorithms. A prime example of this approach is the EELRU algorithm, which we discuss next. EELRU (for "Early-Eviction LRU") is a well-known adaptive algorithm in the research literature, with performance that matches LRU for LRU-friendly workloads and significantly beats LRU in several other instances.

A high-level version of the EELRU logic is:

- Perform LRU replacement unless many references are to pages that were only recently evicted.

- If many references are to pages recently evicted, enable "early evictions": Pick an optimal point e in the recency space and evict the e-th most recently accessed page.

This informal strategy is clearly adaptive, in the intuitive sense. EELRU is effectively checking whether LRU performs well, and, if not, it emulates an MRU-like algorithm. To be more precise, the MRU-like algorithms belong in a family of algorithms developed for a model of program behavior called the "LRU stack model". The LRU stack model assumes that programs behave as random processes with no memory, but the random variable is not which page address they access, but which page they access in the *recency* (also called *reuse-distance*) space. In this way, a program is modeled by a histogram of probabilities, $h(i)$, indicating how likely it is for the program to next reference the i-th most recently accessed page. That is, the program's memory accesses are assumed to be independent random actions, where on each step of the execution the program randomly decides on a number i, with probability $h(i)$, and then accesses the i-th most recently accessed page (at the current moment). If we assume that program locality is primarily determined by loops, the LRU stack model is an excellent model of program behavior, since a histogram with a high probability for a certain i reflects how well the behavior of a program that has a loop touching i distinct pages.

If we know the histogram that best describes the probabilities of program accesses, then we can compute an optimal replacement algorithm for this program (Wood, Fernandez, & Lang, 1983). Specifically, if we pick two points e and l (for "early" and "late" eviction point, respectively) in the recency axis, with e less than and l greater than the memory size, m, then the Wood et al. technique yields a replacement algorithm that has a hit ratio (i.e., proportion of accesses that are in memory) of $H(0,e) + (m-e)/(l-e) \cdot H(e,l)$, where $H(x,y)$, for $x < y$, is the probability that the page accessed is among the y most recently accessed but not among the x most recently accessed—i.e., $H(x,y)$ is the sum of $h(x+1)$, $h(x+2)$, …, $h(y)$.

EELRU is now simple to understand as an algorithm adapting over a large number of component algorithms that each pick a specific e and l position. EELRU keeps a histogram of all program accesses in the recent past, ordered by recency. For each position i, the histogram records how many recent hits were to the i-th most recently accessed page. In this way, this past-behavior-histogram can be used as the probability histogram $h(i)$ of future references. Based on the assumption that the future will look like the past, recency-wise, EELRU tries all its available combinations of e and l points in the histogram and picks the one that maximizes the sum $H(0,e) + (m - e)/(l - e) \cdot H(e,l)$. In the case that the maximum value is $H(0,m)$, LRU is the best algorithm.

To reword this in terms of an ART, EELRU keeps a window of k past misses and it checks (for the program accesses during that time) whether the algorithm that would have performed best is plain LRU or any "early eviction" algorithm for a given e and l value. (We slightly simplify the EELRU logic, but not in important ways.) This is akin to a (multiple) instantiation of an adaptive replacement template ART_k, which is much like ART_∞, but with only the last k misses taken into account. If we view EELRU as a multiple instantiation of

ART_k, the number of instantiations is staggering: the published EELRU experiments are derived by using a total of 40 points in the recency histogram (Smaragdakis, Kaplan, & Wilson, 2003). 15 of those points are below the memory size m, and are thus candidates for the early eviction position e, while another 24 points are above m, and are candidates for the late eviction position l. Hence, there are over 300 possible combinations of e and l points (plus the plain LRU algorithm) that EELRU examines to pick the optimal, based on the program's past behavior. A naïve implementation of EELRU, as consecutive instantiations of ART_k would be catastrophic. The memory needs alone, in order to record the memory contents for all 300+ component algorithms, would be clearly unrealistic.

Nevertheless, the actual implementation of EELRU has modest space requirements. The memory contents of all 300+ component algorithms have very high overlap and can be computed approximately from a single recency queue, holding the 2.5·m most recently accessed pages. (The 2.5 factor applies to the setup in the EELRU publication, but any other factor could be used.) That is, while plain LRU maintains a data structure of the m most recently accessed pages, which also happen to be resident in memory, EELRU does the same for 2.5 times more pages, many of which are not resident in memory, but have been evicted to disk. From this data structure, the memory contents of any component algorithm (for any combination of e and l points) can be approximated: the probability that the i-th most recently accessed page is resident in memory is known, even without knowing which exact pages would be in memory. (It is possible to compute the exact memory contents for any component algorithm, but only by knowing the initial contents, right before the least-recently-accessed page was last touched.) This approximation is used in all adaptivity reasoning and EELRU can imitate effectively any of the component algorithms it chooses to adapt into.

The approximate nature of the EELRU adaptivity means that it would be hard to apply to it robustness results, such as those in the previous section. Yet the robustness property of interest for EELRU is not with respect to all its 300+ component algorithms, but with respect to a specific one: LRU itself. Since LRU is the best known replacement algorithm in practice, it is reasonable to give LRU special status in the EELRU adaptivity. That is, EELRU can be seen as an algorithm that first decides whether to stay with LRU or perform some early evictions, and then chooses which early evictions to perform. In this way, the cumulative performance of past early eviction decisions is taken into account, relative to that of LRU. Effectively, if we see EELRU as an algorithm that applies a sequence of ART_k instantiations then its structure is $ART_k(LRU, ART_k (early1, ART_k(early2, ART_k(...))))$: LRU is always at the top of the composition. This guarantees that EELRU has its tightest robustness result with respect to LRU. Interestingly, LRU is easy to reason about in the context of EELRU, because there is no ambiguity with respect to LRU's memory contents: the EELRU data structure can always tell us precisely whether a certain page would be in memory under the LRU algorithm, since LRU just keeps the m most recently accessed pages in memory. Overall, EELRU can be proven 3-robust with respect to LRU using techniques similar to those presented earlier. (Smaragdakis, Kaplan, & Wilson, 2003 demonstrate a proof for a much simplified version of EELRU, but a proof for a more realistic EELRU is effectively the same as that for algorithm AB(K) by Smaragdakis, 2004.)

In short, EELRU is best understood as a specialized application of an adaptive replacement template. Just like the ARTs examined earlier, EELRU keeps track of recent misses for each of its component algorithms and chooses to imitate the algorithm that has the fewest past misses. For actual implementation, EELRU exploits a mathematical understanding of how its component algorithms behave and approximates their memory contents using a single data structure with little space overhead. At the same time, EELRU can be shown to be robust with respect to LRU by just treating it preferentially.

EMPIRICAL PERFORMANCE OF EELRU

It is interesting to see how the theoretical properties of an adaptive replacement template (e.g., robustness) translate to practice. In particular, is it the case that an adaptive algorithm like EELRU can achieve benefit without hurting performance much in the worst case? In practice, constant factors (e.g., 2x) that represent tight theoretical lower bounds can be unacceptable overheads. We present here a representative sample of a simulated performance evaluation of EELRU on real memory reference sequences. (An extensive empirical evaluation can be found in Smaragdakis, Kaplan, & Wilson, 2003.)

Specifically, we compare EELRU both to LRU—the standard on-line policy—and OPT—the provably optimal, off-line policy. In particular, by comparing EELRU to OPT, we see the amount of the potential improvement over LRU that EELRU obtains. When compared to these two policies, EELRU provides substantial fraction of the available improvement over LRU. Just as

Table 1.

Program name	Mean potential improvement
acrord32	-6.82%
Applu	35.85%
cc1	-6.12%
compress95	78.08%
espresso	10.61%
gcc-2.7.2	9.44%
Gnuplot	89.00%
Go	16.35%
grobner	30.96%
gs3.33	-1.84%
Ijpeg	40.62%
Lindsay	-1.77%
m88ksim	37.95%
Murphi	-2.39%
netscape	-3.73%
p2c	3.56%
perl-etch	34.02%
perl-wisconsin	20.81%
photoshp	-8.69%
powerpnt	-8.10%
Trygtsl	29.31%
Vortex	0.60%
wave5	70.31%
winword	-7.03%

importantly, when EELRU does *not* yield fewer misses than LRU, its adaptive mechanism, in practice, yields at worst approximately a 16% increase in misses over LRU. That is, EELRU commonly improves upon LRU, and when it cannot, it does little to no harm.

First, we examine the how much of the potential improvement over LRU that EELRU obtains. This table shows the percentage of that potential improvement for each of a group of benchmark applications over a wide range of memory sizes. (We filtered out memory sizes for which few misses occur, since differences may seem disproportionately large. We do not show memory sizes for which the program suffers few faults. In particular, we present statistics for all memory sizes m, at which LRU incurs at least m misses.)

For example, consider a program and a memory size where, under the optimal policy, OPT, the system would incur 100 main memory misses, while under LRU, it would incur 200 misses. If EELRU incurred 200 misses, then it would obtain 0% of the potential improvement. At 175 misses, EELRU would obtain 25% of the potential improvement. Finally, at 225 misses, EELRU would obtain -25% of that possible improvement.

On one hand, Table 1 shows that there are

Table 2.

Program name	Increase in number of misses
acrord32	9.45%
applu	5.42%
cc1	9.96%
compress95	0.99%
espresso	4.57%
gcc-2.7.2	8.26%
gnuplot	3.55%
go	3.85%
grobner	3.80%
gs3.33	10.89%
ijpeg	5.68%
lindsay	2.74%
m88ksim	1.66%
murphi	4.13%
netscape	11.23%
p2c	1.57%
perl-etch	-3.46%
perl-wisconsin	7.52%
photoshp	14.87%
powerpnt	16.38%
trygtsl	-1.41%
vortex	4.27%
wave5	-8.86%
winword	9.10%

some programs—nine of them here—for which EELRU, on average, provides no benefit, and only five of those incur more than 5% detriment. Furthermore, for those five programs, the detriment is never more than 10%. In contrast, twelve of these programs enjoy an improvement of more than 10%, up to 89%, of the possible improvement over LRU. On balance, EELRU yields a modest detriment in some cases in exchange for a substantial improvement for others.

Although Table 1 shows means, you may be concerned that there are worst cases in which EELRU performs far worse than LRU. Table 2 shows, for each program, the raw increase in misses that occurs at the memory size for which EELRU's performance is worst in comparison to LRU.

For Table 2, positive values imply more misses for EELRU than LRU. We first see that, at worst, the increase in the raw number of misses is only 16.38%. For most programs, the worst case is no worse than 10%, and for a few programs, the worst case is either a modest detriment (less than 2%) or an improvement (up to -8.86%). Even for a poor combination of application and memory size, the adaptivity of EELRU avoids substantial harm.

CONCLUSION

We presented the idea of adaptive replacement algorithms created by instantiating general "adaptive replacement templates" (ARTs). ARTs are very attractive because of their generality and theoretical guarantees regardless of which algorithms are adapted over. Importantly, ARTs can lead to specialized, efficient instantiations, when the algorithm designers understand well the properties of the component algorithms. We demonstrated how the EELRU algorithm from the research literature can be thought of as an optimized multiple instantiation of an ART, and its performance in practice. We believe that ARTs, rather than EELRU itself, are a very promising idea for future replacement policies, and we have already applied them to different domains, including hardware caching.

REFERENCES

Jiang, S. (2009). Swap Token: Rethink the Application of the LRU Principle on Paging to Remove System Thrashing. In Y. Wiseman & S. Jiang, (Eds.), *The Handbook of Advanced Operating Systems and Kernel Applications: Techniques and Technologies*. Hershey, PA: IGI Global.

Lee, D., Choi, J., Kim, J.-H., Noh, S. H., Min, S. L., Cho, Y., & Kim, C. S. (2001). LRFU: A spectrum of policies that subsumes the least recently used and least frequently used policies . *IEEE Transactions on Computers, 50*(12), 1352–1361. doi:10.1109/TC.2001.970573

Megiddo, N., & Modha, D. S. (2003). ARC: A self-tuning, low overhead replacement cache. In *Proc. File and Storage Technologies (FAST)*. USENIX Association.

Robertson, J., & Devarakonda, M. (1990). Data cache management using frequency-based replacement. In *Proc. SIGMETRICS Conference on Measurement and Modeling of computer systems*. New York: ACM Press.

Smaragdakis, Y. (2004). General Adaptive Replacement Policies. *Proc. International Symposium on Memory Management* (pp. 108-119). New York: ACM Press.

Smaragdakis, Y., Kaplan, S., & Wilson, P. (2003). The EELRU Adaptive Replacement Algorithm. *Performance Evaluation, 53*(2), 93–123. doi:10.1016/S0166-5316(02)00226-2

Subramanian, R., Smaragdakis, Y., & Loh, G. (2006). Adaptive Caches: Effective Shaping of Cache Behavior to Workloads. In *Proc. International Symposium on Microarchitecture (MICRO)* (pp. 385-386). Washington, DC: IEEE Computer Society.

Wiseman, Y. (2009). Alleviating the Trashing by Adding Medium-Term Scheduler. In Y. Wiseman & S. Jiang, (Eds.), *The Handbook of Advanced Operating Systems and Kernel Applications: Techniques and Technologies*. Hershey, PA: IGI Global.

Wood, C., Fernandez, E. B., & Lang, T. (1983). Minimization of Demand Paging for the LRU Stack Model of Program Behavior. *Information Processing Letters, 16*, 99–104. doi:10.1016/0020-0190(83)90034-0

Chapter 14
Enhancing the Efficiency of Memory Management in a Super–Paging Environment by AMSQM

Moshe Itshak
Bar-Ilan University, Israel

Yair Wiseman
Bar-Ilan University, Israel

ABSTRACT

The concept of Super-Paging has been wandering around for more than a decade. Super-Pages are supported by some operating systems. In addition, there are some interesting research papers that show interesting ideas how to intelligently integrate Super-Pages into modern operating systems; however, the page replacement algorithms used by the contemporary operating system even now use the old Clock algorithm which does not prioritize small or large pages based on their size. In this chapter an algorithm for page replacement in a Super-Page environment is presented. The new technique for page replacement decisions is based on the page size and other parameters; hence is appropriate for a Super-Paging environment.

INTRODUCTION

The paging concept is very old and well-known. Super-Paging is an augmentation for this well-known concept. Super-Pages are larger pages that are pointed to by the TLB (Khalidi et al., 1993). The internal memory of modern computers has been drastically increased during the last decades. However, the TLB coverage (i.e. the size of the memory that can be pointed to directly by the TLB) has been increased by a much lower factor during the same period (Navarro, 2004), (Navarro et al., 2002). Therefore, several new architectures like Itanium, MIPS R4x00, Alpha, SPARC and HP PA RISC support multiple page size of the frames pointed to by the TLB. In that way the memory size pointed to directly by the TLB is higher and the overhead of the page table access time is reduced. There are also some particular operating systems

DOI: 10.4018/978-1-60566-850-5.ch014

that support Super-Paging e.g. (Ganapathy and Schimmel, 1998), (Subramanian et al., 1998), (Winwood et al., 2002).

The Super-Paging concept brings up several questions to discuss in the operating systems community. First, when should the Operating System upgrade some base pages into a large Super-Page? This dilemma is even more complicated when the processor supports several sizes of Super-Pages; e.g. the Itanium has 10 sizes of Super-Pages. Second, where should the location of the small pages in the memory be? One possibility is placing them in a location that spares the need for relocation of the base page, once the Operating System upgrades base pages into a Super-Page (Talluri and Hill, 1994). Another policy is placing the base page in the first vacant location in the memory and relocating it when the Operating System upgrades (Romer et al., 1995). Thirdly, who handles the relocation, the hardware or the software (Fang et al., 2001)? Some processors and Operating Systems have addressed these questions as was mentioned above. More about Super-pages can be read at (Wiseman, 2005).

In this chapter a new algorithm for page replacement in a Super-Paging environment is suggested (Itshak and Wiseman, 2009). The new algorithm is based on some parameters including the page size. The results show better TLB miss rate for the benchmarks used for testing.

Multimedia applications typically have large portions of memory that are clustered in few areas. Such applications can benefit Super-Paging enormously (Abouaissa et al., 1999). Also, nowadays computers usually have large memories (Wallace et al., 2006), (Geppert, 2003); hence, larger pages can be used; however using larger pages can apparently cause a higher page fault rate. This is a well-known flaw of the Super-Paging mechanism; however the algorithm suggested in this chapter does not suffer from this flaw and even utilizes the usual behavior of the paging mechanism to reduce the page fault rate. The algorithm actually makes use of the locality principle to prefetch

base-pages that are a part of heavy used Super-pages and the results show that this prefetching makes the memory hit percents better.

We also aim at developing a good technique that finds the best page to be taken out when the page fault mechanism requires this in a Super-Paging environment based on all the available parameters. Here again the locality principle that the Super-paging environment induces helps us to select the victim page better, because if page's neighbors have been accessed, it can imply that the page itself might be accessed as well and it may not be a good choice to swap the page out as the common base-page algorithms would have done.

The question of which page should be taken out also occurs in higher levels as well i.e. Which page should be in the cache and which page should be pointed to by the TLB. The algorithm suggested in this chapter can be also a good alternative for the well-known Clock algorithm in these decisions.

SUPER-PAGES OF THE SUN MICROSYSTEM'S SPARC MACHINES

We recently got a donation of a lab from SUN Microsystems, so our implementation is focused on this platform. In this section we detail the specification of the SultraSPARC CPU of SUN Microsystems and how this processor handles several sizes of page.

UltraSPARC CPU family is the main RISC CPU of Sun Microsystems server line. Multiple Page Size Support (MPSS) has been available by UltraSPARC CPUs since its first generation, but the support may vary between the UltraSPARC CPU family generations and even within one generation (mainly US-III) there might be a change in the support that this generation offers.

UltraSPARC I,II,III,IV cpu families supports 4 page sizes: 8KB, 64KB, 512KB, 4MB, whereas UltraSPARC IV+ supports 6 page sizes: 8KB,

64KB, 512KB, 4MB, 32MB, 256MB. UltraS-PARC T1 cpu supports also 4 page sizes but the sizes are slightly different than the original one. The new sizes are: 8KB, 64KB, 4MB and 256MB.

UltraSPARC MMU which is called sfmmu (spit-fire mmu) supports two mmu units: I-MMU for instructions and D-MMU for data, whereas UltraSPARC I and II have only one I-MMU TLB and one D-MMU TLB that supports the 4 page sizes.

UltraSPARC III TLB support for MPSS is a little bit restricted; even though the number of I-MMU and D-MMU TLB entries has been increased, there is a constraint that the bigger TLB may only use one page size. The next generation - UltraSPARC IV+ TLB support is better because D-TLB and I-TLB have been increased and also it allows more than one page size in the D-TLB. UltraSPARC T1 TLB also supports all page sizes simultaneously.

Solaris 2.6 through Solaris 8 have enabled Super-Paging via a mechanism called Intimate Shared Memory (ISM) that allowed a sharing of a System V IPC "intimate" shared memory in page sizes of 4MB if possible. Solaris 8 update 3 introduced Dynamic ISM allowing a dynamic resizing of ISM areas.

The new Solaris 9 also supports MPSS without the use of ISM (Weinand, 2006), but this support requires the application or an administrator to request the certain page size that he thinks useful for this application. MPSS was also expanded to be used in vnodes (VMPSS), means libraries and text code can be also stored in Super-Pages. The latest work in Solaris selects page sizes for stack, heap and memory mapped segments, text and data based on a simple set of policies. This is known as MPSS out of the box (MPSS-OOB) (Lowe, 2005).

PAGE REPLACEMENT ALGORITHMS

Over the years many replacement algorithms have been published e.g. (O'Neil et al., 1993), (Johnson and Shasha, 1994), (Lee et al., 2001), (Kim et al., 2000), (Jiang and Zhang, 2002), (Smaragdakis et al., 2003), (Zhou et al., 2004); however over the last decades, CLOCK (Corbato, 1968) has been dominated page replacement algorithms.

The "Clock" Page Replacement Algorithm

The CLOCK algorithm looks at the memory pages as a circular linked list and moves around the pages like a clock hand. Each page is associated with a reference bit. This bit is set to 1 when the page is referenced. When a page fault occurs, the page which is pointed to by the hand is checked. If its reference bit is unset it will be swap out; otherwise its reference bit is unset, and the hand moves to the subsequent page. Research and experiences have shown that CLOCK is a close approximation of LRU, thus suffers from the same problems of LRU. Nevertheless, CLOCK is still dominating the vast majority of OS including UNIX, Linux and Windows (Friedman, 1999).

Some variant of CLOCK have been suggested over the years. GCLOCK (Nicola et al., 1992) was published at 1992 as an expansion to CLOCK. This algorithm contains a counter to each page (instead of a reference bit), which is increased in each reference. The clock's hand checks the pages and decrements their counter value, until it finds a page with a zero value. This page is swapped out. Unlike CLOCK, GCLOCK is taking into account the frequency, thus achieves better performance.

CLOCK-Pro (Jiang et al., 2005) counts for each page the number of other distinct pages accesses since its last access. This number is called "reuse distance" and a page with a larger "reuse distance" will be considered as a colder page and will be swap out before a page with a smaller "reuse distance".

The Arc Page Replacement Algorithm

We focused in the above section at CLOCK, because CLOCK dominates the Operating Systems market; however some other methods seem to suffer from two acute problems:

(i)   The need for parameters tuning (e.g 2Q (Johnson and Shasha, 1994)) and LRFU (Lee at. Al, 2001)) and/or

(ii) Non-constant complexity (e.g. LRU-K (O'Neil et al., 1993),

LRFU (Lee at. al, 2001),CLOCK (Corbato, 1968) and GCLOCK (Nicola et al., 1992)).

CLOCK also has a Non-constant complexity, so we prefer to adapt more modern algorithm to the Super-Paging environment.

(O'Neil at el., 1993) found in their experiments that LRU-2 (LRU-K where K=2) achieves most of the advantages of their method. This result motivated Johnson and Shasha to develop 2Q (Johnson and Shasha, 1994), an algorithm which is similar in its performance to LRU-2, and still works in a constant time. 2Q in its simplified version has two buffers A1 and Am, where A1 is managed as a FIFO queue, whereas Am as a regular LRU queue. At the first reference to a page, 2Q places the page in A1 queue. If the page is re-referenced while it is in A1, the algorithm will assume it is probably a hot page. So, if a page in A1 is referenced, it will be moved to the Am queue, and if a page is not referenced while it is in A1, it the algorithm will assume that the page is probably a cold page and 2Q will remove the page from the memory. 2Q's main disadvantage is its offline property - 2Q requires two static parameters tuning (Kin and Kout) before running. Tuning these parameters can be sometime a very difficult task. Johnson and Shasha reported

that according to their experiments 2Q gives an improvement of 5-10% in hit ratio over LRU for a wide variety of applications and buffer sizes and never damaging. But these results were not convincing enough.

Recently, N. Megiddo and S. Modha took the 2Q algorithm and make the size of A1 and Am adaptive. They proposed a new "online" tunable algorithm called ARC (Stands for Adaptive Replacement Cache) (Megiddo and Modha, 2003a), (Megiddo and Modha, 2003b), (Megiddo and Modha, 2004). The unique capability of this algorithm is its ability to adapt itself "online" according to the systems properties e.g. from the Stack Depth Distribution (SDD) model to the Independence Reference Model (IRM) and vice versa.

The main concept of ARC is having two lists of active pages (one for the frequently used pages and one for the most recent pages) and to endow the list that is performing the best with a larger memory space. The two lists that ARC maintains are variably-sized lists called L1 and L2. L1 contains the pages that have been accessed only once and L2 contains the pages that have been accessed twice or more. The algorithm always holds that $0 \leq L1+L2 \leq 2C$, where C is the number of pages in the memory. L1 consists of two buffers - T1 which consists of the most recent pages in the memory and B1 which consists of the history of the most recent pages that were in the memory. Similarly L2 is partitioned into T2 and B2. In addition p which always holds $p \leq c$, is the automatic adaptive parameter of the algorithm which sets the target size for T1.

The algorithm in a simplify version is for any page request:

*   If the requested page is in T_1 or in T_2:
    ○   Move the page to the MRU of T_2.
*   If the requested page is in B_1:
    ○   If $|B_1| \geq |B_2|$
        ▪ $\delta_1 = 1$
    ○   Else

- $\delta_1 = |B_2|/|B_1|$
  - $P = \text{Min}(P + \delta_1, C)$
  - Move the page from B_1 to be the LRU of T_2 (swap out page according to P).
- If the requested page is in B_2:
  - If $|B_2| \geq |B_1|$
    - $\delta_2 = 1$
  - Else
    - $\delta_2 = |B_1|/|B_2|$
  - $P = \text{Max}(P - \delta_2, 0)$
  - Move the page from B_2 to be the LRU of T_2 (swap out page according to P).
- If the requested page is not in $T_1 \cup T_2 \cup B_1 \cup B_2$:

o Move the new page to be the MRU of T_1 (swap out page according to P).

As we mentioned above, CLOCK can move its clock hand over many pages, until a page with an unset bit is found. Unlike CLOCK, ARC has a constant complexity - O(1). In addition, ARC is tunable i.e. ARC can adapt itself according to the characteristics of the data that the processes use. These are the reasons why we chose to adapt ARC to the Super-Paging mechanism.

SUPER-PAGES AND ARC

When adapting ARC for super-paging environment, some considerations should be taken into account. In this section, we would like to discuss these considerations and to see how they can affect the ARC algorithm.

Larger Pages

When using super-pages the pages that are used by the operating system are usually larger. In such a case the recency is less important than the frequency. If a page is frequently accessed, it can hint the operating system that this page is important, even if the page is very large, whereas

the importance of the last access time to a larger page is less weighty.

Fragmentation

ARC and LRU do not take into their considerations the location of the "victim" that is chosen to be swapped out; therefore, they can leave many holes within a super-page, because some of the base pages that the super-page consists of can be in the memory whereas some others can be out of memory. When not all of the base pages are in the memory, a promotion can be costly. A better page replacement algorithm must check the "neighborhood" of the victim page. A similar scheme was suggest by Romer et al., 1995), but the authors of this paper have preferred to use LRU.

Thrashing

Usually supper-pages supported systems are less thrashing-proof than the old traditional paging systems. They cause a more extensive memory consuming that can lead to a memory pressure and even a thrashing (Wiseman, 2009), (Jiang, 2009). Obviously, when the memory is very large this deficiency is not critical. However, one of the importance advantages of the ARC over the "recency" algorithms is the thrashing-proof feature; hence the thrashing argument is clearly in favor of the use of ARC.

Coarse Granularity

The use of super-pages causes all the super-page's base pages to be considered as important (or unimportant) pages, whereas usually just several base pages are important or sometimes even just a single base page is important. In such cases, the LRU algorithm gives poor results, because it has no mechanism to distinguish between super-pages containing many important base pages and super-pages containing just a small number of important base pages. "Recency" algorithms cannot notice this difference; therefore LRU will not be a good choice in cases where just a small number of base pages are indeed important. ARC, however, takes into account the "frequency"; thus ARC can be a better choice for these cases.

Gathering the Accesses

When the size of page is small, an access to a specific location by the readings/writings is not significant. However, one can think that a gather can imply an important page, while scattered readings/writings will mean arbitrary accesses. However, practically this assumption is not proved as correct.

THE AMSQM PAGE REPLACEMENT ALGORITHM

The ARC page replacement algorithm has been utilized to develop a new algorithm - Adaptive Multiple Super-Pages Queues Management (AMSQM) (Itshak and Wiseman, 2008) which is an expansion of the ARC algorithm that supports Super-Paging. AMSQM algorithm has two levels - the high level manages the different Super-Page queues (sizes and allocations); whereas the low level is the internal management of each Super-Page's queue. In addition, there is a special buffer for each Super-Page size that collects fractions of bigger Super-Pages. The purpose of these buffers is in case of demotion, giving the demoted Super-Pages a chance to get a better priority if they are hot pages.

The suggested algorithm uses a reservation-based scheme, in which region is reserved for a super-page at the page fault time and the promotion is done when the number of the super-page's populated base pages gets to a promotion threshold. Since we would like a partially populated super-page to have the opportunity of being promoted,

the decision for preempting reservation of a super-page candidate or swapping out its base-pages is taken based on the super-page "recency" in the page lists and not based on the number of currently resident base-pages that the super-page consists of. This is actually a known technique of information filtering in order to achieve a better decision (Wang, 2008).

Hardware maintains only a single reference bit; thus it is difficult to decide whether all (or at least most) of the base-pages that the super-page consists of are actually in use. Sometimes, only a small percentage of the base pages should be in the memory. Therefore, AMSQM manages several queues for each super-page size, preventing from cold super-pages to be retained in the cache occupying the space of some potential hotter smaller super-pages or base pages.

Finally, in order to wisely balance the different queues length, the algorithm counts the number of times that each page has been referenced and checks the relative "recency" of each super-page's queue.

Similarly to ARC, AMSQM has B and T lists, but AMSQM has T and B list for each super-page size that is denoted as $Ti1$, $Ti2$, $Bi1$ and $Bi2$ where i is the super-page size. Therefore, the pseudo-code briefly should be:

- Find the super-page that contains the requested page.
- If the page is in $Ti1$ or $Ti2$, the size of lists is good and no need to change it.
- If the page is in $Bi1$, the size of $Li1$ should be increased.
- If the page is in $Bi2$, the size of $Li2$ should be increased.
- If the page is not in the memory, the size of lists is good and no need to change it.

The detailed AMSQM algorithm in pseudo-code is written herein below:

Let us define:

C- The memory size.

ci - Physical size of the super (and base) pages buffers. $\Sigma\, c_i \leq C$.

si - Target size of each buffer.

Qi- Queue (FCFS) that saves demoted Super-Pages (or base-pages), which are a fraction of bigger Super-pages.

Ti1 - The most recent pages in the memory of every Super (or base) page, which were accessed only once.

Bi1 - The most recent pages in the history of every Super (or base) page, which were accessed only once.

Ti2 - The most recent pages in the memory of every Super (or base) page, which were accessed more than once.

Bi2 - The most recent pages in the history of every Super (or base page), which were accessed more than once.

Pi - Tunable parameter - the recommended size of Ti1.

sizei - Super-Page size in base pages.

boundi=$\beta\cdot$sizei/size1

count(x) - The number of times that Super-Page x was referenced.

ranki - Determines which queue removes an entry. ranki=$\alpha\cdot$difi+$(1-\alpha)\cdot$reci, where difi is the difference between si and ci; i. e. max(0, sizei$\cdot$(ci-si)) and reci is the relative recency of the LRU of Super-Page i among the LRU of the other Super-Pages.

threshold - threshold for promoting a partially occupied (candidate) super-page to a fully occupied super-page.

SP(xj) - The superpage which the base page xj belongs to. xj =SP(xj) iff xj does not belong to any super-page (a solitary base page).

ω(x) - The number of occupied base pages in super-page x.

α,β,γ - Parameters that should be set according to the data characteristic; where $0\leq\alpha\leq1$, $\beta\geq1$ and $0\leq\gamma\leq\frac{1}{2}$.

The algorithm AMSQM is:

AMSQM(c, Stream of base pages requests: $x_1,x_2,..,x_n$)

- $c_1=c_2=...=c_k=0$
- For each x_j
  - Call **HandleSuperPage**($x_j,| SP(x_j)|$)
  - If $\omega(SP(x_j))\geq threshold\cdot size_{|SP(xj)|}$
  - Promote $SP(x_j)$
- if the access type is "write", recursively demote $SP(x_j)$ to clean base/super pages and move them to the suitable Q lists.

HandleSuperPage(x_j,i)

- If $SP(x_j)$ is in T^i_1,
  - If x_j is valid
    - Move $SP(x_j)$ to be the MRU of T_2
  - Else
    - Fetch x_j to the cache.
    - Move $SP(x_j)$ to be the MRU of T_1
  - If (count($SP(x_j)$)= $bound_i$)
    - count($SP(x_j)$)=$\gamma\cdot bound_i$
  - Else
    - count($SP(x_j)$)= count($SP(x_j)$)+1
- If $SP(x_j)$ is in T^i_2 or Q_i
  - If x_j is invalid
    - Fetch x_j to the cache.
  - Move $SP(x_j)$ to be the MRU of T_2
  - count($SP(x_j)$)= count($SP(x_j)$)+1
- If $SP(x_j)$ is in B^i_1
  - If the size of B^i_1 is at least the size of B^i_2
    - $\delta=1$
  - Else
    - $\delta=|B^i_2|/|B^i_1|$
  - P_i=min(P_i +δ, c_i)
  - Call **Release** (x_j,i)
  - Fetch x_j to the cache.
  - Move $SP(x_j)$ to be the MRU of T_2
  - count($SP(x_j)$)= count($SP(x_j)$)+1
- If $SP(x_j)$ is in B^i_2
  - If the size of B^i_2 is at least the size of B^i_1

- $\delta=1$
  ○ Else
    - $\delta=|B^i_1|/|B^i_2|$
  ○ $P_i=\max(P_i-\delta,0)$
  ○ If count$(SP(x_j))\leq 2\cdot\gamma\cdot bound_i$
    - Call **Release** (x_j,i)
    - Fetch x_j to the cache.
    - Move $SP(x_j)$ to be the MRU of T_2
  ○ If count$(SP(x_j))>2\cdot\gamma\cdot bound_i$
    - If $0\leq C-\sum c_i<size_i$
    - Call **IncreaseBuffer** (x_j,i)
    - If we couldn't allocate a continuous space of $size_i$
    - Call **Release** (x_j,i)
    - Else
    - Call **Allocate** (x_j,i)
    - Count$(x_j)=\gamma\cdot bound_i$
    - $s_i=s_i+1$
- If $SP(x_j)$ is not in T^i_1, T^i_2, B^i_1 or B^i_2
  ○ If (i>1) and ($SP(x_j)$ has ever been in lists B^i_1 or B^i_2)
    - Call Demote (x_j,i)
  ○ o Else
    - If $0\leq C-\sum c_i<size_i$
    - If $(|Q_i|+|T^i_1|+|B^i_1|=c_i)$
    - If $(|Q_i|+|T^i_1|<c_i)$
    - Remove the LRU of B^i_1
    - Call **Release** (x_j,i)
    - Else
    - Remove the LRU among Q_i and T^i_1.
    - Else
    - If $(|Q_i|+|T^i_1|+|B^i_1|+|T^i_2|+|B^i_2|>c_i)$
    - If $\quad(|Q_i|+|T^i_1|+|B^i_1|+|T^i_2|+|B^i_2|=2\cdot c_i)$
    - Remove the LRU of B^i_2
    - Call **Release** (x_j,i)
    - Fetch x_j to the cache.
    - Move $SP(x_j)$ to be the MRU of T^i_1
    - Else
    - Call **Allocate** (x_j,i)

IncreaseBuffer (x_j,i)

- Do until $size_i$ base-pages are released:
  ○ r=max $rank_i$
  ○ Remove LRU among T_1, T_2 and Q_r
  ○ $c_r=c_r-1$
  ○ If $(c_r<s_r)$
    - $s_r=s_r-1$
- Call **Allocate** (x_j,i)

Release (x_j,i)

- If $((|T^i_1|>P_i)$ or $(|T^i_1|=P_i$ and x_j is in $B^i_2)$
  ○ Take the LRU page between the LRU of T^i_1 and the LRU of Q_i and put it as the MRU of B^i_1.
- Else
  ○ Take the LRU page between the LRU of T^i_2 and the LRU of Q_i and put it as the MRU of B^i_2.

Allocate (x_n,i)

- If there is a contiguous empty space of $size_i$ in the cache
  ○ Fetch x_j to the cache.
  ○ Move $SP(x_j)$ to be the MRU of T^i_2
  ○ $c_i=c_i+1$

Demote (x_n,i)

- Cancel $SP(x_j)$
- If(i>1)
  ○ $Dsize=size_{i-1}$
- Else
  ○ $Dsize=1$
- $free$=The biggest available continuous empty space of maximum $Dsize$.
- if $(free>0)$
  ○ o Create superpage x'$_j$ of size $free$ which must contain x_j
  ○ o Move x'$_j$ to the MRU of Q_{free}.
- Else
    - Call **Release**$(x_j,1)$.
    - Fetch x_j to the cache.
    - move x_j to the MRU of Q_1.

EVALUATION AND RESULTS

Actually, the best way to evaluate the AMSQM page replacement algorithm is by considering its performance results. In the following subsections, an extensive evaluation that has been made to the medium term scheduler is described.

Testbed and Benchmarking

We implemented the standard CLOCK algorithm, the ARC algorithm and the AMSQM algorithm. We used Valgrind (Nethercote and Seward, 2007) to capture the pages that were used by some of the SPEC–cpu2000 (SPEC, 2000). The SPEC manual explicitly notes that attempting to run the suite with less than 256Mbytes of memory will cause a measuring of the paging system speed instead of the CPU speed. This suits us well, because our aim is precisely to measure the paging system speed; hence, we simulated a machine with just 128MB of RAM, although it is obviously a very small memory.

The sizes of the Super-pages that we used were 8 KB, 16 KB, 32 KB, 64 KB, 128 KB and 256 KB. We assumed a tagged TLB of 32 entries for instructions and 64 entries for data.

Both AMSQM and ARC outperform CLOCK by all the parameters in our simulation, so we found no point in presenting the results of CLOCK; therefore, the results presented here are only the ratio between strict ARC and AMSQM.

Let us define:

n - Number of memory requests by the benchmark.
p - Number of pages that the benchmark accesses.
tmARC - Number of TLB misses when ARC is the replacement algorithm.
tmAMSQM - Number of TLB misses when AMSQM is the replacement algorithm.
pfARC - Number of the benchmark's page faults when ARC is the replacement algorithm.
pfAMSQM - Number of the benchmark's page faults when AMSQM is the replacement algorithm.

$$tm\_ratio=1-((tmAMSQM-p)/(tmARC-p))$$

$$pf\_ratio=1-((pfAMSQM-p)/(pfARC-p))$$

The TLB misses are shown as the ratio between the TLB misses that AMSQM produces and the TLB misses that ARC produces. When a page is accessed at the first time, any algorithm will have to induce a TLB miss and obviously there is no way to eliminate this TLB miss, so we calculated only the TLB misses of the pages just from the second time they are accessed. The page faults are shown also as the ratio between the page faults that AMSQM produces and the page faults that ARC produces counting for each page only the second and further accesses.

tm_ratio and pf_ratio are the values that represent the calculation of the TLB miss ratio and the page fault ratio respectively.

Benchmarking Using Spec-2000

Figure 1 and Figure 2 show the extra overhead of ARC over AMSQM. Figure 1 shows the tm_ratio of several selected SPEC2000 benchmarks whereas Figure 2 shows the pf_ratio of the same SPEC2000 benchmarks. It can be clearly seen in Figure 1 that AMSQM achieves a higher TLB ratio, because of the super-pages usage.

Furthermore, AMSQM memory hit ratio is also higher than ARC memory hit ratio in most of the benchmarks as can be noticed in Figure 2. The improvement of the memory hit ratio is because AMSQM takes advantage of the locality principle as is mentioned above in the introduction section. The other SPEC benchmarks show similar results, so we do not include these benchmarks in this paper.

The Threshold Setting Considerations

Figure 3 and Figure 4 show the influence of threshold on the system performance. Too high threshold harms the TLB hit ratio, whereas too low threshold harms the page fault ratio; hence, it

Figure 1. The TLB miss reduction of AMSQM

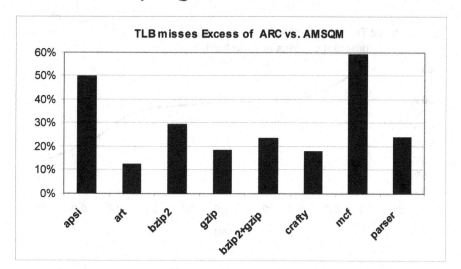

can be concluded from Figure 3 and Figure 4 that the best balance of the TLB ratio requirements and the page faults requirements is setting threshold to 0.5. On one hand choosing a threshold less than 0.5 will yield a good TLB miss ratio, but on the other hand choosing a threshold more than 0.5 will yield a good page fault ratio. Setting threshold to exactly 0.5 will produce a reasonable result for both the TLB ratio and the page fault ratio.

We also tested the running of both of the algorithms using the subroutine "clock()" in "time.h"

of GNU C compiler. We found the results quite similar, so we do not include these results in this paper as well.

The βEta Setting Considerations

According to experiments, we found that AMSQM gives the best results if its parameters are set to the following values:

- $\alpha = 0.5$

Figure 2. The page fault reduction of AMSQM

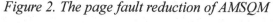

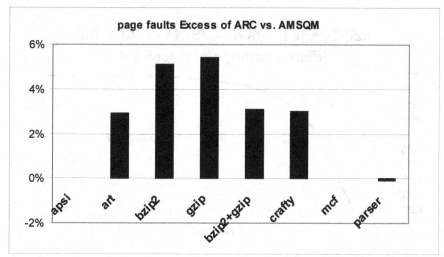

Figure 3. The influence of threshold on TLB misses

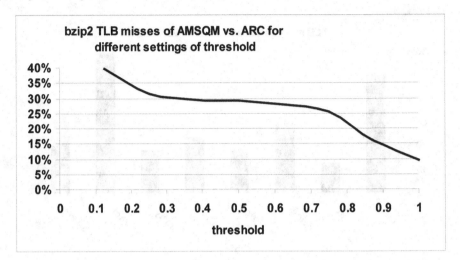

- β=4
- γ=0.25

Figure 5 and Figure 6 show the effect of different β values on the TLB miss ratio and the number of Page faults. It can be clearly concluded from these figures that setting β to 4 gives the best performance in terms of TLB hit ratio and the number of page faults. It can be noticed as well that setting β with low values, or alternatively with big values causes a poorer performance of the algorithm. Similar tests were taken to determine the best value of α and γ. The conclusion was that the best value for α is 0.5 and the best value for γ is 0.25.

Heavy Memory Consuming Benchmarks

As we have mentioned above, during last years the TLB size has been increased slowly comparing to the memory increasing rate; hence the TLB coverage has been dramatically reduced. We find it very commonsensical to assume that in the

Figure 4. influence of threshold on page faults

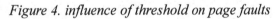

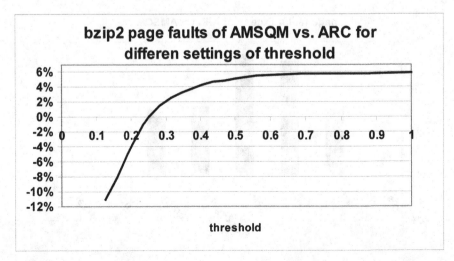

Figure 5. The influence of Beta on TLB miss ratio

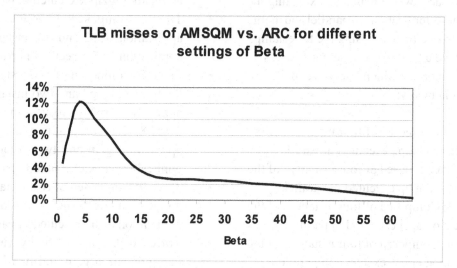

coming years the ratio between the memory size and the TLB size will be even smaller than the current ratio.

It is very uncommon to publish nowadays a new memory management technique or system that is not tested by a heavy workload benchmarking system (Hristea et al., 1997), because the future anticipates a significant increase in the memory usage of the applications; hence we also checked the heavy memory workload scenario.

With the aim of simulated this scenario, we modeled a machine with a TLB coverage that is even smaller than the one we have simulated above. For this purpose, we simulated a machine with 512 MB of RAM and a tagged TLB consists of 32 entries for instructions and 64 entries for data.

Consequently, we had to create new benchmarks that will request for many pages that a machine with 512 MB of RAM cannot handle without causing a thrashing. With the purpose of overloading the memory, we have chosen the heaviest memory consuming benchmarks among the SPEC-CPU2000 benchmarks. The applications which were selected are: apsi, crafty, bzip2 and gzip.

Figure 6. The influence of Beta on Page faults

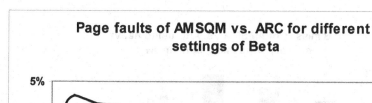

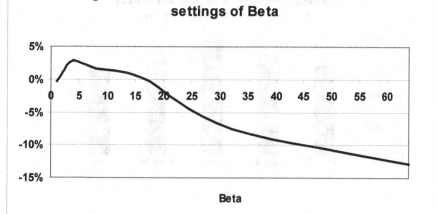

The new traces were created by executing instances of these applications in parallel and merging them into one trace by using the timestamps which we have added to each memory access.

The benchmarks which we have built are defined herein below:

- Trace 1: Composed of four instances of the application bzip2 executed in parallel.
- Trace 2: Composed of four instances of the application gzip executed in parallel.
- Trace 3: Composed of four instances of the application apsi executed in parallel.
- Trace 4: Composed of four instances of the application crafty executed in parallel.
- Trace 5: Composed of two instances of the application bzip2 and two instances of the

application gzip, executed in parallel.
- Trace 6: Composed of two instances of the application bzip2 and two instances of the application apsi, executed in parallel.
- Trace 7: Composed of two instances of the application bzip2 and two instances of the application crafty, executed in parallel.
- Trace 8: Composed of two instances of the application gzip and two instances of the application apsi, executed in parallel.
- Trace 9: Composed of two instances of the application crafty and two instances of the application apsi, executed in parallel.
- Trace 10: Composed of two instances of the application gzip and two instances of the application crafty, executed in parallel.
- Trace 11: Composed of the instances of

Figure 7. a. First group of heavy traces TLB misses; b. Second group of heavy traces TLB misses

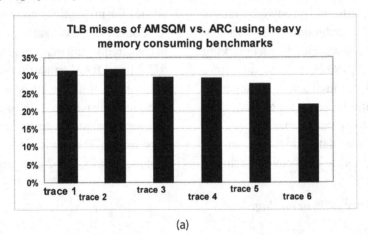

(a)

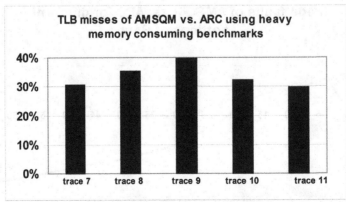

(b)

apsi, crafty, bzip2 and gzip, executed in parallel.

Figures 7a and 7b show the TLB miss ratio of AMSQM vs. ARC. It can be easily seen that AMSQM TLB misses are significantly fewer than ARC TLB misses. It can be noticed that trace 2 achieves a higher TLB hit ratio comparing to strict gzip. This can be explained as a result of the TLB coverage in this experiment which is significantly smaller than the TLB coverage in the previous experiment; thus a base page replacing algorithm such as ARC will experience enormous number of TLB misses, whereas an algorithm such AMSQM that utilizes wisely the Super-paging mechanism will gain a higher TLB coverage and hence will produce relatively less TLB misses comparing to

ARC. The significant improvement in the TLB ratio of AMSQM comparing to ARC can be similarly explained in the other traces.

Figures 8a and 8b show the page faults of AMSQM vs. to ARC. It can be clearly seen that AMSQM achieves a higher memory hit ratio in all the benchmarks, because of a good utilization of superpages and based on the locality principle. However, the improvements vary from 0.2% for trace 4 up to 10.4% for trace 1. We found out that ARC performs efficiently in trace 4 (and trace 3) i.e. does not produce many page faults, because there is enough space in the main memory, and therefore AMSQM's improvement is relatively small.

Yet, we found it very encouraging that for an extreme heavy memory consumer benchmarks

Figure 8. a. First group of heavy traces page faults; 8b. Second group of heavy traces page faults

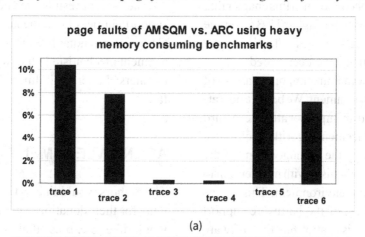

(a)

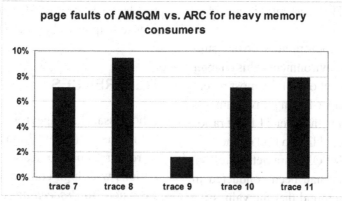

(b)

(such as: trace 1, trace 2, trace 5, trace 6, trace 7, trace 8 and trace 11), AMSQM achieves a notably higher memory hit ratio, since contemporary applications require a big portion of the memory and reducing the number of the page faults in such applications can significantly improve the overall performance.

CONCLUSION AND FUTURE WORK

In conclusion, there is a need for a faster and more suitable page replacement algorithm. AMSQM seems to meet this need. The speed and super-paging suitability offered by AMSQM will help page replacement algorithm avoid being a performance bottleneck in computer systems for years to come. AMSQM is an innovative adaptive page replacement algorithm for Super-paging environment. It has been shown in this chapter that AMSQM usually achieves a higher TLB coverage than ARC and also a better page fault ratio in most of the benchmarks that have been tested.

This chapter shows another important aspect of the Super-Paging environment. We believe operating systems have had an improper attitude toward the Super-Page replacement algorithm selection. They usually just copy the old algorithms of the traditional paging mechanism with no attention to the new Super-Paging environment. This brings about an improvement of the hardware support for a smaller TLB miss ratio, but the software support for a smaller TLB miss ratio is considerably poorer.

So as to achieve an appropriate software support for Super-Paging environments, this chapter has shown a way to adapt one of the most recent algorithms to these Super-Paging environments with the aim of obtaining a better TLB hit ratio.

In the future we would like to find methods to dynamically set the AMSQM parameters (α, β, γ). In the experiments that had been conducted in this research, we have found that the values we used for these parameters are the best for most of benchmarks; however, there is a very few

benchmarks that have a preference of other values and there are also a small number of benchmarks that will have a preference of adaptively modified values. Therefore, we believe that adaptively modified values can improve the performance of several benchmarks. Another issue that should be addressed as well is the mutual influence of the processes scheduled together (Wiseman and Feitelson, 2003).

In addition, we would like to find a pattern for super-pages reoccurrence. Such a pattern can improve the efficiency of the super-page promotion decisions. The traditional threshold parameter seems to be insufficient for taking the most beneficial decision. Some applications like (Wiseman et al., 2004), (Wiseman, 2001), (Wiseman and Klein, 2003) have a pattern of supper-pages reoccurrence and the Operating System can take an advantage of it.

The current results are encouraging and they support our belief that the new page replacement algorithm can notably enhance the memory management mechanism in the two above mentioned manners: better TLB hit ratio and fewer page faults.

ACKNOWLEDGMENT

The authors would like to thank SUN Microsystems for their donation. Specifically, the authors would like to express their sincere thankfulness to Mr. Yosi Harel of SUN and Mr. Haim Zadok whose help was above and beyond.

REFERENCES

Abouaissa, H., Delpeyroux, E., Wack, M., & Deschizeaux, P. (1999). Modelling and integration of resource communication in multimedia applications with high constraints using hierarchical Petri nets. In *Proceedings of IEEE International Conference on Systems, Man, and Cybernetics (SMC-99)*, (Vol. 5, pp. 220-225), Tokyo, Japan.

Corbato, A. (1968). *Paging Experiment with the Multics System*. MIT Project MAC Report, MAC-M-384.

Fang, Z., Zhang, L., Carter, J., McKee, S., & Hsieh, W. (2001). Re-evaluating Online Superpage Promotion with Hardware Support. In *Proceedings of the Seventh International Symposium on High Performance Computer Architecture*, (pp. 63-72).

Friedman, M. B. (1999). Windows NT Page Replacement Policies. In *Proceedings of 25th International Computer Measurement Group Conference*, (pp. 234-244).

Geppert, L. (2003). The New Indelible Memories. *IEEE Spectrum*, *40*(3), 48–54. doi:10.1109/MSPEC.2003.1184436

Hristea, C., Lenoski, D., & Keen, J. (1997). Measuring Memory Hierarchy Performance of Cache-Coherent Multiprocessors Using Micro Benchmarks. In *Supercomputing, ACM/IEEE 1997 Conference*, (p.45).

Itshak, M., & Wiseman, Y. (2008). AMSQM: Adaptive Multiple SuperPage Queue Management. In *Proc. IEEE Conference on Information Reuse and Integration (IEEE IRI-2008)*, Las Vegas, Nevada.

Itshak, M., & Wiseman, Y. (2009). AMSQM: Adaptive Multiple SuperPage Queue Management. *International Journal of Information and Decision Sciences (IJIDS)*, (Special issue on the best papers of IEEE Conference on Information Reuse and Integration (IEEE IRI), 2009).

Jiang, S., Chen, F., & Zhang, X. (2005). CLOCK-Pro: an Effective Improvement of the CLOCK Replacement. In *Proceedings of 2005 USENIX Annual Technical Conference*, (pp. 323-336), Anaheim, CA.

Jiang, S., & Zhang, X. (2002). LIRS: An Efficient Low Inter-reference Recency Set Replacement Policy to Improve Buffer Cache Performance. In *Proceeding of 2002 ACM SIGMETRICS*, Marina Del Rey, California, (pp. 31-42).

Johnson, T., & Shasha, D. (1994). 2Q: a low overhead high performance buffer management replacement algorithm. In *Proceedings of the Twentieth International Conference on Very Large Databases, VLDB' 94*, Santiago, Chile, (pp. 439-450).

Khalidi, Y. A., Talluri, M., Nelson, M. N., & Williams, D. (1993). Virtual memory support for multiple page sizes. In *Proceedings of the Fourth IEEE Workshop on Workstation Operating Systems*, Napa, CA, October.

Kim, J., Choi, J., Kim, J., Noh, S., Min, S., Cho, Y., & Kim, C. (2000). A Low-Overhead, High-Performance Unified Buffer Management Scheme that Exploits Sequential and Looping References. In *4th Symposium on Operating System Design and Implementation*, San Diego, California, (pp. 119-134).

Klein, S. T., & Wiseman, Y. (2003). Parallel Huffman Decoding with Applications to JPEG Files. *The Computer Journal*, *46*(5), 487–497. doi:10.1093/comjnl/46.5.487

Lee, D., Choi, J., Kim, J.-H., Noh, S. H., Min, S. L., Cho, Y., & Kim, C. S. (2001). LRFU: A spectrum of policies that subsumes the least recently used and least frequently used policies. *IEEE Transactions on Computers*, *50*(12), 1352–1360. doi:10.1109/TC.2001.970573

Lowe, E. (2005). *Automatic Large page selection policy*. Retrieved from http://www.opensolaris.org/os/project/muskoka/virtual_memory/policy_v1.1.pdf.

Megiddo, N., & Modha, D. S. (2003). ARC: A Self-Tuning, Low Overhead Replacement Cache. In *Proc. of the 2nd USENIX Conference on File and Storage Technologies (FAST'2003)*, San Francisco, (pp. 115-130).

Megiddo, N., & Modha, D. S. (2003). One Up on LRU;login. *The Magazine of the USENIX Association*, 28(4), 7–11.

Megiddo, N., & Modha, D. S. (2004). Outperforming LRU with an Adaptive Replacement Cache Algorithm. *IEEE Computer*, (pp. 4-11).

Navarro, J. (2004). *Transparent operating system support for superpages*, Ph.D. Thesis, Department of Computer Science, Rice University.

Navarro, J., Iyer, S., Druschel, P., & Cox, A. (2002). *Practical, Transparent Operating System Support for Superpages*. Fifth Symposium on Operating Systems Design and Implementation (OSDI '02), Boston, USA. Ganapathy, N. & Schimmel, C. (1998). General purpose operating system support for multiple page sizes. In *Proceedings of the USENIX Annual Technical Conference*, New Orleans.

Nethercote, N., & Seward, J. (2007). Valgrind: A Framework for Heavyweight Dynamic Binary Instrumentation. In *Proceedings of ACM SIGPLAN 2007 Conference on Programming Language Design and Implementation (PLDI 2007)*, San Diego, CA.

Nicola, V. F., Dan, A., & Diaz, D. M. (1992). Analysis of the generalized clock buffer replacement scheme for database transaction processing. *ACM SIGMETRICS Performance Evaluation Review*, 20(1), 35–46. doi:10.1145/149439.133084

O'Neil, E., O'Neil, P., & Weikum, G. (1993). *The LRU-K Page Replacement Algorithm for Database Disk Buffering*. Proceedings of SIGMOD '93, Washington, DC.

Romer, T. H., Ohllrich, W. H., Karlin, A. R., & Bershad, B. N. (1995). Reducing TLB and memory overhead using online superpage promotion. In *Proceedings of the 22nd International Symposium on Computer Architecture* (ISCA), (pp. 87-176), Santa Margherita Ligure, Italy.

Smaragdakis, Y., Kaplan, S., & Wilson, P. (2003). The EELRU adaptive replacement algorithm. *Performance Evaluation (Elsevier)*, 53(2), 93–123. doi:10.1016/S0166-5316(02)00226-2

SPEC. (2000). *CPU-2000*. Warrenton, VA: Standard Performance Evaluation Corporation. Retrieved from http://www.spec.org/.

Subramanian, M. C., Peterson, K. & Raghunath, B. (1998). *Implementation of multiple pagesize support in HP-UX*. Proceedings of the USENIX Annual Technical Conference, New Orleans.

Talluri, M., & Hill, M. D. (1994). *Surpassing the TLB Performance of Superpages with Less Operating System Support*. Sixth International Symposium on Architectural Support for Programming Languages and Operating Systems (ASPLOS), San Jose, CA, (pp. 171-182).

Wallace, R. F., Norman, R. D. & Harari, E. (2006). *Computer memory cards using flash EEPROM integrated circuit chips and memory-controller systems*. [US Patent no. 7106609].

Wang, J. (2008). Improving Decision-Making Practices Through Information Filtering. [IJIDS]. *International Journal of Information and Decision Sciences*, 1(1), 1–4.

Weinand (2006). *A survey of large page support*. Retrieved from http://www.gelato.unsw.edu.au/~ianw/litreview/report.pdf, 2006.

Winwood, S., Shuf, Y., & Franke, H. (2002, June). *Multiple Page Size Support in the Linux Kernel*, Ottawa Linux Symposium, Ottawa, Canada.

Wiseman, Y. (2001). A Pipeline Chip for Quasi Arithmetic Coding. *IEICE Journal - Trans. Fundamentals, Tokyo, Japan . E (Norwalk, Conn.)*, *84-A*(4), 1034–1041.

Wiseman, Y. (2005). ARC Based SuperPaging. *Operating Systems Review*, *39*(2), 74–78. doi:10.1145/1055218.1055225

Wiseman, Y., & Feitelson, D. G. (2003). Paired Gang Scheduling. *IEEE Transactions on Parallel and Distributed Systems*, *14*(6), 581–592. doi:10.1109/TPDS.2003.1206505

Wiseman, Y., Schwan, K., & Widener, P. (2004). Efficient End to End Data Exchange Using Configurable Compression. In *Proc. The 24th IEEE Conference on Distributed Computing Systems (ICDCS 2004)*, Tokyo, Japan, (pp. 228-235).

Zhou, Y., Chen, Z., & Li, K. (2004). Second-Level Buffer Cache Management. [TPDS]. *IEEE Transactions on Parallel and Distributed Systems*, *15*(7), 505–519. doi:10.1109/TPDS.2004.13

Compilation of References

Abouaissa, H., Delpeyroux, E., Wack, M., & Deschizeaux, P. (1999). Modelling and integration of resource communication in multimedia applications with high constraints using hierarchical Petri nets. In *Proceedings of IEEE International Conference on Systems, Man, and Cybernetics (SMC-99)*, (Vol. 5, pp. 220-225), Tokyo, Japan.

Abrossimov, V., Rozier, M., & Shapiro, M. (1989). Virtual Memory Management for Operating System Kernels. In *Proceedings of the 12th ACM Symposium on Operating Systems Principles*, Litchfield Park, AZ, December 3-6, (pp. 123-126). New-York: ACM SIGOPS.

Acharya, S., & Muthukrishnan, S. (1998). Scheduling on-demand broadcasts: New metrics and algorithms. In *Proceedings of the International Conference on Mobile Computing and Networking*, Dallas, Texas, USA.

Acharya, S., Alonso, R., et al. (1995). Broadcast disks: Data management for asymmetric communication environments. In *Proceedings of the ACM SIGMOD International Conference on Management of Data*.

Acharya, S., Franklin, M. J., et al. (1995). Dissemination-based data delivery using broadcast disks. IEEE *Personal Communications, 2*(6), 50-60.

Acharya, S., Franklin, M. J., et al. (1996). Prefetching from broadcast disks. In *Proceedings of the International Conference on Data Engineering*.

Acharya, S., Franklin, M. J., et al. (1997). Balancing push and pull for data broadcast. In *Proceedings of the ACM SIGMOD International Conference on Management of Data*.

Aksoy, D., & Franklin, M. J. (1998). Scheduling for large-scale on-demand data broadcasting. In *Proceedings of the IEEE Conference on Computer Communications*.

Albers, S., & Mitzenmacher, M. (2000). Average-Case Analyses of First Fit and Random Fit Bin Packing. *Random Structures Alg., 16*, 240–259. doi:10.1002/(SICI)1098-2418(200005)16:3<240::AID-RSA2>3.0.CO;2-V

Alderson, A., Lynch, W. C., & Randell, B. (1972). *Thrashing in a Multiprogrammed System. Operating Systems Techniques*. London: Academic Press.

Altinel, M., Aksoy, D., et al. (1999). DBIS-toolkit: Adaptable middleware for large scale data delivery. In *Proceedings of the ACM SIGMOD International Conference on Management of Data*, Philadelphia, Pennsylvania, USA.

Alverson, G., Kahan, S., Korry, R., McCann, C., & Smith, B. (1995). Scheduling on the Tera MTA. In *Proceedings of the 1st Workshop on Job Scheduling Strategies for Parallel Processing, In Conjunction with IPPS '95* Fess Parker's Red Lion Resort, Santa Barbara, California, April 25, (pp. 19-44). Berlin: Springer-Verlag.

Analysis of the Linux kernel (2004). San Francisco, CA: Coverity Corporation.

Anti rootkit software, news, articles and forums. *(n.d.)* *Retrieved from* http://antirootkit.com/.

Anzinger, G., & Gamble, N. (2000). *Design of a Fully Preemptable Linux Kernel*. MontaVista Software.

Arnold, J. B. (2008). *Ksplice: An automatic system for rebootless linux kernel security updates*. Retrieved from http://web.mit.edu/ksplice/doc/ksplice.pdf.

Arnold, M., & Ryder, B. G. (2001). A framework for reducing the cost of instrumented code. In *Proceedings of the SIGPLAN Conference on Programming Language Design and Implementation*, (pp. 168-179).

Arpaci-Dusseau, R. H., Arpaci-Dusseau, N. C., Burnett, T. E., Denehy, T. J., Engle, H. S., Gunawi, J., & Nugent, F. I. Popovici. (2003). *Transforming Policies into Mechanisms with Infokernel*. 19th ACM Symposium on Operating Systems Principles.

Artho, C., & Biere, A. (2005). Combined static and dynamic analysis. In *Proceedings of the 1st International Workshop on Abstract Interpretation of Object-oriented Language (AIOOL 2005)*, ENTCS, Paris. Elsevier Science Publishing.

Bacic, E. M. (n.d.). UNIX & Security. Canadian System Security Centre, Communications Security Establishment. Retrieved January 7, 2005 from http://andercheran. aiind.upv.es/toni/unix/Unix_and_Security.ps.gz

Baliga, A. (2009). *Automated Detection and Containment of Stealth Attacks on the Operating System Kernel*. Ph. D Thesis, Department of Computer Science, Rutgers University.

Baliga, A., Ganapathy, V., & Iftode, L. (2008). Automatic Inference and Enforcement of Kernel Data Structure Invariants. In *Proceedings of the 2008 Annual Computer Security and Applications Conference*, Anaheim, CA.

Baliga, A., Iftode, L., & Chen, X. (2008). Automated Containment of Rootkit Attacks. *Elsevier Journal on Computers and Security*, 27(Nov), 323–334.

Baliga, A., Kamat, P., & Iftode, L. (2007). Lurking in the shadows: Identifying systemic threats to kernel data. In *Proceedings of the 2007 IEEE Symposium on Security and Privacy*, Oakland, CA.

Baratloo, A., Tsai, T., & Singh, N. (2000). Transparent Run-Time Defense Against Stack Smashing Attacks. In *Proceedings of the USENIX annual Technical Conference*.

Barham, P., Dragovic, B., Fraser, K., Hand, S., Harris, T., Ho, A., et al. (2003). Xen and the art of virtualization. In *Proceedings of the 19th ACM Symposium on Operating Systems Principles*.

Batat, A., & Feitelson, D. G. (2000). Gang scheduling with memory considerations. In *Proceedings of the 14th International Parallel and Distributed Processing Symposium (IPDPS'2000)*, Cancun, Mexico, May 1-5, (pp. 109-114). Los Alamitos, CA: IEEE.

Bates, R. (2004). Buffer overrun madness. *ACM Queue*, 2(3).

Baxter, I. (2004). DMS: Program transformations for practical scalable software evolution. In *Proceedings of the 26th International Conference on Software Engineering*, (pp. 625-634).

Beck, M., Bohme, H., Dziadzka, M., Kunitz, U., Magnus, R., & Verworner, D. (1998). *Linux Kernel Internals* (2nd Ed.). Harlow, MA: Addison Wesley, Longman

Belady, L. A. (1966). A Study of Replacement Algorithms for Virtual Storage Computers. *IBM Systems Journal*, 5(2), 78–101.

Benchmark, B. E. N. C. H.-M. A. T. L. A. B. (2004). *Matlab Performance Tests*. Natick, MA: The MathWorks, Inc. Retrieved from http://www.mathworks.com/

Bershad, B. N., Chambers, C., Eggers, S., Maeda, C., McNamee, D., & Pardyak, P. et al (1995). SPIN - An Extensible Microkernel for Application-specific Operating System Services. *ACM Operating Systems Review*, 29(1).

Bhattacharya, S., Tran, J., Sullivan, M., & Mason, C. (2004). Linux AIO Performance and Robustness for Enterprise Workloads. In . *Proceedings of the Linux Symposium*, 1, 63–78.

Binder, W. (2005). A portable and customizable profiling framework for Java based on bytecode instruction counting. In *Proceedings of the Third Asian Symposium on Programming Languages and Systems (APLAS 2005)*, (LNCS 3780, pp. 178-194).

Binder, W., & Hulaas, J. (2004, October). A portable CPU-management framework for Java. *IEEE Internet Computing*, 8(5), 74-83.

Binder, W., Hulaas J., &Villaz A. (2001). Portable resource control in Java. In *Proceedings of the 2001 ACM SIGPLAN Conference on Object Oriented Programming, Systems, Languages and Applications*, (Vol. 36, No. 11, pp. 139-155).

Black, D., Carter, J., Feinberg, G., MacDonald, R., Mangalat, S., Sheinbrood, E., et al. (1991). *OSF/1 Virtual Memory Improvements*. USENIX Mac Symposium.

Boner, J. (2004, March). AspectWerkz—Dynamic AOP for Java. In *Proceedings of the 3rd International Conference on Aspect-oriented development (AOSD 2004)*. Lancaster, UK.

Borland Software Corporation. (2006). *Borland Optimize-it Enterprise Suite* (Computer software). Retrieved March 11, 2008, from http://www.borland.com/us/products/optimizeit/index.html

Bovet, D., & Cesati, M. (2003). *Undersatnding the Linux Kernel*, (2nd Ed.). Sebastopol, CA: O'Reilly Press.

Broberg, M., Lundberg, L., & Grahn, H. (1999, April). Visualization and performance prediction of multi-threaded solaris programs by tracing kernel threads. In *Proceedings of the 13th International Parallel Processing Symposium*, (pp. 407-413).

Brose, G. (1997, September). JacORB: Implementation and design of a Java ORB. In *Proceedings of IFIP DAIS'97*, (pp. 143-154).

Brown, A. D., Mowry, T. C., & Krieger, O. (2001). Compiler-based i/o prefetching for out-of-core applications. *ACM Transactions on Computer Systems*, *19*, 111–170. doi:10.1145/377769.377774

Bruening, D. L. (2004). *Efficient, transparent, and comprehensive runtime code manipulation*. Unpublished doctoral dissertation, Massachusetts Institute of Technology.

Bryant, R. E., & O'Hallaron, D. R. (2003). Computer Systems: A Programmer's Perspective. Prentice Hall, pp.294.

Buck, B., & Hollingsworth, J. K. (2000). An API for runtime code patching. *International Journal of High Performance Computing Applications*, 317-329.

Butler, J. (2005). Fu rootkit. http://www.rootkit.com/project.php?id=12.

Butt, A. R., Gniady, C., & Hu, Y. C. (2007). The Performance Impact of Kernel Prefetching on Buffer Cache Replacement Algorithms. *IEEE Transactions on Computers*, *56*(7), 889–908. doi:10.1109/TC.2007.1029

Cantrill, B., & Doeppner, T. W. (1997, January). Threadmon: A tool for monitoring multithreaded program performance. In *Proceedings of the 30th Hawaii International Conference on Systems Sciences*, (pp. 253-265).

Cao, G. (2002). Proactive power-aware cache management for mobile computing systems. *IEEE Transactions on Computers, 51*(6), 608-621.

Cao, P., & Irani, S. (1997). *Cost-Aware WWW Proxy Caching Algorithms*. USENIX Annual Technical Conference.

Cao, P., Felten, E. W., Karlin, A. R., & Li, K. (1995). A study of integrated prefetching and caching strategies. In *Proceedings of the 1995 ACM SIGMETRICS joint international conference on Measurement and modeling of computer systems*, (pp. 188-197).

Cao, P., Felten, E. W., Karlin, A. R., & Li, K. (1996). Implementation and performance of integrated application-controlled file caching, prefetching, and disk scheduling. *ACM Transactions on Computer Systems*, *14*, 311–343. doi:10.1145/235543.235544

Card, R., Dumas, E., & Mevel, F. (1998). *The Linux Kernel Book*. New York: John Wiley & Sons.

CERT1 (2004). CERT, [Data File]. Accessed on December 20, 2004 from http://www.cert.org/cert_stats.html

CERT2 (2003). Incident note IN-2001-09, Code Red II: Another worm exploiting buffer overflow In IIS indexing service DLL. Retrieved on December 20, 2004 from http://www.cert.org/incident_notes/IN-2001-09.html

CERT3 (2005). CERT Vulnerability Note VU#596387, Icecast vulnerable to buffer overflow via long GET request. US-CERT Vulnerability Notes Database. Retrieved on January 4, 2005 from http://www.kb.cert.org/vuls/id/596387

Chen, B. (2000). *Multiprocessing with the Exokernel Operating System*. Unpublished.

Chen, H., Chen, R., Zhang, F., Zang, B., & Yew, P.-C. (2006). Live updating operating systems using virtualization. *Proceedings of the 2nd international conference on Virtual execution environments,* Ottawa, Canada.

Chou, A., Yang, J. F., Chelf, B., Hallem, S., & Engler, D. (2001). An Empirical Study of Operating Systems Errors. In *Proceedings of the 18th ACM, Symposium on Operating System Principals (SOSP)*, (pp. 73-88), Lake Louise, Alta. Canada.

Chow, C.-Y., Leong, H. V., et al. (2004). Group-based cooperative cache management for mobile clients in a mobile environment. In *Proceedings of the International Conference on Parallel Processing (ICPP)*.

Chow, C.-Y., Leong, H. V., et al. (2005). Distributed group-based cooperative caching in a mobile broadcast environment. In *Proceedings of the International Conference on Mobile Data Management.*

Chu, Y., & Ito, M. R. (2000). The 2-way Thrashing-Avoidance Cache (TAC): An Efficient Instruction Cache Scheme for Object-Oriented Languages. In *Proceedings of 17th IEEE International Conference on Computer Design (ICCD2000)*, Austin, Texas, September 17-20, (pp. 93-98). Los Alamitos, CA: IEEE.

Clarke, E. M., Grumberg, O., & Peled, D. A. (2000). *Model checking. Massachusetts Institute of Technology*. Cambridge, MA: The MIT Press.

Clauss, P., Kenmei, B., & Beyler, J.C. (2005, September). The periodic-linear model of program behavior capture. In *Proceedings of Euro-Par 2005* (LNCS 3648, pp. 325-335).

Coffman, E. G. Jr., & Ryan, T. A. (1972). A Study of Storage Partitioning Using a Mathematical Model of Locality. *Communications of the ACM, 15*(3), 185–190. doi:10.1145/361268.361280

Coffman, E. G., Jr., Garey, M. R., & Johnson, D. S. (1997). Approximation Algorithms for Bin Packing: A Survey. In D. Hochbaum (ed.), *Approximation Algorithms for NP-Hard Problems,* (pp. 46-93). Boston: PWS Publishing.

Collins, R. (1997, September). In-circuit emulation: How the microprocessor evolved over time. *Dr. Dobbs Journal*. Retrieved March 11, 2008, from http://www.rcollins.org/ddj/Sep97

Corbato, A. (1968). *Paging Experiment with the Multics System*. MIT Project MAC Report, MAC-M-384.

Cordy, R., Halpern C., & Promislow, E. (1991). TXL: A rapid prototyping system for programming language dialects. In *Proceedings of the International Conference on Computer Languages* (Vol. 16, No. 1, pp. 97-107).

Corporation, H. P. (1995). *HP-UX 10.0*. Memory Management White Paper.

Cowan, C., Pu, C., Maier, D., Hinton, H., Walpole, J., Bakke, P., et al. (1998). StackGuard: Automatic Adaptive Detection and Prevention of Buffer-Overflow Attacks. In *Proceedings of the 7th USENIX Security Conference,* San Antonio, TX.

Dandekar, H., Purtell, A., & Schwab, S. (2002). AMP: Experiences with Building and Exokernel-based Platform for Active Networking. In *Proceedings: DARPA Active Networks Conference and Exposition*, (pp. 77-91).

Dankwardt, K. (2001). *Real Time and Linux, Part 3: Sub-Kernels and Benchmarks*. Retrieved from

Davies, J., Huismans, N., Slaney, R., Whiting, S., & Webster, M. (2003). *An aspect-oriented performance analysis environment*. AOSD'03 Practitioner Report, 2003.

Denning, P. (1970). Virtual Memory. [CSUR]. *ACM Computing Surveys, 2*(3), 153–189. doi:10.1145/356571.356573

Denning, P. J. (1968). The Working Set Model for Program Behavior. *Communications of the ACM, 11*(5), 323–333. doi:10.1145/363095.363141

Denning, P. J. (1968). Thrashing: Its Causes and Prevention. In *Proceedings of AFIPS Conference*, (pp. 915-922).

Denning, P. J. (1970). Virtual Memory. *Computer Survey*, *2*(3), 153–189. doi:10.1145/356571.356573

Ding, X., Jiang, S., Chen, F., Davis, K., & Zhang, X. (2007). *DiskSeen: Exploiting Disk Layout and Access History to Enhance I/O Prefetch*. USENIX Annual Technical Conference.

Dini, G., Lettieri, G., & Lopriore, L. (2006). Caching and prefetching algorithms for programs with looping reference patterns. *The Computer Journal*, *49*, 42–61. doi:10.1093/comjnl/bxh140

Dmitriev, M. (2001). *Safe evolution of large and long-lived Java applications*. Unpublished doctoral dissertation, Department of Computing Science, University of Glasgow, Glasgow G12 8QQ, Scotland.

Dmitriev, M. (2001). Towards flexible and safe technology for runtime evolution of Java language applications. In *Proceedings of the Workshop on Engineering Complex Object-Oriented Systems for Evolution* (pp. 14-18). In Association with OOPSLA 2001 International Conference, Tampa Bay, FL, USA.

Dmitriev, M. (2002). Application of the HotSwap technology to advanced profiling. In *Proceedings of the First Workshop on Unanticipated Software Evolution*, held at ECOOP 2002 International Conference, Malaga, Spain.

Dmitriev, M. (2004). Profiling Java applications using code hotswapping and dynamic call graph revelation. In *Proceedings of the 4th International Workshop on Software and Performance*, Redwood Shores, CA, (pp. 139-150).

Draves, R. P., Bershad, B. N., Rashid, R. F., & Dean, R. W. (1991). Using continuations to implement thread management and communication in operating systems. In *Proceedings of the thirteenth ACM symposium on Operating systems principles*, Pacific Grove, CA, (pp. 122-136).

Druschel, P., Pai, V., & Zwaenepoel, W. (1997). Extensible Kernels and Leading the OS Research Astray. In *Operating Systems*, (pp. 38-42).

Ellard, D., & Seltzer, M. (2003). NFS Tricks and Benchmarking Traps. In *Proceedings of the FREENIX 2003 Technical Conference*, (pp. 101-114).

Ellard, D., Ledlie, J., Malkani, P., & Seltzer, M. (2003). Passive NFS Tracing of Email and Research Workloads. In *Proceedings of the Second USENIX Conference on File and Storage Technologies (FAST'03)*, (pp. 203-216).

Engler, D. R., Kaashoek, M. F., & O'Toole, J. (1995). Exokernel: an Operating System Architecture for Application-level Resource Management. In *15th ACM Symposium on Operating Systems Principles* (pp. 251-266).

Ernst, M. D., Perkins, J. H., Guo, P. J., McCamant, S., Pacheco, C., Tschantz, M. S., & Xiao, C. (2007). The Daikon system for dynamic detection of likely invariants. *Science of Computer Programming*, *69*.

Esfahbod, B. (2006). *Preload - An Adaptive Prefetching Daemon*. PhD thesis. Graduate Department of Computer Science, University of Toronto, Canada.

Etsion, Y., Tsafrir, D., & Feitelson, D. G. (2004). Desktop Scheduling: How Can We Know What the User Wants? In *Proceedings of the 14th ACM International Workshop on Network & Operating Systems Support for Digital Audio & Video (NOSSDAV'2004)*, Cork, Ireland, June 16-18, (pp. 110-115). New York: ACM.

Fang, Z., Zhang, L., Carter, J., McKee, S., & Hsieh, W. (2001). Re-evaluating Online Superpage Promotion with Hardware Support. In *Proceedings of the Seventh International Symposium on High Performance Computer Architecture*, (pp. 63-72).

Feiertag, R. J., & Organick, E. I. (1971). The multics input/output system. In *Proceedings of the third ACM symposium on Operating systems principles*, (pp. 35-41).

Fekete, S. P., & Schepers, J. (2001). New Classes of Fast Lower Bounds for Bin Packing Problems. *Mathematical Programming*, *91*(1), 11–31.

Fernandez, M., & Espasa, R. (1999). Dixie: A retargetable binary instrumentation tool. In *Proceedings of the Workshop on Binary Translation, held in conjunction with the International Conference on Parallel Architectures and Compilation Techniques.*

Franklin, M., & Zdonik, S. (1996). Dissemination-based information systems. *IEEE Data Engineering Bulletin, 19*(3), 20-30.

Frantzen, M., & Shuey, M. (2001). StackGhost: Hardware facilitated stack protection. In *Proceedings of the 10th conference on USENIX Security Symposium* – Washington, D.C. (Vol. 10, p. 5).

Fraser, K., Hand, S., Neugebauer, R., Pratt, I., Warfield, A., & Williamson, M. (2004). Safe hardware access with the Xen virtual machine monitor. In *Workshop on Operating System and Architectural Support for the On-Demand IT Infrastructure.*

Freund, S. N., & Qadeer, S. (2003). *Checking concise specifications of multithreaded software.* Technical Note 01-2002, Williams College.

Friedman, M. B. (1999). Windows NT Page Replacement Policies. In *Proceedings of 25th International Computer Measurement Group Conference,* (pp. 234-244).

Fuchs, P., & Pemmasani, G. (2005). *NdisWrapper.* Retrieved from http://ndiswrapper.sourceforge.net/

Galvin, P. B., & Silberschatz, A. (1998). *Operating System Concepts* (6th Ed.). Harlow, MA: Addison Wesley Longman.

Ganger, G., & Kaashoek, F. (1997). *Embedded Inodes and Explicit Groups: Exploiting Disk Bandwidth for Small Files.* USENIX Annual Technical Conference.

Ganger, G., Engler, D., Kaashoek, M. F., Briceño, H., Hunt, R., & Pinckney, T. (2002). Fast and Flexible Application-level Networking on Exokernel Systems. *ACM Transactions on Computer Science, 20*(1), 49–83. doi:10.1145/505452.505455

Garfinkel, T., & Rosenblum, M. (2003). A virtual machine introspection based architecture for intrusion detection. In *Proceedings of the Network and Distributed Systems Security Symposium,* San Diego, CA.

Gent, I. (1998). Heuristic Solution of Open Bin Packing Problems. *Journal of Heuristics, 3,* 299–304. doi:10.1023/A:1009678411503

Geppert, L. (2003). The New Indelible Memories. *IEEE Spectrum, 40*(3), 48–54. doi:10.1109/MSPEC.2003.1184436

Gifford, D. K. (1990). Polychannel systems for mass digital communications. *Communications of ACM, 33*(2), 141-151.

Gill, B. S., & Bathen, L. A. D. (2007). Optimal multistream sequential prefetching in a shared cache. *ACM Transactions on Storage, 3*(3), 10. doi:10.1145/1288783.1288789

Gill, B. S., & Modha, D. S. (2005). Sarc: sequential prefetching in adaptive replacement cache. *Proceedings of the USENIX Annual Technical Conference 2005 on USENIX Annual Technical Conference,* (pp. 33-33).

Gontla, P., Drury, H., & Stanley, K. (2003, May 2003). An introduction to OVATION—Object viewing and analysis tool for integrated object networks. *CORBA News Brief, Object Computing Inc.* [Electronic media]. Retrieved March 11, 2008, from http://www.ociweb.com/cnb/CORBANewsBrief-200305.html

Gonzalez, A., Valero, M., Topham, N., & Parcerisa, J. M. (1997). Eliminating Cache Conflict Misses through XOR-Based Placement Functions. In *Proceedings of the International Conference on Supercomputing,* Vienna, Austria, July 7-11, (pp. 76-83). New-York: ACM.

Gorman, M. (2004). *Understanding The Linux Virtual Memory Management* (Bruce Peren's Open Book Series).

Gorman, M. (2004). Understanding The Linux Virtual Memory Manager. Upper Saddle River, NJ: Prentice Hall, Bruce Perens' Open Source Series.

Gosling J. (1995, January 23). Java intermediate byte-codes. In *Proceedings of the ACM SIGPLAN Workshop on Intermediate Representations (IR'95).* (pp. 111-118), San Francisco, CA, USA.

Grassi, V. (2000). Prefetching policies for energy saving and latency reduction in a wireless broadcast data delivery system. In *Proceedings of the International Workshop on Modeling Analysis and Simulation of Wireless and Mobile Systems.*

Gray, J., & Shenoy, P. J. (2000). Rules of Thumb in Data Engineering. *Proceedings of International Conference on Data Engineering, 2000,* 3–12.

Greenhouse, A. (2003). *A programmer-oriented approach to safe concurrency.* Unpublished doctoral dissertation, Carnegie Mellon University School of Computer Science.

Grehan, R. (1995). *BYTEmark Native Mode Benchmark,* Release 2.0, [Computer software]. BYTE Magazine.

Griffioen, J., & Appleton, R. (1994). Reducing file system latency using a predictive approach. Proceedings of the USENIX Summer Conference, June 1994, pp. 197-208.

Grimm, R. (1996). *Exodisk: Maximizing Application Control Over Storage Management.* Unpublished.

Guo, Y., Pinotti, M. C., et al. (2001). A new hybrid broadcast scheduling algorithm for asymmetric communication systems. *SIGMOBILE Mobile Computing and Communications Review, 5*(3), 39-54.

Gutterman, Z., Pinkas, B., & Reinman, T. (2006). Analysis of the linux random number generator. In *Proceedings of the 2006 IEEE Symposium on Security and Privacy,* Oakland, CA.

Hameed, S. & Vaidya, N. H. (1997). Log-time algorithms for scheduling single and multiple channel data broadcast. In *Proceedings of the International Conference on Mobile Computing and Networking.*

Hand, S. Warfield, A. Fraser, K. Kotsovinos E. & Magenheimer, D. (2005). Are Virtual Machine Monitors Microkernels Done Right? In *Proceedings of the Tenth Workshop on Hot Topics in Operating Systems (HotOS-X),* June 12-15, Santa-Fe, NM.

Hara, T. (2002). Cooperative caching by mobile clients in push-based information systems. In *Proceedings of the Conference on Information and Knowledge Management.*

Hartig, H. Hohmuth, M. Liedtke, J. Schonberg, & S. Wolter, J. (1997). The Performance of μ-Kernel-Based Systems. In *Proceedings of the sixteenth ACM symposium on Operating systems principles,* Saint Malo, France, (p.66-77).

Herder, J. N., Bos, H., Gras, B., Homburg, P., & Tanenbaum, A. S. (2006). Minix 3: a highly reliable, self-repairing operating system. *ACM Operating Systems Review, 40*(3), 80–89. doi:10.1145/1151374.1151391

Herder, J. N., Bos, H., Gras, B., Homburg, P., & Tanenbaum, A. S. (2007). Failure resilience for device drivers. In *The 37th Annual IEEE/IFIP International Conference on Dependable Systems and Networks,* (pp. 41-50).

Hill, J., Schmidt, D.C., & Slaby, J. (2007). *System execution modeling tools for evaluating the quality of service of enterprise distributed real-time and embedded systems.* In P. F. Tiako (Ed.). *Designing software-intensive systems: Methods and principles.* Langston University, OK.

Hilyard, J. (2005, January). No code can hide from the profiling API in the .NET framework 2.0. *MSDN Magazine.* Retrieved March 11, 2008, from http://msdn.microsoft.com/msdnmag/issues/05/01/CLRProfiler/

Hollingsworth, J. K., Miller, B. P., & Cargille, J. (1994). Dynamic program instrumentation for scalable performance tools. In *Proceedings of the Scalable High-Performance Computing Conference, Knoxville, TN,* (pp. 841-850).

Howell, J. & Kotz, D. (2000). End-to-end authorization. *Proceedings of the 4th Symposium on Operating Systems Design and Implementation* (151 164). San Diego, CA.

Hristea, C., Lenoski, D., & Keen, J. (1997). Measuring Memory Hierarchy Performance of Cache-Coherent Multiprocessors Using Micro Benchmarks. In *Supercomputing, ACM/IEEE 1997 Conference,* (p.45).

Hsu, W. W., Young, H. C., & Smith, A. J. (2003). *The Automatic Improvement of Locality in Storage Systems.* Technical Report CSD-03-1264, UC Berkeley.

Hu, H., Xu, J., et al. (2003). Adaptive power-aware prefetching schemes for mobile broadcast environments. In *Proceedings of the International Conference on Mobile Data Management.*

Hu, Q., Lee, W. C., et al. (1999). Indexing techniques for wireless data broadcast under data clustering and scheduling. In *Proceedings of the Eighth International Conference on Information and Knowledge Management,* Kansas City, Missouri, USA.

Hughes Network Systems, LLC. (2008). DIRECWAY. Retrieved May 25, 2008, from http://www.direcway.com/

Hunt, G., & Brubacher, D. (1999). Detours: Binary interception of Win32 functions. In *Proceedings of the 3rd USENIX Windows NT Symposium,* (pp. 135-144).

Hunt, G., & Larus, J. (2007). Singularity: Rethinking the software stack. *Operating Systems Review, 41*(2), 37–49. doi:10.1145/1243418.1243424

IBM Corporation (1996). *AIX Versions 3.2 and 4 Performance Tuning Guide.*

IBM Corporation. (1998). *PowerPC 604e RISC microprocessor user's manual with supplement for PowerPC 604 microprocessor* (Publication No. G522-0330-00) [Electronic media]. Retrieved March 11, 2008, from http://www-3.ibm.com/chips/techlib/

IBM Corporation. (2000). *Jikes Bytecode toolkit* [Computer Software]. Retrieved March 11, 2008, from http://www-128.ibm.com/developerworks/opensource/

IBM Corporation. (2003). *Develop fast, reliable code with IBM rational PurifyPlus.* Whitepaper. Retrieved March 11, 2008, from ftp://ftp.software.ibm.com/software/rational/web/whitepapers/2003/PurifyPlusPDF.pdf

IEEE. (2001). *IEEE standard test access port and boundary-scan architecture.* IEEE Std. 1149.1-2001.

IEEE-ISTO. (2003). *The Nexus 5001 forum standard for global embedded processor debug interface, version 2.0* [Electronic media]. Retrieved March 11, 2008, from http://www.ieee-isto.org

Imielinski, T., Viswanathan, S., et al. (1994). Energy efficient indexing on air. In *Proceedings of the ACM SIGMOD International Conference on Management of Data.*

Imielinski, T., Viswanathan, S., et al. (1997). Data on air: Organization and access. *IEEE Transactions on Knowledge and Data Engineering, 9*(3), 353-372.

Intel Corporation. (2006). *Intel 64 and IA-32 architectures software developer's manual (Vol. 3B, System Programming Guide, Part 2).* Retrieved March 11, 2008, from www.intel.com/design/processor/manuals/253669.pdf

Intel Corporation. (2006). Intel's tera-scale research prepares for tens, hundreds of cores. *Technology@ Intel Magazine.* Retrieved March 11, 2008, from http://www.intel.com/technology/magazine/computing/tera-scale-0606.htm

Intel Pentium Processor User's Manual. (1993). Mt. Prospect, IL: Intel Corporation. *IA-32 Intel Architecture Software Developer's Manual,* (2005). Volume 3: System Programming Guide. Mt. Prospect, IL: Intel Corporation.

Itshak, M., & Wiseman, Y. (2008). AMSQM: Adaptive Multiple SuperPage Queue Management. In *Proc. IEEE Conference on Information Reuse and Integration (IEEE IRI-2008),* Las Vegas, Nevada, (pp. 52-57).

Itshak, M., & Wiseman, Y. (2008). AMSQM: Adaptive Multiple SuperPage Queue Management. In *Proc. IEEE Conference on Information Reuse and Integration (IEEE IRI-2008),* Las Vegas, Nevada.

Iyer, S., & Druschel, P. (2001). Anticipatory Scheduling: A Disk Scheduling Framework to Overcome Deceptive Idleness in Synchronous I/O. *18th ACM Symposium on Operating Systems Principles.*

Jackson, D., & Rinard, M. (2000). Software analysis: A roadmap. In *Proceedings of the IEEE International Conference on Software Engineering,* (pp. 133-145).

Jacob, B. (2002). Virtual Memory Systems and TLB Structures. In *Computer Engineering Handbook*. Boca Raton, FL: CRC Press.

Jiang, S. (2009). Swap Token: Rethink the Application of the LRU Principle on Paging to Remove System Thrashing. In Y. Wiseman & S. Jiang, (Eds.), *The Handbook of Advanced Operating Systems and Kernel Applications: Techniques and Technologies*. Hershey, PA: IGI Global.

Jiang, S., & Zhang, X. (2001). Adaptive Page Replacement to Protect Thrashing in Linux. In *Proceedings of the 5th USENIX Annual Linux Showcase and Conference, (ALS'01)*, Oakland, California, November 5-10, (pp. 143-151). Berkeley, CA: USENIX.

Jiang, S., & Zhang, X. (2002). LIRS: An Efficient Low Inter-reference Recency Set Replacement Policy to Improve Buffer Cache Performance. In *Proceeding of 2002 ACM SIGMETRICS*, Marina Del Rey, California, (pp. 31-42).

Jiang, S., & Zhang, X. (2002). TPF: a System Thrashing Protection Facility. *Software, Practice & Experience, 32*(3), 295–318. doi:10.1002/spe.437

Jiang, S., & Zhang, X. (2005). Token-ordered LRU: An Effective Page Replacement Policy and Implementation in Linux systems. *Performance Evaluation, 60*(1-4), 5–29. doi:10.1016/j.peva.2004.10.002

Jiang, S., Chen, F., & Zhang, X. (2005). CLOCK-Pro: an Effective Improvement of the CLOCK Replacement. In *Proceedings of 2005 USENIX Annual Technical Conference*, (pp. 323-336), Anaheim, CA.

Johnson, T., & Shasha, D. (1994). 2Q: A Low Overhead High Performance Buffer Management Replacement Algorithm. In *International Conference on Very Large Data Bases*, (pp. 439-450).

Johnson, T., & Shasha, D. (1994). 2Q: a low overhead high performance buffer management replacement algorithm. In *Proceedings of the Twentieth International Conference on Very Large Databases, VLDB' 94*, Santiago, Chile, (pp. 439-450).

Jouppi, N. P., & Wall, D. W. (1989). Available Instruction Level Parallelism for Superscalar and Superpipelined Machines. In *Proc. Third Conf. On Architectural Support for Programming Languages and Operation System IEEE/ACM*, Boston, (pp. 82-272).

Kadrich, M. (2007). *Endpoint security*. New York: Addison-Wesley Professional.

Karp, R. M. (1972). Reducibility Among Combinatorial Problems. In R.E. Miller & J.M. Thatcher, (Eds.) *Complexity of Computer Computations*, (pp. 85-103). New York: Plenum Press.

Karsten, W. (n.d.). Fedora Core 2, SELinux FAQ. Retrieved on January 5, 2005 from http://fedora.redhat.com/docs/selinux-faq-fc2/index.html#id3176332

Kenah, L. J., & Bate, S. F. (1984). *VAX/VMS Internals and Data Structures*. Digital Press.

Kerberos1 (n.d.). Kerberos: the Network Authentication Protocol. Retrieved January 5, 2005 from http://web.mit.edu/kerberos/www/

Khalidi, Y. A., Talluri, M., Nelson, M. N., & Williams, D. (1993). Virtual memory support for multiple page sizes. In *Proceedings of the Fourth IEEE Workshop on Workstation Operating Systems*, Napa, CA, October.

Kiczale, G., Hilsdale, E., Hugunin, J., Kersten, M., Palm, J., & Griswold, W. G. (2001). *An overview of AspectJ*. (LNCS, 2072, pp. 327-355).

Kim, J., Choi, J., Kim, J., Noh, S., Min, S., Cho, Y., & Kim, C. (2000). A Low-Overhead, High-Performance Unified Buffer Management Scheme that Exploits Sequential and Looping References. In *4th Symposium on Operating System Design and Implementation*, San Diego, California, (pp. 119-134).

Klein, S. T., & Wiseman, Y. (2003). Parallel Huffman Decoding with Applications to JPEG Files. *The Computer Journal, 46*(5), 487–497. doi:10.1093/comjnl/46.5.487

Koch, H.-J. (2008). The Userspace I/O HOWTO. Revision 0.5. In *Linux kernel DocBook documentation*.

Kogge, P. M. (1981). The Architecture of Pipelined Computers. New-York: McGraw-Hill.

Komarinski, M. F., & Collett, C. (1998). *Linux System Administration Handbook*. Upper Saddle River, NJ: Prentice Hall.

Kroeger, T. M., & Long, D. D. E. (2001). Design and implementation of a predictive file prefetching algorithm. In *Proceedings of the General Track: 2002 USENIX Annual Technical Conference*, (pp. 105-118).

Kuhn, B. (2004). *The Linux real time interrupt patch*. Retrieved from http://linuxdevices.com/articles/AT6105045931.html.

Lampson, B. (1974). Protection. *SIGOPS Operating System Review, 8*, 18-24.

Lampson, B. (2004). Computer security in the real world. *IEEE Computer, 37*, 37-46.

Larus, J., & Schnarr, E. (1995). EEL: Machine-independent executable editing. In *Proceedings of the ACM SIGPLAN Conference on Programming Language Designes and Implementation*, (pp. 291-300).

Lau, W. H. O., Kumar, M., et al. (2002). A cooperative cache architecture in support of caching multimedia objects in MANETs. In *Proceedings of the International Symposium on a World of Wireless, Mobile and Multimedia Networks*.

Lazowska, E. D., & Kelsey, J. M. (1978). *Notes on Tuning VAX/VMS*. Technical Report 78-12-01. Dept. of Computer Science, Univ. of Washington.

Lee, D., Choi, J., Kim, J.-H., Noh, S. H., Min, S. L., Cho, Y., & Kim, C. S. (2001). LRFU: A spectrum of policies that subsumes the least recently used and least frequently used policies. *IEEE Transactions on Computers, 50*(12), 1352–1360. doi:10.1109/TC.2001.970573

Lee, E. A. (2006). The problem with threads. *IEEE Computer, 39*(11), 33-42.

Lee, H. B. (1997, July). *BIT: Bytecode instrumenting tool*. Unpublished master's thesis, University of Colorado, Boulder, CO.

Lee, S., Carney, D., et al. (2003). Index hint for on-demand broadcasting. In *Proceedings of the International Conference on Data Engineering*.

Lemos, R. (2003). Cracking Windows passwords in seconds. CNET News.com. Retrieved July 22, 2003 from http://news.zdnet.com/2100-1009_22-5053063.html

Leschke, T. (2004). Achieving speed and flexibility by separating management from protection: embracing the Exokernel operating system. *Operating Systems Review, 38*(4), 5–19. doi:10.1145/1031154.1031155

Leschke, T. R. (2004). Achieving Speed and Flexibility by Separating Management From Protection: Embracing the Exokernel Operating System. *Operating Systems Review, 38*(4), 5–19. doi:10.1145/1031154.1031155

Li, C., & Shen, K. (2005). Managing prefetch memory for data-intensive online servers. In *Proceedings of the 4th conference on USENIX Conference on File and Storage Technologies*, (pp. 19).

Li, C., Shen, K., & Papathanasiou, A. E. (2007). Competitive prefetching for concurrent sequential i/o. In *Proceedings of the ACM SIGOPS/EuroSys European Conference on Computer Systems 2007*, (pp. 189-202).

Li, J. (2002). *Monitoring of component-based systems* (Tech. Rep. No. HPL-2002-25R1. HP). Laboratories, Palo Alto, CA, USA.

Li, Z., Chen, Z., & Zhou, Y. (2005). Mining block correlations to improve storage performance. *ACM Transactions on Storage, 1*, 213–245. doi:10.1145/1063786.1063790

Li, Z., Chen, Z., Srinivasan, S., & Zhou, Y. (2004). C-Miner: Mining Block Correlations in Storage Systems. Proceedings of 3rd USENIX Conference on File and Storage Technologies (FAST04), March 2004.

Li, Z., Lu, S., Myagmar, S., & Zhou, Y. (2004). CP-Miner: A Tool for Finding Copy-paste and Related Bugs in Operating System Code. In *The 6th Symposium on Operating Systems Design and Implementation (OSDI '04)*, San Francisco, CA.

Liang, S., Jiang, S., & Zhang, X. (2007). STEP: Sequentiality and Thrashing Detection Based Prefetching to

Improve Performance of Networked Storage Servers. *27th International Conference on Distributed Computing Systems (ICDCS'07)*, (p. 64).

Liedtke, J. (1995). On Micro-Kernel Construction. In *Proceedings of the 15th ACM Symposium on Operating System Principles*. New York: ACM.

Liedtke, J. (1996). Toward Real Microkernels. *Communications of the ACM, 39*(9). doi:10.1145/234215.234473

LINUX Pentiums using BYTE UNIX Benchmarks (2005). Winston-Salem, NC: SilkRoad, Inc.

Liu, Y., & Knightly, E. (2003). Opportunistic fair scheduling over multiple wireless channels. In *Proceedings of the IEEE Conference on Computer Communications*.

Lo, S.-C., & Chen, A. L. P. (2000). Optimal index and data allocation in multiple broadcast channels. In *Proceedings of the 16th International Conference on Data Engineering*.

London, K., Moore, S., Mucci, P., Seymour, K., & Luczak, R. (2001, June 18-21). The PAPI cross-platform interface to hardware performance counters. In *Proceedings of the Department of Defense Users' Group Conference*.

Loscocco, P. A., Smalley, S. D., Mucklebauer, P. A., Taylor, R. C., Turner, S. J., & Farrell, J. F. (1998). The inevitability of failure: The flawed assumption of security in modern computing national security agency.

Love, R. (2003). *Linux Kernel Development* (1st Ed.). Sams.

Lowe, E. (2005). *Automatic Large page selection policy*. Retrieved from http://www.opensolaris.org/os/project/muskoka/virtual_memory/policy_v1.1.pdf.

Lu, X., & Smith, S. F. (2006). A Microkernel Virtual Machine: Building Security with Clear Interfaces. *ACM SIGPLAN Workshop on Programming Languages and Analysis for Security*, Ottawa, Canada, June 10, (pp. 47-56).

Luk, C., Cohn, R., Muth, R., Patil, H., Klauser, A., Lowney, G., et al. (2005). Pin: Building customized program analysis tools with dynamic instrumentation.

In *Proceedings of the ACM SIGPLAN Conference on Programming Language Design and Implementation*, (pp. 190-200).

MacAfee AVERT Labs. (2006). *Rootkits, part 1 of 3: A growing threat*. MacAfee AVERT Labs Whitepaper.

Maeda, T. (2002). *Kernel Mode Linux: Execute user process in kernel mode*. Retrieved from http://www.yl.is.s.u-tokyo.ac.jp/~tosh/kml/

Maeda, T. (2002). *Safe Execution of User programs in Kernel Mode Using Typed Assembly Language*. Master Thesis, The University of Tokyo, Tokyo, Japan.

Maeda, T. (2003). Kernel Mode Linux. *Linux Journal, 109*, 62–67.

Manber, U. (1989). *Introduction to Algorithms – A Creative Approach*, (pp.130-131). Harlow, MA: Addison-Wesley.

Mantegazz, P., Bianchi, E., Dozio, L., Papacharalambous, S., & Hughes, S. (2000). *RTAI: Real-Time Application Interface*. Retrieved from http://www.linuxdevices.com/articles/ AT6605918741.html.

Marsaglia, G. (1996). *The marsaglia random number cdrom including the diehard battery of tests of randomness*. Retrieved from http://stat.fsu.edu/pub/diehard

Martello, S., & Toth, P. (1990). Lower Bounds and Reduction Procedures for the Bin Packing Problem. *Discrete Applied Mathematics, 28*, 59–70. doi:10.1016/0166-218X(90)90094-S

Marti, D. (2002). System Development Jump Start Class. *Linux Journal, 7*.

McCalpin, J. D. (1995). Memory bandwidth and machine balance in current high performance computers. *IEEE Technical Committee on Computer Architecture newsletter*.

McKusick, M. K., Bostic, K., Karels, M. J., & Quarterman, J. S. (1996). *The Design and Implementation of the 4.4 BSD Operating System*. Reading, MA: Addison Wesley.

McKusick, M. K., Joy, W. N., Leffler, S. J., & Fabry, R. S. (1884). A Fast File System for UNIX. *Transactions on Computer Systems, 2*(3), 181–197. doi:10.1145/989.990

McMahan, S. (1998). Cyrix Corp. *Branch Processing unit with a return stack including repair using pointers from different pipe stage*. U.S. Patent No. 5,706,491.

McVoy, L., & Staelin, C. (1996). Lmbench: portable tools for performance analysis. In *Proceedings of the USENIX Annual Technical Conference*, May 1996.

Megiddo, N., & Modha, D. S. (2003). ARC: A Self-Tuning, Low Overhead Replacement Cache. In *Proc. of the 2nd USENIX Conference on File and Storage Technologies (FAST'2003)*, San Francisco, (pp. 115-130).

Megiddo, N., & Modha, D. S. (2003). One Up on LRU;login. *The Magazine of the USENIX Association, 28*(4), 7–11.

Megiddo, N., & Modha, D. S. (2004). Outperforming LRU with an Adaptive Replacement Cache Algorithm. *IEEE Computer*, (pp. 4-11).

Microsoft (2006). *Architecture of the user-mode driver framework*. Version 0.7. Redmond, WA: Author.

Microsoft Corporation. (2007). *Windows server 2003 performance counters reference*. Microsoft TechNet [Electronic media]. Retrieved March 11, 2008, from http://technet2.microsoft.com/WindowsServer/en/library/3fb01419-b1ab-4f52-a9f8-09d5ebeb9ef21033.mspx?mfr=true

Microsoft Corporation. (2007). *Using the registry functions to consume counter data*. Microsoft Developer Network [Electronic media]. Retrieved March 11, 2008, from http://msdn2.microsoft.com/en-us/library/aa373219.aspx

Microsoft Corporation. (2007). *Using the PDH functions to consume counter data*. Microsoft Developer Network [Electronic media]. Retrieved March 11, 2008, from http://msdn2.microsoft.com/en-us/library/aa373214.aspx

Microsoft. (2008). MSN Direct. Retrieved May 25, 2008, from http://www.msndirect.com/

Microsoft-1, Microsoft Security Bulletin MS03-026, Buffer Overrun In RPC Interface Could Allow Code Execution (823980) revised September 10, 2003, Retrieved on January 7, 2005 from http://www.microsoft.com/technet/security/bulletin/MS03-026.mspx

Microsoft-2, Microsoft, Inc. (2005). *Loading and Running a GINA DLL*. (n.d.). Retrieved January 7, 2005 from http://whidbey.msdn.microsoft.com/library/default.asp?url=/library/en-us/security/security/loading_and_running_a_gina_dll.asp

Miller, B.P., Callaghan, M.D., Cargille, J.M., Hollingsworth, J.K., Irvin, R.B., & Karavanic, K.L. (1995, December). The Paradyn parallel performance measurement tool. *IEEE Computer, 28*(11), 37-46.

Milojicic, D. (1999). Operating Systems - Now and in the Future. *IEEE Concurrency, 7*(1), 12–21. doi:10.1109/MCC.1999.749132

Mock, M. (2003). Dynamic analysis from the bottom up. In *Proceedings of the ICSE 2003 Workshop on Dynamic Analysis (WODA 2003)*.

Moore, D., Shannon, C., Brown, D. J., Voelker, G. M., & Savage, S. (2006). Inferring internet denial-of-service activity. *ACM Transactions on Computer Systems*.

Morris, J. B. (1972). Demand Paging through Utilization of Working Sets on the MANIAC II. *Communications of the ACM, 15*(10), 867–872. doi:10.1145/355604.361592

Morris, R., & Thompson, K. (1979). Password security: A case history. *Communications of the ACM, 22*, 594-597.

MPI Forum (1997). MPI-2: Extensions to the Message-Passing Interface, URL: http://www.mpi-forum.org/docs/mpi-20-html/mpi2-report.html

MSDN Technical Library, Interactive Authentication (GINA). Retrieved on December 21, 2004 from http://msdn.microsoft.com/library/default.asp?url=/library/en-us/secauthn/security/interactive_authentication.asp

Murayama, J. (2001, July). *Performance profiling using TNF. Sun Developer Network*. Retrieved March 11,

2008, from http://developers.sun.com/solaris/articles/tnf.html

Myricom: Pioneering high performance computing. (n.d.). Retrieved from http://www.myri.com

Navarro, J. (2004). *Transparent operating system support for superpages*, Ph.D. Thesis, Department of Computer Science, Rice University.

Navarro, J., Iyer, S., Druschel, P., & Cox, A. (2002). *Practical, Transparent Operating System Support for Superpages*. Fifth Symposium on Operating Systems Design and Implementation (OSDI '02), Boston, USA. Ganapathy, N. & Schimmel, C. (1998). General purpose operating system support for multiple page sizes. In *Proceedings of the USENIX Annual Technical Conference*, New Orleans.

Necula, G. C., McPeak, S., Rahul, S. P., & Weimer, W. (2002). Cil: Intermediate language and tools for analysis and transformation of c programs. In *Proceedings of the 11th International Conference on Compiler Construction*, Grenoble, France.

Nethercote, N. (2004). *Dynamic binary analysis and instrumentation*. Unpublished doctoral dissertation, University of Cambridge, UK.

Nethercote, N., & Seward, J. (2007). Valgrind: A Framework for Heavyweight Dynamic Binary Instrumentation. In *Proceedings of ACM SIGPLAN 2007 Conference on Programming Language Design and Implementation (PLDI 2007)*, San Diego, CA.

Nick, J., Petroni, L., & Hicks, M. (2007). Automated detection of persistent kernel control-flow attacks. In *Proceedings of the 14th ACM conference on Computer and Communications Security*, Alexandria, VA.

Nick, J., Petroni, L., Fraser, T., Walters, A., & Arbaugh, W. A. (2006). An architecture for specification-based detection of semantic integrity violations in kernel dynamic data. In *Proceedings of the USENIX Security Symposium*, Vancouver, Canada.

Nicola, V. F., Dan, A., & Diaz, D. M. (1992). Analysis of the generalized clock buffer replacement scheme for database transaction processing. *ACM SIGMETRICS Performance Evaluation Review*, *20*(1), 35–46. doi:10.1145/149439.133084

Nikolopoulos, D. S. (2003). Malleable Memory Mapping: User-Level Control of Memory Bounds for Effective Program Adaptation. In *Proceedings of the 17th International Parallel and Distributed Processing Symposium (IPDPS'2003)*, Nice, France, April 22-26, [CD-ROM]. Los Alamitos, CA: IEEE.

Nimmer, J., & Ernst, M. D. (2001). Static verification of dynamically detected program invariants: Integrating Daikon and ESC/Java. In *Proceedings of the 1st International Workshop on Runtime Verification*.

Norcott, W. (2001). *Iozone benchmark*. Retrieved from http://www.iozone.org

NT Security (2005). Network strategy report: Windows NT security. Retrieved on January 5, 2005 from http://www.secinf.net/windows_security/Network_Strategy_Report_Windows_NT_Security.html

O'Neil, E., O'Neil, P., & Weikum, G. (1993). *The LRU-K Page Replacement Algorithm for Database Disk Buffering*. Proceedings of SIGMOD '93, Washington, DC.

Object Computing Incorporated. (2006). *A window into your systems* [Electronic media]. Retrieved March 11, 2008, from http://www.ociweb.com/products/OVATION

OMG. (2002). *Object Management Group: the common object request broker: Architecture and specification, revision 3.0*. OMG Technical Documents, 02-06-33 [Electronic media]. Retrieved March 11, 2008, from http://www.omg.org/cgi-bin/doc?formal/04-03-01

Ousterhout, J. (1989). *Why Aren't Operating Systems Getting Faster as Fast as Hardware*. Unpublished. Carver, L., Chen, B., & Reyes, B. (1998). *Practice and Technique in Extensible Operating Systems*. Manuscript submitted for publication. Engler, D. R. (1998). *The Exokernel Operating System Architecture*. Unpublished.

Packetstorm. (n.d.). Retrieved from http://packetstorm-security.org/UNIX/penetration/rootkits/.

Pai, R., Pulavarty, B., & Cao, M. (2004). Linux 2.6 performance improvement through readahead optimization. In . *Proceedings of the Linux Symposium, 2*, 391–402.

Papadopouli, M., & Schulzrinne, H. (2001). Effects of power conservation, wireless coverage and cooperation on data dissemination among mobile devices. In *Proceedings of the International Symposium on Mobile Ad Hoc Networking and Computing*.

Papathanasiou, A. E., & Scott, M. L. (2005). Aggressive prefetching: An idea whose time has come. In *Proceedings of the 10th Workshop on Hot Topics in Operating Systems (HotOS)*.

Paris, J.-F. Amer, A. & Long, D. D. E. (2003). A stochastic approach to file access prediction. In *Proceedings of the international workshop on Storage network architecture and parallel I/Os*, (pp. 36-40).

Patel, P. (2002). An Introduction to Active Network Node Operating Systems. *Crossroads, 9*(2), 21–26. doi:10.1145/904067.904072

Patterson III, Russel. H. (1997). *Informed Prefetching and Caching*. PhD thesis, School of Computer Science, Carnegie Mellon University, Pittsburgh, PA.

Patterson, D. A., & Hennessy, J. L. (1997). *Computer Organization and Design* (pp. 434-536). San Francisco, CA: Morgan Kaufmann Publishers, INC.

Patterson, R. H., Gibson, G. A., & Satyanarayanan, M. (1993). A status report on research in transparent informed prefetching. *SIGOPS Operating Systems Review, 27*(2), 21–34. doi:10.1145/155848.155855

Patterson, R. H., Gibson, G. A., Ginting, E., Stodolsky, D., & Zelenka, J. (1995). Informed prefetching and caching. In *Proceedings of the fifteenth ACM symposium on Operating systems principles*, (pp. 79-95).

Petroni, N., Jr., Fraser, T., Molina, J., & Arbaugh, W. A. (2004). Copilot - a coprocessor-based kernel runtime integrity monitor. In *Proceedings of the USENIX Security Symposium*, San Diego, CA.

Pietrik, M. (1998, May). Under the hood. *Microsoft Systems Journal*. Retrieved March 11, 2008, from http://www.microsoft.com/msj/0598/hood0598.aspx

Red Hat-1, Red Hat Linux Reference Guide, Shadow Passwords. Retrieved January 6, 2005 from http://www.redhat.com/docs/manuals/linux/RHL-9-Manual/ref-guide/s1-users-groups-shadow-utilities.html

Reiss, S. P. (2003). Visualizing Java in action. In *Proceedings of the 2003 ACM Symposium on Software Visualization*, (p. 57).

Reiss, S. P. (2005). Efficient monitoring and display of thread state in java. In *Proceedings of the IEEE International Workshop on Program Comprehension* (pp. 247-256). St. Louis, MO.

Reuven, M., & Wiseman, Y. (2005). *Reducing the Thrashing Effect Using Bin Packing, Proc. IASTED Modeling, Simulation, and Optimization Conference*, MSO-2005, Oranjestad, Aruba, (pp. 5-10).

Reuven, M., & Wiseman, Y. (2006). Medium-Term Scheduler as a Solution for the Thrashing Effect. *The Computer Journal, 49*(3), 297–309. doi:10.1093/comjnl/bxl001

Riechmann, T., & Kleinöder, J. (1996). *User-Level Scheduling with Kernel Threads*. Unpublished.

Rinard, M. (2001). *Analysis of multithreaded programs*. (LNCS 2126, pp. 1-19).

Ritchie, D. M. & Thompson, K. (1978). The UNIX time-sharing system. *The Bell System Technical Journal, 57*, 1905-1920.

Ritchie, D. M. (1979). *On the Security of UNIX*, in UNIX SUPPLEMENTARY DOCUMENTS, AT & T.

Robbins, A. (2004). *Linux Programming by Example*. Upper Saddle River, NJ: Pearson Education Inc.

Robertson, J., & Devarakonda, M. (1990). Data cache management using frequency-based replacement. In *Proc. SIGMETRICS Conference on Measurement and Modeling of computer systems*. New York: ACM Press.

Romer, T. H., Ohllrich, W. H., Karlin, A. R., & Bershad, B. N. (1995). Reducing TLB and memory overhead using online superpage promotion. In *Proceedings of the 22nd*

International Symposium on Computer Architecture (ISCA), (pp. 87-176), Santa Margherita Ligure, Italy.

Romer, T., Voelker, G., Lee, D., Wolman, A., Wong, W., Levy, H., et al. (1997). Instrumentation and optimization of Win32/Intel executables using Etch. In *Proceedings of the USENIX Windows NT Workshop*.

Rutkowska, J. (2007). Defeating hardware based ram acquisition. *Blackhat Conference*, Arlington, VA.

Saltzer, J. H., & Schroeder, M. D. (1975). The protection of information in computer systems. *Proceedings of the IEEE, 63*, 1278-1308.

Saltzer, J. H., Reed, D. P., & Clark, D. D. (1984). End-to-end arguments in system design. *ACM Transactions on Computer Systems, 2* , 277-288.

Samar, V. & Schemers, R. (1995). *Unified Login with Pluggable Authentication Modules (PAM)*. Request For Comments: 86.0, Open Software Foundation (October 1995).

Schindler, J., & Ganger, G. R. (2000). Automated Disk Drive Characterization. Proceeding of 2000 ACM SIG-METRICS Conference, June 2000.

Schindler, J., Griffin, J. L., Lumb, C. R., & Ganger, G. R. (2002). Track-Aligned Extents: Matching Access Patterns to Disk Drive Characteristics. Proceedings of USENIX Conference on File and Storage Technologies, January 2002.

Schlosser, S. W., Schindler, J., Papadomanolakis, S., Shao, M., Ailamaki, A., Faloutsos, C., & Ganger, G. R. (2005). On Multidimensional Data and Modern Disks. Proceedings of the 4th USENIX Conference on File and Storage Technology, December 2005.

Schmid, P. (2006). *15 years of hard drive history: Capacities outran performance*. Retrieved from http://www.tomshardware.com/reviews/15-years-of-hard-drive-history,1368.html

Schmidt, D. C., Natarajan, B., Gokhale, G., Wang, N., & Gill, C. (2002, February). TAO: A pattern-oriented object request broker for distributed real-time and embedded systems. *IEEE Distributed Systems Online, 3*(2).

Schmidt, D. C., Stal, M., Rohnert, H., & Buschmann, F. (2000). *Pattern-oriented software architecture patterns for concurrent and networked objects*. John Wiley & Sons.

Schmuck, F., & Haskin, R. (2002). GPFS: A Shared-Disk File System for Large Computing Clusters. Proceedings of USENIX Conference on File and Storage Technologies, January 2002.

Scholl, A., Klein, R., & Jurgens, C. (1997). BISON: A Fast Hybrid Procedure for Exactly Solving the One-Dimensional Bin Packing Problem. *Computers & Operations Research, 24*, 627–645. doi:10.1016/S0305-0548(96)00082-2

Schuba, C. L., Krsul, I. V., & Kuhn, M. G. spafford, E. H., Sundaram, A. & Zamboni, D. (1997). Analysis of a denial of service attack on tcp. In *Proceedings of the 1997 Symposium on Security and Privacy*, Oakland, CA.

Shamir, A., & van Someren, N. (1999). Playing "hide and seek" with stored keys. In *Proceedings of the Third International Conference on Financial Cryptography*, London, UK.

Shellcode Security Research Team. (2006). *Registration weakness in linux kernel's binary formats*. Retrieved from http://goodfellas.shellcode.com.ar/own/binfmt-en.pdf.

Shen, H., Joseph, M. S., et al. (2005). PReCinCt: A scheme for cooperative caching in mobile peer-to-peer systems. In *Proceedings of the International Parallel and Distributed Processing Symposium*.

Shivakumar, N., & Venkatasubramanian, S. (1996). Efficient indexing for broadcast based wireless systems. Mobile *Networks and Applications, 1*(4), 433-446.

Shriver, E., Small, C., & Smith, K. A. (1999). Why does file system prefetching work? In *Proceedings of the Annual Technical Conference on 1999 USENIX Annual Technical Conference*, (pp. 71-84).

Smaragdakis, Y. (2004). General Adaptive Replacement Policies. *Proc. International Symposium on Memory Management* (pp. 108-119). New York: ACM Press.

Smaragdakis, Y., Kaplan, S., & Wilson, P. (2003). The EELRU Adaptive Replacement Algorithm. *Performance Evaluation*, *53*(2), 93–123. doi:10.1016/S0166-5316(02)00226-2

Smaragdakis, Y., Kaplan, S., & Wilson, P. (2003). The EELRU adaptive replacement algorithm. *Performance Evaluation (Elsevier)*, *53*(2), 93–123. doi:10.1016/S0166-5316(02)00226-2

Soloman, D. A. (1998). *Inside Windows NT (2nd ed)*. Redmond: Microsoft Press.

Spear, M., Roeder, T., Hodson, O., Hunt, G., & Levi, S. (2006). Solving the starting problem: Device drivers as self-describing artifacts. In *Proceedings of the 2006 EuroSys Conference*, pages 45-58.

SPEC. (2000). *CPU-2000. Standard Performance Evaluation Corporation, Warrenton, VA*. Retrieved from http://www.spec.org/

Spinczyk, O., Lohmann, D., & Urban, M. (2005). Aspect C++: An AOP extension for C++. *Software Developer's Journal*, 68-76.

Srivastava, A., & Eustace A. (1994). *ATOM: A system for building customized program analysis tools* (Tech. Rep. No. 94/2). Western Research Lab, Compaq Corporation.

Stallings, W. (1998). *Operating Systems Internals and Design Principles*, (3rd Ed., p. 383). Upper Saddle River, NJ: Prentice-Hall.

Staniford, S., Paxson, V., & Weaver, N. (2002). How to own the Internet in your spare time. *Proceedings of the 11th Usenix Security Symposium*, 149-167.

Su, C.-J., & Tassiulas, L. (1998). Joint broadcast scheduling and user's cache management for efficient information delivery. In *Proceedings of the International Conference on Mobile Computing and Networking*.

Subramaniam, K., & Thazhuthaveetil, M. (1994). Effectiveness of sampling based software profilers. In *Proceedings of the 1st International Conference on Reliability and Quality Assurance*, (pp. 1-5).

Subramanian, M. C., Peterson, K. & Raghunath, B. (1998). *Implementation of multiple pagesize support in HP-UX*. Proceedings of the USENIX Annual Technical Conference, New Orleans.

Subramanian, R., Smaragdakis, Y., & Loh, G. (2006). Adaptive Caches: Effective Shaping of Cache Behavior to Workloads. In *Proc. International Symposium on Microarchitecture (MICRO)* (pp. 385-386). Washington, DC: IEEE Computer Society.

Sun Microsystems Corporation. (2002). *The Java native interface programmer's guide and specification* [Electronic media]. Retrieved March 11, 2008, from http://java.sun.com/docs/books/jni/html/jniTOC.html

Sun Microsystems Corporation. (2004). *JVM tool interface* [Computer software]. Retrieved March 11, 2008, from http://java.sun.com/j2se/1.5.0/docs/guide/jvmti/

Sutter, H. (2005). The free lunch is over: A fundamental turn towards concurrency in software. *Dr. Dobb's Journal*, *30*(3).

Sutter, H., & Larus J. (2005). Software and the concurrency revolution. *ACM Queue Magazine*, *3*(7).

Swift, M. M., Bershad, B. N., & Levy, H. M. (2005). Improving the reliability of commodity operating systems. *ACM Transactions on Computer Systems*, *23*(1). doi:10.1145/1047915.1047919

Swift, M., Annamalau, M., Bershad, B. N., & Levy, H. M. (2006). Recovering device drivers. *ACM Transactions on Computer Systems*, *24*(4). doi:10.1145/1189256.1189257

Talluri, M., & Hill, M. D. (1994). *Surpassing the TLB Performance of Superpages with Less Operating System Support*. Sixth International Symposium on Architectural Support for Programming Languages and Operating Systems (ASPLOS), San Jose, CA, (pp. 171-182).

Tan, K.-L., & Ooi, B. C. (2000). D*ata dissemination in wireless computing environments*. Norwell, MA. USA: Kluwer Academic Publishers.

Tennenhouse, D. L., & Wetherall, D. J. (1996). Towards an Active Network Architecture. *Computer Communications Review, 26* (2).

Tennenhouse, D. L., Smith, J. M., Sincoskie, W. D., Wetherall, D. J., & Minden, G. J. (1997). A Survey of Active Network Research. *IEEE Communications Magazine, 35*(1), 80–86. doi:10.1109/35.568214

Thompson, K. (1984). Reflections on trusting trust. *Communication of the ACM, 27*, 761-763.

Vahalia, U. (1996). *UNIX Internals: The New Frontiers* (pp. 112-148). Upper Saddle River, NJ: Prentice Hall.

Vaswani, K., & Srikant, Y. N. (2003), Dynamic recompilation and profile-guided optimizations for a .NET JIT compiler. In *Proceedings of the IEEE Software Special on Rotor .NET,* (Vol. 150, pp. 296-302). IEEE Publishing.

Visser, E. (2001). *Stratego: A language for program transformation based on rewriting strategies.* (LNCS 2051, pp. 357).

Waddington, D. G., & Yao, B. (2005). High fidelity C++ code transformation. In *Proceedings of the 5th Workshop on Language Descriptions, Tools and Applications.*

Waddington, D. G., Amduka, M., DaCosta, D., Foster, P., & Sprinkle, J. (2006, February). *EASEL: Model centric design tools for effective design and implementation of multi-threaded concurrent applications* (Technical Document). Lockheed Martin ATL.

Wallace, R. F., Norman, R. D. & Harari, E. (2006). *Computer memory cards using flash EEPROM integrated circuit chips and memory-controller systems.* [US Patent no. 7106609].

Wang, H., Zhang, D., & Shin, K. (2002). Detecting syn flooding attacks. In *Proceedings of the INFOCOM Conference,* Manhattan, NY.

Wang, J. (2008). Improving Decision-Making Practices Through Information Filtering. [IJIDS]. *International Journal of Information and Decision Sciences, 1*(1), 1–4.

Wang, Y., Beck, D., Vo, B., Roussev, R., & Verbowski, C. (2005). Detecting stealth software with strider ghostbuster. *Proceedings of the 2005 International Conference on Dependable Systems and Networks,* Yokohama, Japan.

Weinand (2006). *A survey of large page support.* Retrieved from http://www.gelato.unsw.edu.au/~ianw/litreview/report.pdf, 2006.

Wetherall, D. (1999). Active Network Vision and Reality: Lessons From a Capsule-based System. *Operating Systems Review, 34*(5), 64–79. doi:10.1145/319344.319156

Whaley, J. (2000). A portable sampling-based profiler for Java virtual machines. In *Proceedings of ACM Java Grand* (pp. 78-87).

Whittle, G. A. S., Paris, J.-F., Amer, A., Long, D. D. E., & Burns, R. (2003). Using multiple predictors to improve the accuracy of file access predictions. In *Proceedings of the 20th IEEE/11th NASA Goddard Conference on Mass Storage Systems and Technologies (MSS'03),* (pp. 230).

Wilander, J., & Kamkar, M. (2003). A Comparison of Publicly Available Tools for Dynamic Buffer Overflow Prevention. In *Proceedings of the 10th Network and Distributed System Security Symposium (NDSS'03),* San Diego, CA, (pp. 149-162).

Williams, C. (2002). *Linux Scheduler Latency.* Raleigh, NC: Red Hat Inc.

Winwood, S. J., Shuf, Y., & Franke, H. (2002). Multiple page size support in the Linux kernel. *Proceedings of Ottawa Linux Symposium,* Ottawa, Canada. Bovet, D. P. & Cesati, M. (2003). Understanding the Linux Kernel (2nd Ed). Sebastol, CA: O'reilly.

Winwood, S., Shuf, Y., & Franke, H. (2002, June). *Multiple Page Size Support in the Linux Kernel,* Ottawa Linux Symposium, Ottawa, Canada.

Wiseman, Y. (2001). A Pipeline Chip for Quasi Arithmetic Coding. *IEICE Journal - Trans. Fundamentals, Tokyo, Japan . E (Norwalk, Conn.), 84-A*(4), 1034–1041.

Wiseman, Y. (2005). ARC Based SuperPaging. *Operating Systems Review, 39*(2), 74–78. doi:10.1145/1055218.1055225

Wiseman, Y. (2009). Alleviating the Trashing by Adding Medium-Term Scheduler. In Y. Wiseman & S. Jiang, (Eds.), *The Handbook of Advanced Operating Systems and Kernel Applications: Techniques and Technologies.* Hershey, PA: IGI Global.

Wiseman, Y., & Feitelson, D. G. (2003). Paired Gang Scheduling. *IEEE Transactions on Parallel and Distributed Systems, 14*(6), 581–592. doi:10.1109/TPDS.2003.1206505

Wiseman, Y., Schwan, K., & Widener, P. (2004). Efficient End to End Data Exchange Using Configurable Compression. In *Proc. The 24th IEEE Conference on Distributed Computing Systems (ICDCS 2004)*, Tokyo, Japan, (pp. 228-235).

Wolf, F., & Mohr, B. (2003). Hardware-counter based automatic performance analysis of parallel programs. In *Proceedings of the Mini-symposium on Performance Analysis, Conference on Parallel Computing (PARCO)*. Dreseden, Germany.

Wood, C., Fernandez, E. B., & Lang, T. (1983). Minimization of Demand Paging for the LRU Stack Model of Program Behavior. *Information Processing Letters, 16*, 99–104. doi:10.1016/0020-0190(83)90034-0

Wright C., Cowan C., Morris J., Smalley S. & Kroah-Hartman G. (2002). Linux security modules: General security support for the Linux kernel. *Proceedings of Usenix 2002.*

Wu, F., Xi, H., & Xu, C. (2008). On the design of a new linux readahead framework. *ACM SIGOPS Operating Systems Review, 42*(5), 75–84. doi:10.1145/1400097.1400106

Wu, F., Xi, H., Li, J., & Zou, N. (2007). Linux readahead: less tricks for more. In . *Proceedings of the Linux Symposium, 2*, 273–284.

Wu, W., & Tan, K.-L. (2005). Cooperative prefetching strategies for mobile peers in a broadcast wnvironment. In *Proceedings of the International Workshop on Databases, Information Systems and Peer-to-Peer Computing.*

Wu, W., & Tan, K.-L. (2006). Global cache management in non-uniform mobile broadcast. In *Proceedings of the International Conference on Mobile Data Management*, Nara, Japan.

Wyatt, D. (1997). *Shared Libraries in an Exokernel Operating System.* Unpublished.

Xu, B., & Wolfson, O. (2004). Data management in mobile peer-to-peer networks. In *Proceedings of the International Workshop on Databases, Information Systems and Peer-to-Peer Computing.*

Xu, J., Hu, Q., et al. (2000). SAIU: An efficient cache replacement policy for wireless on-demand broadcasts. In *Proceedings of the Conference on Information and Knowledge Management.*

Xu, J., Hu, Q., et al. (2004). Performance evaluation of an optimal cache replacement policy for wireless data dissemination. IEEE *Transactions on Knowledge and Data Engineering, 16*(1), 125-139.

Yegneswaran, V., Barford, P. & Ullrich, J. (2003). *Internet intrusions: Global characteristics and prevalence,* 138-147. New York: ACM Press.

Yin, L., & Cao, G. (2004). Supporting cooperative caching in ad hoc networks. In *Proceedings of the IEEE Conference on Computer Communications.*

Zahorjan, J., Lazowsk, E., & Eager, D. (1991). The Effect of Scheduling Discipline on Spin Overhead in Shared Memory Multiprocessors. *IEEE Transactions on Parallel and Distributed Systems, 2*(2), 180–198. doi:10.1109/71.89064

Zhang, X., van Doorn, L., Jaeger, T., Perez, R., & Sailer, R. (2002). Secure coprocessor-based intrusion detection. In *Proceedings of the 10th workshop on ACM SIGOPS European workshop*, St-Emilion, France.

Zheng, B., & Lee, D. L. (2005). Information dissemination via wireless broadcast. *Communications of ACM, 48*(5), 105-110.

Zheng, B., Wu, X., et al. (2005). TOSA: A near-optimal scheduling algorithm for multi-channel data broadcast. In *Proceedings of the 6th International Conference on Mobile Data Management*, Ayia Napa, Cyprus.

Zhou, F., Condit, J., Anderson, Z., Bagrak, I., Ennals, R., Harren, M., et al. (2006). SafeDrive: Safe and recoverable extensions using language-based techniques. In

Proceedings of the 7th USENIX Symposium on Operating Systems Design and Implementation.

Zhou, P., Pandey, V., Sundaresan, J., Raghuraman, A., Zhou, Y., & Kumar, S. (2004). Dynamically Tracking Miss-Ratio-Curve for Memory Management. In *Proceedings of the Eleventh International Conference on Architectural Support for Programming Languages and Operating Systems (ASPLOS'04)*, Boston, MA, October 7-13, (pp.177-188). New York: ACM.

Zhou, Y., Chen, Z., & Li, K. (2004). Second-Level Buffer Cache Management. [TPDS]. *IEEE Transactions on Parallel and Distributed Systems, 15*(7), 505–519. doi:10.1109/TPDS.2004.13

About the Contributors

Yair Wiseman got his PhD from Bar-Ilan University and did two Post-Doc - one at the Hebrew University of Jerusalem and one in Georgia Institue of Technology. Dr. Wiseman is now with the Computer Science department of Bar-Ilan University. His research interests are Process Scheduling, Hardware-Software Codesign, Memory Management, Asymmetric Operating Systems and Computer Clusters.

Song Jiang got his PhD from the Department of Computer Science and Engineering at the Ohio State University. He is now an assistant professor at the Department of Electrical and Computer Engineering at Wayne State University. His research interests include operating system, file and storage system, fault tolerance in parallel systems, and distributed systems.

* * *

Arati Baliga has completed her Ph.D degree from the department of Computer Science at Rutgers University. Her research interests lie in the area of system security, operating systems, distributed systems, web based systems, covert systems and applied cryptography.

Feng Chen is a Ph.D student in the Department of Computer Science and Engineering at The Ohio State University. He received his B.S. degree and M.S. degree in Computer Science from Zhejiang University, Hangzhou, China. His research interest is focused on improving performance and optimizing energy efficiency for storage systems.

Vinod Ganapathy got his PhD from the Computer Science Department of University of Wisconsin-Madison. He is now an Assistant Professor of Computer Science at Rutgers University. He is broadly interested in computer security and reliability, particularly in techniques and tools to improve the security and robustness of system software. He also maintains an active interest in software engineering, program analysis, formal methods, operating systems and computer architecture.

Liviu Iftode got his PhD in Computer Science from Princeton University. He is now an Associate Professor of Computer Science and the Graduate Program Director at the Department of Computer Science of Rutgers University. His research interests are Operating Systems, Distributed Systems, Mobile and Pervasive Computing and Vehicular Computing and Networking.

Joel Isaacson has worked as a independent consultant at the cutting edge of high technology for over 30 years. He concentrates his efforts on consulting and actively developing software. He has been promoting open software solutions for over 15 years. For the last 20 years, he has taught various advanced computer science courses at Bar-Ilan University and has advised tens of students in their advance degree theses. He has a Ph.D. degree in theoretical Physics from the University of Pennsylvania.

Moshe Itshak got his MSc from Bar-Ilan University. He is a memory management expert. He is now with Radware.

Pandurang Kamat was a Ph.D. student in the Computer Science department of Rutgers University and a graduate researcher at WINLAB. After completing his Ph.D. he has been working at Ask.com (IAC corp.). He is interested in security and privacy issues in computer and communication systems.

Scott Kaplan is an Associate Professor and the Chair of the Department of Computer Science at Amherst College. Dr. Kaplan performs experimental systems research, primarily in the area of OS- and runtime-level memory systems. Dr. Kaplan is interested in understanding the ways in which a program can use memory, and how a system can find and then respond to patterns of memory use.

Timothy R. Leschke is a Doctoral student in Computer Science at the University of Maryland, Baltimore County. His research interests include extensible operating systems and digital forensics pertaining to computers, cell-phones, and GPS navigation devices.

Eliad Lubovsky got his MSc from Bar-Ilan University. He is an Operating Systems and Linux expert. He has worked for several Hi-Tech companies like Smart Link Technologies and Sungard. Now he is with Alcatel-Lucent at Miramar, Florida.

Moses Reuven got his MSc from Bar-Ilan University. He is an Operating Systems and Linux expert. He has worked for several Hi-Tech companies like Seabridge Networks and Expand Networks. Now he is with Cisco.

Yannis Smaragdakis got his PhD from the University of Texas at Austin. He was an assistant professor at Georgia Institute of Technelogy and an associate professor at university of Oregon. He is now an associate professor at the Department of Computer Science, University of Massachusetts, Amherst. He research interests are programming language tools, object-oriented language design and implementation and memory management (virtual memory management, caching).

Michael M. Swift received a B.A. from Cornell University in 1992. After college, he worked at Microsoft in the Windows group, where he implemented authentication and access control functionality in Windows Cairo, Windows NT, and Windows 2000. From 1998 to 2005, he was a graduate student at the University of Washington working with Professors Hank Levy and Brian Bershad. After getting his PhD he has joint the Computer Sciences Department of University of Wisconsin where he has studied large-scale clusters, simultaneous multithreading and operating system reliability.

Pinchas Weisberg got his MSc from Bar-Ilan University. He is an Operating Systems and Computer Communication expert. He is the system administrator of the Computer Science department and the Engineering School of Bar-Ilan University.

Fengguang Wu got his PhD from the University of Science and Technology of China (USTC). His main focus on Linux kernel is I/O optimization, which hopefully will enable FTP servers to offer better service for us and make desktop Linux boot faster. Dr. Wu is now with Intel Corporation.

Index